CASES IN CONTEMPORARY STRATEGY ANALYSIS

Todd Exler

texler@tulane.edu

(504) 301-4319

Cases in Contemporary Strategy Analysis

Robert M. Grant and Kent E. Neupert

Georgetown University and *Boise State University*

THIRD EDITION

Blackwell
Publishing

350 Main Street, Malden, MA 02148-5018, USA
108 Cowley Road, Oxford OX4 1JF, UK
550 Swanston Street, Carlton South, Melbourne, Victoria 3053, Australia
Kurfürstendamm 57, 10707 Berlin, Germany

First edition published 1996
Second edition published 1999
Reprinted 2000, 2001, 2003
Third edition published 2003 by Blackwell Publishing Ltd

Library of Congress Cataloging-in-Publication Data

Grant, Robert M., 1948–
Cases in contemporary strategy analysis / Robert M. Grant, Kent E.
Neupert. – 3rd ed.
p.   cm.
Includes bibliographical references and index.
ISBN 1–40511–180–1 (pbk : alk. paper)
1. Strategic planning – Case studies.   2. Decision making – Case
studies.   I. Neupert,
Kent E.   II. Title.

HD30.28. G716 2003
658.4′012 – dc21

2002151887

A catalogue record for this title is available from the British Library.

Set in 10/12 Photina
by SNP Best-set Typesetter Ltd., Hong Kong
Printed and bound in the United Kingdom
by TJ International, Padstow, Cornwall

For further information on
Blackwell Publishing, visit our website:
http://www.blackwellpublishing.com

Contents

1 Madonna *(Robert M. Grant)*   1

Madonna Ciccone has been one of the world's leading female entertainers for two decades. Madonna shows an inexhaustible capacity to defy changes in style and her own aging by continually reinventing herself. What can we learn from Madonna's remarkable career about the nature of strategy and the foundations of success?

2 Laura Ashley Holdings plc: The Battle for Survival *(Robert M. Grant)*   11

In February 1999 Ng Kwan Cheong took over as the seventh CEO of Laura Ashley Holdings since the death of its founder in 1985. During this period, the company's performance had been mostly downhill. Cheong faced a critical situation: despite several years of cost cutting and restructuring, sales were declining and operating losses were mounting. Cheong must determine the sources of Laura Ashley's problems, and determine what can be done to stem the losses and protect the interests of Laura Ashley's long-suffering shareholders.

3 The US Airline Industry in 2002 *(Robert M. Grant)*   28

During 2002, the US airline industry was still struggling with the aftermath of the terrorist hijackings of September 11, 2001. But, as the airlines return to greater normalcy, their attention shifts to the longer-term problems of the industry. Since deregulation in 1978, the airlines have been the least profitable of any major industry sector in the US. Given the structure of the industry and the characteristics of the product, is the airline doomed to price wars and low profits, or are there strategies that offer the airline companies opportunities for improving their dismal financial performance?

DaimlerChrysler's ability to improve its financial performance depends critically upon the future of the world automobile industry. Internationalization and maturity in the world automobile industry have been associated with increasing competition and declining profitability. The industry's structure continues to change: against a backdrop of weak demand and excess capacity, the industry is consolidating rapidly. Why has the industry been so unprofitable in recent years and what will be the effects of current changes in industry structure on competition and profitability?

From its humble origins in Bentonville, Arkansas, Wal-Mart has grown to be the world's largest retailer and the world's biggest corporation (in revenue). In so competitive an industry as discount retailing, what is the basis of Wal-Mart's competitive advantage? Understanding the basis of Wal-Mart's success requires careful analysis of the resources and capabilities that Wal-Mart has built over time. Will these strengths in resources and capabilities be sufficient to sustain Wal-Mart's competitive advantage into the future?

Eastman Kodak faced a dilemma as technology was changing within its core photographic market from chemical imaging to digital imaging. The company had staked its future on being a leader in digital imaging. Yet, despite massive investment and a string of acquisitions and strategic alliances, Kodak's ability to establish competitive advantage within the digital imaging sector and to generate satisfactory returns from its investments remained in doubt. The case describes Kodak's digital imaging strategy and explores the challenges of developing new organizational capabilities in a competitive, fast-moving sector.

During 2000, the Royal Dutch/Shell Group of companies was emerging from one of the most ambitious and far-reaching reorganizations of its 91-year history. However, despite reducing complexity and creating worldwide business sectors, central direction remained weaker than in most other major energy companies and Shell's national operating companies retained considerable autonomy. The new structure was helping to squeeze costs, control capital expenditure, and refocus strategy; but has enough been done to create an organizational structure that would allow Shell to compete effectively in an increasingly turbulent industry environment?

Harley-Davidson had begun the twenty-first century in spectacular style with strong revenue and profit growth. However, despite expectations that 2001 would be another record year, CEO Jeff Bluestein knew that Harley-Davidson could not afford to be complacent. If Harley was to maintain its superior performance against powerful rivals such as Honda and BMW, it would need to carefully examine the sources of its competitive advantage and implement strategies that would broaden and deepen these competitive advantages in order to meet the challenges of a changing market and competitive environment.

The advent of the internet resulted in established brokerage firms being challenged by a host of online upstarts riding on the back of the late 1990s technology boom. By 2001, the game has changed – declining trading volumes are putting pressure on the whole industry and on the online brokers especially. How should E*Trade (an online broker), Schwab (a discount broker), and Merrill Lynch (a full-service broker) adjust to the new market conditions, and which business model is likely to be most successful in the future?

EMI, a British music and electronics company, has developed a revolutionary medical imaging technology. What is the best strategy for exploiting this innovation? The subsequent [B] case revisits EMI five years after the successful introduction of its CT scanner. EMI faces competition on all sides, including the imminent entry of General Electric. Can EMI sustain its competitive advantage as the industry evolves? How can it best respond to the changing circumstances in the market for CT scanners?

Since its beginnings in the 1970s, the world video games industry has evolved through four periods of market domination. Atari's early leadership was overturned by Nintendo, then by Sega, and finally by Sony. In this winner-take-all industry, what strategies have allowed different hardware manufacturers to achieve market leadership? In 2002, the industry was entering a new period of uncertainty. After several years of leadership by Sony, the industry had now become a three-way race with Ninendo and Microsoft introducing technologically advanced new products. What strategies could best exploit hardware–software complementarities, the presence of network externalities, and the opportunities made available by new technology?

During the 1950s and 1960s, Unilever subsidiary, Birds Eye Foods, used a strategy of vertical integration to develop and dominate the British frozen foods industry. Birds Eye invested heavily in a national network of cold stores and refrigerated trucks, while securing supplies of fresh produce through contracts with growers and fishing boats. As the industry developed, Birds Eye lost market share to competitors that concentrated on a few stages of the value chain, outsourcing most other activities. As the industry evolved, the competitive advantages that Birds Eye had derived from vertical integration were transformed into disadvantages.

Walt Disney's decision to build a European theme park was its biggest and riskiest project since the Epcot Center a decade earlier. What considerations explained the complex mode of entry that Disney adopted for EuroDisney? Unlike Tokyo Disneyland in which Disney held no equity stake and the US parks that were wholly owned, Disney held minority ownership in Euro Disney as well as licensing and management contracts. However, despite the careful planning of the project, huge losses at Euro Disney were forcing Disney to reassess its strategy.

During 1998–2002, Richard Branson's Virgin group of companies had continued to diversify into an ever-widening set of industries – wireless telephony, financial services, an Australian airline, soft drinks, and internet sales of cars, motorcycles, and wine. At the same time, many of his larger business were making losses, and cash flow was strongly negative. Branson needs to consider the strategy of his loose-knit corporate empire. What is the logic, if any, that links together this motley collection of business ventures? Should any of the businesses be divested? What criteria should be used to guide future diversification? Are changes needed in the financial and management structure of the group?

In summer 2001, Jeffrey Immelt succeeded Jack Welch as chairman and CEO of General Electric. Following "the greatest CEO of the twentieth century" at the "world's most admired company" was a difficult act to follow, and during his first ten months in the job GE's shares fell by almost half their value. During two decades as CEO of GE, Welch had transformed GE's portfolio of businesses, and created the organizational structure, management systems, and corporate culture that could mesh the benefits of massive size and diversity with the agility and entrepreneurial drive of much small enterprises. Where was Immelt to go from here?

AES was like no other company in the electricity-generation industry. It was committed to social responsibility and providing fun for employees. Its management system had been described as "empowerment gone mad." During the 1990s it had enjoyed phenomenal growth and startling shareholder returns. By early 2002, it was reeling from the effects of Enron, the California power crisis, and overseas difficulties – notably in Venezuela, Brazil, Argentina, and Pakistan. Should AES maintain its commitment to social responsibility, fun, and employee empowerment, or is a more conventional approach to management needed?

Preface

This third edition of *Cases in Contemporary Strategy Analysis* represents a continuing commitment to examining the concepts and techniques of business strategy analysis in the context of real business situations.

The cases have been written and selected to accompany Robert Grant's *Contemporary Strategy Analysis* (Fourth Edition) which is also published by Blackwell. Thus, each case presents issues that illuminate the ideas, concepts, and analytical techniques contained in one or more chapters of the textbook. For example, Cases Three and Four ("The US Airline Industry in 2002" and "DaimlerChrysler and the World Automobile Industry") are industry cases that permit readers to apply the tools of industry and competitive analysis found in Chapters Three and Four of the textbook. Cases Five and Six ("Wal-Mart: The World's Most Successful Retailer" and "Eastman-Kodak: Meeting the Digital Challenge") are primarily cases in the analysis of resources and capabilities that apply the tools of Chapter Five of the textbook.

The cases in this collection represent the challenges faced by managers at the beginning of a new century. Most of the cases relate to company situations in 2001 and 2002, though a few of the cases look at situations further back in time. However, no matter how up to date at the time of writing, by the time the book reaches the market, the business environment of 2003 will be different from that which existed in 2001 and 2002. This use of teaching cases that refer to recent history rather than the immediate present is not a significant problem. The challenge for students and their teachers is to address the business situation as it existed at the time of the case. The danger here is that hindsight does not necessarily yield wisdom. We now know that Vodafone and the other wireless telecom companies overpaid for their 3G licenses. However, the critical strategic issue is this: given the information available in 1999, how much should the companies pay for these licenses?

The cases outline situations where decision making is required: How can Laura Ashley avoid disaster? What can Wal-Mart do to sustain its competitive advantage into the future? How can Microsoft supplant Sony as leader of the worldwide market for video game consoles? Other cases focus more on gaining understanding of strategy formulation and the determinants of competitive advantage: How has a niche player like

Harley-Davidson become one the most profitable motorcycle companies in the world? What lessons can we learn from Kodak's difficulties in adjusting to the digital revolution in photography? By being more focused than the typical strategy cases, the cases are typically shorter than is normal for business strategy teaching cases. Brevity means also limits on the amount of information that is supplied to students. Does this mean that students should seek out additional information? Preferably not – the cases provide all the data needed to identify and analyze the key issues. More data permits more detailed analysis, but at the cost of slowing and overloading the decision process. For most companies strategic decisions must be taken with only a fraction of the relevant information available – events are moving too quickly to allow the luxury of extensive, in-depth research.

We hope you will find the cases instructive and enjoyable. We intend to update the case book regularly and we should appreciate any comments and suggestions that you have. We should also appreciate any suggestions for new cases that you might have.

Rob Grant (rgrant2208@aol.com)
Kent Neupert (kneupert@boisestate.edu)

Acknowledgments

The editor and publishers gratefully acknowledge the following for permission to reproduce copyright material:

Bakhru, A., and Brown, A. (2002). *On-line broking strategies: Merrill Lynch, Charles Schwab, and E*Trade*. London: City University Business School. Copyright © 2002 A. Bakhru and A. Brown. Reprinted with permission.

Bartlett, Christopher, A. (1993). *EMI and the CT Scanner [A] and [B]*. Copyright © 1993 President and Fellows of Harvard College. Reprinted with permission.

Costa, Peter R., Harned, Doug. S., and Lundquist, Jerrold T. (2002). "Rethinking the Aviation Industry", *The McKinsey Quarterly* No. 2, 2002. This article was originally published in *The McKinsey Quarterly 2002, Number 2, Risk and Resilience*, and can be found on the publication's website, www.mckinseyquarterly.com. Copyright © 2002 McKinsey & Company. All rights reserved. Reprinted with permission.

Will, George (2002). "Always a Bumpy Ride", *Washington Post* May 9, 2002. Copyright © 2002 Washington Post Writers Group. Reprinted with permission.

The publishers apologize for any errors or omissions in the above list and would be grateful to be notified of any corrections that should be incorporated in the next edition or reprint of this book.

case one

Madonna

Robert M. Grant

■ THE STRUGGLE ■

In July 1978, shortly before her 20th birthday, Madonna Louise Ciccone arrived in New York City with $35 in her pocket. She had left the University of Michigan at Ann Arbor where she was midway through her bachelor's program majoring in dance. Circumstances were far from auspicious. Madonna was brought up in the suburbs of Detroit, the third of eight children whose mother died when she was six years old. Despite her training in dance, she had almost no musical background and had no contacts in the world of show business.

For the first few years, life was a struggle. "I worked at Dunkin' Donuts, I worked at Burger King, I worked at Amy's. I had a lot of jobs that lasted one day. I always talked back to people and they'd fire me. I was a coat-check girl at the Russian Tea Room. I worked at a health club once a week."[1] She spent several months training with the Alvin Ailey Dance Theater and had a succession of modeling engagements for photographers and artists. Early in 1979, Madonna decided that popular music rather than dance might be a better career path for her. She moved in with new boyfriend Dan Gilroy, and joined him and his brother in their efforts to form a successful rock band. Later that year she landed a job as a dancer and backup singer with French singing star Patrick Hernandez, spending six months based in Paris and touring Europe and North Africa. Returning to New York and Dan Gilroy, Madonna became increasingly focused upon developing her talents as a musician, singer, and songwriter. "Breakfast Club" featured Ed Gilroy on guitar, bassist Angie Smit, and Madonna and Dan Gilroy sharing drums and vocals. Between gigs in Sixth Avenue bars and up to five hours a day practicing drums, Madonna continued her modeling while scouring theatrical and movie magazines for casting calls. In August 1979, Madonna was offered the lead role in underground movie director Stephen Lewicki's low-budget film A *Certain Sacrifice*.

After breaking up with Dan Gilmore, Madonna was nomadic, sleeping on the couches of various friends and acquaintances before finding a commercial loft in the garment district "There was no hot water. There wasn't even a fucking shower."[2] "At one point I was living in a New York flophouse and eating out of garbage cans."[3]

During this time, Madonna invited her old Michigan boyfriend, Steve Bray, to New York to help her form a band. They moved into the Music Building – a converted 12-story building crammed with studios, rehearsal rooms, and striving, impoverished young bands. Together they worked on writing songs and developing their sound. The resulting rock band "Emmy" made little impression, but Madonna maintained a continuous stream of calls to managers, agents, record companies, and club owners. Camille Barbone offered her a management contract, but only for Madonna – Steve Bray was only allowed back into the band later. However, Barbone was unable to deliver success fast enough for Madonna and after 18 months Madonna fired her manager.

Finding a Sound, Finding a Style

During 1981, Madonna's music and image moved in a new direction. Influenced by the emerging dance scene in New York, Madonna moved increasingly from Pretenders/Pat Benatar rock to the dance music that was sweeping New York clubs. In addition to working with Steve Bray to develop songs and mix demo tapes, she worked on her image – a form of glam-grunge that featured multilayered, multicolored combinations of thrift-store clothing together with scarves and junk jewelry. She adopted "Boy Toy" as her "tag name" and prominently displayed it on her belt buckle. It was a look that she would continue to develop with the help of jewelry designer Maripole. Within a few years her trademark look of messy, badly dyed hair, neon rubber bracelets, black lace bras, white lace gloves, and chunky belt buckles would be seen on teenage girls throughout the world.

Madonna was quick to recognize the commercial implications of the new musical wave – it was the dance clubs that were key inroads and the DJs who were the key gatekeepers. Armed with her demo tapes, Madonna and her friends increasingly frequented the hottest dance clubs where they would make a splash with their flamboyant dancing and provocative clothing. At Danceteria, one of the staff referred to her as a "heat-seeking missile in targeting the hottest DJs." There she attracted the attention of DJ Mark Kamins who introduced her to Mike Rosenblatt and Seymour Stein of Sire Records – a recording contract and $5,000 were soon hers.

The first release was a 12-inch single with different versions of "Everybody" on each side. The record gained extensive play across the dance clubs of America. Madonna began working on her first album. Although she had promised both longtime friend and music collaborator Steve Bray and DJ Mark Kamins the job of producer, she dumped both in favor of Warner Records' house producer, Reggie Lucas. Together with Warner Records' national dance promoter, Bobby Shaw, Madonna began a relentless round of courting DJs and pushing her record for play time. Central to her promotion plan was a new boyfriend, New York's hottest DJ, John "Jellybean" Benitez whom she began dating in November 1982.

Her second single, "Burning Up," with "Physical Attraction" (written by Reggie Lewis) on the B-side, was released in March 1983. It too was a dance club hit and bounded up the dance charts to number three. Madonna now had the full attention and full resources of Warner Brothers and was ready to press ahead with her full album. One key resource was missing, however. Despite the backing and expertise of key movers in the music scene such as John Benitez, Reggie Lucas, Mark Kamins, and Seymour Stein, Madonna recognized the need for someone who was in her pay, under her control and would work to push her into the major league. She started at the top. Early in 1983 she flew to Los Angeles to visit Freddie DeMann, the then manager of megastar Michael Jackson. DeMann remembers the meeting vividly: "I was knocked off my feet. I've never met a more physical human being in my life." In a short time DeMann dropped Michael Jackson in favor of managing Madonna.

Breakthrough

The record album, "Madonna" was released in July 1983. By the end of 1983, the record was climbing the US album charts supported by the success of single release "Holiday." In April 1984, another single release from the album, "Borderline," became Madonna's first top-10 hit. At Madonna's national TV debut on "American Bandstand," presenter Dick Clark asked Madonna, "What do you really want to do when you grow up?" "Rule the world," she replied.

Within little more than a year Madonna was partway there. The fall of 1984 saw Madonna filming in *Desperately Seeking Susan*. Although initially hired as support for the movie's star, Rosanna Arquette, Madonna soon turned the movie into a vehicle for herself. By the time the shooting was complete, *Desperately Seeking Susan* had become a movie that was essentially about Madonna playing herself, wearing her own style of clothes, and featuring her own music. The release of the movie coincided with a surge of Madonna-mania. Her second album, "Like a Virgin," had gone triple-platinum in February 1985, while the singles charts were featuring a succession of individual tracks from the album. Madonna's first concert tour was a sell-out, and her stormy relationship with soon-to-be-husband Sean Penn was seldom far from the popular press headlines. When Madonna took up residence in Los Angeles during 1985, she was already a star.

■ FAME, FORTUNE, NOTORIETY ■

During the next five years, there was little to come between Madonna and her quest for fame. Between 1986 and 1990, she released six record albums. Her 16 single releases during these same years gave her an almost continuous presence in the charts, including a remarkable seven number one hits.[4] Yet, Madonna's approach was far from the established industry wisdom of "Find a winning formula and stick to it." Madonna's career was a continuous experimentation with new musical ideas and new images, and a constant quest for new heights of fame and acclaim. Having established herself as the queen of popular music, Madonna did not stop there. By the end of the 1980s she was destined to be "the most famous woman on the planet."

Madonna in Charge

Madonna's driving ambition and her appetite for hard work has been widely acknowledged. "I'm tough, I'm ambitious, and I know exactly what I want – and if that makes me a bitch, that's okay," she told the London *News of the World* newspaper in 1985. On the set of *Desperately Seeking Susan* she maintained a blistering pace. "During the shoot we'd often get home at 11 or 12 at night and have to be back at 6 or 7 the next morning. Half the time the driver would pick up Madonna at her health club. She'd get up at 4:30 in the morning to work out first."[5]

There was never any doubt as to who was in charge of managing and developing Madonna's career. While Madonna relied upon some of the best minds and strongest companies in the entertainment business, there was never any ambiguity as to who was calling the shots. In addition to Freddie DeMann as manager, Madonna hired top lawyer Paul Schindler to represent her business deals. Her swift exit from her marriage with Sean Penn further emphasized her unwillingness to allow messy personal relationships to compromise her career goals. When it came to her third album – "True Blue" – released in June 1986, Madonna insisted on being co-producer.

The best evidence of her hands-on management style is the documentary of her 1990 "Blonde Ambition" tour, *Truth or Dare*. The tour itself was a masterpiece of the pop concert as multimedia show embracing music, dance, imagery, and theater. The tour's planning began in September 1989. Madonna was involved in every aspect of the show's design and planning, including auditioning dancers and musicians, planning, costume design, and choice of themes. For example, Madonna worked closely with Jean-Paul Gaultier on the metallic, cone-breasted costumes that became one of the tour's most vivid images. On the tour itself, the *Truth or Dare* movie revealed Madonna as both creative director and operations supremo. In addition to her obsessive attention to every detail of the show's production, she was the undisputed organizational leader responsible for building team spirit among the diverse group of dancers, musicians, choreographers, and technicians, motivating the troupe when times were tough; resolving disputes between her fractious and highly strung male dancers; and establishing the highest standards of commitment and effort.

The summer of 1990 marked new heights of international obsession with Madonna. The "Blonde Ambition" tour was the must-see concert of that summer in North America, Europe, and Japan. The tour coincided with the release of *Dick Tracy*, the Disney movie that was a vehicle for the high-profile lovers – Madonna and Warren Beatty. The film did much to rectify a string of Hollywood flops and scathing reviews of Madonna's own acting capabilities. Madonna's portrayal of Breathless Mahoney exuded her natural talents for style and seductiveness and became her biggest box office hit to date, and allowed her to indulge in her seductiveness. At the MTV annual music awards on September 4, Madonna yet again stole the show with a version of her "Vogue" single in which she portrayed French queen, Marie Antoinette.

Fame and Controversy

From her initial launch into stardom, Madonna's fame was tinged with notoriety. While her capacity to create controversy was seemingly limitless, it was also apparent that her challenges to conventional norms of decency and morality were a carefully managed aspect of her self-promotion. From the early days of her singing career, her overt sexuality was reinforced by her "Boy Toy" moniker. This combined with her sexually audacious, expletive-laced talk and use of crucifixes as items of jewelry raised disquiet among conservative and religious circles. Madonna's explanation only added fuel to the fire: "Crucifixes are sexy because there's a naked man on them." With every video and interview, Madonna was pushing a little harder against the boundaries of acceptable language, behavior, and imagery. Her *Like a Prayer* album, released in March 1989, proved to be a landmark in this process.

The strongly autobiographical content of many of the songs on the album created a rising tide of interest. Pepsi Cola saw the opportunity to piggy-back on the surge of Madonna-mania by making an advertising video based upon the album's title track "Like a Prayer." Madonna received $5 million for appearing in the video. What Pepsi had not taken into account was that Madonna was making her own music video of "Like a Prayer" to accompany the launch of the record. The day after the first broadcast of the Pepsi commercial, Madonna's own *Like a Prayer* video appeared on MTV. The video was a stunning mixture of sex and religion that featured Madonna dancing in front of burning crosses, making love on an altar, and revealing stigmata on her hands. The video outraged many Christian groups and the American Family Association threatened to boycott Pepsi products. Pepsi pulled its Madonna commercial, leaving Madonna with $5 million in the bank.

The explicit sexuality of the "Blonde Ambition" tour and its mixing of sexual and religious imagery resulted in Madonna achieving new heights of controversy – and public awareness. In Toronto, city authorities threatened canceling the show after a deluge of phone calls from concerned parents. In Europe, the Vatican condemned the show as "blasphemous." Her *Justify My Love* video released in November 1990 set a new record for Madonna – it was banned by MTV on the basis of its inclusion of homosexuality, voyeurism, nudity, sado-masochism, and oral sex. Again, Madonna was quick to turn controversy into profit: as soon as MTV refused to air *Justify My Love*, the video was rush-released for retail sale. The publicity generated helped the "Justify My Love" single to quickly establish itself at the top of the singles charts.

During the early 1990s, Madonna continued to break new ground in sexual explicitness. Her photographic "art" book *Sex* featured Madonna in an array of sexual poses. The book itself featured a number of marketing and design innovations from its unusual size (14 by 11 inches), its stainless steel covers and spiral binding, its sale in sealed wrapping, and its inclusion of Madonna's latest CD, "Erotica." And it was a smash hit. Despite its high price ($49.95 for 120 pages) the book sold half a million copies in its first week. The record too went beyond any of Madonna's prior albums in terms of sexually explicit lyrics and scandalous supporting videos.

■ EVITA ■

While Madonna has been compared to previous superstars and goddesses of sex and glamour – Greta Garbo, Marilyn Monroe, Mae West, Brigitte Bardot – she has gone beyond any of these in creating a persona that transcends her work as an entertainer. All the prior-mentioned female superstars have been defined by their movie roles. The same has been true of the big names in popular music, from Lena Horne to Janet Jackson. Madonna achieved a status that was no longer defined by the type of work that she did. By the 1990s, Madonna was no longer famous as a rock singer or an actress; she was famous for being Madonna. Over the remainder of the decade she worked to reinforce this status. Strategically, superstar status has much to commend it. Joining the pantheon of superstars acts as insulation from comparison with lesser mortals. As a singer Madonna is competent but unexceptional, as an actress she is barely proficient – but such mundane comparisons are immaterial; as her website proclaims, she is "icon, artist, provocateur, diva, and mogul."

In her acting roles the key has been to take roles which are primarily vehicles for Madonna to be Madonna. Her success in *Desperately Seeking Susan* and *Dick Tracy* was the result of roles where Madonna could be herself. However, both these roles were to be eclipsed by Madonna's success in playing Eva Peron in the movie version of the Andrew Lloyd Webber musical. Madonna had coveted the role for years and mounted a vigorous campaign to gain the support of director Alan Parker and Argentine President Carlos Menem. While, in previous roles, Madonna had been able to use her talents as a singer, a poser, a sharp talker and a seductress, in *Evita* Madonna was able to play her own character and her own life. Like Madonna, Evita had working class origins, a burning ambition, and had used sex and shrewd judgment to become a legend in her time. The film, released in December 1996, was a huge commercial and critical success. As *Q* magazine's Paul Du Noyer remarked, "If ever there was an ideal vehicle for Madonna's dream of transcendent stardom, this must be it."[6]

■ MOTHERHOOD, AND MORE ■

During most of the filming of *Evita*, Madonna was coping with her pregnancy. On October 14, 1996, she gave birth to Lourdes Maria Ciccone Leon at the Good Samaritan Hospital in Los Angeles. The baby's father was Carlos Leon, Madonna's personal trainer.

In terms of her life, image, and career, motherhood was a major discontinuity for Madonna. The press began reporting a host of lifestyle changes: Madonna abandoned pumping iron in favor of yoga, she had begun to study Kabbalah ("A mystical interpretation of the Old Testament," she explained), she developed a closer circle of women friends, she spent increasing amounts of time writing music, she became less available to the media. Her interviews were amazingly devoid of sex, expletives, and shock value. "I think [motherhood] made me face up to my more feminine side. I had a much more masculine view of the world. What I missed and longed for was that unconditional love that a mother gives you. And so, having my daughter is the same kind of thing. It's like that first, true, pure, unconditional love."[7]

The clearest revelation of these changes was in Madonna's new album. "Ray of Light" was unlike any previous Madonna album. Working with William Orbit, the album incorporated a host of new influences: electronic music; traditional Indian music; Madonna's thoughts about the troubles of the world and the hollowness of fame; Madonna's own emotional development and her reflection on her unhappy childhood. In performing tracks from the album both on TV and on video, Madonna revealed a series of entirely new looks, including Madonna as Goth-Girl (black hair, black clothes, black nail polish), Madonna as Shiva (multi-armed with henna tattoos on her hands), Madonna as geisha (straight black hair, kimono, and white makeup).

The new persona was the most ambitious and risky reinvention of Madonna's career, insofar as it was the first that was not founded upon sexuality and sexual aggression. Yet this transformation was met with no loss of popularity or worldwide acclaim. "Ray of Light" hit number two on the album charts and went triple platinum (over 3 million copies) on the basis of US sales alone, and at the MTV Music Video Awards she walked away with a total of six awards followed by three Grammy Awards.

■ MADONNA AS INVESTOR AND BUSINESS MANAGER ■

Not only did Madonna maintain control over her own content; she increasingly wanted a cut in distribution too. In April 1992 she signed a $60 million deal with Time Warner, Inc. to form a joint venture, Maverick Records. Maverick was a music production company with TV, video, and music publishing offshoots that was to provide a vehicle for Madonna's creative and promotional talent. Warner Records provided distribution. Although Madonna remained contracted to Warner Records for her own recordings, Maverick offered an avenue for her to develop and promote other singers and musicians.

During the late 1990s her efforts became increasingly focused towards identifying and nurturing emerging young singers and musicians relying upon her creative and promotional intuition and experience, the wealth of talented specialists and media moguls who were part of her personal networks, and, above all, her ability to open any door in the business. Among Maverick's early signings was Canadian singer/songwriter Alanis Morissette whose "Jagged Little Pill" album sold over 30 million copies. Though Madonna's links with director Mike Myers, Maverick released the soundtrack for the Austin Powers movie *The Spy Who Shagged Me*. Other Maverick artists included William Orbit, Olive, Muse, the Deftones, Erasure, Tantric, and Michelle Branch. Madonna also teamed up with British comedian gangsta rapper, Ali G, and helped him to launch himself on to the US market.

Madonna's interest in new musicians and in developing and producing their music was linked closely to her own widening musical interests. Her involvement with William Orbit on "Ray of Light" was followed by increased interest in both electronic and world music, including collaboration with the French electro-boffin, Mirwais. But Madonna's interests also embraced more standard popular music. In February 2000, Madonna's recording of the 1971 hit "American Pie" became an international best seller.

Madonna's business interests extended beyond records. Through a series of collaborative ventures, Madonna became involved in a series of movie, TV, and pop video productions. With her Maverick Records' partner, Guy Oseary, Madonna set up Madguy

Films. Among the Madguy projects were several television films based on music history and culture, including *The Dusty Springfield Story*. In collaboration with New Line Films, Madguy also produced Ghetto *Superstar* featuring the Fugees' Pras.

Madonna was also an early enthusiast for online music. In February 2000, Madonna took an equity stake in internet music company Listen.com. Later in the year she won a highly publicized legal action to establish her rights to the Madonna.com web address from a rival company.

■ THE NEW DECADE ■

During 2000 and 2001, neither Madonna's career, nor her popularity, showed any sign of flagging. Year 2000 saw her setting up home in London with new partner, actor and director Guy Ritchie. In August, shortly before her 42nd birthday, Madonna gave birth to her second child, Rocco. In the following month, her new album, "Music," was released. The album was an immediate hit, topping the album charts within two weeks. In October, the "Music" single from the album became her 12th number one single in the US.

Year 2001 marked Madonna's return to concert touring after an eight-year lapse. The "Drowned World" tour opened in Europe, with shows in Barcelona and Milan followed by a run of shows at London's Earls Court before moving on to its US leg. Like prior Madonna concert tours, the show was a sophisticated and meticulously planned multimedia event embracing music, light, video projection, elaborate dance scenes, and pure theater – including Madonna riding a mechanical bull. Observations of Madonna's audience for the shows suggested that the adoring fans who bought tickets for Madonna's "Drowned World" concerts were not the same people who had attended her earlier tours – they were, for the most part, simply too young. Unlike the aging fans of aging rock stars from Bob Dylan to Tom Jones, Madonna's successive reinventions had been successful not just in renewing her appeal to existing fans, but in creating new audiences in entirely new generations, some of whom had not been born when she recorded her debut album.

APPENDIX
Madonna's Biographical Timeline

1958	Born August 16 in Bay City, Michigan to Sylvio Ciccone (design engineer for Chrysler and General Motors) and Madonna Ciccone.
1964	Mother dies of breast cancer.
1973	Starts at Rochester Adams High School.
1976	Freshman at University of Michigan, Ann Arbor; majoring in drama.
1977	July, arrives in New York City with $35.
	September, begins training with Alvin Ailey Dance Theater.
1979	Flies to Paris, becomes backup singer for Patrick Hernandez.

Joins Dan and Ed Gilroy to form Breakfast Club.
Lands part of "Bruna" in underground movie *A Certain Sacrifice*.
1980 Forms rock band "Emmy" with Steve Bray.
1982 Establishes friendship with DJ Mark Kamins.
Signs recording contract with Sire Records (division of Warner Brothers).
First record release, "Everybody," goes to #3 on the dance charts.
Begins dating DJ John "Jellybean" Benitez.
1983 Second single, "Burning Up"/"Physical Attraction," reaches #3 in dance charts.
Release of first record album "Madonna"; first Top Ten hit, "Borderline."
Persuades Freddie DeMann (Michael Jackson's manager) to become her manager.
Appears in the movie *Vision Quest*.
1984 TV appearance on "American Bandstand."
Appears and performs on annual MTV Awards.
Release of second record album "Like a Virgin" (produced by Niles Rodgers); sells 7
        million copies worldwide.
Begins work on major studio movie *Desperately Seeking Susan*.
1985 "Virgin Tour" opens April 10 in Seattle.
Signs merchandising deal for official Madonna Boy-Toy clothing designs sold under the
        Wazoo label.
Appears in "Live Aid" charity concert (London/Philadelphia, July 13).
Marries Sean Penn.
1986 Releases "True Blue" album.
Shoots *Shanghai Surprise* with Sean Penn.
Establishes her own film production company, Siren Productions, backed by Universal
        Studios.
1987 "Who's That Girl" tour opens Osaka, Japan on June 14; closes in Turin, Italy.
"Who's That Girl" album and film also released.
1989 Divorce with Sean Penn (January 10).
Signs contract with Pepsi to produce video commercial based upon "Like A Prayer."
Pepsi pays Madonna $5 million.
Madonna's own video *Like a Prayer* creates storm of protest from Christian groups.
        Pepsi pulls its commercial after just one showing.
Releases "Like A Prayer" album.
Plays Breathless Mahoney in *Dick Tracy*, co-starring with Warren Beatty.
Begins affair with Warren Beatty.
1990 Album releases: "I'm Breathless" and "The Immaculate Collection."
"Blonde Ambition" world concert tour kicks off in Tokyo, April 13. Shows in Toronto
        and Italy threatened with closure because of their explicit sexual content.
MTV refuses to screen Madonna's "Justify My Love" video because of its portrayal of
        homosexuality, lesbianism, nudity, sado-masochism, and voyeurism.
1991 *Truth or Dare* documentary of "Blonde Ambition" tour is released.
Appears in Woody Allen's *Shadows and Fog*.
1992 Grammy Award: Best Music Video (Long Form), *Madonna: Blonde Ambition World Tour
        Live*; award shared with Dave Mallet, Mark "Aldo" Miceli and Tony Eaton.
Release of photographic book *Sex*: sells 500,000 copies in first week, tops New York
        Times best-seller list.
Release of feature movie, *A League of Their Own*.
Madonna signs deal with Time Warner to create Maverick, her own record label.
1993 Movie releases: *Body of Evidence* and *Dangerous Game*.
1994 "Bedtime Stories" album released.

1995 Releases "Something to Remember" album.
    Movie releases include *Blue in the Face* and *Four Rooms*.

1996 Release of *Evita* in which Madonna plays Eva Peron. Wins Golden Globe Award for Best
    Actress in a Motion Picture (Musical or Comedy).
    Also release of the movie *Girl 6*.
    Gives birth to Lourdes Maria Ciccone Leon, October 14; father is Carlos Leon.

1997 Release of "Ray of Light" album which in 1998 wins three Grammy Awards in the
    categories Dance Recording, Pop Album, and Music Video, and two MTV Video
    Music awards.

1999 Grammy Award for "Beautiful Stranger" – best song written for a motion picture,
    television or other visual media (shared with William Orbit).
    Release of movie *The Next Best Thing*.

2000 Son, Rocco Ritchie, born August 11, 2000; father is actor/director Guy Ritchie.
    Release of new album, "Music".
    Wins WIPO arbitration to gain control of Madonna.com domain name.
    Marries Guy Ritchie at Dornoch Castle, Scotland.

2001 July–Sept. "Drowned World" concert tour kicks off in London prior to US.

NOTES

1. Mark Bego, *Madonna: Blonde Ambition*, Cooper Square, New York, 2000, p. 46.
2. Bill Zehme, "Madonna: Candid about music, movies, and marriage," Rolling Stone, March 23, 1989.
3. Scott Cohen, "Confessions of Madonna," *Spin*, May 1985.
4. Her Billboard number ones during 1986–90 were: "Live to Tell" (1986), "Papa Don't Preach" (1986), "Open Your Heart" (1986), "Who's That Girl" (1987), "Like a Prayer" (1988), "Vogue" (1990), "Justify My Love" (1990).
5. Carl Arrington, "Madonna," *People*, March 11, 1985.
6. "Commanding" (Review of Evita), *Q*, December 1996.
7. Mary Murphy, "Madonna Confidential," *TV Guide*, April 11–17, 1998.

case two

Laura Ashley Holdings plc:
The Battle for Survival

Robert M. Grant

On February 1, 1999, Ng Kwan Cheong took over as chief executive of Laura Ashley Holdings. Cheong was the company's seventh CEO since the death of Laura Ashley in 1985. Indeed, the life expectancy of Laura Ashley CEOs was shortening. John James was CEO from 1976 to 1990, Jim Maxmin from 1991 to 1993, A. Schouten from 1993 to 1995, Ann Iverson from 1995 to 1997, David Hoare from 1997 to 1998, while Cheong's immediate predecessor, Victoria Egan, had held the job a mere five months.

The top management turmoil coincided with a downward spiral for the company. In the financial year ended January 31, 1999, sales were down 17 percent on the previous year, and net income was a negative £33 million (representing a return on sales of −11 percent and a return on average equity of −73 percent).

Ng Kwan Cheong was one of the senior management team of MUI Asia Group, a diversified Malaysian corporation which acquired 40 percent of Laura Ashley's equity in May 1998. He had been chief executive of MUI's retailing arm Metrojaya Berhad, as well as holding board positions with several other Malaysian companies. However, despite a succession of senior management positions as well as familiarity with the UK (Cheong was a graduate of Middlesex University), little in his prior experience could have prepared him for the situation at Laura Ashley. Despite a succession of restructurings and strategy redirections since 1990, the company continued on its downhill trajectory. Laura Ashley continued to bleed cash – cash outflow from operations was £11.4 million during the most recent financial year and MUI's cash injection of £43.5 million had been absorbed by debt repayment and covering operating losses. Many outside observers wondered whether there was any future for this icon of the 1970s, or whether Laura Ashley Holdings would follow its founder to the grave.

■ THE HISTORY ■

Development of the Business, 1953–85

Bernard and Laura Ashley began designing and printing scarves and tablemats in their flat in Pimlico, London in 1953.[1] The products combined Laura's interest in color and design with Bernard's expertise in printing and dyeing. The product range was extended to include Victorian-styled aprons and linen kitchen towels. Laura's designs drew upon British traditional country styles, patterns, and colors. The designs were mainly floral, and the colors predominantly pastel. They sold mainly to department stores such as John Lewis, Heals, and Peter Jones. In 1957 the Ashleys opened a showroom in London, and in 1961 they transferred their production operations to a disused railway station at Carno, Wales which used a flatbed printing process designed by Bernard.

The popularity of Laura's first dress designs encouraged the Ashleys to open a London retail store in Pelham Street, South Kensington in 1968. Although sales were initially slow, advertisements on the London Underground stimulated a surge of interest in Laura Ashley's dresses and fabrics. Throughout the early 1970s, the reaction against modernism, pop art, and other trends of the 1960s rekindled a strong interest in the rural English styles and traditions of the Victorian and Edwardian eras. Laura Ashley's positioning between English bourgeois tradition and hippie abandon, and her ability to evoke nostalgia for the comfort and simplicity of pre-industrial Britain, placed her styles in the vanguard of contemporary fashion. During the early 1970s Laura Ashley expanded the company's product range from furnishing fabrics, clothes, and housewares into wallpaper and house paints. What Laura Ashley offered was a coordinated approach to home décor and clothing with a perfect matching of designs and colors across fabrics, wallpapers, paints, and ceramic tiles. The company expanded internationally too, with shops in Geneva, Paris, Amsterdam, and Dusseldorf. In Canada, Australia, and Japan licenses were sold to local companies to open Laura Ashley stores. In 1974 Laura Ashley entered the US, initially by licensing McCall's Patterns of New York to distribute its fabrics, and then with an office and retail store in San Francisco.

The company was highly vertically integrated. By the early 1980s, almost all products were designed by Laura Ashley and 85 percent of the products were manufactured either by the production facilities based in Wales or by subcontractors. The majority of sales were through Laura Ashley retail stores. The company became expert in the fast, flexible production of good quality fabrics manufactured in small runs. By the early 1980s there were eight garment making-up plants close to Carno in Wales, a fabric plant in Dublin, and two plants in England making home furnishing products and made-to-measure curtains and blinds. Distribution from plants and warehouses to retail stores was done by the company's own transport division. Products for the North American stores were air-freighted weekly; others were manufactured under contract at a plant in Kentucky.

The distinctive design of Laura Ashley products was extended to the retail stores. The dark-green Laura Ashley storefronts were clearly recognizable in the High Street, and the interiors with their wooden fittings projected an image of quality and homeliness. The company was an early adopter of electronic point-of-sale systems, which linked retail sales to inventory planning, distribution, and production planning. Laura Ashley also offered mail order sales.

The family ownership and management of the group (in 1982 Nick Ashley took over from his mother, Laura, as director of design) was reflected in relationships with employees. The family atmosphere of the company was evident in a cooperative, non-hierarchical working environment with a high level of job security and generous employee benefits.

Continued growth resulted in the adoption of a divisional structure. The six divisions were:

- *Laura Ashley Design Services* responsible for design and product development.
- *The Product Division* responsible for production, production contracting, and purchasing.
- *The UK Retail Division*, which included Laura Ashley shops, concession stores within Sainsbury Homebase stores, and the mail order operation.
- *The North America Division* with Laura Ashley stores mainly in shopping malls and mainly concentrating on clothing.
- *The Continental Europe Division* with 46 Laura Ashley stores mainly in Germany, Switzerland, the Netherlands, France, and Italy.
- *The Asia-Pacific Division* with Laura Ashley stores located in Australia, Japan, and Southeast Asia, together with a number of franchised stores in other countries.

In November 1985, the company went public. The offer for 23 percent of Laura Ashley Holdings plc was oversubscribed 34 times. Just one month before the public offering, Laura Ashley died after a fall in her home. *The Economist* wrote:

> Her popularity lay in the taste she stamped on her international empire, not so much for the elegance and smartness as for the prettiness and comfort. Nobody was intimidated by the look or price of a Laura Ashley design. Her home furnishings offered a cheap and feminine alternative to the drab, the posh, and the sternly post-war Habitat Scandinavian. She made it possible to look smart without paying Liberty prices. Her company's success has been the acceptable face of British capitalism in the past two decades. She was deputy chairman to her husband and her power has been considerable. She prized the loyalty of her staff and cared for their welfare. There was no smoking and no fried fish in the canteens, no night shift in the factories.

Expansion 1986–89

Fuelled with capital from the public offering, Laura Ashley Holdings launched a new phase of its growth. Between 1986 and 1989 a series of acquisitions extended the product range and geographical scope of the company. These included Sandringham Leather Goods Ltd, Bryant of Scotland (a knitwear company), Willis and Geiger (a US outdoor clothing company with both production facilities and retail outlets), and Penhaligon's (an old-established producer of perfumes and toiletries).

The company also continued its internal expansion. In 1985 a 135,000 square foot textile factory in Wales was completed. This increased the company's production capacity by 50 percent. The new capacity was supported by heavy investment in a new computer-aided design system, computerized fabric-cutting equipment, and a computerized material-handling system.

In 1988 the company was organized into a more conventional multidivisional structure comprising seven divisions, each with a divisional managing director and with profit and loss responsibility to the main board:

- Laura Ashley Group Services – head office functions;
- Laura Ashley Brand Management – design, sourcing, licensing;
- Laura Ashley Industries – manufacture and distribution;
- Laura Ashley UK Retail;
- Laura Ashley Inc. – retailing in North America;
- Laura Ashley Continental Europe;
- Laura Ashley Pacific Basin – retailing in Australia, Japan, and Asia.

Emerging Problems 1990–91

The expansion of the late 1980s was followed by a deteriorating bottom line as the UK recession of 1989–92 coincided with a series of internal difficulties. Problems included:

- massive overproduction of Laura Ashley catalogs in 1989;
- losses at the Willis and Geiger subsidiary;
- the 1989 autumn range arriving at the shops three months late;
- high costs of producing in Britain due to the rising value of the pound sterling;
- higher interest expenses due to a rising cost of borrowing;
- exceptional charges resulting from the sale or closure of non-core businesses including Penhaligons, Bryant of Scotland, Sandringham Leather Goods, and the Units chain of stores;
- the closure or sale of several production plants.

As the company shifted from expansion to retrenchment, it simultaneously searched for a new design look that would be faithful to Laura Ashley values while appealing more to the 1990s consumer. Table 2.1 shows financial performance during the 1990s.

■ THE IVERSON ERA ■

In June 1995, Ann Iverson was appointed Laura Ashley's chief executive. Iverson was one of the most sought-after executives in the retail sector after a successful retailing career on both sides of the Atlantic. She had been a vice president at Bloomingdales, the US department store, a senior vice president at Bonwit Teller, CEO of Kay-Bee Toys, and, most significantly, leader of the turnaround of Mothercare, the British mother and baby chain.

Table 2.1 Laura Ashley Holdings plc: summary of selected financial data, 1989–99 (£ million)

	Financial year to January 31										
	1999	1998	1997	1996	1995	1994	1993	1992	1991	1990	1989
Turnover	288.3	344.9	327.6	336.6	322.6	300.4	247.8	262.8	328.1	296.6	252.4
Operating (loss)/profit before exceptional items	(15.2)	(23.6)	14.8	9.1	4.1	2.3	1.1	(0.6)	3.4	n.a.	n.a.
Exceptional operating costs	(2.9)	(12.4)	(0.4)	0.1	(33.4)	—	—	—	—	—	—
Operating (loss)/profit	(16.6)	(36.0)	14.4	9.2	(29.3)	2.3	1.1	(0.6)	3.4	6.1	23.6
Income from associated cos.	(0.2)	0.5	2.1	2.0	1.5	1.8	1.5	1.9	0.1	(0.2)	42.0
Exceptional items	(13.8)	(11.4)	0.4	—	(1.0)	—	—	(8.1)	(2.6)	(3.1)	—
Net interest payable	(1.3)	(2.4)	(0.7)	(0.9)	(1.8)	(1.1)	(0.8)	(2.3)	(12.4)	(8.6)	(5.0)
(Loss)/profit before taxation	(31.9)	(49.3)	16.2	10.3	(30.6)	3.0	1.8	(9.1)	(11.5)	(4.7)	20.3
Taxation	(1.1)	—	(6.1)	(3.3)	(0.9)	(1.9)	(1.0)	—	2.5	(2.1)	(7.1)
(Loss)/profit after taxation	(33.0)	(49.3)	10.1	7.0	(31.5)	1.1	0.8	(9.1)	(9.0)	(6.8)	13.1
Dividends	—	—	(2.4)	(1.2)	—	(0.2)	(0.1)	(0.1)	(0.1)	(1.7)	(4.7)
Retained (loss)/profit	(33.0)	(49.3)	7.7	5.8	(31.5)	0.9	0.7	(9.2)	(9.1)	(9.8)	8.4
Fixed assets	22.0	42.2	49.5	45.2	48.3	71.7	66.3	60.5	67.1	81.5	80.2
Net current assets	36.7	27.6	49.7	27.0	43.7	50.2	53.9	52.8	66.9	n.a.	n.a.
Long term creditors	(0.9)	(30.4)	(21.8)	(0.9)	(15.0)	(35.1)	(34.4)	(28.0)	(41.4)	3.5	44.7
Provisions for liabilities/charges	(27.4)	(19.7)	(7.3)	(8.3)	(21.3)	(0.7)	(0.3)	(0.5)	(0.4)	2.9	2.2
Net assets	30.4	19.7	70.1	63.0	55.7	86.1	85.5	84.8	92.2	72.9	79.8
Share capital	19.9	11.9	11.9	11.8	11.7	11.7	11.7	11.7	11.7	10.0	10.0
Reserves	10.5	7.8	58.2	51.2	44.0	74.4	73.8	73.1	80.5	n.a.	n.a.
Equity shareholders' funds	19.7	70.1	63.0	55.7	86.1	85.5	84.8	92.2	72.9	79.8	n.a.
Employees											
Total	3,634	3,657	4,104	4,173	4,430	n.a.	n.a.	n.a.	7,800	8,350	8,100
Manufacturing	n.a.	582	617	859	1,019	1,010	n.a.	n.a.	n.a.	n.a.	n.a.
Retail	2,452	2,415	2,592	2,459	2,639	n.a.	n.a.	n.a.	n.a.	n.a.	n.a.
Administrative	n.a.	600	625	653	695	781	n.a.	n.a.	n.a.	n.a.	n.a.

n.a. = not available.
Source: Laura Ashley Holdings plc, Annual Reports (various).

Ann Iverson was joined by James Walsh as finance director, previously CFO of Harrods and House of Fraser and CEO of Kurt Geiger Ltd. The remuneration packages offered the pair put them among the highest-earning retail executives in Britain. In their first year, Iverson received £883,000 and Walsh £360,000.

Iverson moved quickly to restructure Laura Ashley's manufacturing, purchasing, and merchandising. Processes were redesigned, decision making was centralized, international procedures were standardized, unprofitable businesses sold, smaller shops closed, and cost controls tightened. In March 1996, Iverson outlined her strategy for the future (see exhibit 2.1).

Exhibit 2.1: Ann Iverson's Strategy

I was delighted to become Group Chief Executive in June 1995 because I saw a retail business that could be fixed and also a brilliant brand with great potential. However, it was a time of great unrest for the organization, as it was showing no signs of improvement or turnaround.

The restructuring program announced last year was needed for the business. With that said, there were many business issues this program did not address. It only looked at overhead costs, it had no retail focus, it identified no change to our business processes and nothing was mentioned about sales growth and improving gross margins. All of these elements are vital to the turnaround of this business and if not addressed could allow history to repeat itself.

When I joined the business I had many impressions that needed validation. I reacted from three different points of reference: as a customer, as a non-executive and finally as the new Group Chief Executive. I saw a business not led by a single point of view; we had multi-design, multi-buying, multi-merchandising and even multi-catalogues.

In other words, each market or business category was defining what they thought the Laura Ashley brand was all about. As you and I know, every successful brand has a single message consistently delivered to their customer. That was not the case at Laura Ashley.

I also found serious supply chain inefficiencies and, most importantly, shops that were too small to show the extensive range in garments and home furnishings. There were also no clear lines of accountability, which is an unproductive and demotivating culture to have. It doesn't allow hardworking people to really know what their job is, how they are going to be measured and where to go for answers.

So in my first three months we set about making things right. We consolidated design, buying and merchandising, the pivotal areas of our business, into our Fulham office.

We began the necessary changes in the buying process, reducing the width of the product ranges by 25% and also developing a common catalogue worldwide. We delivered the head count reduction that was identified in the restructuring program, changed and eliminated tasks and put the right structure in place. Simply said, we set about establishing a retail culture.

Additionally, I identified six key initiatives which were critical to the consolidation and turnaround of the Group. They have proved to be exactly the right priorities to have aggressively focused on for the second half of the financial year.

These initiatives are ongoing and I would like to describe them:

- *Product ranges and gross margins.* Improvement of product ranges and gross margins are the most important for topline growth. The key to this is modernizing the fashion offer in garments and expanding our strengths in home furnishings. The improved product offer in fashion will increase sales and reduce mark-downs and is absolutely essential for repositioning this international lifestyle brand. The home furnishings ranges are already very strong and offer the greatest opportunity for growth. They must be expanded, however, to reflect the developments in the market sector and realize the strength of the Laura Ashley brand.
- *Supply chain.* Development of efficient product sourcing is critical in achieving supply chain improvement. This will be accomplished by developing and working closely with our suppliers so they are more reactive to the needs of the business.

- *Manufacturing review.* A total review of manufacturing continues, within the context of the overall supply chain, focusing primarily on home furnishings where we produce 80% of our own product. It is essential that we ensure our factories are competitive as a supplier to a worldwide retailer.
- *Distribution.* In the area of distribution, our costs are well above industry standards. Work is being done to reduce these costs and we will begin to see these reductions coming through in the next financial year. We will strive to achieve best practice industry standards in this important supply chain category.
- *Shop portfolio.* The assessment of our shop portfolio with regard to both location and shop size is under way. Increasing the size of our shops is absolutely necessary to remain competitive in today's retail environment.
- *The US market.* And lastly, determining the potential of the US market. This market should be our greatest vehicle for topline growth and profit improvement. Our brand values, reaffirmed through customer research, show a potential audience of over 19 million female shoppers. But our shops are too small to even begin presenting the width of the range that supports customer perception and demand. We have started to change this and have already opened the first of our new shops, much larger in format, positioned in premier locations.

The strategy of the Laura Ashley brand is already clearly defined. We are the quintessential English company with a timelessness and spirit understood and embraced worldwide. Our research supports the brand values our customer identifies with: love of flowers, family, romanticism, freedom and simplicity and the tradition which directly relates to the enduring brand qualities and its uniqueness.

In the past the business has talked too much about strategy and not about results. It is time we delivered to our customers and shareholders. As a retailer I see clearly what needs to be done and how to do it.

The way forward continues to be about focus and implementation of the key initiatives which are fundamental to the Company's turnaround. Additionally, we have identified two new initiatives, namely: to establish an appropriate infrastructure for licensing, franchising and wholesaling and to build a new mail order business.

I am pleased we were able to deliver profit improvement this year coming from hard work and focused efforts. We have a strong and highly experienced results driven team and working together we look forward to delivering the profits we know this brand is capable of generating.

Source: Ann Iverson's Strategy, from "Chief Executive's Statement," *Laura Ashley Holdings plc Annual Report 1996*, London 1996.

The strategy involved combining better controls through tighter budgeting, more rigorous financial reporting, and more effective management systems, with a strong emphasis on top-line growth through expanding retail square footage, especially in the US (see table 2.2).

Iverson's first year at Laura Ashley was hailed by investors and industry observers as the long-awaited turnaround in the fortunes of the beleaguered group. *Business Week* enthused:

Since becoming CEO of Laura Ashley Holdings, plc last July, Ann Iverson has replaced most of top management, cut the payroll, slashed costs, and unveiled an aggressive expansion plan in the US. "I'm the kind of person who has a steamroller behind her back," says Iverson, 52, who was recruited when shareholders were getting fed up. Now the market's applauding. On April 18, the company reported pretax income of $15.6 million for 1995, compared with a $46.5 million loss a year before. Since Iverson's appointment, Laura Ashley's stock has more than doubled . . . [but] no one knows yet if Iverson can solve the

Table 2.2   Laura Ashley Holdings plc: retail stores and floor space

	Number of stores				Square footage (000s) (at January 31)			
	1999	1998	1997	1996	1999	1998	1997	1996
UK	234	237	189	174	587	561.5	441.8	394.1
North America	106	132	155	168	301	379.3	349.6	276.8
Continental Europe	69	72	74	76	112	114.1	115.9	117.7
Total	409	441	418	418	1,000	1,055.2	907.3	788.6

Source: Laura Ashley Holdings plc, Annual Reports 1996–9.

biggest problem: the apparel line with its signature floral prints and long, girlish dresses, is deeply unfashionable in the minimalist 1990s. . . . Iverson acknowledges that the company's Victorian look is dated, but cites recent research showing that the brand could appeal to 19 million women in America and Britain. She hopes the new designer she lured from Carole Little, Basha Cohen, will help freshen the line, but still keep the flowing romantic look. More important, she is betting that home furnishings will boost sales. The company's wallpaper, bedspreads, linens and curtains have proven much more resistant to fashion's whims than the frocks have.[2]

Even long-serving Laura Ashley executives were heartened by Iverson's clarity of vision and effective leadership. Visiting the first new-style US Laura Ashley store in North Carolina, Sir Bernard Ashley commented, "I almost cried, it was so marvelous."

During 1996, the company's capital expenditures increased as the number of stores and their average size increased. Yet, any prospects of the new strategy delivering improved sale profit performance soon evaporated. Despite the emphasis on expansion in the US, North American sales fell during 1996. Then, in the spring of 1997, problems of poor coordination caused losses to mount. Overoptimistic sales projections for garments resulted in excessive levels of inventories, while in home furnishings demand was also weak. Clearance sales during spring and early summer devastated margins. Table 2.3 shows sales by region.

In April 1996, John Thornton, a partner at Goldman Sachs, succeeded Lord Hooson as Chairman of the Board, and in November 1996, Ann Iverson was replaced as CEO by David Hoare, formerly a partner with management consultants Bain & Company and chief executive of the diversified holding company Cope Allman plc.

■ RETRENCHMENT: NOVEMBER 1996–APRIL 1998 ■

Almost immediately, David Hoare and new finance director Richard Pennycock began undoing much of the previous strategy. Plans for further new store openings were

Table 2.3 Laura Ashley Holdings plc: sales by product group and by region (£ million)

	UK and Ireland	North America	Continental Europe
Year to 1.31.99			
Garments	70.0	37.1	19.4
Furnishings	85.4	25.9	21.1
Year to 1.31.98			
Garments	85.9	57.0	23.0
Furnishings	90.0	34.5	24.7
Year to 1.31.97			
Garments	82.3	49.7	21.7
Furnishings	76.9	34.5	24.1
Year to 1.31.96			
Garments	80.8	60.1	28.6
Furnishings	67.4	35.9	31.9
Year to 1.31.95			
Garments	78.3	61.8	27.2
Furnishings	59.9	36.6	30.1

Source: Laura Ashley Holdings plc, Annual Reports 1996–9.

radically pruned and several existing stores were closed both in the US and in Britain. Attention was focused on cost reduction, particularly on reducing inventory. By the close of 1997, Hoare and Pennycock were exploring opportunities to staunch losses and raise finance through disposing of non-core businesses. In January 1998, several manufacturing plants were sold, and a 13 percent stake in Laura Ashley Japan Ltd was sold to Laura Ashley's Japanese partner Jusco, for £9.5 million.

In March 1998, David Hoare reported on his progress since September 1997 and on his plans for the future (see exhibit 2.2).

Exhibit 2.2: David Hoare's Three-Phase Strategy

I am pleased to have joined Laura Ashley in September 1997. I am well aware that over the past 12 years, since flotation, Laura Ashley's financial performance has been most disappointing. A number of serious problems face our business and need to be addressed. However, we have an opportunity to build a successful business on the back of a strong international brand.

■ **KEY PROBLEMS FACING LAURA ASHLEY** ■

- *Complexity of the Business.* Laura Ashley is too complex for a business of its size. We attempt to be experts in design, manufacturing, distribution, retailing in 13 countries, franchising, licensing and mail order. Our management information systems are outdated and our cost base is too high. We have not been sufficiently focused on our core competencies of brand management and retailing.
- *Garment Design.* Over the past three years, the garment range has been repositioned towards the High Street and a younger market. However, it has been taken too quickly and too far in this most competitive sector of the market. We have confused our loyal customers and not attracted sufficient new ones.

- *North American Expansion.* In 1996, we operated 168 stores in North America, with an average size of 1,600 sq. ft. This small-store format was not profitable. Over the past two years our North American store portfolio was restructured by closing 68 smaller stores and opening 32 larger stores (5,000 sq. ft.) in prestige mall locations. Store merchandising was centralized in London. This program was implemented rapidly without sufficient planning and knowledge of market conditions and with an inadequate supply chain. Costs, particularly rents, have increased whilst sales have not grown significantly.

Overall, these problems led to a shortfall in sales against expectations and excess stocks in both garments and home furnishings, across all markets, which was cleared throughout the year with heavy discounting. As a result, gross profit margins reduced by 10% from 48% to 38% on sales of £345 million, a £34 million adverse gross profit variance. In addition, operating costs rose by 8% or £11.5 million, principally due to a 16% increase in floor space in North America and the UK. As a result, we have reported an operating loss before exceptional items and tax of £25.5 million for 1997/98 against £16.2 million profit last year. In addition, exceptional charges of £23.8 million have been taken mainly to restructure our North American and manufacturing business.

■ RECOVERY PROGRAM ■

Whilst it is clear that we have had a number of significant problems at Laura Ashley, and that it will take time to fix them, it is also clear that there are great opportunities for our business. Laura Ashley is one of the best known international brand names, representing the quintessential English country lifestyle. We trade in 34 countries, in over 550 owned and franchised stores. We have a base of loyal customers who, though disappointed in the recent past, will return provided we can develop products and services that meet their aspirations.

In order to tackle our current problems and take advantage of the significant opportunities, we have put in place a three-phase recovery plan to be implemented over the next five years.

- *Phase I. Stabilize the Business*
  - stop significant new store development
  - rebuild the senior management team
  - generate cash by reducing stocks and selling non-core assets
  - raise additional finance
- *Phase II. Improve the Profitability of the Business*
  - return to full price retailing
  - redesign the product to meet the wishes of our core customers
  - fix the North American retail business
  - reduce business complexity and costs
  - invest in systems
- *Phase III. Grow the Business*
  - focus on core competence of brand management
  - build our brand internationally with new products, new distribution channels and new partners

■ PHASE I ■

In late 1997/98 good progress was made to stabilize the business. Store expansion was stopped, and we refocused on managing the existing business. We strengthened our senior management team by recruiting Richard Pennycock as our new Group Finance Director. A new Designer, and an interim Chief Executive Officer for our North American business, were also appointed.

Our worsening trading position in the autumn of 1997 required us to renegotiate with our banks. They supported us with a 15-month £170 million committed bank facility through to April 1999. Cash outflow was minimized by reducing year end stock by 32% from £93 million to £63 million. In addition, following the year end, we announced the sale of part of our shareholding in our Japanese licensee, Laura Ashley Japan, to Jusco, the majority owner ... in a transaction which realized aggregate gross proceeds of 9.5 million pounds. The transaction included a revision of the terms of the license agreement between us.

■ PHASE II ■

Progress has also been made in improving the profits of the existing business. Following our January 1998 end of year sale, we returned to more normal full price retailing with occasional marketing promotions. As expected, sales have slowed. However, the key to maintaining satisfactory margins is having the right produce for our customers. We recognize that our garment range has moved too far towards the High Street and a younger market and has lost an element of its Laura Ashley signature. We are redesigning our product range, which, because of lead times, will be only partly evident in our Autumn/Winter 1998 collection. More substantial change will be seen in Spring/Summer 1999.

North America remains a major challenge. Our business there has suffered disproportionately from the problems affecting the Group. The product range was not right, the large-stores format did not work and the complexity of the business led to severe supply problems. Significant losses were incurred. However, research shows that there is a major opportunity in North America for lifestyle brands aimed at discerning 30–50-year-old customers, and we believe that our quintessential English country brand can succeed in this market.

In order to fix our North American business we have strengthened the management team with the appointment of an interim Chief Executive Officer. They will be given the ability to select products from our global range and greater freedom in store merchandising. It has become clear to the Board that these management actions alone will be insufficient to turn around the business. Rather, a decisive program of restructuring, cost reduction, store closures and carefully targeted new investment will be required. As part of this program, we intend to close a number of larger stores while investing in information systems, store refurbishment and brand development.

Throughout the Group, our overheads are too high, partly as a result of the complexity of the business and partly due to the weakness of our systems which require significant investment. Some steps have been taken to reduce costs but greater progress will need to be made in 1998.

As a first step to simplifying our business we announced, in January 1998, our intention to sell our manufacturing operations with a continuing supply agreement. Our manufacturing operations in Wales and the Netherlands, although good businesses, are not part of our core. They will be better off owned and managed by a team whose primary focus is manufacturing. They will become a better supplier and we, with greater clarity, will become a better customer. The sale process is continuing.

■ PHASE III ■

We have significant opportunities to expand our franchise, license and wholesale activities internationally. In 1997/98 we opened 22 new franchised stores. In addition, we continue to expand our range of licensed products. However, we will pursue this expansion program only once we are satisfied that we have the right product, service and infrastructure to give the required levels of support.

■ CURRENT TRADING ■

Store sales, at constant exchange rates, in the first 10 weeks of the year were 13% below last year with substantially lower stock levels. However, last year excess garment stock was being cleared at very low margin.

■ **EQUITY** ■

In the light of last year's results, the investment need in North America, the opportunities in the rest of the business and the current levels of debt, we have added additional equity capital essential to improve the financial stability and operational health of the Group. On 17 April 1998 we announced that we intend to raise new equity of £43.7 million net in a subscription by the Malayan United Industries Group. The Board believes that raising this new equity is essential in order to implement the recovery plan.

■ **1998/99** ■

We start the year with our Organization focused on stabilizing, simplifying and fixing our base business, without the pressure of an expansion program and excess stock. Although we recognize that an enormous amount of work needs to be done, and that it will take time, we are excited by the prospect of building the Laura Ashley brand worldwide to satisfy our customers, and to reap the rewards for our shareholders.

I would like to thank all our staff for their continued dedication, in what has been a very difficult year. With their support, we will make progress.

Source: David Hoare's Three-Phase Strategy, from "Chief Executive's Statement," *Laura Ashley Holdings plc Annual Report 1998*, London 1998.

By the end of 1997, Laura Ashley's need for new financing became increasingly evident. Debt had more than doubled during the year to £30.6 million and the company's bankers had become increasingly restive. By the end of 1997, Laura Ashley had been forced to renegotiate its bank facility, with the result that Laura Ashley was permitted to retain for use within the business the £9.5 million received from the sale of shares in Laura Ashley Japan, but was not permitted to draw further on its banking facility, nor could it use funds available from outside of North America to fund continued losses within North America.

■ MUI TO THE RESCUE: APRIL 1998 ■

In April 1998, the Board agreed to increase the issued equity of Laura Ashley Holdings and to sell the new equity to the MUI Group, a diversified Malaysian group with interests in retailing, hotels and resorts, food and confectionery, cement and building materials, real estate, and financial services. After the equity sale, MUI would own 40 percent of Laura Ashley's equity and would appoint four board members, including Mrs Victoria Egan, president of MUI's retail subsidiary in the Philippines, who would become chief executive, and Mr Paul Ng Tuand an Tee, executive director of Metrojaya, who would become President of Laura Ashley North America.

The £43.5 million that the equity sale would raise (net of expenses) would put Laura Ashley on a sounder financial footing. Extensive restructuring and repositioning were needed, especially in North America. (Tables 2.4 and 2.5 show the deteriorating financial performance of the North American business, while table 2.6 shows performance by business segment.) The North America recovery program would require about £20

Table 2.4 Laura Ashley Holdings plc: retail sales and contribution by geographical segment (£ million)

	UK and Ireland	North America	Continental Europe	Total retail
Turnover				
Year to Jan. 31, 1999	155.4	63.0	40.5	258.9
Year to Jan. 31, 1998	175.9	91.5	47.7	315.1
Year to Jan. 31, 1997	159.2	84.2	45.8	289.2
Contribution				
Year to Jan. 31, 1999	15.0	(7.1)	6.9	14.8
Year to Jan. 31, 1998	14.9	(12.9)	7.3	9.3
Year to Jan. 31, 1997	24.5	7.6	10.7	42.8

Source: Laura Ashley Holdings plc, *Annual Reports* 1997 and 1999.

Table 2.5 Laura Ashley Holdings plc: sales, profit, and net assets by geographical segment (£ million)

	Year to 1.31.99	Year to 1.31.98	Year to 1.31.97	Year to 1.31.96	Year to 1.31.95
Sales:					
UK and Ireland	176.1	197.2	175.1	160.0	145.2
North America	68.2	96.4	92.7	104.6	107.0
Continental Europe	42.5	50.2	57.7	65.8	57.4
Other	1.5	1.1	1.1	1.3	0.9
Profit before tax (after exceptionals):					
UK and Ireland	(21.7)	(12.6)	8.6	(0.5)	(29.5)
North America	(20.0)	(29.4)	3.3	1.7	(1.2)
Continental Europe	10.7	(7.8)	1.4	5.6	(0.8)
Other	(0.9)	0.5	3.2	3.5	1.6
Net assets:					
UK and Ireland	(3.6)	16.0	25.7	15.4	14.1
North America	(5.6)	(18.6)	11.4	13.3	14.3
Continental Europe	38.0	19.9	29.2	32.5	26.4
Other	1.6	2.4	2.3	1.8	0.9

Source: Laura Ashley Holdings plc, *Annual Reports* 1996 to 1999.

million, mainly for closing up to six large-format stores, refurbishment of continuing stores, and implementing a new merchandising approach that would allow North American management the freedom to select from the Laura Ashley global product range. Worldwide, Laura Ashley needed to upgrade its logistics and information systems. This would require investing some £6.5 million outside of North America. The Board agreed with its banks to reduce its existing £50 million revolving credit facility to £35 million pounds by the end of 1998. This would be financed by cash flow from operations and proceeds from asset disposal.

Table 2.6 Laura Ashley Holdings plc: sales, contribution, and net assets by business segment (£ million)

	Year to 1.31.99	Year to 1.31.98	Year to 1.31.97
Turnover:			
Retail	258.9	315.1	289.2
Non-retail	29.4	29.8	22.9
Contribution:			
Retail	14.8	9.3	42.8
Non-retail	7.8	7.6	12.1
Net assets:			
Retail	14.6	(0.6)	40.7
Non-retail	15.8	20.3	27.9

Retail includes Laura Ashley managed retail stores and mail order. Non-retail includes wholesale, licensing, franchising, and manufacturing.
Source: Laura Ashley Holdings plc, *Annual Reports* 1997 and 1999.

Victoria Egan's approach was to continue with the three-phase strategy developed by the previous CEO with a particular emphasis on reducing losses, restructuring the North American business, and disposing of assets. In August 1998, a reorganization plan was announced involving creating three profit centers: Europe, North America, and Franchising. A £2.5 million provision was made to cover the redundancy costs associated with this reorganization. However, during 1998, the business continued to deteriorate – especially in the US (tables 2.4 to 2.6 show financial performance by region). Although inventories were reduced and the costs of closing US large-format stores remained within budget, sales were sharply lower than the year-ago period. The half-yearly results (to August 1, 1998) were greeted with a fall in Laura Ashley's share price to 17 pence – an all-time low.

■ FEBRUARY 1999 ■

As he prepared for his first board meeting as group chief executive of Laura Ashley Holdings, Ng Kwan Cheong reviewed the company's financial statements for the financial year ended January 31, 1999 (see Appendix). His immediate concerns were for Laura Ashley's cash position. MUI had pumped £43.5 million into Laura Ashley in order to underpin its recovery program. This sum, plus the £7.9 million raised from the sale of 13 percent of Laura Ashley Japan, had been eaten up by debt repayment, restructuring and closure costs, and continuing operating losses. With continuing operating losses together with the need to close unprofitable stores, and refurbish profitable stores, Laura Ashley would need to find new sources of finance during the coming financial year. Given the weakness of Laura Ashley's balance sheet in relation to the continuing cash drain, it was unlikely that the banks would be willing to lend. It seemed as though the parent company, MUI, was the only possible source of additional funding. With Chairman John Thornton stepping down in order to take up the position as president and chief operating officer of Goldman Sachs, and MUI Berhad CEO, Khoo Kay Peng, taking over the chairmanship of Laura Ashley, this might be an opportune moment to press MUI for additional funding.

But did it make sense for MUI to continue to invest in Laura Ashley? Despite an improvement in margins, sales had continued to decline. Did a profitable market exist for Laura Ashley products? If so, was this market primarily within Britain, or did it extend overseas? And what should Laura Ashley's approach be in accessing and developing this market?

APPENDIX

Table 2.A1   Laura Ashley Holdings plc: profit and loss statement (£ million)

	Year to 1.31.99	Year to 1.31.98	Year to 1.31.97
Turnover	288.3	344.9	327.6
Cost of sales	(159.9)	(214.0)	(168.9)
Gross profit	128.4	130.9	158.7
Operating expenses	(146.5)	(166.9)	(144.3)
Other operating income	1.5	—	—
Operating profit/(loss)	(16.6)	(36.0)	14.4
Share of operating (loss)/profit of associate cos.	(0.2)	0.5	2.1
Profit on sale of investment in associate	7.5	—	—
Profit on sale of freehold property	2.0	—	—
Amounts written-off investment	—	(2.4)	—
Provision for disposal of businesses	(23.3)	(9.0)	—
(Loss)/profit on ordinary activities before interest	(30.6)	(46.9)	16.9
Net interest payable	(1.3)	(2.4)	(0.7)
(Loss)/profit on ordinary activities before taxation	(31.9)	(49.3)	16.2
Taxation on (loss)/profit on ordinary activities	(1.1)	—	6.1
(Loss)/profit on ordinary activities after tax	(33.0)	(49.3)	16.2
Dividend		—	(2.4)
Retained (loss)/profit for the period	(33.0)	(49.3)	7.7

Source: Laura Ashley Holdings plc, Annual Reports 1997 and 1999.

Table 2.A2 Laura Ashley Holdings plc: balance sheet (£ million)

	At 1.31.99	At 1.31.98	At 1.31.98
Fixed assets			
Tangible fixed assets	19.5	38.9	44.0
Investment in associated undertaking	1.7	2.5	2.2
Own shares	0.8	0.8	3.3
Total	22.0	42.2	49.5
Current assets			
Stocks (inventories)	56.4	63.2	93.1
Debtors	19.7	21.2	24.4
Short-term deposits and cash	8.4	10.2	6.2
Total	84.5	94.6	123.7
Creditors: amounts due within one year			
Borrowings	0.1	9.9	—
Trade and other creditors	47.7	57.1	72.6
Total	47.8	67.0	74.0
Net current assets	36.7	27.6	49.7
Total assets less current liabilities	58.7	69.8	99.2
Creditors: amounts due after 1 year			
Borrowings	—	29.2	21.0
Trade and other creditors	0.9	1.2	0.8
Total	0.9	30.4	21.8
Provisions for liabilities and charges	27.4	19.7	7.3
Net assets Capital and reserves	30.4	19.7	70.1
Share capital	19.9	11.9	11.9
Share premium account	87.1	51.6	51.5
Profit and loss account	(76.6)	(43.8)	6.7
Equity shareholders' funds	30.4	19.7	70.1
Ordinary shares issued (millions)	398	236	236

Source: Laura Ashley Holdings plc, Annual Reports 1997 and 1999.

Table 2.A3 Laura Ashley Holdings plc: cash flow statement (£ million)

	Year to 1.31.99	Year to 1.31.98	Year to 1.31.97
Net cash flow from operating activities	(11.4)	5.2	(0.7)
Returns on investments and servicing of finance:			
Interest received	0.5	1.2	0.8
Interest paid	(1.6)	(3.3)	(1.2)
Interest element of lease payments	(0.2)	(0.3)	(0.3)
Dividends received from associates	0.1	0.2	0.1
Net cash outflow for returns on investments and the servicing of financeTax paid	(1.3)	(2.2)	(0.6)
	(1.6)	(5.5)	(1.6)
Capital expenditure and financial investment:			

Table 2.A3 *continued*

	Year to 1.31.99	Year to 1.31.98	Year to 1.31.97
Acquisition of tangible fixed assets	(3.9)	(9.6)	(14.2)
Disposal of tangible fixed assets	4.6	0.1	0.2
Net cash flow for capital investment	0.7	(9.5)	(14.0)
Acquisitions and disposals	7.9	—	—
Equity dividends paid	—	(1.4)	(2.1)
Net cash outflow before financing	(5.6)	(13.4)	(18.8)
Financing:			
Issue of ordinary share capital	44.6	0.1	1.4
Expenses of share issue	(1.1)	—	—
Settlement of currency swaps	—	0.5	4.0
Loans taken out	—	18.1	21.0
Repayment of loans	(39.0)	—	(5.0)
Capital element of lease payments	(0.8)	(0.9)	(1.2)
Net cash inflow from financing	3.7	17.8	20.2
Increase in cash	(1.9)	4.4	1.4

Source: Laura Ashley Holdings plc, Annual Reports 1997 and 1999.

Table 2.A4 Financial ratios: Laura Ashley compared with other clothing retailers

	Laura Ashley	Abercrombie & Fitch	Next plc	Ann Taylor Stores	The Limited	Monsoon plc
Sales ($,m.)	478	815	2,041	912	9,347	212
Gross profit margin (%)	44.4	42.2	30.1	48.8	32.1	61.0
SGA/Sales (%)	50.8	21.7	17.6	38.4	24.6	45
Operating margin (%)	(5.8)	20.5	12.7	10.4	7.5	15.1
Net profit margin (%)	(11.5)	12.5	10.0	14.3	22.0	9.9
Inventory turns*	5.1	16.3	8.7	6.6	7.6	10.2
Total asset turns*	2.7	2.5	1.5	1.2	2.8	2.5
Current ratio*	1.8	1.8	1.8	2.3	1.0	1.3
ROE (%)*	(108.6)	99.8	22.8	7.9	72.0	47.5

*Based upon year end balance sheet values.
Source: Companies' financial statements.

NOTES

1. This section draws upon "Laura Ashley: History," Laura Ashley Holdings plc; and J. L. Heath, *Laura Ashley Holdings PLC (A) and (B)*, European Case Clearing House, 1991.
2. "Giving Laura Ashley a Yank," *Business Week*, May 27, 1997, p. 147.

The US Airline Industry in 2002

Robert M. Grant

*Here's a list of 129 airlines that in the past 20 years filed for bank-
ruptcy. Continental was smart enough to make that list twice. As of
1992, in fact – though the picture would have improved since then –
the money that had been made since the dawn of aviation by all of this
country's airline companies was zero. Absolutely zero.*

*Sizing all this up, I like to think that if I'd been at Kitty Hawk in 1903
when Orville Wright took off, I would have been farsighted enough,
and public-spirited enough – I owed this to future capitalists – to shoot
him down. I mean, Karl Marx couldn't have done as much damage to
capitalists as Orville did.*

Warren Buffett, chairman, Berkshire Hathaway

For most of the first half of 2002, US airlines were still reeling from the aftermath of
the terrorist attacks of September 11, 2001. Despite a recovery of passenger numbers
and the US economy more generally, the industry's financial results for the first quarter
of 2002 were dire. Compared to the first quarter of 2001, revenues were down by over
20 percent and a net profit of $2 billion in 2000 was transformed into a loss of over
$7 billion for 2001 (table 3.1). All the airlines battled to restore profitability through
cost reductions and cutbacks in capacity. Although most airlines had reinstated some
of their flights, the Mohave Desert looked much the same as in the dark days of the
Persian Gulf war – it was a massive parking lot for unwanted jets. As a result of September 11, 350 passenger jets were retired or parked by US airlines.[1]

While the focus of most airline executives was on survival in the short term, there
were also longer-run issues that needed to be addressed. All the airlines were being
courted by Airbus and Boeing for orders for the revolutionary new passenger jets that
they were developing. Airbus had staked its future on the giant A380 – a plane that
would carry up to 560 passengers and would have, it hoped, a similar impact on mass

Table 3.1 Revenues and profits for the seven largest US airlines, first quarter 2002

	Revenue Q1 2002 $, million	Change on Q1, 2001 (%)	Operating Q1 2002 $, million	Income Q1 2001 $, million	Net income Q1 2002 $, million	Net income Q1 2001 $, million
AMR	4,136	−13.1	(729)	17	(575)	(45)
UAL	3,288	−25.7	(629)	(319)	(510)	(313)
Delta	2,863	−28.7	n.a.	n.a.	(354)	(133)
Northwest	2,180	−17.5	n.a.	n.a.	(171)	(171)
Continental	1,993	−19.7	(187)	76	(166)	9
US Airways	1,709	−23.7	n.a.	n.a.	(269)	(171)
Southwest	1,257	−12.0	49	210	21	121
TOTAL	17,426	−20.6	n.a.	n.a.	(2,024)	(703)

Source: Companies' quarterly financial statements.

air transportation as the Boeing 747 over 30 years earlier. At the same time, Boeing was realizing an alternative vision of the future of commercial air transport. In 2001, Boeing began developing its Sonic Cruiser, a high-speed, high-altitude jet designed to substantially reduce travel times on long-distance flights.

Even if, as most airline executives expected, air traffic recovered from its recent setback and the US demand for airline travel was to achieve the long-term growth trend of 4 percent per annum projected by the Federal Airline Administration (FAA), it was unclear whether market growth would translate into profits for the industry. If profitability in the US airline industry was going to be much the same in the future as it had been in the past (table 3.2), how could the companies justify capital investments in civil aviation if these investments were not going to yield a rate of return that covered their cost of capital?

■ FROM REGULATION TO COMPETITION ■

There have been two major phases in the development of the US airliner industry: the period of regulation up until 1978, and the period of deregulation since then.

The Airlines Under Regulation (Pre-1978)

The US civil airline industry began in the 1920s when scheduled services began, primarily for carrying mail rather than passengers. As a result, the postmaster-general exercised regulatory control over the industry, and by the early 1930s, transcontinental routes were controlled by three airlines: United Airlines in the north, American Airlines in the south, and TWA through the middle. New entry and growing competition (notably from Delta and Continental) led to the threat of instability in the industry, and

Table 3.2 Financial and operating data for the US airline industry, 1978–2001

	Available seat miles (billions)	Load factor (%)	Break-even load factor (%)	Operating revenue ($, billion)	Operating margin (%)	Rate of return on investment (%)
1978	369	61.5	57.4	22.9	5.2	13.3
1979	416	63.0	62.5	27.2	1.3	6.5
1980	433	59.0	59.1	33.7	0.1	5.3
1981	425	58.6	59.2	36.7	(0.8)	4.7
1982	440	59.0	60.0	36.4	(2.5)	2.1
1983	465	60.7	60.1	39.0	0.5	6.0
1984	515	59.2	56.3	43.8	1.9	9.9
1985	548	61.4	59.7	46.7	1.8	9.6
1986	607	60.3	58.7	50.5	(0.5)	4.9
1987	649	62.4	59.6	57.0	1.0	7.2
1988	677	62.5	58.9	64.6	2.6	10.8
1989	684	63.2	61.6	69.3	0.2	6.3
1990	733	62.4	64.0	76.1	(5.1)	(6.0)
1991	715	62.6	64.1	75.2	(2.6)	(0.5)
1992	753	63.6	65.6	78.1	(3.1)	(9.3)
1993	771	63.5	62.4	83.8	1.7	(0.4)
1994	784	66.2	66.8	88.3	(0.4)	5.2
1995	807	67.0	64.9	94.6	2.4	11.9
1996	835	69.3	66.9	101.9	2.8	11.5
1997	861	70.3	65.0	109.6	4.7	14.7
1998	874	70.7	66.7	113.5	4.3	12.0
1999	918	71.0	66.4	119.0	4.5	11.1
2000	957	72.4	70.2	129.5	2.0	6.6
2001	930	70.0	77.0	115.4	(6.7)	(6.9)

Source: Air Transport Association.

in 1938 Congress responded with the Civil Aeronautics Act. The legislation established the Civil Aeronautics Board (CAB) with authority to administer the structure of the industry and competition within it. The CAB awarded interstate routes to the existing 23 airlines, established safety guidelines priorities, and strict rules for passenger fares, airmail rates, route entry and exit, mergers and acquisitions, and inter-firm agreements. Fares were set by the CAB on the basis of cost plus a reasonable rate of return. The result was that cost increases could be passed on to customers. The outcome was an ossification of industry structure – despite more than 80 applications from firms seeking to operate scheduled domestic flights, not a single new carrier was approved between 1938 and 1978. Instead, new entrants set up as local carriers offering intrastate routes.

Rapid expansion of the industry after World War II and a wave of technological innovations – notably the jet – led to increasing concerns over airline safety. Following an aircraft collision in 1956 that killed 128 people, a new safety regulatory agency, the Federal Aviation Agency (later renamed the Federal Aviation Administration), was created in 1958.

During the 1970s, two factors created the impetus for reform. First, the oil shock of 1974 led to rapidly rising costs and attempts by the CAB to protect the airlines through large fare increases, a four-year moratorium on new routes, and agreements among the airlines to limit capacity on major routes. The result was the public's growing dissatisfaction with the high cost and inefficiency of air travel. Second, a major shift was occurring in political opinion. The system of airline regulation was an outcome of the New Deal. During the 1970s, the principles of economic liberalism were attracting increasing support. Politicians, particularly on the right, were pushing for less reliance on government regulation and a greater role for market forces.

Political arguments for deregulation were supported by new developments in economics. The case for regulation had been based traditionally upon arguments about "natural monopoly" – competition was impossible in industries where scale economies and network effects were particularly important. During the early 1970s, the theory of contestable markets was developed. The main argument was that industries did not need to be competitively structured in order to result in competitive outcomes. So long as barriers to entry and exit were low, then the potential for "hit and run" entry would cause established firms to charge competitive prices and earn competitive rates of return[2].

These arguments were supported by evidence that unregulated intrastate airfares were substantially lower than fares for interstate flights of comparable distances.

By the mid-1970s, pressures for regulatory reforms were gathering pace. In 1976, a Senate Subcommittee chaired by Ted Kennedy concluded that lifting government constraints on competition would cause efficiency and innovation in the airline industry to rise and prices to fall. In the same year, Alfred Kahn, the new chairman of the CAB, pushed the agency to liberalize entry and pricing. In October 1978 the Airline Deregulation Act abolishing the CAB was approved by Congress and signed into law by President Carter.

The Impact of Deregulation

The elimination of restrictions over domestic routes and schedules and over domestic fares resulted in a wave of new entrants – by 1980, 20 new carriers including People Express, Air Florida, and Midway had set up – and an outbreak of price competition.

Deregulation was quickly followed by the oil shock of 1979, the onset of worldwide recession, and the air traffic controllers' strike of 1981. During 1978–82, the industry incurred massive losses (see table 3.2), and the outcome was a widespread bankruptcy (between 1978 and 1988 over 150 carriers went bust) and a wave of mergers and acquisitions. By 1982, expansion had resumed and during the 1980s and into the 1990s mileage flown grew at a trend rate of 4 percent per annum. At the same time, competition and the quest for efficiency resulted in a continuous decline in real prices.

■ FIRM STRATEGY AND INDUSTRY EVOLUTION AFTER DEREGULATION ■

Changes in the structure of the airline industry during the 1980s and 1990s were primarily a result of the strategies of the airlines as they sought to adjust to the new conditions of competition in the industry and gain competitive advantage.

Route Strategies: The Hub and Spoke System

During the 1980s a system of predominantly point-to-point routes was replaced by one where the major airlines concentrated their routes on a few major airports linked by frequent services using large planes, with smaller, nearby airports connected to these hubs by shorter routes using smaller planes. This "hub-and-spoke" system offered two major benefits:

- It allowed greater efficiency through concentrating traveler facilities and maintenance and refueling facilities in fewer locations, while permitting cost savings through higher levels of capacity utilization and the use of larger, more cost efficient aircraft for inter-hub travel. The efficiency benefits of the hub-and-spoke system were reinforced by scheduling flights such that incoming short-haul arrivals were concentrated at particular times to allow passengers to be pooled for the longer-haul flights on large aircraft. The efficiency benefits of hub-and-spoke over point-to-point in terms of economizing on routes and aircraft distance traveled may be illustrated by a hypothetical example. An airline with two hubs, each hub linking through 10 spokes to other cities, can provide one-stop service with 21 routes. Non-stop, point-to-point service between all these cities would require 190 routes. In addition, the carrier can increase their overall load factor (and thus revenues) and flight frequencies and decrease costs by serving all these markets with fewer aircraft and fewer crewmembers.
- It allowed major carriers to establish dominance in major regional markets and on particular routes. In effect, the major airlines became more geographically differentiated in their route offerings. The ability of a single airline to dominate individual hubs was reinforced by mergers. For example, when TWA acquired Ozark in 1986, it controlled over 80 percent of flights in and out of St Louis. Northwest accounted for 65 percent of traffic in and out of Detroit Metropolitan Airport. The hub-and-spoke system also created a barrier to the entry of new carriers who often found it difficult to obtain gates and landing slots at the major hubs.

The hub and spoke system also allowed the major airlines to offer a more integrated, through-ticketing service by establishing alliances with local ("commuter") airlines. Thus, American Eagle, United Express, and Delta Shuttle were franchise systems established by AMR, UAL, and Delta respectively whereby commuter airlines used the reser-

Table 3.3 Concentration in the US airline industry

	Four-firm concentration ratio		Four-firm concentration ratio
1935	88%	1982	54.2%
1939	82%	1987	64.8%
1949	70%	1990	61.5%
1954	71%	1999	66.4%
1977	56.2%		

Notes: The four-firm concentration ratio measures the share of the industry's passenger-miles accounted for by the four largest companies. During 1935–54, the four biggest companies were United, American, TWA, and Eastern. During 1982–99 the four biggest companies were United, American, Delta, and Northwest.
Source: Civil Aeronautics Board and US Dept of Transport.

vation and ticketing systems of the major airlines and coordinated their operations and marketing policies with those of their bigger partners.

Mergers

New entry during the period of deregulation had reduced seller concentration in the industry (see table 3.3).

The consolidation of the industry is shown in figure 3.1.

Pricing

The growth of competition in the post-deregulation era was most apparent in the prices of air tickets. The instigators of lower prices were mainly established airlines suffering from weak revenues and excess capacity and eager for cash flow, and new entrants into the industry. The new, low-cost entrants played a critical role in stimulating the price wars that came to characterize competition after deregulation. People Express, Braniff, New York Air, and Southwest all sought aggressive expansion through rock-bottom fares made possible by highly efficient cost structures and a bare-bones service (the low-cost airlines typically offered no in-flight meals or entertainment and no baggage handling). Although most of the low-cost newcomers failed during the early years of airline deregulation, new entry continued during the 1980s and 1990s.

In response to the price initiatives of the low-cost airlines, the major carriers sought to cut prices selectively. Fare structures became increasingly complex as airlines sought to separate price-sensitive leisure customers from price-inelastic business travelers. As a result, fare structures became wider: advanced purchased economy fares with Saturday night stays were often just 15 percent of the first class fare for the same journey.

Price cuts were also selective by route. Typically the major airlines offered low prices on those routes where they faced competition from low-cost rivals. Southwest, the

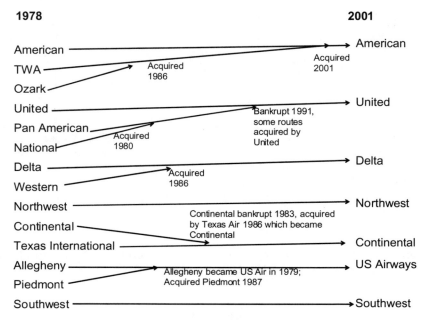

Figure 3.1 Consolidation in the US airline industry after deregulation
Source: Updated from S. Borenstein, "The evolution of US airline competition," *Journal of Economic Perspectives*, Vol. 6, No. 2, 1992, p. 48.

biggest and most successful of the economy carriers, complained continually of predatory price cuts by its larger rivals.

However, the ability of the major airlines to compete against the budget airlines was limited by the majors' cost structures. Their ability to reduce costs was constrained by their complex, restrictive labor agreements, their infrastructure, and their commitments to provide scheduled services over vast route networks. Hence, to meet the competition of low-cost newcomers, several of the majors set up new subsidiaries to imitate the strategies and cost structures of the budget airlines. Continental launched CALite in 1994, and was followed the next year by UAL's "Shuttle by United." American Airlines, on the other hand, sought to compete with Southwest and other budget airlines (such as ValuJet) by forging agreements with smaller airlines such as Midway and Reno Air in which it ceded some of its most price competitive (and loss making) routes to its smaller partners.

The Quest for Differentiation

Under regulation, the inability to compete on price resulted in airline competition shifting to non-price dimensions – customer service and in-flight food and entertainment.

Deregulation brutally exposed the myth of customer loyalty: most travelers could not distinguish major differences between the offerings of the different major airlines and were increasingly indifferent as to which airline they flew on a particular route. Increasing evidence that airline seats were fundamentally commodity products did not stop the airlines from attempts to differentiate their offerings and build customer loyalty.

For the most part, efforts to attract customers through enhanced services and facilities were directed towards business travelers. The high margins on first and business class tickets provided a strong incentive to attract these customers by means of spacious seats and intensive in-flight pampering. For leisure travelers it was unclear whether their choice of carrier was responsive to anything other than price, and the low margins on these tickets limited the willingness of the airlines to increase costs by providing additional services. Some airlines – notably TWA and American – experimented with cabin configurations that offered coach passengers more legroom.

The most widespread and successful initiatives to build customer loyalty was the introduction of frequent flyer schemes. American's frequent flyer program was introduced in 1981 and was soon followed by all the other major airlines. By offering free tickets and upgrades on the basis of number of miles flown, and building in different threshold levels for receiving benefits, the airlines encourage customer loyalty and discourage customers from switching airlines in response to small price differentials. By the end of the 1990s, these frequent flyer programs had become a major part of the airlines' operations. *The Economist* estimated that unredeemed frequent flyer miles had surged to 8 trillion miles by the end of 2001, worth roughly $500 billion.[3] Through involving other companies as partners – car rental companies, hotel chains, credit card issuers – frequent flyer programs had become an important source of additional revenue for the airlines worth about $10 billion in 2001.[4]

■ THE INDUSTRY IN 2002 ■

The Airlines

At the end of 2001, the US airline industry comprised almost 100 companies ranging from the major airlines to small local companies (table 3.4).

The industry was dominated by the seven major passenger airlines – United, American, Delta, Northwestern, Continental, US Airways, and Southwest (table 3.5).

A number of airlines are linked together in alliances. Thus, American, United, Delta, Northwest, and US Airways all have alliances with smaller airlines for coordinating schedules and routes and using the reservations and ticketing systems of the larger carriers.

Given the mergers already in process (notably American's acquisition of TWA and United's attempt to acquire US Airways) and the perilous financial state of many other airlines, most observers were expecting the industry's consolidation to continue into the future.

Table 3.4 The US airline companies in 2001

Major airlines (13)	National airlines (34)	Regional airlines (45)
Alaska	Air Transport Int'l	Accessair
America West	Air Wisconsin	Air South
American	Air Tran	Allegiant
Continental	Aloha	AmeriJet
Delta	Atlantic Southeast	Ameristar
DHL Airways	Atlas Air	Asia Pacific Int'l
FedEx	Challenge	Capital Cargo
Northwest	Comair	Casino Express
Southwest	Continental Express	Champion Air
Trans World	Continental Micronesia	Custom Air
United	Emery Worldwide	Eastwind
United Parcel Services	Evergreen Int'l	Express National
US Airways	Executive	Falcon Air
	Express One	Florida West
	Fine	Gemini
	Frontier	Gulf and Caribbean
	Hawaiian	Kiwi
	Horizon Air	Laker
	JetBlue	Lorair
	Kitty Hawk	Lynden
	Mesaba	Miami Air
	Midway	Nations Air
	Midway Express	North American
	National	Northern Air
	Polar Air Cargo	Omni
	Ryan Int'l	Pace Aviation
	Spirit Air	Pan American
	Sun Country	Panagra
	Tower	Prestige
	Trans States	Pro Air
	USA Jet	Reeve Aleutian
	US Airways Shuttle	Reliant
	Vanguard	Renown
	World	Sierra Pacific
		Skytrek
		Southeast
		Sun Pacific
		Sunworld
		Tatonduk
		Trade Winds
		Trans Air Link
		Trans Continental
		Transmeridian
		UFS
		Zantop

Source: Air Transport Association.

Table 3.5 Operating data for the larger airlines

Carrier	Available seat miles Sept. 2001 (billions)	Available seat miles Sept. 2000 (billions)	Load factor Sept. 2001 (%)	Load factor Sept. 2000 (%)	Average cost per available seat mile (cents)
Total System	64.9	79.2	58.6	69.6	
United	11.4	14.5	61.2	69.9	67.5
American	10.0	12.9	59.7	70.0	65.0
Delta	10.1	12.3	56.6	68.9	82.5
Northwest	6.9	8.3	64.0	76.8	62.3
Continental	5.5	6.9	61.5	72.6	79.2
Southwest	4.9	5.0	52.5	65.7	61.3
US Airways	4.6	5.7	56.2	67.0	99.9
TWA	1.9	3.0	50.0	71.0	65.0
America West	1.9	2.2	59.7	64.0	66.6
Alaska	1.1	1.3	60.8	62.9	78.1
American Trans Air	0.9	1.0	64.7	72.2	66.6
American Eagle	0.4	0.4	44.3	56.4	201.4

Source: Air Transport Association.

Market for Air Travel

At the beginning of the twenty-first century, airlines provided the dominant mode of long-distance travel in the US. For shorter journeys, cars provided the major alternative. Alternative forms of public transportation – namely bus and rail – accounted for a small and diminishing proportion of journeys in excess of a hundred miles, except on a few routes (e.g., between Washington, New York, and Boston trains provided a viable alternative to air).

Most forecasts point to the continued growth in the demand for air travel, probably below the trend rate of 5 percent per year of past two decades, but most likely faster than the rate of population growth. There was little evidence of growing competition from alternative modes of transport. With Amtrak mired in financial and political difficulties, there seemed little chance that the US would develop high-speed train services similar to those of Europe and Japan. Meanwhile, the communications revolution seemed to have done little to relieve business people of the need for face-to-face meetings.

More important changes were occurring within the structure of market demand. Of particular concern to the airlines was evidence that the segmentation between business and leisure customers was breaking down. Conventional wisdom dictated that while the demand for air tickets among leisure travelers was fairly price elastic, that of business travelers was highly inelastic. As a result, while US ticket prices had declined by 8 percent in 2001, business class fares had increased. However, the huge premium of full-price coach and first class fares to advanced-purchased leisure fares was causing many employers to baulk. During 2001, the demand for first and business class travel declined sharply.[5]

Major changes were occurring within the distribution side of the industry. Historically, the primary channel of distribution of airline tickets was travel agencies: retailers that specialized in the sale of travel tickets, hotel reservations, and vacation packages and provided travel consulting and reservations services to travelers. During the 1990s, the airlines made substantial reductions in the commission rates paid to travel agents. By 1996, most airlines were paying a base commission rate of 8% on fares, with a $50 cap on domestic round-trip fares. By 2000, the maximum commission rates offered by most airlines was 5 percent, while in 2001 Northwest led the way in withdrawing commissions from independent travel agents altogether. In the early 1990s commissions amounted to 10–11 percent of total costs, by 1998 they represented only about 6 percent of total costs. At the same time they developed their direct sales organizations using both telephone and internet reservations and ticket purchase systems. While the internet offered greater opportunity for airlines to deal directly with their customers, it also created a set of new players, online travel agents. Expedia, Travelocity, Cheap Tickets, Priceline, and a host of other online travel agents quickly established themselves as the biggest distributors of airline tickets in the US. Not only did their size allow them to wield greater bargaining power than traditional travel agencies, but they provided consumers with unparalleled transparency of prices, permitting the lowest price deals to be quickly spotted. Meanwhile, in the traditional travel agent sector major changes were afoot as fragmentation gave way to consolidation (led by large international players such as American Express, Thomas Cook, and Carlson). During 2001 and 2002, the airlines were attempting to gain greater control over ticket distribution. They offered their own online ticket agency, Orbitz, to compete with Expedia and Travelocity, while some of the budget airlines attempted to move towards complete direct selling. In 2002, Southwest withdrew its business from Travelocity and increased its proportion of ticket sales through its own online reservations system to 70 percent.

Airline Cost Conditions

Less than one-third of airline operating costs are accounted for by flying operations; servicing and maintenance account for a whopping 28 percent, while promotion and sales activities make up the next major cost activity (see table 3.6).

Among the items which make up the airlines' total operating costs, labor costs are the most important, followed by fuel and equipment costs. Table 3.7 shows the breakdown of the industry's costs by cost item.

LABOR

Wages and salaries account for about 35 percent of total costs. The industry's labor costs are boosted by the high level of employee remuneration – average pay in airlines

Table 3.6   The cost structure of the US airline industry: breakdown by activity

	Percentage of total operating costs
Flying operations	31.0
Aircraft and traffic servicing	15.7
Maintenance	12.3
Promotion and sales	10.9
Transport related	10.3
Passenger services	8.6
Administrative	5.6
Depreciation and amortization	5.6

Source: Air Transport Association, *2000 Airline Industry Review*.

Table 3.7   Airline costs by expense item, 1991 and 2001

	Cost index 1991	Cost index 2001	% of total operating expenses 1991	% of total operating expenses 2001
Labor cost	129	184	32.5	38.2
Fuel cost	89	78	14.5	12.0
Fleet cost	187	288	8.6	9.4
Interest cost	81	53	2.4	2.1
Insurance cost	81	68	0.3	0.5
Maintenance materials	183	180	3.4	2.7
Landing fees	153	202	1.9	1.9
Advertising and promotion	94	52	1.0	1.0
Traffic commission costs	188	65	10.4	3.4

Source: Air Traffic Association.

is 47 percent higher than the average for all private industries – and by low labor productivity that results from rigid working practices agreed with unions. Most airline workers belong to one of a dozen major unions: the Association of Flight Attendants, the Air Line Pilots Association, the International Association of Machinists and Aerospace Workers, etc. Labor unions provide the key institutional force through which high salaries have been maintained. Despite intense competition, falling real ticket prices, and the financial weakness of the industry, labor costs have continued to increase as airlines have awarded pay increases that far outstrip the rate of inflation. Labor relations in the industry have been historically adversarial, with work stoppages and strike threats becoming increasingly frequent as contracts come up for renewal. United has typically set the lead in pay increases. In summer 2000, United pilots refused to work overtime, which resulted in delays and canceled flights, which severely disrupted the summer travel plans of thousands of passengers. In order to solve the problem with its pilots, United agreed to extraordinary pay raises which led to parity demands among pilots at other airlines.

The *Washington Post* observed:

Before deregulation, the Civil Aeronautics Board governed fares and generally allowed airlines to pass along labor costs. That, together with the dread of work stoppages, disposed the carriers to generous labor contracts. In the 1990s, wages went up. Today the process is protracted, workers become angry, then surly with customers (remember United's pilots sabotaging their airline in 2000, when they had a miserable 40 percent on-time rate and 20,000 flights were canceled), so profits decline with service.

The industry could benefit from mandatory, binding arbitration of the sort baseball has. Each side would make a proposal and the arbitrator would pick one or the other proposal. Because the arbitrator could not split the difference, the process would pull each side toward the other.

Meanwhile, United pilots recently won a 28 percent raise, just before the company lost $600 million in the *first* half of 2001. Other carriers' pilots want parity. Other workers want their earnings pulled up by those of the pilots. Turbulence ahead. Situation normal.[6]

FUEL

Jet fuel (kerosene) is the airlines' second largest cost, accounting for 10 to 12 percent of total expenses. How much a carrier spends on fuel depends on the age of its aircraft and its average flight length. Newer planes and longer flights equate to higher fuel efficiency. Also, the fuel efficiency of different aircraft varies widely, primarily dependent on the number of engines. Fuel prices represent the most volatile and unpredictable cost item for the airlines due to fluctuations in the price of crude. Since January 1999 crude prices have fluctuated between $14 and $40 a barrel. Although there is strong competition between different refiners in the supply of petroleum products (including jet fuel), ultimately, fuel prices depend upon crude prices whose level is determined by the OPEC cartel. As OPEC has become increasingly effective in enforcing adherence to production quotas among its members, so the price of crude has remained high.

EQUIPMENT

Aircraft are the biggest capital expenditure item for the airlines. At prices of up to $150 million apiece (the A380 will be over $200 million), the purchase of new planes represents a major source of financial strain for the airlines. While Boeing and Airbus compete fiercely for new business (especially when, as in 2002, they have spare capacity), aggressive discounts and generous financing terms for the purchase of new planes disguises the fact that a major source of profits for the aircraft manufacturers are in aftermarket sales of parts, upgrades, and training. Over the past 20 years the number of manufacturers of large jets has declined from four to two. Lockheed ceased civilian jet manufacture in 1984; McDonnell Douglas was acquired by Boeing in 1997.

AIRPORT FACILITIES

Airports play a critical role in the US aviation industry. They are hugely complex, expensive facilities and few in number. Only the largest cities are served by more than one airport. Despite the rapid, sustained growth in air transport over the 25 years since deregulation, only one major new airport has been built – Denver. Most airports are owned by municipal or state governments and generate substantial revenue flows for these government authorities. Landing fees are set by contracts between the airport and the airlines, and are typically based upon aircraft weight. In 1993, Los Angeles International airport raised its landing fees by 200 percent, and increased them again by 33 percent in 1995. Threatened with the withdrawal of their landing rights, the airlines soon fell into line. Although the fees airlines pay to airports account for only about 5 percent of their total operating costs, airport landing fees and terminal rents have been one of the industry's fastest-growing costs. Between 1992 and 1999, airport charges, including passenger facility charges, rose 70 percent.[7]

COST DIFFERENCES BETWEEN AIRLINES

One of the arguments for deregulation had been that there were few major economies of scale in air transport, hence large and small airlines could coexist. Indeed, there is little evidence that large airlines have systematically lower average costs than smaller airlines. However, there are economies associated with network density – the greater the number of routes within a region, the easier is it for an airline to gain economies of utilization of aircraft, crews, and passenger and maintenance facilities. In practice, differences in average costs between airlines far exceed those predicted by economies of scale, scope, density, or any other external factor. The critical issues seem to be company-specific managerial and organizational factors. The industry's cost leader, Southwest, has a strategy and management systems committed to lowering costs. By offering services from minor airports, with limited customer service, a single type of airplane, job-sharing among employees, and salary levels substantially less than those paid by other major carriers, Southwest achieves the industry's lowest cost per available seat mile (CASM), despite flying relatively short routes. Conversely, US Airways had the highest operating costs of the majors (its CASM in 2001 was 12.46 cents compared with 7.54 cents for Southwest, 10.14 cents for Delta and 11.14 cents for American). US Airways' high costs were partly a result of eternal factors – short routes, smaller planes, and routes concentrated on the eastern seaboard and subject to adverse weather conditions – but mainly the consequence of managerial factors such as highly restrictive labor agreements, poor employee relations, and deficiencies in operational management.

A critical factor determining average costs was capacity utilization. Because most costs, at least in the short run, were fixed, profitable operation was acutely dependent upon achieving break-even levels of capacity operation. When airlines were operating below break-even capacity there were big incentives to cut price in order to attract additional business. The industry's periodic price wars tended to occur during periods of slack demand and on routes where there were several competitors and considerable excess capacity.

Achieving high load factors while avoiding ruinously low prices is a major preoccupation for the airlines. Yield management systems are highly sophisticated computer models that combine historical data, models, and rigorous financial analysis to provide flexible price determination. The goal is to earn as much revenue on each flight as possible. Achieving this goal has meant a proliferation of pricing categories and a plethora of special deals ranging from "weekend internet specials" to the auctioning of tickets over internet auction sites such as eBay.

Entry and Exit

Hopes by the deregulators that the US airline business would be a case study of competition in a contestable industry were thwarted by evidence of significant barriers to both entry and exit. Evidence on price levels showing significantly higher prices on routes with a single carrier suggested that potential competition was no substitute for actual competition. The key issue is that, while the capital costs of entry are fairly low (it is possible to set up a new airline with a single leased plane), offering airline service requires gates, airline and aircraft certification, takeoff and landing slots, baggage handling services, and the marketing and distribution of tickets. Airport congestion together with the increasing dominance of gates and landing slots at hub airports by a few major carriers has often meant that new entrants have been forced to use secondary airports. Despite the unprofitable state of the industry, there appeared to be a continual stream of entrepreneurs attracted to the apparent glamour of owning an airline. However, in the future the most likely source of significant new entry is foreign airlines which in 2002 were still restricted from either acquiring US airlines or offering internal service within the US.

Once established, there are significant barriers to the exit of companies from the industry. A notable feature of the industry has been the tendency for loss-making airlines to continue in the industry for long periods of time. The unwillingness or inability of airlines to exit can be attributed to the contracts (especially with employees) which give rise to large closure costs and optimism of executives and investors that things will get better in the future. A key factor maintaining otherwise insolvent airlines has been the provisions of Chapter 11 bankruptcy. The ability of financially failed airlines to enter Chapter 11 has allowed them to survive through suspending many of their contracts. A critical problem for otherwise financially healthy airlines has been meeting competition from bankrupt airlines which have the benefit of artificially lowered costs.

■ FUTURE PROSPECTS ■

Looking to the future, most of the major airlines looked to short-run benefits from the recovery of the aviation market from the aftermath of September 11, but only limited prospects for longer-run changes that might improve fundamental industry economics. The Air Transport Association's outlook statement offered little basis for optimism:

It is impossible to predict with certainty when air traffic demand will return to normal . . . Looking at the Gulf War as a point of reference, it took approximately six months for traffic to return to its previous levels. The declines following September 11 were dramatically deeper and the recovery is expected to reflect the changing world situation. Under normal circumstances the recovery would track the strengthening of US economy. However, because the events of September 11 and aftermath have no precedent, recovery remains less certain. A return to pre-September 11 levels of service sometime in the 3rd quarter of 2002 is the current expectation.

Unprecedented challenges for the airline industry lie ahead. Airlines must focus on cost control, cash preservation, and cautious growth. Losses are expected for the full year 2002, and it is not until 2003 that the airlines as a group see a hope of return to profitability. The net profit margin for airlines is slim, even at the best of times . . . Because cash from operations has declined significantly, many carriers will be forced to borrow . . . Debt will increase well above norms for other industries. Airline debt-to-capital ratios have risen to 60 percent as compared with 35 percent for US industry.[8]

Consultants at McKinsey & Company were even more pessimistic about the industry's outlook:

In times of low demand, airlines are badly hampered by high fixed costs. As an example, the newest Boeing or Airbus wide-body jetliners cost between $80 million and $150 million each, and lease or loan payments are due whether a plane is parked on a tarmac or cruising with a cabin full of paying passengers. Meanwhile, strong unions have historically made it difficult to reduce labor costs. From 1995 to 2000, operating costs for the US majors stayed roughly constant, with costs rising even higher in 2001 prior to September 11. After September 11, costs moved still higher to pay for increased security and insurance provisions (probably 1 to 2 percent of revenues) – and that is before adding the high cost of increased debt levels.

Cutting capacity is considered critical to cost reduction, but the full impact on profits still takes time to emerge. Analysts estimate that after September 11, airlines reduced the number of seats available for each kilometer they were flying by more than 20 percent in the United States. However, more than three-quarters of these reductions came from using active aircraft less, with the remaining cuts coming from putting aircraft into storage. Both measures allow airlines to lower variable costs, notably fuel and maintenance, by dropping unprofitable flights, but fixed costs such as lease and debt payments remain. What is more, because the excess capacity is readily available, it can come back quickly. In early 2002, airlines were already bringing back capacity into their networks rather than lose market share on key routes. This is particularly important, since available excess capacity in the present downturn exceeds that at similar points in the past two cycles.

As scheduled deliveries arrive during the next two years, the record surplus may continue growing despite the fact that the number of orders as a percentage of total fleet size is lower than it was at this point during the most recent cycle.

Another important element in recovery is passenger yield – the price paid for each passenger-kilometer flown. The problem here is that, given near-term fixed costs, airlines must sacrifice yield to keep seats filled. Business travel has been the primary source for high-yield passengers, critical to the economic viability of the hub-and-spoke model used by the major airlines. However, over the past several years, business travel has accounted for an ever smaller share of airline revenues. In 2001 before September 11, the share had dropped to 23 percent, from more than 35 percent in 1999, in the United States. While some of this drop is normal cyclicality as companies cut back on travel, other factors indicate that the decline may be longer term. After September 11, the inconveniences caused by time-consuming new security measures have made business travel even less attractive, and the likelihood is that these inconveniences will continue for the foreseeable future.

In order to reduce the cost of travel, companies have made several fundamental changes that are likely to have long-lasting effects on business travel revenues. Large corporations have used their purchasing power to negotiate volume discounts on fares, with price reductions on some routes often as high as 20 to 30 percent. Furthermore, most corporations are now enforcing the travel restrictions tied to these volume agreements.

Some alternatives to business travel on commercial airlines may now finally take hold. Companies are turning increasingly to travel substitutes such as videoconferencing and have been experimenting with shared corporate jets as a replacement for first-class travel for top executives. New advances such as web conferencing have boosted demand for videoconferencing services, with a 30 percent year-over-year increase prior to September 11. Forced behavioral changes in the aftermath of the terrorist attacks have pushed the growth rate for these services up to 40 percent. In addition, the expansion of fractional jet models for business aircraft significantly increases the availability of business jets as a travel alternative. The corporate jet option, which is becoming more attractive given the increased time required to negotiate security procedures at major airports, may take away at least 10 percent of first-class travelers by 2005. In view of these changes in the way corporations work and purchase travel, we believe that business travel revenues will remain under pressure even when the world economy recovers.

In the 1980s, increased yields drove recovery in the airline business. This time around, given the high levels of excess capacity and projected weakness in business travel revenues, we do not believe that yields will come back as strongly as in previous downturns. Instead, any recovery will have to come from long-term, structural cost reductions. For major airlines using the high-coverage hub-and-spoke model, such reductions may be difficult to achieve, and these airlines may struggle beyond 2004. In contrast, competitors that utilize a lower-cost strategy – such as Ryanair and easyJet in Europe, Southwest Airlines and WestJet in North America, and Virgin Blue in Australia – look well positioned to expand their operations and profitability.[9]

Many industry experts believed that more fundamental changes in industry structure would be necessary to create a financially healthy airline industry in the US. The major airlines looked to consolidation as one means of reducing cut-throat competition and managing excess capacity in the system. With American's acquisition of TWA and United's proposed takeover of US Airways, industry concentration seemed likely to increase significantly. Other executives believed that the industry would always be unprofitable as long as it was subject to the power of organized labor. American's Don Carty believed that there was a case for Congressional intervention to mandate the arbitration of labor disputes in the industry.

NOTES

1.   Air Transport Association, State of the US Airline Industry: A Report on Recent Trends for US Airline Carriers, 2002 (http://www.airlines.org/public/industry/bin/state.pdf).

2. For a review of contestability as applied to the airline industry, see S. Borenstein, "The evolution of US airline competition," *Journal of Economic Perspectives*, Vol. 6, No. 2, 1992, pp. 45–73.

3. "Fly me to the moon," *The Economist*, May 4, 2002, p. 80.

4. Ibid.

5. "Saturday night fever," *The Economist*, April 20, 2002, p. 72.

6. George Will, "Always A Bumpy Ride," *Washington Post*, May 9, 2002, p. 34. Copyright © 2002 Washington Post WritersGroup, reprinted with permission.

7. Air Transport Association, *Airline Handbook*, 2000.

8. Air Transport Association, State of the US Airline Industry: A Report on Recent Trends for US Airline Carriers, 2002, pp. 9–11 (http://www.airlines.org/public/industry/bin/state.pdf).

9. Peter R. Costa, Doug S. Harned, and Jerrold T. Lundquist, "Rethinking the aviation industry," *The McKinsey Quarterly, No. 2, 2002*. This article was originally published in *The McKinsey Quarterly, 2002, Number 2, Risk and Resilience*, and can be found on the publication's website, http://www.mckinseyquarterly.com. Copyright © 2002 McKinsey & Company. All rights reserved. Reprinted by permission.

DaimlerChrysler and the World Automobile Industry

Robert M. Grant

■ THE MERGER ■

The merger between Daimler Benz and Chrysler Corporation announced in May 1998 was the biggest industrial merger in history. It created the world's third largest automotive company (after GM and Ford) with 421,000 employees worldwide and sales of over $130 billion.[1] The prospects for the merger looked good. Because of the two companies' complementary product ranges, regional concentrations, and capabilities, its logic was acclaimed by both investors and auto industry analysts. The extent of the companies' pre-merger and post-merger planning by the two companies.was also *unusual.* Under the vision of "one company, one vision, one chairman, two cultures," the merged company established an elaborate structure of joint Chrysler – Daimler integration teams which began work on reconciling and integrating almost every aspect of the two companies' development, technology, operations, and marketing with a view to achieving the $3 billion in cost savings that the merger anticipated.

Within a year, however, the merger had run into trouble. The rapid exodus of Chrysler's senior managers made it clear that the deal was not so much a merger of equals as a German takeover. Despite the efforts of the post-merger integration teams, few of the anticipated cost savings had been realized. Most serious was the rapidly deteriorating performance of Chrysler. With its dominance in the once-lucrative sport-utility and minivan sectors eroding, and a dearth of new product, revenues and profits sagged during 2000. By September 2000, DaimlerChrysler's share price had almost halved from its post-merger high, and Chrysler's losses for the second half of the year were forecast to reach $700 million. Moreover, the task of integrating Daimler and Chrysler had been complicated by further acquisitions: in order to build the group's position in Asia it acquired a third of Mitsubishi motors in March 2000 and 10 percent of Hyundai in June.

In February 2001, DaimlerChrysler launched a turnaround plan for Chrysler and Mitsubishi Motors. Restructuring at Chrysler involved plans to reduce material costs by 15 percent, reduce the workforce by 20 percent, and close six plants. Over the medium term cost reduction would require increased global integration between Chrysler, Mitsubishi, and Mercedes Benz. The number of platforms used by Chrysler and Mitsubishi were to be cut from 29 to between 13 and 16, the number of engines cut by between 15 and 30 percent, and Mercedes technology would be shared more widely. A restructuring charge of $3.9 billion was taken in the first quarter of 2001, and for the whole year Chrysler's anticipated operating losses were $2.2 billion.

Restructuring was accompanied by a tightening of top management control. In place of the automotive and sales councils that Daimler Benz and Chrysler set up after the merger, Chairman Jurgen Schrempp created a tightly knit executive auto committee headed by himself and Mercedes Benz chief Jurgen Hubbert and including Chrysler CEO Dieter Zetsche, commercial vehicles director Eckhard Cordes, Mitsubishi board member Manfred Bischoff, and corporate strategy director Rudiger Grube. The new committee would make all key strategic decisions and coordinate production and marketing across the group's divisions.

For 50-year-old Rudiger Grube, his position as head of corporate development, including corporate strategy, mergers and acquisitions as well as corporate e-business, represented both continuity and change. During the years following the merger, he had taken charge of the post-merger integration initiative. His most pressing responsibilities for the remainder of 2001 would be to continue and accelerate the effort to build a truly global business and in doing so release the potential efficiencies from integrating the activities of Mercedes, Chrysler, and Mitsubishi. However, once the cost savings from the restructuring plan had been achieved, Grube realized that DaimlerChrysler's performance – and its strategy – would be increasingly dependent upon the future prospects for the automobile industry as a whole.

As Grube began working on DaimlerChrysler's corporate strategy, he asked his team to look more closely at the development of the world automobile industry over the next four years. The primary focus of the strategy team was on the outlook for the world economy. With the US and Europe threatening to join Japan in recession and with only hesitant recovery by Southeast Asia, Latin America, and Russia from the financial crisis of 1998, the prospects for automobile demand were poor. But market demand was only one factor affecting the industry's profitability over the period 2002–5. During the past five years, the demand for new cars had been fairly buoyant – supported in particular by the booming US economy. Nevertheless, the final performance of even the major producers had been poor. Grube was struck by a recent report by Stern Stewart and Company on the industry: throughout the 1990s the industry's return on capital employed had been far below its cost of capital with the result that EVA (economic value added) was negative in every year from 1991 to 1999 (see table 4.1).

To what extent would DaimlerChrysler's financial performance in the future be constrained by adverse industry economics? If the auto industry's future profitability was to be similar to that of past, and unless DaimlerChrysler was able to achieve a level of profitability far in excess of its rivals, it seemed unreasonable for the company to risk the destruction of shareholder value through continuing to make multi-billion dollar

Table 4.1 Economic Value Added of major automobile producers (in $, millions)

	1991	1992	1993	1994	1995	1996	1997	1998	1999
General Motors	(10,719)	(8,765)	(7,807)	(4,430)	(2,963)	(6,593)	(4,807)	(7,669)	(6,160)
Ford	(6,821)	(9,386)	(6,805)	(230)	(5,412)	1,102	341	(3,980)	2,864
DaimlerChrysler	(3,332)	(1,038)	1,560	2,653	488	2,271	759	5,210	588
Toyota	(506)	(2,215)	(3,481)	(4,039)	(5,133)	(3,630)	(2,027)	(345)	(742)
VW	(214)	(1,964)	(3,489)	(2,210)	(2,445)	(2,395)	(2,319)	402	76
Nissan	(1,819)	(3,651)	(4,993)	(6,795)	(4,095)	(2,225)	(2,426)	(2,537)	(2,337)
Honda	(674)	(497)	(920)	(699)	(2,687)	(1,602)	(233)	1,100	1,372
Fiat	(633)	(2,658)	(3,292)	(576)	(554)	(703)	(1,371)	(1,456)	(1,888)
Renault	n.a.	n.a.	n.a.	n.a.	(1,647)	(4,040)	(2,888)	(349)	(932)
Peugeot	n.a.	n.a.	n.a.	n.a.	(389)	(1,033)	(759)	462	133
Hyundai	n.a.	n.a.	n.a.	n.a.	n.a.	144	(231)	(547)	(547)
Suzuki	(112)	(49)	(120)	(195)	(298)	(182)	(93)	(94)	n.a.
BMW	n.a.	(630)	(661)	(466)	(891)	(820)	(698)	(730)	48

Source: "Economic value added of major automobile producers," *Best of Times, Worst of Times*, Stern Stewart & Co., December 2000.

projects that were unlikely to cover their cost of capital. The prospects for profitability in the world automobile in the future depended critically upon the evolving structure of the industry. The problems of the 1990s had been caused not so much by lack of demand as by the pressure of competition created by too many producers, each of which was investing in too much capacity. The recent wave of consolidation in the industry offered a possible solution to these past problems of excessive competition. Yet it was also likely that the industry might be transformed by new forces that would also have huge implications for competition and profitability in the industry as a whole, and the basis for competitive advantage.

■ THE MARKET ■

Trends in Market Demand

From its beginnings in Europe and the United States during the 1890s, the automobile industry had grown almost continuously until the mid-1980s. However, market growth had followed different time-paths in different parts of the world. The US market entered its period of rapid growth during 1910–28. In Europe, the growth phase was both later and more subdued. By the late 1950s and early 1960s, the US market had reached maturity, though in Europe and Japan, market penetration of the automobile continued during the 1960s and 1970s. During the last two decades of the twentieth century, the advanced industrial world had seen little growth in automobile demand and in the US, even during the booming 1990s, production failed to surpass the peak reached in 1973 (see table 4.2). The problem of market saturation has been compounded by the tendency for cars to last longer. Table 4.3 shows the increase in the average age of cars in use in the US.

As a result, the automobile producers have looked increasingly to the newly industrializing countries for market opportunities. During the 1980s and 1990s countries such as Korea, Malaysia, Taiwan, Thailand, Turkey, Brazil, and Argentina offered the best growth prospects. As these markets became increasingly saturated, so China, India, and the former Soviet Union were seen as the "next wave" of attractive markets. With the opening of many of these countries to trade and direct investment, the world production of cars and trucks has continued to grow (table 4.4 shows world production).

The Evolution of the Automobile

The early years of the industry were characterized by considerable uncertainty over the design and technology of the motor car. Early "horseless carriages" were precisely that – they followed design features of existing horse-drawn carriages and buggies. Early motor cars demonstrated a bewildering variety of technologies. During the early years, the internal-combustion engine vied with the steam engine. Among internal-combustion engines there was a wide variety of cylinder configurations. Transmission systems, steering systems, and brakes all displayed a remarkable variety of technologies and designs, as well as considerable ingenuity.

Table 4.2 US motor vehicle production

	Passenger cars	Trucks and buses	Total
1900	4,192	n.a.	4,192
1905	24,250	750	25,000
1910	181,000	6,000	187,000
1915	895,930	74,000	969,930
1920	1,905,560	321,789	2,227,349
1925	3,735,171	530,659	4,265,830
1930	2,787,456	575,364	3,362,820
1935	3,273,874	697,367	3,971,241
1940	3,717,385	754,901	4,472,286
1945	69,532	655,683	725,215
1950	6,665,863	1,337,193	8,003,056
1955	7,920,186	1,249,105	9,169,291
1960	6,674,796	1,194,475	7,869,271
1965	9,305,561	1,751,805	11,057,366
1967	7,436,764	1,539,462	8,976,226
1970	6,546,817	1,692,442	8,239,259
1975	6,712,852	2,272,160	8,985,012
1977	9,200,849	3,411,521	12,612,370
1980	6,400,026	1,667,283	8,067,309
1985	8,002,259	3,464,327	11,466,586
1990	6,049,749	3,718,781	9,768,530
1991	5,407,120	3,375,422	8,782,542
1992	5,684,221	4,042,486	9,726,707
1993	5,981,046	4,883,157	10,864,203
1994	6,601,223	5,648,767	12,249,990
1995	6,350,367	5,634,742	11,985,109
1996	6,083,000	5,749,000	11,832,000
1997	5,927,000	6,169,000	12,096,000
1998	5,554,390	6,451,689	12,006,079
1999	5,637,949	7,387,029	13,024,978
2000	5,542,217	7,228,497	12,770,714

Source: Based on *Ward's Automotive Yearbook 2001* and earlier editions.

Over the years the technologies and designs of different manufactured parts tended to converge as many approaches (and their manufacturers) were eliminated through competition. The Ford Model T represented the first "dominant design" in automobiles – the technologies and design features of the Model T set a standard for other manufacturers to imitate. During the 1920s, the process of development continued, especially in car bodies with the general adoption of the enclosed, all-steel body.

During the post-war period, technological and design convergence continued. During the 1970s and 1980s, most of the models which were "outliers" in terms of distinctively different design disappeared: the VW Beetle with its rear, air-cooled engine,

Table 4.3 Average age of passenger cars in the US (years)

	Mean	Median
2000	8.8	8.3
1998	8.7	8.1
1996	8.5	7.4
1994	8.4	7.4
1992	8.1	7.0
1990	7.8	6.5
1988	7.6	6.8
1984	7.5	6.7
1980	6.6	6.0
1976	6.2	5.5
1972	5.7	5.1
1968	5.6	4.7
1962	6.0	5.7
1958	5.6	5.1
1952	6.8	4.5
1948	8.8	8.0
1941	5.5	4.9

Source: R.L. Polk & Co.

Table 4.4 World motor vehicle production (passenger cars and commercial vehicles)

	Total (mil.)	US and Canada as % of total		Total (mil.)	US and Canada as % of total
1950	10.58	79.4	1990	48.35	24.2
1955	13.63	70.9	1991	46.50	23.0
1960	16.49	50.4	1992	47.69	24.5
1965	24.27	49.4	1993	46.40	28.3
1970	29.40	32.1	1994	49.69	29.4
1975	33.00	31.4	1995	49.93	28.8
1980	38.51	24.8	1996	52.50	28.2
1985	44.81	30.3	1997	54.15	28.0
1986	45.30	29.1	1998	53.50	27.3
1987	45.90	27.4	1999	55.74	28.7
1988	48.21	27.3	2000	57.43	27.4
1989	49.10	26.2			

Sources: Annual Statistical Reports of the American Automobile Manufacturers Association (AAMA) (various years) and *Ward's Automotive Yearbook* (various years).

the Citroen 2-CV and its idiosyncratic braking and suspension system, Daf with its "Variomatic" transmission. The fall of the Berlin Wall was followed by the disappearance of other automotive idiosyncrasies, such as the 3-cylinder Wartburg and the 2-cycle Trabant. Engines became more similar: typically 4 or 6 cylinders, usually in-line (although V-6 and V-8 configurations are common in larger engines) with overhead

Table 4.5 Pounds of material in a typical family automobile

	1978	2001
Steel	2,128	1,781
Iron	512	345
Plastic and plastic composites	180	253
Aluminum	112	257
Copper and brass	37	46
Zinc castings	31	11
Glass	86	99
Rubber	146	146
Other	337	371
Total	3,569	3,309

Source: *Ward's Automotive Yearbook 2001*.

camshafts. Front-wheel drive and disc, anti-lock brakes became standard; suspension and steering systems became more standard; body shapes became increasingly alike. Although the automobile continued to evolve, technological progress has tended to be incremental: innovations have included application of electronics to ignition, braking, and engine control; safety features such as air bags; and developments such as multi-valve cylinders, traction control systems, all-wheel drive, variable suspensions, and inter-cooled turbos. The key design innovations of the 1990s was the "cab forward" design (pioneered by Honda), which increased the ratio of passenger space to engine space. The quest for fuel economy resulted in the substitution of lighter materials (aluminum, plastics, ceramics, and composites) for iron and steel (see table 4.5).

During the 1990s, electronic components accounted for an increasing proportion of the value of cars. A 1950 Mercedes had about 10 meters of wiring. A 1995 SL 500 with full options had 3,000 meters of wiring and 48 different microcomputers. The 1998 Ford Taurus embodied more computing power than was used in the 1969 moon landing. Current development, including satellite navigation systems, communications technology (telematics), emergency signaling, collision-avoidance radar, and intelligent monitoring systems, will only increase the importance of electronic technology within cars. Yet, despite the adoption of new, technology-based accessories and design improvements, there is little in today's family cars that is radically new (see table 4.6).

Designs and technologies have converged among manufacturers. While different types of vehicle (family cars, sports cars, passenger minivans, sport-utility vehicles) retain distinctive design features, within each of these categories manufacturers' product offerings have become increasingly similar. By 2000, GM was using wireless telephony-based "vehicle locators" to help motorists find their vehicles among the ranks of similar-looking automobiles. Convergence of technology and design meant a quest for new types of differentiation. All the major manufacturers strive to develop new "concept cars," and introduce novel design features. Recent years have seen a flood of new small car designs aimed particularly at the European market: Ford's Ka, Toyota's Yaris, and DaimlerChrysler's Smart car. Some manufacturers have experimented with retrodesign features (e.g., DaimlerChrysler's PT Cruiser).

Table 4.6 From option to standard: convergence in automobile features

Feature	Introduction	General adoption
Speedometer	1901 by Oldsmobile	Circa 1915
Automatic transmission	First installed 1904	Introduced by Packard as an option 1938. Standard on Cadillacs and other luxury cars early 1950s
Electric headlamps	GM introduced 1908	Standard equipment by 1916
All-steel body	Adopted by GM 1912	Becomes standard early 1920s
Steel enclosed body	Dodge 1923	Becomes standard late 1920s
Radio	Optional extra 1923	Standard equipment 1946
Four-wheel drive	Appeared 1924	Only limited availability by 1994
Hydraulic brakes	Introduced 1924	Become standard 1939
Shatterproof glass	First used in cars 1927	Standard feature in Fords 1938
Power steering	Introduced 1952	Standard equipment by 1969
Anti-lock brakes	Introduced 1972	Standard on GM cars in 1991
Air bags	Introduced by GM 1974	Standard in most new cars by 1994

Source: *Washington Post*.

Convergence also occurred across countries. US cars downsized, Japanese and Italian cars became larger. Although the automobile market remained highly segmented, the increased convergence of national markets was evident from the tendency for the same market segments to emerge in different countries. Thus, Mercedes, BMW, Jaguar, and the upmarket brands of the Japanese (Lexus, Infiniti, etc.) dominated the luxury segment throughout most of the world. Toyota, Land Rover, Chrysler (Jeep), Suzuki, and a few other manufacturers led the worldwide sport-utility segment (4-wheel drive vehicles designed for off-road use). The passenger minivan segment established by the Chrysler Caravan in North America appeared in Europe as the "multi-purpose vehicle" (MPV) segment led by the Renault Espace. The major differences between countries were in the *sizes* of the various segments. Thus, in the US, the "mid-size" family sedan was the largest segment, with the Ford Taurus, Honda Accord, and Toyota Camry the leading models. In Europe and Asia, small family cars ("subcompacts") formed the largest market segment. Other national differences were also apparent. In North America, pickup trucks, used as commercial vehicles in most of the world, increasingly displaced passenger cars.

The Evolution of Manufacturing Technology

At the beginning of the twentieth century, car manufacture, like carriage-making, was a craft industry. Cars were built to order according to individual customers' preferences and specifications. In Europe and North America there were hundreds of companies producing cars, few with annual production exceeding 1,000 vehicles. When Henry Ford began production in 1903, he used a similar approach. Even with fairly long runs of a single model (the first version of the Model T, for example), each car was individually built. The development of more precise machine tools permitted interchangeable parts, which ushered in mass production: batch or continuous production of components which were then assembled on moving assembly lines by semi-skilled workers. The productivity gains were enormous. In 1912 it took 23 man-hours to assemble a Model T, just 14 months later it took only 4. The resulting fall in the price of cars opened up a new era of popular motoring. By the 1920s automobile manufacturers were emerging among the ranks of the world's biggest industrial enterprises.

If "Fordism" was the first major revolution in process technology, then Toyota's "lean production" was the second. The system was developed by Toyota in post-war Japan at a time when shortages of key materials encouraged extreme parsimony and a need to avoid inventories and waste through defects. Key elements of the system were statistical process control, just-in-time scheduling, quality circles, teamwork, and flexible production (more than one model manufactured on a single production line). Central to the new manufacturing was the transition from static concepts of efficiency optimization towards continuous improvement to which every employee contributed. During the 1980s and 1990s all the world's car manufacturers redesigned their manufacturing processes to incorporate variants of Toyota's lean production.

New manufacturing methods required heavy investments by the companies in both capital equipment and training. The 1980s were a period of unprecedented high investment expenditures. However, as GM was to learn after spending more than $10 billion in upgrading its plants, the essence of the Toyota system was not new manufacturing "hardware" in the form of robotics and computer-integrated manufacturing systems. The critical elements were the "software" – new employee skills, new methods of shop-floor organization, redefined roles for managers, and new relationships with suppliers.

The new flexible manufacturing technology together with modular designs reduced the extent of scale economies in assembly. During the 1960s and 1970s it was believed that efficiency required giant assembly plants with outputs of at least 400,000 units a year. During the past decade, most of the new plants established had output capacities of between 150,000 and 300,000 units.

New Product Development

The declining importance of scale economies in assembly has done little to assist smaller automobile producers. The critical scale issues are related to the huge and increasing costs of new product development.

Despite the modest pace of technological innovation, the cost of developing new model development rose steeply as a result of increasing complexity of automobiles, the application of electronics and new materials, higher safety requirements, quality improvements, new environmental standards and the need for increased fuel efficiency. By the late 1980s the cost of creating an entirely new, mass-production passenger car from drawing board to production line was about $1.25 billion. By the early 1990s, the costs of major new models had escalated substantially above this level (see table 4.7).

Table 4.7 New car development costs during the 1990s

Ford Mondeo/Contour	$6 billion
GM Saturn	$5 billion
Ford Taurus (1996 model)	$2.8 billion
Ford Escort (new model)	$2 billion
Chrysler Neon	$1.3 billion
Renault Clio (1999 model)	$1.3 billion
Honda Accord (1997 model)	$0.6 billion
Rolls Royce Silver Seraph	$0.33 billion

Source: Assembled from various newspaper reports.

For smaller manufacturers, the costs of developing entirely new models were entirely beyond their means. One way for smaller producers to remain competitive was to avoid new model changes: at the time of its acquisition by Ford, Jaguar's two models, the XJ-6 and XJ-S, were almost two decades old and almost no investment had been made in developing a new model. The tiny Morgan car company economized on product development costs by building the same model from the late 1930s on. The alternative was to license designs from larger manufacturers. Thus, Tofas of Turkey builds Fiat-designed cars, Proton of Malaysia builds Mitsubishi-designed cars, and Maruti of India produces Suzuki-designed cars.

The high cost of new product development has been the major source of the cost-uncompetitiveness of smaller producers. The result has been mergers among smaller manufacturers, and the acquisition of smaller producers by bigger ones. The desire to share development costs also results in increased collaboration and joint ventures: Renault and Peugeot established joint engine manufacturing; GM established collaborations with Suzuki, Daewoo, Toyota, and Fiat to build cars and share components. In China and India most new auto plants were joint ventures between local and overseas companies.

During the 1990s, new product development emerged as the critical organizational capability differentiating car manufacturers. Designing, developing, and putting into production a completely new automobile is a hugely complex process involving every function of the firm, up to 3,000 engineers, close collaboration with several hundred suppliers, and up to five years from drawing board to market launch. If the primary competitive advantage of the Japanese manufacturers during the 1970s was low production cost, and during the 1980s was superior quality, by the 1990s the critical Japanese advantage was shorter new product development times and lower development costs. By the early 1990s, US and European carmakers were studying the Japanese companies' use of product development teams as a means of achieving improved functional integration and accelerated product development cycles.

Attempts to lower product development costs have focused around modular designs and "virtual prototyping" – the use of 3D computer graphics to design and test prototypes.

■ THE INDUSTRY ■

The Manufacturers

The major automobile manufacturers are shown in table 4.8. The ranks of the leading producers are dominated by US, Japanese, and European companies. All the major manufacturers are multinational. Thus, both GM and Ford produce more cars outside the US than within it. Similarly, Honda produces more Accords in the US than in Japan As a result some countries – notably Canada, Spain and the UK – are significant auto producing countries without having any domestic auto companies (other than small specialist producers).

Table 4.8 The world's leading auto manufacturers

		Production ('000s of autos and CVs)							
		1992	1994	1995	1996	1997	1998	1999	2000
GM	US	6,764	8,254	8,619	8,176	8,310	8,155	8,236	8,114
Ford	US	5,742	6,679	6,462	6,611	6,943	6,850	6,665	7,206
Toyota	Japan	4,249	4,565	4,465	4,794	4,850	4,643	5,496	5,897
DaimlerChrysler	Germany	—	—	—	—	—	—	4,822	4,666
Chrysler	US	1,983	2,880	2,808	3,080	3,051	3,120	—	—
Daimler Benz	Germany	799	884	930	1,002	1,149	1,442	—	—
Volkswagen	Germany	3,286	2,436	3,299	3,977	4,325	3,320	4,786	5,106
Nissan	Japan	2,963	2,702	2,839	2,712	2,801	2,610	2,457	2,698
Peugeot	France	2,437	2,027	1,890	1,975	1,146	1,294	2,515	2,879
Renault	France	1,929	1,881	1,761	1,755	1,868	2,234	2,345	2,515
Fiat	Italy	1,800	1,967	2,143	2,545	2,486	2,341	2,624	2,639
Honda	Japan	1,762	1,725	1,765	2,021	2,269	2,298	2,425	2,469
Mitsubishi	Japan	1,599	1,504	1,529	1,452	1,529	1,353	1,555	1,613
Mazda	Japan	1,248	1,215	974	984	1,052	1.030	967	972
Suzuki	Japan	888	1,076	510	1,387	1,458	1,450	1,521	1,434
Hyundai	S. Korea	874	1,153	1,255	1,402	1,370	889	1,970	2,488
AutoVAZ	Russia	674	528	585	562	575	n.a	680	756
Fuji	Japan	648	434	419	525	542	n.a.	578	581
Daihatsu	Japan	610	554	606	691	683	724	—	—
BMW	Germany	598	573	563	641	672	706	1,147	835
Kia	S. Korea	502	675	691	847	750	498	648	735
Isuzu	Japan	473	487	456	462	481	461	520	572
Rover	UK	405	485	503	510	479	502	400	345
Volvo	Sweden	365	439	448	446	466	487	504	n.a.
Daewoo	S. Korea	179	419	523	710	819	758	569	834

Volkswagen's production for 1996 and 1997 includes Skoda and Seat.
Sources: *Ward's Automotive Yearbook, Fortune.*

Table 4.9 Mergers and acquisitions among automobile manufacturers, 1986–2001

2001	GM (US)	Daewoo (S. Korea)	
2000	GM (US)	Fiat (Italy)	20% of equity acquired
2000	DaimlerChrysler (Germ.)	Hyundai (S. Korea)	10% of equity acquired
2000	DaimlerChrysler (Germ.)	Mitsubishi Motors (Japan)	34% of equity acquired
1999	Renault (France)	Nissan (Japan)	38.6% of equity acquired
1999	Ford (US)	Volvo (Sweden)	Car business acquired from Volvo
1999	Ford (US)	Land Rover (UK)	Acquired from BMW
1998	Daimler Benz (Germany)	Chrysler (US)	
1998	VW (Germany)	Rolls Royce Motors (UK)	
1998	Hyundai (S. Korea)	Kia (S. Korea)	
1998	Daewoo (S. Korea)	Sssangyong Motor (S. Korea)	
1998	Daewoo (S. Korea)	Samsung Motor (S. Korea)	
1997	Proton (Malaysia)	Lotus (UK)	
1997	BMW (Germany)	Rover (UK)	
1996	Daewoo (S. Korea)	FSO (Poland)	
1996	Daewoo (S. Korea)	FS Lublin (Poland)	
1995	Fiat (Italy)	FSM (Poland)	
1995	Ford (US)	Mazda (Japan)	
1994	Daewoo (S. Korea)	Oltcit/Rodae (Romania)	
1991	VW (Germany)	Skoda (Czech Republic)	
1990	GM (US)	Saab-Scandia (Sweden)	50% of equity acquired
1990	Ford (US)	Jaguar (UK)	
1987	Ford (US)	Aston Martin (UK)	
1987	Chrysler (US)	Lamborghini (Italy)	
1986	VW (Germany)	Seat (Spain)	

The key trend of the past decade has been consolidation through mergers and acquisitions. Table 4.9 lists the principal deals. At the beginning of the new century, the trend to consolidation appeared to be accelerating. The financial problems of Japanese and Korean auto companies have accelerated the process. The Korean car industry has been reduced from five to two manufacturers (both of which are partly owned by western producers). In Japan both Nissan and Mitsubishi Motor have fallen under western control.

Despite this consolidation, a number of small producers survive in protected markets. Many of these will be threatened by continued trade liberalization. For example, it is unlikely that many of China's 30-odd motor vehicle manufacturers will survive China's accession to the World Trade Organization (see table 4.10).

Outsourcing and the Growing Role of Suppliers

Henry Ford's system of mass production tended to be supported by heavy backward integration. In Ford's giant River Rouge plant, iron ore entered at one end, Model Ts

Table 4.10 Major motor vehicle manufacturers in China, 2000 (companies producing more than 100,000 vehicles annually)

Manufacturer	Production	Notes
First Auto	322,687	Includes 110,005 vehicles produced by First Auto–VW joint venture.
Shanghai-VW	221,524	Mainly VW Santanas.
Changlan Machine	195,432	
Dongfeng Auto Co.	157,038	Includes Dongfeng-Citroen joint venture producing Citroen ZX under "Fukang" badge
Beijing Automobile	124,824	Includes joint venture with Chrysler to build Jeep Cherokees
Hafei Company	122,007	
Liuzhou Auto	111,908	
Tianjin Auto	101,763	License agreement with Daihatsu.

Sources: *Ward's Automotive Yearbook, Financial Times.*

emerged at the other. Ford even owned rubber plantations in the Amazon basin. The trend of the past 20 years has been towards increasing outsourcing of materials, components, and subassemblies. This has been led primarily by the desire for lower costs and increased flexibility. Again, leadership came from the Japanese: Toyota and Nissan have traditionally been much more reliant upon their supplier networks than their US or European counterparts.

Moreover, the Japanese companies' relationships with their suppliers were much different. In contrast to the US model of arm's-length relationships and written contracts, the Japanese manufacturers developed close, collaborative long-run relationships with their "first-tier" suppliers. During the 1980s and 1990s, all the world's auto manufacturers outsourced more manufacturing and technology development while greatly reducing the number of their suppliers.

The result has been growing size and power of the parts manufacturers, especially those that develop and supply sophisticated subassemblies such as transmissions, braking systems, and electrical and electronic equipment. By the end of the 1990s, Bosch, TRW, Johnson Controls, Denso, and other suppliers were key global players in the automotive sector, with size and geographical scope similar to many of the automobile manufacturers (see table 4.11). The spin-off of Visteon from Ford and Delphi-Delco from GM helped spur the creation of a new tier of "mega-suppliers" through mergers and acquisitions among tier I suppliers.

Most recent developments have shifted power from the automobile manufacturers to the key suppliers of components and technologies. However, The launch of Covisint – an online auction forum for components and materials created jointly by Ford, GM, DaimlerChrysler, Renault, and Nissan – may shift bargaining power in the opposite direction through bringing parts suppliers into more open competition with one another.

Table 4.11 Leading suppliers of automotive components ($ billion)

	Revenues				ROE 2000 (%)
	1994	1996	1998	2000	
Delphi Automotive	—	—	—	29.1	28.2
Robert Bosch (Germany)	19.6	16.3	17.8	29.1	16.7
Visteon (US)	—	—	—	19.5	n.a.
Denso Corp. (Japan)	11.0	13.9	11.7	18.2	4.7
Johnson Controls (US)	7.1	6.3	12.6	17.2	17.9
TRW (US)	7.9	6.5	11.9	17.2	17.3
Dana (US)	5.5	7.7	12.5	12.7	13.0
Eaton (US)	4.4	7.0	6.6	8.3	10.2
Lucas-Varity (UK–US)[1]	3.9	7.2	6.6	—	—
Aisin Seiki (Japan)	7.3	7.8	6.5	8.9	12.5
Lear Corp (US)	3.1	6.2	9.0	14.1	17.0
Valeo SA (France)	3.8	5.0	5.7	8.9	n.a.
Magna International (Canada)	—	—	—	10.5	14.3

[1] Acquired by TRW.

Sources: *Ward's Automotive Yearbook, Business Week* "Global 1000."

The Quest for Cost Reduction

Increasing competition in the industry has intensified the quest for cost reduction among automobile manufacturers. Cost-reduction measures have included:

- Worldwide outsourcing. The tendency for increased outsourcing of components has been referred to above. In addition, auto firms have developed OEM supply arrangements amongst themselves: Daewoo supplies several of GM's models, Mitsubishi supplies engines and complete cars to Chrysler, BMW supplied engines to Rolls Royce (prior to its acquisition by VW).
- Just-in-time scheduling has radically reduced levels of inventory and work-in-progress.
- Component production and some assembly activities have been shifted to lower-cost locations: VW's North American production is based in Mexico and the company has also shifted production from Germany to the Czech Republic, Spain, and Hungary; the Japanese companies have moved more and more production to lower-cost locations in Southeast Asia; Daimler Benz and BMW have developed greenfield plants in the Deep South of the US.
- In high-cost locations (North America, Western Europe, and Japan) increased automation has reduced labor input.

Different companies have faced different cost issues. While European manufacturers were constrained by rigid working conditions, restrictions on layoffs, and generous

Table 4.12 Capacity utilization in motor vehicle manufacturing (%)

	2000	1998	1996	1994	1992	1990
United States	81.2	76.8	77.4	83.5	69.9	71.6
Western Europe	71.8	71.5	72.0	69.8	75.8	77.8
Asia	64.5	61.2	68.5	69.8	75.1	76.7

Sources: AAMA, *The Economist*, economagic.com.

benefits, US companies were hit by increased provisions for pensions and healthcare. In Japan the critical issue for most of the 1990s was the escalating value of the yen.

The quest for economies of scale and scope in relation to product development meant that companies sought to spread rising development costs over larger production and sales volumes. Increasingly during the 1990s the auto manufacturers attempted to introduce single global products. After failing to reach agreement between its European and US designers over a common Escort model, Ford's Mondeo/Contour was the company's first truly global model.

This desire for scale economies in development, manufacture, and purchasing also resulted in the standardization of designs and components across the different models of each manufacturer. The major work of DaimlerChrysler's Executive Automotive Committee during the summer of 2001 was directed towards achieving commonalties of platforms, engines, and components between the group's different models. For example:

- Common platforms were agreed between Chrysler and Mitsubishi (Neon/ Lancer and Stratus/Galant) and between Mitsubishi and Smart.
- On engines, the number of four-cylinder engines was to be cut from 14 to 9, six-cylinder engines from 11 to 8, and 8/10/12-cyclinder engines from 10 to eight.
- A common electrical and electronics architecture was agreed.

Excess Capacity

A major problem for the industry has been the tendency for the growth of production capacity to outstrip the growth in demand. During the 1980s and early 1990s, Japanese companies were major investors in new capacity with a number of greenfield "transplants" in North America and Europe. During the 1990s all the world's major car companies responded to the quest for globalization with new plants (many of them joint ventures) in the growth markets of Southeast Asia, China, India, South America, and Eastern Europe. During 1992–7, the Korean car companies were especially aggressive investors in new capacity. The resulting overhang of excess capacity was a key factor exacerbating intense competition in the industry. Table 4.12 shows excess capacity in the industry.

Internationalization

The driving force behind capacity expansion was internationalization. Although international growth extends back to 1920s, when Ford and General Motors established their European subsidiaries, until the 1970s the world auto industry was made up of fairly separate national markets. Each of the larger national markets was supplied primarily by domestic production, and indigenous manufacturers tended to be market leaders. For example in 1970, the Big Three (GM, Ford, and Chrysler) held close to 85 percent of the US market, VW and Daimler Benz dominated the market in Germany, as did Fiat in Italy, British Leyland (later Rover) in the UK, Seat in Spain, and Renault, Peugeot, and Citroen in France. By 1998, the industry was global in scope: in almost every significant national market, all the world's leading manufacturers had established themselves.

Internationalization has occurred through trade and foreign direct investment. Despite the efforts by the US and Europe to protect their markets against Japanese imports by means of quotas, growth in trade has been stimulated by declining tariffs and the convergence of national preferences.

During the 1970s and 1980s, Japanese car manufacturers displaced the American Big Three as the pioneers of internationalization. The patterns of international expansion were also different. While Ford and GM had established self-sufficient, fully integrated subsidiaries in overseas countries, the Japanese companies preferred to export from their home plants. The Japanese companies' transfer of production outside of Japan was initially the result of import barriers imposed by the US and Europe, and subsequently the result of the rising value of the yen. Table 4.13 shows some of the North American auto plants established by overseas (mainly Japanese) companies. By contrast, the Continental Europeans focused mainly upon Europe and the developing world. VW acquired carmakers in Spain (Seat), Czech Republic (Skoda), Britain (Rolls Royce), and elsewhere. Fiat, PSA, and VW all established plants in Latin America, Africa, and Asia. During the mid-to-late 1990s some of the most aggressive overseas expansion was by the Korean auto producers. Daewoo has also moved rapidly into Eastern Europe with plants in Poland, Romania, and Uzbekistan, as well as starting joint ventures in India and elsewhere. However, the Korean expansionism was quickly halted by the 1998 financial crisis.

The emerging market economies of Eastern Europe, Asia, and Latin America provided a magnet for foreign investment. China and India were identified as particularly important markets within which to establish a presence. However, the tendency has been for capacity in these markets to outstrip demand growth, with the implication that returns on these investments have typically been meager. Despite the tremendous internationalization of the auto industry, national producers still retain leadership in their home markets. For example, Fiat is market leader in Italy, VW in Germany, Renault and PSA in France, Hyundai and Daewoo in Korea (see table 4.14). This is partly a legacy of import protection, partly a reflection of nationalism among domestic consumers, and partly a reflection of the importance of well-established dealership networks and intimate local knowledge of domestic manufacturers.

Table 4.13   Japanese and European "transplants" in North America

Company	Parent(s)	Location	Production of cars and lt. trucks 2000
Honda of America	Honda	E. Liberty and Marysville, OH	677,090
Toyota USA	Toyota	Georgetown, KY	995,000
NUMMI,	Toyota & GM	Fremont, CA	344,000
CAMI Automotive	Suzuki and GM	Ontario	113,000
Toyota Canada	Toyota	Ontario	186,000
Honda of Canada	Honda	Ontario	152,000
Diamond-Star Motors	Mitsubishi/Chrysler	Normal, IL	223,000
Subaru-Isuzu Auto	Fuji and Isuzu	Lafayette, IN	207,000
Nissan Motor Mfr. USA	Nissan	Sryrna, TN	475,898
BMW	BMW	Spartanburg, NC	78,000
Mercedes Benz	DaimlerChrysler	Vance, AL	119,462
AutoAlliance International	Mazda/Ford	Flat Rock, MI	108,000
Volkswagen	Volkswagen	Puebla, Mexico	440,000

Source: *Ward's Automotive Yearbook, Ward's Auto World.*

Industry Location

Given the shift demand to the emerging market countries and the producers quest for lower production costs, it might be expected that the geographical distribution of the industry would have changed substantially over recent decades (in the same way that other manufacturing industries – consumer electronics, small appliances, textiles, and semiconductors – have relocated in newly industrializing countries). Yet, in automobiles, such shifts have been surprisingly small. The main feature of 1950–80 was the rise of production in Japan, but since 1980, changes have been small, with the three major manufacturing regions – Western Europe, North America, and Japan – each accounting for close to 30 percent of world production. The continuing dominance of this triad is despite the attempts of newly industrializing countries to develop their domestic industries, either by protecting domestic manufacturers or by encouraging inward investment. (Tables 4.15 and 4.16 show production by different regions and countries in recent years.)

The advantages of these countries lie primarily in labor costs, which are often a fraction of those in the older industrialized countries (see table 4.17). Nevertheless, with the exception of Korea, none of the new auto-manufacturing countries has emerged as a major auto-producing locality. The ability of the established auto-manufacturing countries to sustain their leadership points to the importance of factors other than wage rates in driving international competitiveness in the auto industry. Table

Table 4.14 Automobile market shares in individual countries (%)

	2000	1997	1994	1992	1988
Japan					
Toyota	28.5	30.6	33.7	35.3	43.9
Honda	16.2	10.1	8.5	10.5	10.8
Nissan	11.8	14.0	18.0	19.9	23.2
Suzuki	10.0	8.6	n.a.	n.a.	n.a.
Mitsubishi	6.9	7.9	9.2	7.5	4.9
Mazda	6.0	4.3	6.3	7.3	6.7
*Korea**					
Hyundai	50.3	46.6	46.5	46.7	55.9
Kia	19.7	23.0	26.5	25.8	25.0
Daewoo	24.8	30.2	16.0	15.5	19.1
Australia					
GM-Holden	22.0	17.7	21.3	19.6	20.9
Toyota	16.8	13.4	19.0	15.5	15.3
Ford	15.9	19.6	24.4	23.3	28.1
Mitsubishi	9.6	11.9	10.1	11.5	12.2
Hyundai	8.1	11.1	8.9	n.a.	n.a.
Nissan	4.7	3.6	3.8	11.5	9.9
Taiwan					
Ford	13.9	16.2	17.8	23.0	n.a.
Toyota	23.8	18.1	20.0	15.9	n.a.
Yulon/Honda	13.3	17.3	11.8	14.5	n.a.
Nissan	22.6	17.2	n.a	n.a	n.a.
France					
Renault	28.2	27.4	30.0	29.4	29.1
Peugeot	30.9	28.8	31.1	30.1	34.2
VW	11.2	11.4	8.0	9.7	9.2
Ford	6.2	8.0	8.1	8.2	7.1
Italy					
Fiat	35.5	43.0	46.0	43.0	59.9
VW	11.8	9.9	10.4	14.8	11.7
Ford	8.8	9.3	9.6	10.8	3.7
Peugeot	7.6	6.3	n.a.	n.a.	n.a.
Renault	7.0	6.8	7.0	7.6	7.1
UK					
Ford	20.7	18.7	22.2	22.5	26.3
GM	14.2	14.3	16.9	17.6	13.7
Peugeot	12.3	11.4	12.1	11.8	8.7
VW	9.8	7.9	n.a.	n.a.	n.a.
BMW/Rover	7.7	12.9	12.8	13.5	15.0
Germany					
VW	27.8	25.0	20.9	26.4	28.3
GM	12.5	15.6	16.5	16.7	16.1
Ford	7.6	11.0	9.9	9.3	10.1
Mercedes	12.8	8.5	8.2	6.5	9.2
Japanese	11.7	12.3	12.5	13.4	15.2

*Domestic producers only (excludes imports).

Source: *Ward's Automotive Yearbook 2001* and earlier years.

Table 4.15 World motor vehicle production by countries and regions (% of world total)

	1960	1989	1992	1994	1997	1998	2000
United States	52.0	23.8	20.6	24.5	22.0	23.0	22.2
Western Europe	38.0	31.7	32.5	31.2	32.6	32.6	29.9
Russia and E. Europe	2.0	4.8	—	4.3	5.6	4.3	4.6
Japan	1.0	18.2	26.7	21.2	20.5	19.2	17.7
Korea	—	1.8	3.7	4.6	4.8	3.4	5.0
Other	7.0	19.7	16.4	14.4	14.5	17.5	20.6
Total units (millions)	12.8	49.5	47.5	50.0	55.0	53.3	57.4

Products for E. Europe and USSR included in "Other" for 1991 and 1992.
Sources: AAMA, *Automotive News*.

Table 4.16 Automobile production by country (thousands of cars)

	2000	1998	1997	1995	1994	1992	1990	1987
US	5,542	5,554	5,884	6,338	6,601	5,664	6,077	7,099
Canada	1,551	1,481	1,374	1,339	1,215	1,020	1,072	810
Mexico	1,130	958	833	710	840	778	346	266
Total N. America	8,223	7,993	8,091	8,387	8,657	7,463	7,496	8,176
Germany	5,132	5,348	4,678	4,360	4,040	4,864	4,805	4,604
France	2,883	2,582	3,326	3,051	3,175	3,320	3,295	3,052
Italy	1,442	1,378	1,580	1,422	1,341	1,477	1,874	1,701
UK	1,641	1,748	1,868	1,532	1,467	1,292	1,296	1,143
Spain	2,445	2,216	1,961	1,959	1,822	1,799	1,679	1,403
Sweden	260	368	373	390	353	294	336	432
Total W. Europe	14,853	14,790	14,687	14,350	13,844	13,520	13,672	13,471
Japan	8,363	8,055	8,494	7,664	7,801	9,379	9,948	7,891
Korea	1,881	1,434	2,088	1,893	1,805	1,307	987	793
Australia	324	349	323	284	286	270	361	225
China	620	543	543	356	313	208	n.a.	n.a.
India	541	406	380	n.a.	n.a.	n.a.	n.a.	n.a.
Taiwan	265	285	258	271	263	283	277	175
Former USSR	967	836	1,066	834	798	1,050	1,260	1,329
Poland	533	574	426	260	250	212	256	301
Brazil	1,348	1,223	1,680	1,312	1,249	816	663	789

Sources: Japan Automobile Manufacturers Association, Korean Automobile Manufacturers Association, *Marketing Systems*.

Table 4.17 Hourly compensation for motor vehicle workers (US$ per hour including benefits)

	1975	1981	1984	1986	1988	1990	1992	1994	1998
US	9.55	17.03	19.02	20.09	20.80	22.48	25.12	26.56	27.49
Mexico	2.94	5.27	2.55	2.03	1.96	2.79	4.35	4.05	2.94
Japan	3.56	7.61	7.90	11.80	16.36	15.77	19.97	26.36	23.38
Korea	0.45	1.33	1.74	1.84	3.20	5.78	7.05	8.83	7.75
Taiwan	0.64	1.86	2.09	2.23	3.50	5.72	6.57	6.76	6,68
France	5.10	9.11	8.20	11.06	13.54	15.94	17.42	17.66	19.32
Germany	7.89	3.34	11.92	16.96	23.05	27.58	32.61	36.10	36.70
Italy	5.16	8.21	8.00	11.03	14.51	17.97	20.48	16.74	18.56
Spain	—	7.03	5.35	7.74	10.85	15.00	17.52	15.17	14.72
UK	4.12	8.10	7.44	9.22	11.95	13.87	16.80	15.07	19.63

Source: US Dept. of Labor, Bureau of Labor Statistics.

Table 4.18 The cost of producing a compact automobile, US and Mexico, 1992 ($)

	US	Mexico
Parts and components	7,750	8,000
Labor	700	140
Shipping costs	300	1,000
Inventory	20	40
Total	8,770	9,180

Source: US Office of Technology Assessment, October 1992.

4.18 shows that, although wage costs are much lower in Mexico than in the US, this cost advantage is outweighed by other factors.

Market Segments and Market Positioning

Despite the globalization of the leading automakers, the world still lacks a single global market. The need for manufacturers to build extensive dealership chains in the markets they supply, differences in national regulations and customer preferences, differences in affluence and infrastructure, and trade restrictions all continue to segment the world market. The world market is also segmented by types of product. The US market has traditionally been segmented by sizes of automobile: full size, medium size, compact, subcompact, and so on. At the top end of the market are "luxury cars" distinguished primarily by their price. There are also specific types of vehicle: sports cars, sport-utility vehicles, small passenger vans ("minivans"), and light pickup trucks, for example.

Margins vary considerably between product segments. Chrysler's position as one of the world's most profitable auto manufacturers during the late 1980s and for much of the 1990s was primarily a result of its strong position in SUVs (through Jeep) and minivans (through its Dodge Caravan and Plymouth Voyager models). The luxury car segment too has traditionally been associated with high margins. However, mobility barriers between segments tend to be low. Over the past decade, all the major manufacturers have broadened their product range in order to access economies of scope in technology, production, and marketing, and to exploit higher margins in specialty segments. In the luxury car segment, traditionally dominated by specialist producers such as Mercedes, Jaguar, Rolls Royce, and BMW, mass manufacturers have entered, either by creating new divisions and models (e.g., Honda's Acura, Toyota's Lexus, and Nissan Infiniti) or through acquisition (Jaguar and Volvo acquired by Ford, Rolls Royce by VW, Lancia and Alfa-Romeo by Fiat, Saab by GM). Similarly, there has been an influx by the volume auto manufacturers into the minivan and SUV sector.

As the pressure of competition has increased across all market segments, manufacturers have sought differentiation advantage through introducing models that combine design features from different segments (e.g., four-wheel drive minivans, luxury SUVs, and smaller SUVs based on small-car platforms).

Vertical segmentation was also an issue for the industry. Profitability varied across the different stages of the auto industry's value chain. The prevailing wisdom was that downstream activities offered better profit potential than manufacturing activities. It was this logic that had encouraged the auto companies to outsource and spin off most of their production of components and invest in downstream activities such as consumer finance, insurance, and after-market services (for example, Ford had acquired the repair and parts supplier Kwik Fit and Hertz car rental in 1999).

■ THE OUTLOOK ■

Meetings between Rudiger Grube, his corporate planning staff, and automotive experts from both within the group and from outside consulting companies produced both consensus and dissent. With much of the world moving into either recession or stagnation during the latter part of 2001, it was agreed that the prospects for any significant growth in market demand looked remote over the medium term. Given the growth in industry capacity resulting from the heavy investments by auto manufacturers in new production capacity, it seemed likely that the industry would continue to be dogged by a substantial overhang of excess capacity. The ability of the industry to control excess capacity and limit the tendency towards price competition (including discounts and favorable trade-in allowances and credit terms) would depend greatly upon the impact of the current wave of consolidation. The spate of mergers and acquisitions had reduced the number of independent automobile manufacturers producing over 400,000 units a year from 23 in 1995 to 13 in 2001. Many industry experts believed that this consolidation would continue: as early as 1999 *Business Week* had forecast that only manufacturers with annual production of five million vehicles or over would survive, leading to the emergence of a global "Big Six": GM, Ford, DaimlerChrysler, Toyota, VW, and Honda.[2] Others disagreed; Peugeot and BMW were adamant that the benefits of huge volume and broad scope were offset by advantages of flexibility, design innovation, and brand strength that medium-sized players could muster.

Looking longer term, there was disagreement over whether the industry would mature through steady, gradual evolution, or would be subject to more radical change. The auto makers had adapted to electronics, new materials, and other technological changes without any major impact on basic automotive design. The prospects for more radical technological change were linked closely with environmental issues. Fears for the demise of the internal combustion engine had proved groundless and most of the investments by the companies in electrical propulsion had been viewed as wasted money. Yet, the threat of global warming was growing, and in several cities of the world problems of pollution were already encouraging government measures to substitute electrical propulsion for gasoline propulsion.

Important developments were also occurring within the value chain. The transfer of manufacturing and technology development from the auto producers to component suppliers seemed likely to continue. Many manufacturers seemed to be unconcerned about losing control over production and technology so long as they could control marketing and distribution. But here too some disturbing developments were occurring. The auto companies controlled their markets through their networks of franchised dealers, through which they supplied not only new cars but also consumer finance and spare parts. These established dealer networks were being threatened by several developments, including the emergence of new automobile "megastores" (e.g., Republic Industries' Auto Nation stores and Circuit City's CarMax group) and the impact of sales through the internet. As *Business Week* observed, "Retailers have historically been the apparatus auto makers use to find homes for all the new cars they crank out. Powerful new buyers could be a threat, the relationship could change to one where the retailer tells the auto maker what to do and what price to sell at."[3]

Changes in the industry's structure over time would influence not just the overall intensity of competition and the prospects of industry profitability, but also how that profit was shared among the different companies. As the companies had converged in terms of technology, design and even quality levels, so cost had emerged as the critical success factor. This in turn had created the drive to exploit economies of scale and scope. Now that all manufacturers were following similar strategies to exploit economies of scale and scope through common vehicle platforms, common components, global models, and global sourcing, what factors would emerge as the critical determinants of competitive advantage during the remainder of the decade?

APPENDIX

The World's Major Automobile Producers, Sales and Profitability 1980–2000

Table 4.A1 Sales ($ billion)

	2000	1999	1998	1997	1996	1995	1994	1993	1992	1991	1990	1985–9	1980–4
GM	185	167	161	178	168	169	155	134	113	124	125	110	68
Ford	170	163	144	154	147	137	128	109	100	59	98	77	42
DaimlerChrysler	152	151	142	—	—	—	—	—	—	—	—	—	—
Chrysler	—	—	—	61	61	53	52	44	37	29	31	28	13
Daimler Benz	—	—	—	70	72	72	64	59	62	57	54	34	12
Toyota	121	120	113	84	109	111	88	85	95	78	65	42	18
VW	79	70	60	64	67	61	50	46	54	46	44	28	16
Honda	58	57	60	43	47	44	40	36	39	31	27	18	8
Fiat	53	45	56	51	51	46	41	35	40	47	48	27	18
Nissan	55	61	54	47	59	63	59	54	59	43	40	26	16
Peugeot	41	38	39	31	34	33	30	26	29	28	29	19	13
Renault	37	35	43	35	36	37	32	30		29	31	31	15
BMW	33	33	35	34	35	32	30	18	20	18	17	10	5
Mitsubishi	30	32	27	n.a	33	37	34	27	26	19	17	14	12
Hyundai Motor	29	21	15	n.a.	n.a.	n.a.	n.a.	n.a.	n.a.	n.a.	n.a.	n.a.	n.a.
Mazda	16	20	17	15	17	19	22	20	25	19	17	12	n.a.

Table 4.A2 Return on Equity (%)

	2000	1999	1998	1997	1996	1995	1994	1993	1992	1991	1990	1985–9	1980–4
GM	14.8	29.9	19.7	37.1	21.2	29.5	39.2	44.1	(46.0)	(16.3)	(6.6)	11.8	11.4
Ford	18.6	26.3	94.3	22.9	16.6	16.9	24.5	16.2	2.6	(10.0)	3.7	21.8	0.4
DaimlerChrysler	18.3	15.9	15.9	—	—	—	—	—	—	—	—	—	—
Chrysler	—	—	—	24.6	30.5	18.5	34.7	(37.3)	6.6	(12.9)	1.0	20.8	66.5
Daimler Benz	—	—	—	12.0	10.5	43.8	5.0	3.6	7.7	9.4	9.0	18.3	24.3
Toyota	7.5	6.5	6.8	8.0	7.5	5.4	2.4	3.3	5.0	7.2	10.8	10.6	12.6
VW	18.0	13.2	6.2	14.6	5.9	3.4	1.3	(19.0)	1.2	7.2	7.2	6.3	1.6
Honda	11.8	14.9	17.3	18.8	17.5	6.8	5.3	2.3	3.5	7.0	8.3	11.8	18.1
Fiat	4.9	3.4	4.8	10.6	9.7	9.7	5.1	10.6	3.5	4.8	9.1	18.7	10.9
Nissan	39.2	(3.8)	(2.2)	(8.0)	6.3	7.2	10.2	(5.2)	3.1	2.7	7.2	4.68	10.3
Peugeot	13.8	9.5	5.7	(4.7)	1.3	3.1	5.6	18.4	10.4	9.8	18.4	36.7	(15.2)
Renault	11.0	6.5	17.0	12.6	14.2	4.8	8.2	3.3	18.1	8.5	6.7	51.1	(152.4)
BMW	20.6	11.3	(63.2)	14.1	9.4	8.5	8.5	8.0		11.1	11.0	10.4	14.8
Mitsubishi	(123.2)	(26.8)	0.2	n.a.	2.6	2.9	2.3	1.3	2.2	10.3	6.9	7.9	10.0
Hyundai Motor	8.9	7.7	1.0	n.a.	n.a.	n.a.	n.a.	n.a.	n.a.	n.a.	n.a.	n.a.	n.a.
Mazda	(110.7)	11.6	10.9	(1.0)	5.6	4.3	11.2	(12.9)	14.4	6.4	6.6	4.8	n.a.

Notes

1. "Merger agreement signed: Daimler-Benz and Chrysler combine to form leading global automotive company," Press Release, Chrysler Corporation, May 1998.
2. *Business Week* "Autos: The Global Six," January 25, 1999.
3. *Business Week*, February 24, 1997, p. 89.

case five

Wal-Mart Stores Inc., May 2002

Robert M. Grant

How did a peddler of cheap shirts and fishing rods become the mightiest corporation in America?

***Fortune*, April 12, 2002**

In May 2002, Wal-Mart published first quarter results for its new financial year (February 1, 2002 to January 31, 2003). Compared to the same period of the previous year, sales were up by 14 percent and net income had increased by 20 percent – the deteriorating US economy and plunging consumer confidence had failed to dent Wal-Mart's continued progress. The *Fortune* 500 rankings list, published in April 2002, showed that Wal-Mart was America's largest company (in terms of revenue); this also implied that Wal-Mart would head *Fortune*'s Global 500 (that would be published in July). International expansion had also extended Wal-Mart's global reputation. In February 2002, *Fortune* had identified Wal-Mart as the world's second "most admired company" (after General Electric). Unlike most other high-flying companies, Wal-Mart also seemed to be impervious to the stock market meltdown: Wal-Mart's share price at the end of May was $54 – barely changed from the level prior to September 11, 2001.

Wal-Mart's transformation from a small chain of discount stores in Arkansas, Missouri, and Oklahoma in 1970 to the world's largest retailer was one of the most remarkable corporate success stories of the twentieth century. Its founder, Sam Walton, had combined folksy charm and home-spun business wisdom with cutting-edge information technology and supply chain management to create the world's most efficient retail organization.

During the financial year ending January 2003, Wal-Mart would continue its expansion. CEO, Lee Scott, outlined plans for over 300 new Wal-Mart stores in the US, together with 130 new stores overseas. In total, some 46 million square feet would be added over the 12-month period. In addition, Wal-Mart announced its intention to acquire 24 Supermercado Amigo supermarkets in Puerto Rico and a majority equity stake in the Japanese retailer Seiyu. Capital expenditures for the year would amount to approximately $10.2 billion.

Despite Wal-Mart's ability to grow its sales and profits throughout economic cycles, technological changes, and continual challenges from new retailing formats, Scott recognized that in the fast-moving, hypercompetitive retail sector, size offered no guarantee of continued success. Previous decades had witnessed the decline of many of America's greatest retailing empires – Sears Roebuck, Montgomery Ward, A&P, and Federated Department Stores – to mention just a few. Wal-Mart's success had been built upon a unique culture founded by Sam Walton and forged in rural Arkansas. But Sam Walton has been dead for ten years and Wal-Mart had far outgrown its Arkansas home base. By 2002, Wal-Mart was operating retail outlets, not only in all 50 states of the Union, but also in nine overseas countries. Wal-Mart's ability to offer its customers lower prices and better service than its competitors depended, ultimately, upon its trying harder – in particular the continual striving of its employees to find new ways to reduce costs and better serve customers. How far would size and success blunt Wal-Mart's drive for efficiency, responsiveness, and innovation? Would existing competitors imitate the Wal-Mart's strategy and systems? And would new competitors emerge with new and superior approaches to retailing?

■ HISTORY ■

Sam Walton opened his first store – a franchised Ben Franklin variety store – in 1945. Over the next 15 years, Sam together with his brother, Bud, developed a chain of 15 Ben Franklin stores throughout rural Arkansas. During this period, Sam Walton became aware of the increasing price competition from discount retailers – large format stores that offered a broad range of products that included apparel, appliances, toiletries, household goods, and sometimes groceries as well. This new category of retailer emerged in the US following World War II. Discount stores were located within large towns – it was generally believed that a minimum population of 100,000 was necessary for a discount store to be viable. Sam Walton believed that discount stores could be viable in smaller communities: if the prices were right, the stores would attract customers from a wide area: "Our strategy was to put good-sized stores into little one-horse towns that everyone else was ignoring."[1] Walton opened his first Wal-Mart in 1962 and within eight years had 30 discount stores in small and medium-sized towns in Arkansas, Oklahoma, and Missouri.

Distribution was a problem for Wal-Mart:

Here we were in the boondocks, so we didn't have distributors falling over themselves to serve us like our competitors in larger towns. Our only alternative was to build our own distribution centers so that we could buy in volume at attractive prices and store the merchandise.[2]

In 1970, Walton built his first distribution center, and in the same year took the company public in order to finance the heavy investment involved. With this structure of large distribution hubs serving a group of 15 to 20 discount stores, Wal-Mart began its rapid expansion across the country. At the end of 1980, Wal-Mart had 330 stores in 11 states (Arkansas, Oklahoma, Missouri, Texas, Kansas, Kentucky, Tennessee, Mississippi, Louisiana, Alabama, and Illinois). By the end of 1985, there were 859 stores in 22 southern and mid-western states. At the beginning of 1994, there were 1,953 stores operating in every state except Vermont, Alaska, and Hawaii. Wal-Mart's geographical expansion was incremental. It moved into a new area, first, by building a few stores that were served by extending Wal-Mart's distribution lines from a nearby cluster; eventually, when a critical mass of stores of stores had been established in the new area, Wal-Mart would build a distribution center to serve the new cluster. Expansion bought Wal-Mart into closer competition with other discount chains. In the small towns of the south-west and south, Wal-Mart faced few major competitors. As Wal-Mart became a national retail chain it entered more developed retailing areas, including larger cities. By 1993, 55 percent of Wal-Mart stores faced direct competition form Kmart and 23 percent from Target.[3]

Diversification

During the 1980s, Sam Walton began experimenting with alternative retail formats. These included Sam's Club (1983), Helen's Arts and Crafts (1995), and Dot Deep Discount Drugstores. In addition, very large retail outlets, Wal-Mart Supercenters and Hypermart USA, were introduced. Helen's Arts and Crafts, Dot Drugstores, and Hypermart USA were sold off, but the other two store types – the Sam's warehouse clubs and the Supercenters – grew rapidly to become important components of Wal-Mart's business.

Sam's Clubs imitated a distribution concept established by Price Club. The warehouse clubs were not, in fact, retailers since they were not open to the public. They were clubs where access was through membership. Most members represented small businesses (especially convenience stores and restaurants) and local organizations (churches, charities, civic groups). In practice a high proportion of sales were for household rather than business use. They carried a small number of lines and most items were available in multipacks and catering-sized packs. The clubs were literally warehouses with product available on pallets and minimal customer service. The rationale was to maximize economies in purchasing, minimize operating costs, and pass the savings on to members through very low prices. Competition among warehouse clubs was ferocious, resulting in rapid consolidation of the sector. Wal-Mart acquired The Wholesale Company in 1991 and Kmart's PACE clubs in 1993, while CostCo Wholesale and PriceCo merged in 1993.

Supercenters were Wal-Mart stores with larger floor space – typically 120,000 to 130,000 square feet, about double the size of the average Wal-Mart discount store. Supercenters were modeled upon the European concept of the "hypermarket" that had been pioneered by the French retailer Carrefour. A Supercenter combined a discount store with a grocery supermarket; in addition, a Supercenter incorporated a number of specialty units such as an eyeglass store, hair salon, dry cleaners, and photo lab. The Supercenters were open for 24 hours a day, seven days a week. The Supercenter stores and Sam's Clubs were supplied through a separate distribution network from the Wal-Mart discount stores. In 1990, Wal-Mart acquired McLane – a Texas-based wholesale distributor. Under Wal-Mart's ownership McLane's primary role became distribution to Wal-Mart Supercenters and Sam's wholesale clubs throughout the US.

International expansion

By the end of the 1980s, Wal-Mart was running out of new territory. It had expanded into most areas of the US, and under the leadership of Sam Walton's successor, David Glass, was now looking towards opportunities abroad. In 1992, Wal-Mart established a joint venture with Mexico's largest retailer, Cifra S.A., and began opening both Wal-Mart discount stores and Sam's club outlets in several Mexican cities. Within seven years the two companies had opened 416 stores in Mexico, and Wal-Mart had established a dominant position in the venture through acquiring 51 percent of Cifra.

In 1994, Wal-Mart entered the Canadian market by acquiring 120 Woolco stores from Woolworth and converting them to its own discount stores format. Wal-Mart boosted the sales per square foot of the Woolco stores from $98 in 1994 to $287 in 1999, taking 40 percent of total discount store sales, and establishing Wal-Mart as Canada largest retailer.

In Argentina, Wal-Mart entered by establishing a number of Sam's Club outlets, while in Brazil it concentrated upon opening stores in the Sao Paulo area.

In Europe, Wal-Mart established itself through acquisition. In Germany, Wal-Mart acquired the 21-store Wertkauf chain, and followed this with the purchase of 21 Interspar stores. In the UK, the third largest supermarket chain, Asda Stores, with its 232 retail outlets was purchased for $10.8 billion in 1999.

In Asia, Wal-Mart proceeded more cautiously – aware of the huge market potential but wary of the risks. In South Korea, Wal-Mart acquired four stores, previously operated by the Dutch retailer Makro, from H.S. Chang, a Korean businessman. In China, Wal-Mart initially proposed to enter through an alliance with CP, the Thailand-based conglomerate. Disagreements between CP and Wal-Mart eventually resulted in Wal-Mart going it alone with Sam's Club and Supercenter stores initially in the Shenzhen Economic Zone of southern China. In Indonesia, a joint venture with PT Multipolar involving two stores collapsed amidst acrimony and lawsuits.

Exhibit 5.1 lists major events in Wal-Mart's development.

Sam Walton

Wal-Mart's strategy and management style was inseparable from the philosophy and values of its founder. Until his death in 1992, Sam Walton was the embodiment of Wal-Mart's unique approach to retailing. After his death, Sam Walton's beliefs and business principles continued to be the beacon that guided Wal-Mart from success to success. As Harry Cunningham, founder of Kmart Stores, observed: "Sam's establishment of the Walton culture throughout the company was the key to the whole thing. It's just incomparable. He is the greatest businessman of this century."[4]

Exhibit 5.1: Wal-Mart – Key Historical Facts

1962	Wal-Mart's founder, Sam Walton, opens the first Wal-Mart in Rogers, Arkansas
1970	Wal-Mart opens its first distribution center, Bentonville, Ark.
1970	Wal-Mart goes public
1971	Continued expansion results in Wal-Mart stores in five states: Arkansas, Kansas, Louisiana, issouri and Oklahoma
1972	Wal-Mart listed on NYSE
1975	After visit to Korea, Walton introduces the "Wal-Mart Cheer"
1977	Acquires 16 Mohr-Value stores in Michigan and Illinois
1981	Acquires 92 Kuhn's Big K stores
1983	First Sam's Cub opens, Midwest City, Oklahoma
1983	Woolco's US stores acquired
1985	Sam Walton becomes the wealthiest person in the US
1987	Wal-Mart Satellite Network completed
1988	David Glass takes over from Sam Walton as CEO
1988	First Supercenter opens, Washington, Missouri
1990	Wal-Mart becomes largest retailer in the US
1991	Begins international expansion with store in Mexico City
1992	Death of Sam Walton. S. Robson Walton becomes Chairman
1992	Enters Puerto Rico
1993	91 Pace Warehouse clubs acquired
1994	Enters Canada with acquisition of 122 Woolco stores
1995	Wal-Mart enters its 50th state – Vermont
1995	Enters Argentina & Brazil
1996	Expands into Asia with first Wal-Mart in China
1998	Enters Germany & Korea
1999	Acquires Asda Stores, a major UK discount retailer
2000	H. Lee Scott named president and CEO
2001	Wal-Mart named by Fortune Magazine as the 3rd most admired company in America
2002	Fortune Global 500 identifies Wal-Mart as the world's largest company

For Sam Walton, thrift and value for money was a religion. Undercutting competitors' prices was an obsession, as was the never-ending quest for cost economies that would permit continuing price cutting. Walton established a culture in which every item of expenditure was questioned – was it necessary? Could it be done cheaper? He set an example that few of his senior colleagues could match: he walked rather than took taxis, shared rooms at budget motels while on business trips, and avoided any corporate trappings or manifestations of opulence or success. For Walton, wealth was a threat and an embarrassment, rather than a reward and a privilege. His own lifestyle gave little indication that he was America's richest person (before being eclipsed by Bill Gates). He also felt uncomfortable about the wealth of his associates: "We've had lots of millionaires in our ranks. And it drives me crazy when they flaunt it. Every now and then somebody will do something especially showy, and I don't hesitate to rant and rave about it at the Saturday morning meeting. I don't think that big mansions and flashy cars is what the Wal-Mart culture is supposed to be about."[5]

His attention to detail was legendary. As chairman and chief executive, he was quite clear that his priorities lay with his employees ("associates"), customers, and the operational details through which the former created value for the latter. He shunned offices in favor of spending time in his stores. Most of his life was spent on the road (or, in his case, in the air flying between stores piloting his own plane), making impromptu visits to stores and distribution centers. Collecting information on which products were selling well in Tuscaloosa; why margins were down in Santa Maria; how a new display system for children's clothing in Carbondale had boosted sales by 15 percent. His passion for detail extended to competitors' stores as well as his own: not only did he regularly visit competitors' stores; he was known to count cars in their parking lots.

Central to his leadership role at Wal-Mart was his relationship with his employees – the Wal-Mart associates. In an industry known for low pay and hard working conditions, Walton created a unique feeling of motivation and involvement. He believed fervently in giving people responsibility, trusting them, but also continually monitoring their performance.

Since his death, Sam Walton's habits and utterances have become hallowed principles guiding the values of the company and the behavior of its employees. For example, Wal-Mart's "10-foot attitude" pledge is based upon Sam Walton's request to a store employee that: "I want you to promise that whenever you come within 10 feet of a customer, you will look him in the eye, greet him and ask if you can help him."[6]

Sam Walton's ability to attract the affection and loyalty of both employees and customers owes much to his ability to generate fun and excitement within the otherwise sterile world of discount retailing. Sam Walton brought a sense of unpredictability and fun to the business. He engendered a positive attitude among Wal-Mart employees and he reveled in his role as company cheerleader.

Sam Walton's contribution to the management systems and management style of Wal-Mart was reflected in Wal-Mart's website's description of "The Wal-Mart Culture" (see exhibit 5.2).

Exhibit 5.2: The Wal-Mart Culture

As Wal-Mart continues to grow into new areas and new mediums, our success will always be attributed to our culture. Whether you walk into a Wal-Mart store in your hometown or one across the country while you're on vacation, you can always be assured you're getting low prices and that genuine customer service you've come to expect from us. You'll feel at home in any department of any store . . . that's our culture.

■ **SAM WALTON'S THREE BASIC BELIEFS** ■

Sam Walton built Wal-Mart on the revolutionary philosophies of excellence in the workplace, customer service and always having the lowest prices. We have always stayed true to the Three Basic Beliefs Mr. Sam established in 1962:

Respect the Individual.
"'Our people make the difference' is not a meaningless slogan – it's a reality at Wal-Mart. We are a group of dedicated, hardworking, ordinary people who have teamed together to accomplish extraordinary things. We have very different backgrounds, different colors and different beliefs, but we do believe that every individual deserves to be treated with respect and dignity." – Don Soderquist, Senior Vice Chairman, Wal-Mart Stores, Inc.

Service to Our Customers

We want our customers to trust in our pricing philosophy and to always be able to find the lowest prices with the best possible service. We're nothing without our customers.

"Wal-Mart's culture has always stressed the importance of Customer Service. Our Associate base across the country is as diverse as the communities in which we have Wal-Mart stores. This allows us to provide the Customer Service expected from each individual customer that walks into our stores." – Tom Coughlin, President and chief executive officer, Wal-Mart Stores division

Strive for Excellence

New ideas and goals make us reach further than ever before. We try to find new and innovative ways to push our boundaries and constantly improve. "Sam was never satisfied that prices were as low as they needed to be or that our product's quality was as high as they deserved – he believed in the concept of striving for excellence before it became a fashionable concept." – Lee Scott, President and CEO

■ EXCEEDING CUSTOMER EXPECTATIONS ■

Years ago, Sam Walton challenged all Wal-Mart associates to practice what he called "aggressive hospitality." He said "Let's be the most friendly – offer a smile of welcome and assistance to all who do us a favor by entering our stores. Give better service – over and beyond what our customers expect. Why not? You wonderful, caring associates can do it and do it better than any other retailing company in the world . . . exceed your customers' expectations. If you do, they'll come back over and over again."

As Wal-Mart associates we know it is not good enough to simply be grateful to our customers for shopping in our stores – we want to demonstrate our gratitude in every way we can! We believe that doing so is what keeps our customers coming back to Wal-Mart again and again.

■ HELPING PEOPLE MAKE A DIFFERENCE ■

Sam Walton believed that each Wal-Mart store should reflect the values of its customers and support the vision they hold for their community. As a result, Wal-Mart's Community Outreach Programs are guided by local Associates who grew up in the area and understand its needs. In addition, Wal-Mart Stores, Inc., has launched several national efforts to help the larger, US community.

Locally, Wal-Mart:

- Underwrites college scholarships for high-school seniors.
- Raises funds for nearby children's hospitals through the Children's Miracle Network Telethon.
- Provides money and manpower for fund raisers, school benefits and churches, Boy and Girl Scouts, park projects, police and fire charities, food banks, senior citizen centers, and more.
- Educates the public about recycling and other environmental topics with the help of a "Green Coordinator," a specially trained Associate who coordinates efforts to make an environmentally responsible store.

On the national scope, Wal-Mart Stores, Inc.:

- Provides industrial development grants each year to towns and cities that are attempting to bolster their economic base.
- Encourages American companies to bring offshore manufacturing operations "back home" and bolster the US job base through our Buy American Program.

■ SAM'S RULES FOR BUILDING A BUSINESS ■

People often ask, "What is Wal-Mart's secret to success?"

In response to this ever-present question, in his 1992 book *Made in America*, Sam Walton compiled a list of ten key factors that unlock the mystery. These factors are known as "Sam's Rules for Building a Business."

Rule 1. Commit to your business. Believe in it more than anybody else. I think I overcame every single one of my personal shortcomings by the sheer passion I brought to my work. I don't know if you're born with this kind of passion, or if you can learn it. But I do know you need it. If you love your work, you'll be out there every day trying to do it the best you possibly can, and pretty soon everybody around will catch the passion from you – like a fever.

Rule 2. Share your profits with all your Associates, and treat them as partners. In turn, they will treat you as a partner, and together you will all perform beyond your wildest expectations. Remain a corporation and retain control if you like, but behave as a servant leader in a partnership. Encourage your Associates to hold a stake in the company. Offer discounted stock, and grant them stock for their retirement. It's the single best thing we ever did.

Rule 3. Motivate your partners. Money and ownership alone aren't enough. Constantly, day-by-day, think of new and more interesting ways to motivate and challenge your partners. Set high goals, encourage competition, and then keep score. Make bets with outrageous payoffs. If things get stale, cross-pollinate; have managers switch jobs with one another to stay challenged. Keep everybody guessing as to what your next trick is going to be. Don't become too predictable.

Rule 4. Communicate everything you possibly can to your partners. The more they know, the more they'll understand. The more they understand, the more they'll care. Once they care, there's no stopping them. If you don't trust your Associates to know what's going on, they'll know you don't really consider them partners. Information is power, and the gain you get from empowering your Associates more than offsets the risk of informing your competitors.

Rule 5. Appreciate everything your Associates do for the business. A paycheck and a stock option will buy one kind of loyalty. But all of us like to be told how much somebody appreciates what we do for them. We like to hear it often, and especially when we have done something we're really proud of. Nothing else can quite substitute for a few well-chosen, well-timed, sincere words of praise. They're absolutely free – and worth a fortune.

Rule 6. Celebrate your successes. Find some humor in your failures. Don't take yourself so seriously. Loosen up, and everybody around you will loosen up. Have fun. Show enthusiasm – always. When all else fails, put on a costume and sing a silly song. Then make everybody else sing with you. Don't do a hula on Wall Street. It's been done. Think up your own stunt. All of this is more important, and more fun, than you think, and it really fools the competition. "Why should we take those cornballs at Wal-Mart seriously?"

Rule 7. Listen to everyone in your company. And figure out ways to get them talking. The folks on the front lines – the ones who actually talk to the customer – are the only ones who really know what's going on out there. You'd better find out what they know. This really is what total quality is all about. To push responsibility down in your organization, and to force good ideas to bubble up within it, you must listen to what your Associates are trying to tell you.

Rule 8. Exceed your customers' expectations. If you do, they'll come back over and over. Give them what they want – and a little more. Let them know you appreciate them. Make good on all your mistakes, and don't make excuses – apologize. Stand behind everything you do. The two most important words I ever wrote were on that first Wal-Mart sign, "Satisfaction Guaranteed." They're still up there, and they have made all the difference.

Rule 9. Control your expenses better than your competition. This is where you can always find the competitive advantage. For 25 years running – long before Wal-Mart was known as the nation's largest retailer – we ranked No. 1 in our industry for the lowest ratio of expenses to sales. You can make a lot of different mistakes and still recover if you run an efficient operation. Or you can be brilliant and still go out of business if you're too inefficient.

Rule 10. Swim upstream. Go the other way. Ignore the conventional wisdom. If everybody else is doing it one way, there's a good chance you can find your niche by going in exactly the opposite direction. But be prepared for a lot of folks to wave you down and tell you you're headed the wrong way. I guess in all my years, what I heard more often than anything was: a town of less than 50,000 population cannot support a discount store for very long.

■ **SUNDOWN RULE** ■

One Sunday morning, Jeff, a pharmacist at a Wal-Mart store in Harrison, Ark., received a call from his store. A store associate informed him that one of his pharmacy customers, a diabetic, had accidentally dropped her insulin down her garbage disposal. Knowing that a diabetic without insulin could be in grave danger, Jeff immediately rushed to the store, opened the pharmacy and filled the customer's insulin prescription. This is just one of many ways your local Wal-Mart store might honor what is known by our associates as the Sundown Rule.

It's a rule we take seriously at Wal-Mart. In this busy place, where our jobs depend on one another, it's our standard to get things done today – before the sun goes down. Whether it's a request from a store across the country or a call from down the hall, every request gets same-day service. These are our working principles.

The Sundown Rule was our founder, Sam Walton's, twist on that old adage "why put off until tomorrow what you can do today." It is still an important part of our Wal-Mart culture and is one reason our associates are so well known for their customer service. The observation of the Sundown Rule means we strive to answer requests by sundown on the day we receive them.

Source: "The Wal-Mart Culture" from www.walmartstores.com (includes "Sam's Rules for Building a Business", from Sam Walton and John Huey, *Made in America*, Doubleday, 1992).

■ WAL-MART IN 2002 ■

The Businesses

During the first half of 2002, Wal-Mart's 4,500 stores and 1.3 million employees were selling at the rate of $225 billion annually to the 100 million customers who visited Wal-Mart stores each week. These sales occurred through four major areas of business:

- Wal-Mart Stores. Wal-Mart's core area of business in 2002 was its retail stores within the US. These comprised Wal-Mart's traditional discount stores – large, self-service stores offering a broad range of non-food products that included apparel, shoes, household textiles (bedding, towels, fabrics), appliances, toys and games, sporting goods, electronic products, recorded music, pharmaceuticals, health and beauty products, stationery, auto supplies, jewelry, and candy. However, the most rapidly growing part of the business was the Wal-Mart Supercenters, much larger stores that combined a discount store with a supermarket. Superstores were based upon the European "hypermarket" concept. By 2002, Wal-Mart was the nation's No. 1 food retailer with $56 billion of grocery sales a year – roughly 10.3 percent of the US grocery market. The rationale for entry into food was simple: whereas the average shopper might come to Wal-Mart only once or twice a month, people buy groceries, on average, more than twice a week. Some Supercenters employed over 500 associates and generated over $100 million in sales each year. Most of Wal-Mart's superstores were the result of converting existing Wal-Mart stores. By early 2002, Superstores were generating more sales than the traditional Wal-Mart discount stores.

- Sam's Clubs. Wal-Mart's entry into warehouse clubs in the mid-1980s demonstrated its ability to transfer its retailing capabilities to a very different retail format. These wholesale outlets offered a narrower range of products – typically around 4,000 stock-keeping units (SKUs) as compared with the 50,000 SKUs for most Wal-Mart discount stores – at prices significantly below those of discount stores. The development of Sam's Club also demonstrated Wal-Mart's capacity for continuous improvement and innovation. From the stark, austere warehouses of the 1980s, Wal-Mart had created a unique wholesale distribution experience. During 2002, Wal-Mart planned to upgrade many of its Sam's Clubs to include a member's restaurant, a section featuring premium wines and gourmet foods, a gas station, and an optical department.

- Wal-Mart's international operations comprised a number of separate national subsidiaries, each attempting to interpret the basic Wal-Mart business principles and underlying approach to retailing within a distinctive economic structure and national culture. Wal-Mart's differentiated approach to different countries reflected the different retailing environments of these countries and the different entry opportunities that had presented themselves. Wal-Mart's joint ventures in Mexico and South America reflected its desire to access local knowledge and utilize the resources and capabilities of strong local players. Its acquisition of Asda in the UK was the result of the strong affinities that the two retailers felt for one another. (Asda had long modeled its strategy and management style upon Wal-Mart.) Wal-Mart's international expansion had been a process of learning and adaptation. The 2002 Annual Report noted that, despite the successful acquisition of Asda, "Cultural transitions haven't always been this smooth for Wal-Mart International. In Argentina, for example, Wal-Mart initially faced challenges in adapting its US-based retail mix and store layouts to the local culture." John Menzer, head of the international division, observed: "It wasn't such a good idea to stick so closely to the domestic Wal-Mart blueprint in Argentina or in some other international markets we have entered. In Mexico City we sold tennis balls that wouldn't bounce right in the high altitude. We built large parking lots at some of our Mexican stores only to realize that many of our customers there rode the bus to the store, then trudged across these large parking lots carrying bags of merchandise . . . We're now working smarter internationally to avoid cultural and regional problems on the front end."[7]

- McLane Company Inc. comprises the business segment that Wal-Mart classifies as "other" in its accounts. Wholesales distribution by McLane is to Wal-Mart's Sam's Clubs and Supercenters, and to third-party customers. The sales and profits shown under the "other" category (table 5.2) relates only to McLane's third-party business. In 2001, McLane acquired AmeriServe Food Distribution, Inc.

Table 5.1 lists Wal-Mart stores by types and location. Table 5.2 shows sales and profits for the different business segments.

Table 5.1 Wal-Mart stores by types and location

	Discount stores	Supercenters	Sam's Clubs	Neighborhood markets
USA	1,647	1,066	500	31
Argentina	0	11	0	0
Brazil	0	12	8	2[a]
Canada	196	0	0	0
China	0	15	3	1
Germany	0	95	0	0
South Korea	0	9	0	0
Mexico	443[b]	62	46	0
Puerto Rico	9	1	7	0
United Kingdom	0	250[c]	0	0
TOTAL	2,286	1,521	564	33

[a] Includes *To do Dia* stores.
[b] Includes Bodegas, Suburbia, Superamas, and VIP stores.
[c] Includes 244 Asda stores and 6 Supercenters.
Source: www.wal-mart.com.

Table 5.2 Wal-Mart: performance by segment

	Wal-Mart stores	Sam's Clubs	International	Other
Sales ($, bill.)				
2002	139.1	29.4	35.5	13.8
2001	121.9	26.8	32.1	10.5
2000	108.7	24.8	22.7	8.8
Sales increase				
2002	14.1%	9.7%	10.5%	30.8%
2001	12.1%	8.1%	41.2%	20.3%
2000	14.0%	8.4%	85.6%	23.2%
Operating income ($, mill.)				
2002	10.3	1.03	1.46	(0.71)
2001	9.70	0.94	1.11	(0.29)
2000	8.70	0.85	0.82	(0.26)
Op. income/Sales				
2002	7.4%	3.5%	4.1%	(5.2)%
2001	8.0%	3.5%	3.5%	(2.7)%
2000	8.0%	3.4%	3.6%	(3.0)%

Source: Wal-Mart annual financial statements.

Performance

Table 5.3 summarizes some key financial data for Wal-Mart during the period 1992 to 2002. Table 5.4 shows Wal-Mart's recent performance compared with other discount retailers.

Table 5.3 Wal-Mart Stores Inc.: financial summary 1992–2002

	2002	2001	2000	1999	1998	1997	1996	1995	1994	1993	1992
Income											
Net sales	217,799	191,329	165,013	137,634	117,958	104,859	93,627	82,494	67,344	55,484	43,887
Net sales increase	14%	16%	20%	17%	12%	12%	13%	22%	21%	26%	35%
Same-store sales increase	6%	5%	8%	9%	6%	5%	4%	7%	6%	11%	10%
Other income-net	2,013	1,966	1,796	1,574	1,341	1,319	1,146	914	645	497	404
Cost of sales	171,562	150,255	129,664	108,725	93,438	83,510	74,505	65,586	53,444	44,175	34,786
SGA administrative expenses	36,173	31,550	27,040	22,363	19,358	16,946	15,021	12,858	10,333	8,321	6,684
Interest costs:											
Debt	1,052	1,095	756	529	555	629	692	520	331	143	113
Capital leases	274	279	266	268	229	216	196	186	186	180	153
Provision for income taxes	3,897	3,692	3,338	2,740	2,115	1,794	1,606	1,581	1,358	1,171	945
Minority interests	(183)	(129)	(170)	(153)	(78)	(27)	(13)	4	(4)	4	(1)
Net income	6,671	6,295	5,377	4,430	3,526	3,056	2,740	2,681	2,333	1,995	1,609
Financial Position											
Current assets	28,246	26,555	24,356	21,132	19,352	17,993	17,331	15,338	12,114	10,198	8,575
Inventories (replacement cost)	22,749	21,644	20,171	17,549	16,845	16,193	16,300	14,415	11,483	9,780	7,857
Net property, plant and equipment and capital leases	45,750	40,934	35,969	25,973	23,606	20,324	18,894	15,874	13,176	9,793	6,434
Total assets	83,451	78,130	70,349	49,996	45,384	39,604	37,541	32,819	26,441	20,565	15,443
Current liabilities	27,282	28,949	25,803	16,762	14,460	10,957	11,454	9,973	7,406	6,754	5,004

Long-term debt	15,687	12,501	13,672	6,908	7,191	7,709	8,508	7,871	6,156	3,073	1,722
Long-term lease obligations	3,045	3,154	3,002	2,699	2,483	2,307	2,092	1,838	1,804	1,772	1,556
Shareholders' equity	35,102	31,343	25,834	21,112	18,503	17,143	14,756	12,726	10,753	8,759	6,990
Financial Ratios											
Current ratio	1.0	0.9	0.9	1.3	1.3	1.6	1.5	1.5	1.6	1.5	1.7
Inventories/working capital	23.5	(9.0)	(13.7)	3.9	3.4	2.3	2.7	2.6	2.3	2.7	2.1
Return on assets*	8.5%	8.7%	9.5%	9.6%	8.5%	7.9%	7.8%	9.0%	9.9%	11.1%	12.0%
Return on shareholders' equity**	20.1%	22.0%	22.9%	22.4%	19.8%	19.2%	19.9%	22.8%	23.9%	25.3%	26.0%
Other Year-End Data											
Number of US Wal-Mart stores	1,647	1,736	1,801	1,869	1,921	1,960	1,995	1,985	1,950	1,848	1,714
Number of U.S. Supercenters	1,066	888	721	564	441	344	239	147	72	34	10
Number of U.S. Sam's Clubs	500	475	463	451	443	436	433	426	417	256	208
Number of U.S. Neighborhood Markets	31	19	7	4	—	—	—	—	—	—	—
International units	1,170	1,071	1,004	715	601	314	276	226	24	10	—
Number of Associates ('000s)	1,383	1,244	1,140	910	825	728	675	622	528	434	371

*Net income before minority interest, equity in unconsolidated subsidiaries and cumulative effect of accounting change/average assets.

**Net income/average shareholders' equity.

Source: Wal-Mart annual financial statements.

Table 5.4 Wal-Mart and its competitors: Performance comparisons

	Wal-Mart	Target	Kmart	CostCo	Dollar General
Sales revenue ($, bill.)					
2002	217.8	39.9	36.2	—	5.3
2001	191.3	36.9	37.0	32.2	4.6
2000	165.0	33.7	36.0	27.5	3.9
Cost of goods sold ($, bill.)					
2002	168.3	27.2	29.1	—	3.7
2001	147.4	25.3	28.9	28.1	3.2
2000	127.3	23.0	27.3	24.0	2.7
Gross profit ($, bill.)					
2002	49.5	12.6	7.0	—	1.6
2001	43.9	11.6	8.1	4.1	1.4
2000	37.7	10.7	8.6	3.5	1.2
Gross margin (%)					
2002	22.7	31.7	19.5	—	30.7
2001	23.0	31.5	22.0	12.7	29.9
2000	22.9	31.7	23.9	12.8	29.9
SG&A expense ($, bill.)					
2002	36.2	8.9	7.6	—	1.1
2001	31.6	8.2	6.7	2.8	0.9
2000	27.0	7.5	6.5	2.4	0.7
Depreciation & amortization ($, bill.)					
2002	3.3	1.1	0.8	—	0.1
2001	2.9	0.9	0.8	0.3	0.1
2000	2.4	0.9	0.8	0.2	0.06
Operating income ($, bill.)					
2002	10.1	2.7	(1.4)	—	0.4
2001	9.5	2.5	0.7	1.0	0.3
2000	8.3	2.3	1.3	0.7	0.3
Operating margin (%)					
2002	4.6	6.7	—	—	7.0
2001	5.0	6.7	1.8	3.2	6.9
2000	5.0	6.9	3.6	3.1	9.0
Net income ($, bill.)					
2002	6.7	1.4	(2.4)	—	0.2
2001	6.3	1.3	(0.2)	0.6	0.07
2000	5.4	1.1	0.4	0.4	0.2
Net profit margin (%)					
2002	3.1	3.4	—	—	3.9
2001	3.3	3.4	—	2.0	1.6
2000	3.3	3.4	1.1	1.4	5.6
Cash ($, bil.)					
2002	2.2	0.5	1.2	—	0.3
2001	2.1	0.4	0.4	0.5	0.2
2000	1.9	0.2	0.3	0.4	0.06
Net receivables ($, bill.)					
2002	2.0	3.8	0.0	—	0.0

Table 5.4 *continued*

	Wal-Mart	Target	Kmart	CostCo	Dollar General
2001	1.8	1.9	0.0	0.2	0.0
2000	1.3	1.8	0.0	0.2	0.0
Inventories ($, bill.)					
2002	22.6	4.5	5.8	—	1.1
2001	21.4	4.3	6.4	2.5	0.9
2000	20.0	3.8	7.1	2.2	1.0
Total current assets ($, bill.)					
2002	28.2	9.6	7.9	—	1.6
2001	26.6	7.3	7.6	3.4	1.1
2000	24.4	6.5	8.2	3.3	1.1
Total assets ($, bill.)					
2002	83.5	24.2	14.3	—	2.6
2001	78.1	19.5	14.6	8.6	2.3
2000	70.3	17.1	15.1	7.5	1.5
Short-term debt ($, bill.)					
2002	3.1	0.9	0.0	—	0.4
2001	6.7	0.9	0.06	0.009	0.009
2000	5.4	0.5	0.06	0.0	0.007
Total current liabilities ($, bill.)					
2002	27.3	7.1	0.6	—	1.1
2001	28.9	6.3	3.8	3.4	0.5
2000	25.8	5.9	4.1	2.9	0.5
Long-term debt ($, bill.)					
2002	18.7	8.1	1.2	—	0.3
2001	15.7	5.6	3.0	0.8	0.7
2000	16.7	4.5	2.8	0.9	0.001
Total liabilities ($, bill.)					
2002	48.3	16.3	10.8	—	1.5
2001	46.8	13.0	8.5	4.4	1.4
2000	44.5	11.3	8.8	4.0	0.5
Shareholders' equity ($, bill.)					
2002	35.1	7.9	3.5	—	1.0
2001	31.3	6.5	6.1	4.2	0.9
2000	25.8	5.9	6.3	3.5	0.9

Source: Wal-Mart annual financial statements.

■ WAL-MART STORES' OPERATIONS AND ACTIVITIES[8] ■

Purchasing and Vendor Relationships

The size of Wal-Mart's purchases and its negotiating ability meant that Wal-Mart was both desired and feared among manufacturers. Being accepted as a Wal-Mart vendor offered access to a huge share of the US retail market. At the same time, Wal-Mart buyers were well aware of their ability to take full advantage of economies of scale available to their suppliers and to squeeze their margins to razor-thin level. Purchasing was centralized. All dealing with buyers took place at Wal-Mart's Bentonville headquarters. Here vendors were escorted to interview rooms equipped only with a table and four chairs. Suppliers regarded the experience of selling to Wal-Mart as intimidating and grueling: "Once you are ushered into one of the Spartan little buyer's rooms, expect a steely eye across the table and be prepared to cut your price."[9] Another vendor commented: "all normal mating rituals are verboten. Their highest priority is making sure everybody at all times in all cases knows who's in charge . . . They talk softly, but they have piranha hearts, and if you aren't totally prepared when you go in there, you're in deep trouble."[10] The requirements that Wal-Mart imposed on its suppliers extended well beyond low prices. Increasingly Wal-Mart involved itself in its suppliers' employment policies, including workplace safety, working hours of less than 60 hours a week, and absence of child labor.

All negotiations were directly between manufacturers and Wal-Mart: from 1992 onwards Wal-Mart refused to do businesses with manufacturers' representatives and agents. While Wal-Mart maximized its buying power through centralizing its purchases, it was also anxious that no individual supplier should gain substantial leverage over it. Hence, Wal-Mart was reluctant to allow any single supplier account for more than two-and-a-half percent of its total purchases.

During the 1990s, Wal-Mart established close collaborative arrangements with its larger suppliers. Wal-Mart's cooperation with Procter & Gamble provided a model for these relationships. P&G was Wal-Mart's biggest supplier accounting for about 2 percent of Wal-Mart's purchases, but nearly 10 percent of P&G's sales. The companies began electronic data interchange (EDI) at the beginning of the 1990s, and by 1993 there were 70 P&G employees working at Bentonville to manage sales and deliveries to Wal-Mart.

By the mid-1990s, Wal-Mart had extended EDI to cover about 70 percent of its vendors. Data interchange included point-of-sale data on sales of the vendors' products at individual stores, levels of inventory, Wal-Mart's sales forecasts, the vendors' production planning and delivery scheduling, and electronic funds transfer. Wal-Mart's system of supply-chain management was called "Retail Link."

Through collaboration with Cisco Systems, Retail Link was moved to the internet during the mid-1990s.

Suppliers used modems to dial into the Wal-Mart database for up-to-date, store-by-store information on sales and inventory for their products. This allowed suppliers to work with Wal-Mart company's buyers to manage inventory in the stores – forecasting, planning, producing, and shipping products as needed. The result was faster replenishment, a product mix tuned to the needs of local customers, and lower inventory costs for Wal-Mart. "We transformed it from a traditional dial-in network to an internet application," says Flanagan. "Now it's easier for our vendors to use, because they just need a web browser. More of our international suppliers can get access, because it's on the internet. And it's easier and less expensive for us to maintain." Data transmission was no longer limited to the speed of dial-up modems, further assisting the speed and responsiveness of the system.

Warehousing and Distribution

Wal-Mart distributed a higher proportion of goods to its own stores than any other discount retailer. While most discount retailers relied heavily upon their suppliers to undertake distribution to individual stores, over 80 percent of Wal-Mart's purchases were shipped to Wal-Mart's own distribution centers from where they were distributed in Wal-Mart trucks. The system that operated in 2002 was fundamentally the same as that which a Harvard Business School case described in 1994:

> Each store received an average of five full or partial truckloads a week, and because Wal-Mart stores were grouped together, trucks could resupply several on a single trip. Returned merchandise was carried back to the distribution center for consolidation, and since many vendors operated warehouses or factories within Wal-Mart's territory, trucks also picked up new shipments on the return trip. Roughly 2,500 people drove Wal-Mart's fleet of 2,000 trucks, which ran more than 60 percent full on backhauls. A store could select one of four options regarding the frequency and timing of shipments, and more than half accepted night deliveries. For stores located within a particular distance from the distribution center, an acetated delivery plan was available, which allowed merchandise to be delivered within 24 hours.

A typical distribution center spanned a million square feet and was operated 24 hours a day by a staff of 700 associates. It was highly automated and designed to serve the needs of about 150 stores within a radius of 200 miles. When orders were pulled from stock, an automated "pick to light" system guided associated to the correct locations.

Since the mid-1990s, Wal-Mart had continued to develop its distribution system. It was an early adopter of "cross-docking" – a system where goods arriving on inbound trucks were unloaded and reloaded on outbound trucks without first sitting in warehouse inventory.

In-Store Operations

Wal-Mart's management of its retail stores was based upon its objective of creating customer satisfaction by combining low prices, a wide range of quality products carefully tailored to customer needs, and a pleasing shopping experience. Wal-Mart's management of its retail stores was distinguished by the following characteristics:

- *Merchandising.* Wal-Mart stores offered a wide range of nationally branded products. Although Wal-Mart also sold its own brand – especially in clothing – it gave less emphasis to own brand products than other retailers (e.g., Sears). Each selection of merchandise was carefully tailored to the characteristics of the local market – point-of-sale data for individual stores greatly assisted responsiveness to local needs (see below).
- *Decentralization of store management.* Individual store managers were given considerable decision-making authority in relation to product range, product

positioning within stores, and pricing. This differed from most other discount chains where decisions over pricing and merchandising were made either at head office or at regional offices. Decentralized decision making was also apparent within stores where the managers of individual departments (e.g., toys, health and beauty, consumer electronics) were expected to develop and implement their own ideas for increasing sales and reducing costs.

- *Customer service.* Most Wal-Mart discount stores were open 9 a.m. to 9 p.m. six days a week with shorter hours on Sundays. Supercenters were open continuously. Despite the fanatical emphasis on cost efficiency, Wal-Mart went to great lengths to engage with its customers at a personal level. Stores employed "greeters" – often retired individuals – who would welcome customers and hand out shopping baskets. Within the store, all employees were expected to look customers in the eye, smile at them, and offer a verbal greeting. In order to encourage customer loyalty, Wal-Mart maintained a "Satisfaction Guaranteed" program. This program assured customers that Wal-Mart would accept returned merchandise on a no-questions-asked basis.

Marketing

Wal-Mart's marketing strategy rested primarily upon disseminating its policy of low prices and customer commitment. Central to its marketing was the communication of its slogan "Everyday Low Prices" – the concept that Wal-Mart's price cutting strategy was not restricted to particular products or to particular time periods, but was a basic principle of Wal-Mart's business.

As a result of its customer-focused, value-for-money approach, Wal-Mart was able to rely upon word-of-mouth communication of its merits, and was able to spend comparatively little on advertising and promotion. Advertising spending was limited to one advertisement circular per month per store and some television advertising. During the early 1990s, Wal-Mart spent only 0.5 percent of every sales dollar on advertising, compared to 2.5 percent for Kmart and 3.5 percent for Sears Roebuck and Company.

Wal-Mart placed strong emphasis on patriotism and national causes. During the mid-1980s, at a time of increased public concern about the mounting trade deficit, Wal-Mart launched its "Buy American" program and placed prominent "Made in the U.S.A." signs on its merchandise displays.

Information Technology

In each of its business functions and between functions, Wal-Mart was a pioneer in the application of information and communications technology to support decision making and promote efficiency and customer responsiveness. In 1974, Wal-Mart was among the first retailers to adopt computers to maintain inventory control. In 1977, Wal-Mart initiated the electronic transfer of information to its suppliers – the system known as Electronic Data Interchange, or EDI. In the following year Wal-Mart introduced bar code scanning for use at point-of-sale and also for inventory control systems.

To link stores and cash register sales with supply chain management and inventory control, Wal-Mart invested $24 million in its own satellite in 1984. By 1990, Wal-Mart's satellite system was the largest two-way, fully integrated private satellite network in the world, providing two-way interactive voice and video capability, data transmission for inventory control, rapid credit card authorization, and enhanced EDI transmission.

In its 1999 Annual Report, Wal-Mart outlined some of ways in which it utilized information to promote customer service:

At Wal-Mart, information technology gives us that knowledge in the most direct way: by collecting and analyzing our own internal information on exactly what any given shopping cart contains. The popular term is "data-mining," and Wal-Mart has been doing it since about 1990. The result, by now, is an enormous database of purchasing information that enables us to place the right item in the right store at the right price. Our computer system receives 8.4 million updates every minute on the items that customers take home – and the relationship between the items in each basket. Our merchants use this database to understand what customers want – and to find ways to help them get it into their carts with as much convenience, and at as low a cost, as possible. In any given week, for example, typical Wal-Mart's highest-selling items will include videotapes of *Sleeping Beauty*, Folgers® coffee, bananas and toilet paper – although the chances are that no single shopping cart contains all of those items. That kind of information has significant value in and of itself. Consider Wal-Mart's ability to keep the shelves stocked with exactly what customers want most, but still be able to keep inventories under tight control. The computerized transmission of transactions to our systems, which keep track of what merchandise is needed where, is a key tool as Wal-Mart merchants work to serve our customers. And that's only the beginning. For example, imagine a receipt that records a customer's purchase of Clearasil,® a Backstreet Boys CD and lip gloss. It's a safe guess that this customer's household has a teenage girl in it, and where there are teenagers, there is merchandising to be done.[11]

Point-of-sale data analysis also assisted in planning store layout:

There are some obvious purchasing patterns among the register receipts of families with infants and small children. Well-thought-out product placement not only simplifies the shopping trip for these customers – with baby aisles that include infant clothes and children's medicine alongside diapers, baby food and formula – but at the same time places higher-margin products among the staples.

Seasonal merchandising – a key Wal-Mart focus – offers many opportunities for product placement based on customer buying patterns. For example, as pre-Halloween displays of costumes go up, they can be accompanied by a selection of flashlights – a valuable reminder for busy parents who might not have thought to stop by the hardware department for that important piece of trick-or-treating equipment.

Customers who buy suitcases are likely to be looking for other items they might need for traveling too – such as travel alarms and irons, which now, logically enough, can be found displayed alongside luggage at many Wal-Mart stores.

The common thread is simple: We are here to serve the customer; and customers tend to buy from us when we make it easy for them. That sounds like a simple idea. But first you must understand the customer's needs. And that's where information comes in.[12]

Most important was the role of IT in linking and integrating the whole of Wal-Mart's value chain:

> Wal-Mart web of information systems extends far beyond the walls of any one store. Starting from the basic information compiled at the checkout stand, at the shelves, and gathered by associates equipped with hand-held computer monitors, Wal-Mart works to manage its supplies and inventories not only in the stores, but all the way back to the original source. Wal-Mart has given suppliers access to some of our systems, which enables them to know exactly what is selling, and to plan their production accordingly. This not only helps us keep inventories under control, but also helps the supplier deliver the lowest-cost product to the customer. With sales and in-stock information transmitted between Wal-Mart and our supplier-partners in seconds over the internet, buyers and suppliers are privy to the same facts and negotiate based on a shared understanding – saving a significant amount of time and energy over more traditional, low-tech systems. Our buyer benefits from the supplier's product knowledge, while the supplier benefits from Wal-Mart's experience in the market. Combine these information systems with our logistics – our hub-and-spoke system in which distribution centers are placed within a day's truck run of the stores – and all the pieces fall into place for the ability to respond to the needs of our customers, before they are even in the store. In today's retailing world, speed is a crucial competitive advantage. And when it comes to turning information into improved merchandising and service to the customer, Wal-Mart is out in front and gaining speed. In the words of Randy Mott, Senior Vice President and Chief Information Officer, "The surest way to predict the future is to invent it."[13]

Human Resource Management

Wal-Mart's human resource policies were based closely upon Sam Walton's ideas about relations between the company and its employees and between employees and customers. All employees – from executive-level personnel to checkout clerks – were known as "Associates." Wal-Mart's relations with its Associates were founded upon respect, high expectations, close communication, and effective incentives.

Although Wal-Mart's employees received relatively low pay (in common with most of the retail trade), Wal-Mart offered strong profit incentives for employees and encouraged them to share in its wealth creation through its stock ownership scheme. Numerous employees had retired as millionaires as a result of their participation in the plan. Most of these were managers; however, in 1989, the first millionaire hourly associate retired from the company.

Wal-Mart resisted the unionization of its employees in the belief that union membership created a barrier between the management and the employees in furthering the success of the company and its members. Despite strenuous efforts by unions to recruit Wal-Mart employees, union penetration remained low.

Associates enjoyed a high degree of autonomy and received continuous communication about their company's performance and about store operations. Every aspect of company operations and strategy was seen as depending upon the close collaboration of managers and shop-floor employees. To help control shrinkage (industry jargon for loss from theft and damage), the company instituted a bonus system whereby each associate could receive up to $200 if a store met corporate goals. Wal-Mart's shrinkage was estimated to be just above one percent, versus an industry average of two percent.

Wal-Mart's approach to employee involvement made heavy use of orchestrated demonstration of enthusiasm and commitment. The central feature of Wal-Mart meetings from corporate to store level was the "Wal-Mart Cheer" – devised by Sam Walton after a visit to Korea. The call and response ritual ("Give me a W!" "Give me an A!" . . .), included the "Wal-Mart squiggly" which involved employees shaking their backsides in unison.

Fortune suggested that the Wal-Mart cheer's mixture of homespun and corporate themes provided an apt metaphor for what it called "the Wal-Mart paradox":

> The paradox is that Wal-Mart stands for both Main Street values and the efficiencies of the huge corporation, aw-shucks hokeyness and terabytes of minute-by-minute sales data, fried-chicken luncheons at the Waltons' Arkansas home and the demands of Wall Street.
>
> Critics of Wal-Mart call the homespun stuff a fraud, a calculated strategy to put a human face on a relentlessly profit-minded corporation. What is paradoxical and suspect to people outside Wal-Mart, however, is perfectly normal to the people who work there. It reflects a deal that Sam Walton, Wal-Mart's founder, made with the people who worked for him.
>
> The deal was a lot more than just a matter of the occasional visit from Mr. Sam. Wal-Mart demonstrated its concern for workers in many ways that were small but specific: time and a half for work on Sundays, an "open door" policy that let workers bring concerns to managers at any level, the real chance of promotion (about 70% of store managers started as hourly associates).
>
> Sam Walton died in 1992, but the language of that deal still peppers the dialogue of Wal-Mart executives and the company's official literature. A quote that runs, in large type, across the top of a page in Wal-Mart's associate handbook is typical: "The undeniable cornerstone of Wal-Mart's success can be traced back to our strong belief in the dignity of each individual." Or listen to Wal-Mart spokesman Jay Allen: "If we didn't practice respect for the individual, didn't operate in an open-door environment, we would not be living up to the expectations that our associates have of us." In an interview with *Fortune* two years ago, Coleman Petersen, Wal-Mart's human resources chief, made much the same point: "The higher up in the organization you go, the more of a servant you need to become because of the respect and expectations that Wal-Mart associates have of you as a leader."[14]

Organization and Management Style

Wal-Mart's management structure and management style had been molded by Sam Walton's principles and values. As Wal-Mart grew in size and geographical scope, Walton was determined that corporate executives should keep closely in touch with customers and store operations. The result was a structure in which communication between individual stores and the Bentonville headquarters was both close and

Table 5.5 Wal-Mart's executive team

Name	Position	Years of experience	Previous employment	Education
S. Robson Walton	Chairman of the Board	30+	Wal-Mart: SVP-Secretary & General Counsel, Vice Chairman; Conner & Winters: Partner	Attended Wooster College; University of Arkansas: BS-Business Administration; Columbia University: JD
David D. Glass	Chairman, Executive Committee of the Board, Wal-Mart Stores, Inc.	15+	Wal-Mart: President & CEO; Kansas City Royals: Current Owner, Chairman & CEO	Southwest Missouri State: Bachelor's Degree
H. Lee Scott	President & CEO, Wal-Mart Stores, Inc	22+	Wal-Mart: VP-Transportation, VP Distribution, SVP-Logistics, EVP Logistics, President & CEO-Stores Division, COO & Vice Chairman	Pittsburg State University: Bachelor's in Business; Penn State: Executive Development; Columbia University: Executive Development
Thomas M. Coughlin	President & CEO, Wal-Mart Stores Division	23+	Wal-Mart: VP-Loss Prevention, VP Human Resources, EVP-SAM'S Club Operations, EVP-Specialty Groups, EVP & COO-Wal-Mart Store Operations; RH Macy: West Coast Division; Cook United, Inc.	California State University: BS in Political Science
Paul R. Carter	EVP, Wal-Mart Stores, Inc.; President, Wal-Mart Realty	24+	Wal-Mart: Controller, EVP & CFO, EVP Special Divisions; Howard Discount Centers: Controller, Secretary-Treasurer, SVP & CFO	University of Arkansas at Monticello: Bachelor's in Accounting

Name	Position	Years	Experience	Education
Bob Connolly	EVP, Marketing & Consumer Communications, Wal-Mart Stores, Inc.	15+	Wal-Mart: EVP- Merchandise Stores Division, VP-Merchandise Manager Apparel, SVP & General Merchandise Manager, VP-Women's Apparel, VP Shoes & Jewelry Merchandising; Montgomery Ward: EVP; Carson Pirie Scott: SVP; Sibleys/ Associated Dry Goods: SVP	Rochester Institute of Technology: Bachelor's in Business Administration
Doug Degn	EVP, Food Merchandising, Wal-Mart Stores, Inc.	18+	Wal-Mart: Pharmacy Manager, VP & Divisional Merchandise Manager, VP Pharmacy Merchandising & Support, SVP & General Merchandise Manager-Stores Division	University of Kansas: BS in Pharmacy
David Dible	EVP, Specialty Division, Wal-Mart Stores, Inc	30+	Wal-Mart: Store Manager, Senior Buyer, Divisional Merchandise Manager, VP-Merchandise Systems Development, SVP & General Merchandise Manager – Hardlines, SVP & General Merchandise Manager – Home/Seasonal, EVP Merchandising & Sales	Ft. Hays State University: BS
Michael Duke	EVP, Administration, Wal-Mart Stores, Inc.	28+	Wal-Mart: EVP-Logistics, SVP-Logistics, SVP-Distribution; Federated Department Stores; May Department Stores; Venture Stores	Georgia Tech: Bachelor's in Industrial Engineering

Table 5.5 *continued*

Name	Position	Years of experience	Previous employment	Education
J.J. Fitzsimmons	SVP, Finance & Treasurer, Wal-Mart Stores, Inc.	7+	Wal-Mart: VP-Finance; Prior to War-Mart: VP & Analyst; SVP & CFO	University of Notre Dame: Bachelor's Degree; University of Chicago: Master's Degree; CPA
Thomas Grimm	President & CEO, Sam's Club	23+	PACE Warehouse: President & CEO; Price Savers Wholesale Warehouse: Founder, President & CEO; Target Stores: Buyer	Weber State University: Bachelor's in Business Management
Don Harris	EVP, General Merchandise, Wal-Mart Stores Division	20+	Wal-Mart: Assistant Manager, Store Manager, Buyer, Senior Buyer, Divisional Merchandise Manager, SVP & General Merchandise Manager, EVP Store Operations	
Jim Haworth	EVP, Operations, Wal-Mart	18+	Wal-Mart: Assistant Store Manager, Store Manager, District Manager, Regional VP-Merchandise, Senior Vice President, Regional VP-SAM'S Club	Central Missouri State University: BS in Business Administration
Craig Herkert	SVP & COO, International Division, Wal-Mart Stores	25+	Albertson's: 23 years; Acme Supermarkets: President-East Region	St. Francis College: BS; Northern Illinois University: Master' Degree
Thomas D. Hyde	EVP & Senior General Counsel, Wal-Mart Stores, Inc.	10+	Raytheon: SVP & General Counsel; Manville Corporation; Emerson Electric	University of Kansas: English Degree; University of Missouri: Law Degree; University of Kansas: MBA

Name	Position	Years	Background	Education
John B. Menzer	EVP, President & CEO, International Division, Wal-Mart Stores, Inc.	15+	Wal-Mart: EVP & CFO; Ben Franklin: 10 years	Loyola University: Bachelor's Degree, MBA; CPA
Coleman H. Peterson	EVP, People Division, Wal-Mart Stores, Inc.	25+	Venture Stores: SVP-Human Resources	Loyola University: Bachelor's & Master's Degree
Robert K. Rhoads	EVP, General Counsel & Secretary, Wal-Mart Stores, Inc.	20+	Wal-Mart: Law Clerk, Corporate Counsel, Assistant General Counsel	University of Arkansas: BS Political Science, Juris Doctor
Thomas M. Schoewe	EVP & CFO, Wal-Mart Stores, Inc.	15+	Black & Decker: SVP & CFO, VP Finance, VP Business Planning & Analysis; Beatrice Companies: CFO & Controller	Loyola University: Bachelor's in Business Administration University of Chicago: Executive MBA
Phil Sutterfield	EVP, Merchandising, SAM's Club	35+	American Strevell: VP Merchandising; Price Savers Warehouse: EVP-Merchandising; PACE: EVP-Merchandising	University of Idaho; Utah State University
Celia Swanson	EVP, Membership, Marketing & Admin., SAM'S Club	10+	SAM'S Club: Senior Director-People Group, VP-People Group; PACE: SVP Human Resources & Administration	University of Nebraska: Bachelor's in Fashion Merchandising
Kevin Turner	EVP & CIO, Wal-Mart Stores, Inc.	15+	Wal-Mart: Cashier, Internal Audit, Business Analyst, Strategy Manager, Director, VP, Assistant CIO	East Central University: BS

Source: "Wal-Mart's executive team," Wal-Mart Stores Inc.

personal. Wal-Mart's regional vice presidents were each responsible for supervising between 10 and 15 district managers (who, in turn, were in charge of 8 to 12 stores). The regional VPs spent most of their work-week traveling their territories, meeting with district and store managers. On Thursday night, they returned to Bentonville for the weekly operations meeting on Friday morning at 7:00 a.m. followed by a merchandising meeting later in the day. Information was shared and guidelines were established regarding merchandising strategies, product pricing, and other operational matters. Following the meetings, the regional VPs contacted their district managers through conference calls or voice mail, and the district managers would disseminate information and decisions to the store managers the same day. On Saturday morning at 7:30 a.m., the regional VP, together with other corporate-level staff, would attend a meeting that combined performance reviews, strategy announcements, religion, and entertainment. Announcements of regional sales and market shares were combined with their honoring of individual achievements, and reports of new initiatives and store openings. On Monday mornings the regional VPs would return to their regions.

Wal-Mart placed a strong emphasis on management development. Most senior managers were recruited internally, and there was a strong emphasis placed upon developing managers through moving them between line and staff positions and between functions: "We have always moved our best and brightest talent around the organization to build the broad skills and experience that will carry Wal-Mart into the future. A few years ago we took our CIO, Bobby Martin, and asked him to run our International business. Three years ago we asked Tom Coughlin, who had run our Sam's business and was then running our Specialty Division, to head up our Wal-Mart store operations. At the same time Lee Scott moved from Logistics to lead our Merchandising team. These are three examples of this cross-pollination that occurs throughout our company."[15] Most senior managers were long-serving Wal-Mart veterans. Almost all had spent their entire careers in retailing (see table 5.5).

■ COMPETITION ■

Wal-Mart's expansion had brought it into closer rivalry with a broader range of competitors. When Sam Walton had opened his first discount stores in the rural south, Wal-Mart's competitors were mostly small mom-and-pop stores. Wal-Mart's expansion throughout the US and now internationally had brought Wal-Mart face to face with more powerful competitors. Not only did Wal-Mart face other discount chains – Target, Kmart, and Dollar General – it also faced competition from specialist mass-retailers. Wal-Mart had established superiority over other discount chains relatively easily (Kmart was flirting with bankruptcy for most of 2001 and 2002); however, Wal-Mart's most formidable competitors were the "category killers" that dominated particular product markets: Home Depot in tools and home improvement products, Toys-R-Us in toys, Office Depot in stationary and home office equipment, Best Buy in appliances and consumer electronics.

As Wal-Mart expanded the range of goods and service offerings, so it expanded its competitive front. Its expansion into Supercenters meant competition with supermarket chains (Kroger, Safeway, Giant). Its establishment of gas stations at its stores resulted in its competing with Exxon Mobil and Shell. Its wal-mart.com online shopping business competed with a wide range of internet retailers.

Overseas, Wal-Mart was competing with well-established incumbents. In Britain its Asda subsidiary faced strong competition from the bigger Tesco chain. In Germany, Wal-Mart was up against a number of powerful, long-established retailers.

NOTES

1. Sam Walton, *Sam Walton: Made in America*, New York: Bantam Books, 1992.
2. *Forbes*, August 16, 1982, p. 43.
3. G. C. Strachan, *The State of the Discount Store Industry*, Goldman Sachs, April 1994 (quoted in *Wal-Mart Stores, Inc.* Harvard Business School Case 9–974–024, 1994).
4. From the Wal-Mart website: www.walmart.com.
5. Sam Walton, *Sam Walton: Made in America*, New York: Bantam Books, 1992.
6. http://www.walmart.com/cservice/aw_samsway.gsp.
7. Wal-Mart Stores, Inc. Annual Report, 2000.
8. This description of Wal-Mart's retailing operations refers primarily to its US discount stores division.
9. Bill Saporito, "A week aboard the Wal-Mart Express," *Fortune*, August 24, 1992, p. 79.
10. Ibid.
11. Wal-Mart Stores, Inc. Annual Report, 1999, p. 9.
12. Ibid., p. 9.
13. Ibid., p. 11.
14. "Sam Walton made us a promise," *Fortune*, March 18, 2002.
15. "Steady as she grows" (interview with David Glass), Wal-Mart Annual Report, 1999, p. 6.

Eastman Kodak: Meeting the Digital Challenge

Robert M. Grant

On Monday April 16, 2001, Patricia F. Russo began her new appointment as President and Chief Operating Officer of Eastman Kodak Company, reporting to Chairman and Chief Executive Officer Dan Carp. The press release announcing her appointment stated: "Russo will oversee the day-to-day operations of Kodak's operating divisions and serve as the CEO's strategic partner in pursuing the business opportunities created by the convergence of imaging and information management technologies."[1] In addition to her role as President and COO, Russo also headed up the Consumer Group, Kodak's biggest operating division (see figure 6.1).

Pat Russo's appointment to the number two position in Kodak's top management team marked the high point of an outstanding career in IT and telecommunications. After graduating from Georgetown University with a degree in political science and history, Russo spent eight years with IBM before joining AT&T in 1982. In the tumultuous years following the breakup of AT&T's Bell system, Russo held management positions ranging from human resources to strategic planning, and completed Harvard's Advanced Management Program in 1989. In 1992, Ms Russo took charge of AT&T's business communications equipment division, which was then spun off as part of the new Lucent group. The Kodak press release noted that:

> Russo brings to Kodak more than twenty years of broad management experience in the computing and communications industries:
>
> As President of the Business Communications Systems division of AT&T Corp. and Lucent Technologies Inc. from 1993 through 1997, Russo drove the successful turnaround of a $6 billion technology business.
>
> As Executive Vice President of Lucent, Russo had executive oversight for such corporate functions as Strategy, Procurement, Human Resources, Investor Relations as well as Business Development.

This case was prepared by Robert M. Grant with the help of Zhenyu Shen, Xiaotong Jia, Eddy Rasoanaivo, Joo-Hyung Lee, and Young Suh. Copyright © 2002 Robert M. Grant

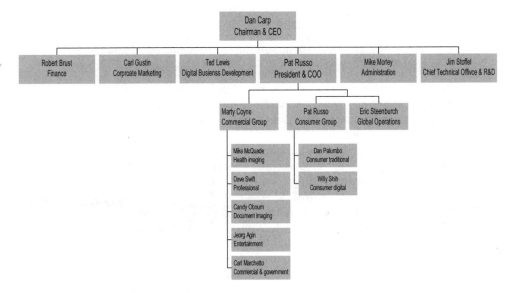

Figure 6.1   Kodak's top management team

Prior to her departure from Lucent in August of last year, Russo headed the $24 billion Service Provider Networks group that developed and delivered networking systems, software and services to communications companies worldwide.

She most recently served as chairman of the board of the Lucent spin-off Avaya . . .

In 1998 and 1999, Russo was named to *Fortune* magazine's list of the Fifty Most Powerful Women in American Business.[2]

Although responsible for operations throughout the Kodak group, it was her potential to lead Kodak's ongoing transition to digital imaging where her primary contribution would be. "Pat's broad management experience in improving operational performance in large global businesses and in generating growth from existing and new markets will serve Kodak well in our transition to the digital age," noted Chairman Dan Carp. "She arrives at Kodak at a time when imaging and information management technologies are converging. Pat's knowledge of the information technology industry will bring a fresh perspective to driving change at Kodak."[3]

At a time when digital technologies were gnawing away at Kodak's traditional market for film and chemical-based photographic products, Russo viewed digital imaging as an area of huge opportunity for Kodak:

Kodak has an enormous set of assets, including its technology, market position and a great brand. I believe these assets are equally relevant to the emerging digital imaging industry. Pictures are the ultimate information form and clearly the most powerful. I see an exciting opportunity to help accelerate Kodak's execution of its digital strategy and position the company as a leader in the new markets created as imaging and information management technologies converge.

Images generate commerce, especially in the digital economy. Kodak's position as the largest producer of traditional photographic products and services will be the foundation of our efforts to become the leading provider of digital imaging products and services, supporting a host of new ways in which images will enrich commercial transactions.[4]

Despite Russo's enthusiasm over her opportunities " . . . to improve the performance of the business, looking for ways of accelerating top and bottom-line growth, and really leveraging the incredible access that Kodak has," [5] she was well aware of the magnitude of the challenge that awaited her.

Kodak's transition from the world's biggest photographic company with a dominant position in photographic film, photographic papers, and several other chemical-based photographic products into a leading supplier of digital imaging products had been far from smooth. Despite investing over $3 billion in digital technology and new digital imaging products since the late 1980s, Kodak had failed to establish either market or technological leadership within the sector, and continued to earn losses on this investment. Two days after Russo joined Kodak, the company announced its first quarter financial results. Compared with the first quarter of 2000, sales were down 4 percent and operating earning down 48 percent. Digital imaging revenues increased by 2 percent to $712 million, representing a little under a quarter of Kodak's total revenues. Losses from digital imaging increased from $1 million to $6 million.[6] In the consumer market, Kodak's sales of digital products and services decreased by 4 percent, adversely affected by strong competition and falling prices. Irrespective of Ms Russo's achievements in the field of digital communication, many outside observers believed that Kodak simply wasn't up to the challenge of digital imaging. After a century of dominating the market for traditional photography, it was unclear whether Kodak could successfully make the transition to the fast-moving world of electronics. Even if Kodak could master the new digital technologies, converting these technologies into market winning products, and converting market success into shareholder value remained massive challenges for the company.

■ BEGINNINGS ■

When George Eastman told a co-worker at the Rochester Savings Bank that he had made plans for a vacation to Santo Domingo, the co-worker suggested that Eastman take photographs to remember it by. Eastman heeded the advice and purchased a state-of-the-art 3-by-4-foot camera, along with all of the developing plates, glass tanks, developing tents, chemicals, jugs of distilled water, tripods, phosphoric flashes, and photographic emulsions he would need. Eastman never made it to Santo Domingo with his heavy load, but he did fall in love with photography and set about the challenge of creating amateur photography as a more convenient and affordable pastime.

Eastman began the commercial manufacture of a new type of dry photographic plate in 1880 and established the Eastman Dry Plate Company the following year. In 1884, Eastman developed silver halide paper-based photographic film, followed by the first fully portable camera in 1888. With these two products, and the processes to develop and print the new film, photography became a leisure activity for the masses. The company changed its name to the Eastman Kodak Company and was incorporated on October 24, 1901. Kodak's strategy was to provide a fully integrated photographic service supplying the camera and film through to processing and printing. Its first advertising slogan was "You push the button, we do the rest." George Eastman remained chairman until his death in 1932, during which period Eastman Kodak came to dominate the world market for photographic film, photographic paper and chemicals, and low-cost cameras.

Eastman established seven basic business principles for Kodak that he felt were vital to the company's future success. Kodak claims that these remain its guiding principles.

- Mass production at low cost
- International distribution
- Extensive advertising
- A focus on the customer
- Fostering growth and development through continuing research
- Treating employees in a fair, self-respecting way
- Reinvesting profits to build and extend the business

After Eastman's death, Kodak continued to build upon its dominant position in the world photographic market. Its approach was one of vertical integration combined with continuous innovation and product development – especially in color photography.

■ THE 1980s: STORM CLOUDS AND NEW HORIZONS ■

By the end of the 1970s, a series of new challenges and market reversals were eroding Kodak's dominance of the world photographic market. In cameras, Kodak's leadership in amateur cameras was undermined by the rise of the Japanese camera industry with its sophisticated, yet easy-to-use 35 mm cameras. In film too, Japanese competition was a growing problem as Fuji Photo Film Company stepped on to the world stage. Fuji's combination of cost leadership, high quality, and market aggressiveness forced Kodak to retaliate through price cuts and bigger advertising budgets, severely denting Kodak's margins. Fuji's sponsorship of the 1984 Los Angeles Olympic Games proclaimed its presence in Kodak's backyard. In instant photography, Kodak was held up by a protracted patent suit that was ultimately settled in 1986 when Kodak was forced into a humiliating withdrawal. Several of Kodak's other innovations were also unsuccessful, most notably the disk camera introduced in 1982.

In July 1983, amidst declining earnings and a falling share price, Colby Chandler took over as Chairman and CEO with Kay Whitmore as President. Under the guidance of these two executives, Kodak embarked upon a decade of diversification and technology-driven business development. Chandler and Whitmore's initiatives were concentrated in two main areas: imaging and life sciences.

Imaging and Data Storage Products

The 1980s and early 1990s were a period of rapid development in imaging technologies and new printing and reprographic products. Chastened by its having passed up the opportunity to acquire Chester Carlson's xerography patents (these were bought by Haliod Corp., which renamed itself Xerox Corp.), Kodak was determined not to be sidelined by new technological opportunities. Kay Whitmore took a leading role in broadening Kodak's imaging interests beyond its traditional area of chemical-based photographic imaging and into electrostatic imaging, electromagnetic imaging, and electronic imaging and thermal printing. Whitmore invested heavily in electronic data storage and data processing products and systems and engaged in acquisitions and joint ventures to access the necessary technologies. For example:

- Eikonix Corp. acquired in 1985 gave Kodak a leading position in commercial digital imaging systems that scanned, edited, and prepared images for printing.
- Kodak developed the world's first electronic image sensor with 1.4 million pixels (1986). This was followed by a number of new products for electronic publishing, scanning, and editing for the printing and publishing industry, including Imagelink for document imaging and Optistar for micrographic or digital capture of images (1989).
- Kodak became a leader in image storage and retrieval systems. Its KAR4000 Information System provided computer-assisted storage and retrieval of microfilm images (1983). The Ektaprint Electronic Publishing System and Kodak Image Management System offered integrated systems to edit, store, retrieve, and print text and graphics (1985).
- Kodak became involved in a range of data storage products including floppy disks (the acquisition of Verbatim Inc. in 1985 placed Kodak among the three leading manufacturers of floppy disks for PCs), a 14-inch optical disk capable of storing 6.8 billion bytes of information (1986), and magnetic recording heads for disk drives (through the 1985 acquisition of Garlic Corp.).
- Through a joint venture with Matsushita, Kodak began supplying alkaline batteries (in competition to Duracell) and videocassettes.

Kodak's electronic sales amounted to a little under 5 percent of total sales in 1984, and increased modestly throughout the 1980s. Most sales of imaging and image processing products were primarily to the commercial sector – especially to publishing and printing. However, by the end of the 1980s, Kodak was putting major efforts into the development of digital imaging products for the consumer market. As a result of its collaboration with Philips, Kodak announced its Photo CD system in 1990. The PhotoCD allowed digitized photographic images to be stored on a compact disk, which could then be viewed and manipulated on a personal computer. Launched in 1992, the PhotoCD was the basis for a number of digital products offered by Kodak.

Life Sciences

The second area of development built upon Kodak's capabilities in chemical technology. Eastman Chemicals had been established in the 1920s to supply photographic chemicals both to Kodak's film and processing division and to third-party customers. By the 1980s, Eastman was a major international supplier of photographic chemicals, fibers, plastics (especially for soft drink packaging), printing inks, and nutrition supplements.

Building upon its capabilities in chemicals and its existing healthcare activities (e.g., nutritional supplements and diagnostic equipment), Kodak established its Life Sciences Division in 1984. The new division forged joint ventures and alliances with a number of pharmaceutical and biotech companies to pursue research and new products in the areas of antiviral compounds, nucleic acid, and recombinant proteins. In 1986 Kodak established Eastman Pharmaceuticals and greatly expanded its pharmaceutical interests with the acquisition of Sterling Drug in 1988 and a series of joint ventures with Sanofi during 1991–2. In addition, Kodak expanded its range of medical imaging products, including its Insight Thoracic Imaging System and X-Omatic RA cassette for pediatric patients.

Organizational Changes and Performance Outcomes

Chandler and Whitmore also sought to change Kodak's internal organization. After 75 years of dominating the world photographic industry, Kodak was perceived as centralized, bureaucratic, slow-moving, and risk averse. Its system of lifetime employment engendered strong employee loyalty but insulated the company from external influences. Pressured by falling profits, Chandler and Whitmore cut costs and reshaped the organizational structure. Employment was cut from 136,500 in 1982 to 110,000 in 1992. To decentralize and increase profit orientation, divisions were subdivided into business units with clear bottom-line responsibilities. To promote entrepreneurship, an internal venturing fund that supported new business proposals was established. To accelerate new product development and improve product-launch quality, Kodak introduced a new product development methodology called the "Manufacturability Assurance Process" based upon a sequence of phases and gates.[7]

Despite the many initiatives of the late 1980s and early 1990s, the deluge of new business ventures added little to Kodak's revenue or profit growth. Two main criticisms of Whitmore's strategy were prevalent: lack of focus and inadequate attention to cost cutting. With regard to the former, the efforts to push Kodak into the future by pioneering computer-based, digital technologies had been dissipated among too many technologies, too many projects, and by the expansion into healthcare. Whitmore was undeterred: "We are not interested in doing more new things. We've got all the new things we need; it's making a success of each of those areas. Silver halide photography is successful. Our chemical company has a very solid base; it's successful. The thing we need to do is to make a success of the commercial applications of digital imaging and make a success of our health strategies."[8] Despite Whitmore's commitment to developing new imaging technologies, the effectiveness of Kodak's digital strategy had been undermined by a lack of integration between Kodak's different digital products and projects, and by spreading its resources too thinly.

With regard to costs, Whitmore's commitment to growth had meant lack of attention to overheads and productivity. Despite a series of restructurings, Kodak earned a dismal return of about 6 percent on capital that cost more than 14 percent while the burden of debt continued to grow. The Kodak board became increasingly skeptical of Whitmore's ability to deliver and in 1993 replaced him with George Fisher, then CEO of Motorola.[9]

■ THE GEORGE FISHER ERA, 1993–2000 ■

Attracting George Fisher was seen as a major coup for Kodak. His success at implementing total quality management at Motorola and building a leading position in hardware for wireless telephony had made him one of the most highly regarded CEOs in America. He was viewed as one of the leaders of America's resurgence in high technology and was on every headhunter's list. He had already turned down the opportunity to become IBM's CEO (IBM's Board subsequently turned to Lou Gerstener). Moreover, with a doctorate in applied mathematics and ten years of R&D experience at Bell Labs, he had a scientist's grasp of electronic technology. From taking up the reins at Eastman Kodak in November 1993 to stepping down as chairman on December 8, 2000, Fisher was the primary architect of Kodak's push into digital imaging.

Refocusing on Imaging

From the outset, Fisher's strategic vision for Kodak was as an imaging company: "We are not in the photographic film business or in the electronics business, we are in the picture business."[10] In order to focus Kodak's efforts and lower debt, Fisher immediately approved proposals to spin off Eastman Chemical Company. This was followed by a string of other divestments. In 1994 the divestment of all healthcare businesses (other than medical imaging) was announced, the most important being the Sterling Winthrop pharmaceutical company. Sterling had been acquired at a cost of $5.1 billion in 1988; it was sold to SmithKline Beecham for $2.9 billion. The funds generated were used mainly to pay off debt.

The intention of the divestments was to enable Kodak to focus all of its resources on its core imaging business. However, developing a coherent strategy for digital imaging business was not easy. After reviewing the company's financials, Fisher was shocked to learn that Kodak had poured several billion dollars into digital imaging research since the mid-1980s yet had little to show for it in terms of world-beating products.

Digital Imaging Strategy

Fisher's digital strategy was to create greater coherence among Kodak's multiple digital projects, in part through creating a single digital projects division headed by newly hired Carl Gustin (previously with Apple Computer and DEC). Having established greater coherence, Fisher's digital strategy emphasized three key themes.

AN INCREMENTAL APPROACH

"The future is not some harebrained scheme of the digital Information Highway or something. It is a step-by-step progression of enhancing photography using digital technology," declared Fisher.[11] This recognition that digital imaging was an evolutionary rather than a revolutionary change would be the key to Kodak's ability to build a strong position in digital technology. If photography was to switch rapidly from the traditional chemical-based technology to a wholly digital technology where customers took digital pictures, downloaded them on to their computers, edited them, and transmitted them through the internet to be viewed electronically, then undoubtedly Kodak would face an extremely difficult time. Apart from Kodak's positions in digital cameras and picture editing software, most of this digital chain was in the hands of computer hardware and software companies. However, fortunately for Kodak, the whole of the 1990s and the early part of the next decade featured only selective incursions of digital technology into traditional photographic imaging. During the 1990s, digital cameras achieved only limited market penetration; the vast majority of photographic images were still captured on traditional film. The critical advantages of digital imaging were in image manipulation and image transmission.

Hence, central to Kodak's strategy was a hybrid approach where Kodak introduced those aspects of digital imaging that could offer truly enhanced functionality for users. Thus, in the consumer market, Kodak recognized that image capture would continue to be dominated by traditional film for some time – digital cameras did not offer the same sharpness of resolution as conventional photography. However, digital imaging offered the potential for image manipulation and transmission that were quite beyond traditional photography.

This hybrid approach involved Kodak in providing facilities in retail outlets for digitizing and editing images from conventional photographs, then storing, transmitting and printing these digital images. Kodak's first walk-up, self-service systems were its Copy-Print Station and Digital Enhancement Station. In 1994, Kodak launched its Picture Maker which allowed digital prints to be made from either conventional photo prints or from a variety of digital inputs. Picture Maker allowed customers to edit their images (zoom, crop, eliminate red-eye, and add text), and print them in a variety of formats. By the end of 2000, some 30,000 retail locations worldwide offered Picture Maker facilities. The internet offered the potential for image storage and image transmission both from retail kiosks and from home PCs. In 1998, Kodak consolidated its position in this market by acquiring Picture Vision which supplied PhotoNet, a rival system of internet-based image storage and print ordering. A particular advantage of these retailer-based digital photography systems was that they allowed Kodak to exploit a key resource – its extensive distribution presence. Ultimately, digital imaging had the potential to bypass retailers and photofinishers completely; however, during the transition period, Kodak viewed its huge retail presence as a means of bringing digital imaging to the mass market.

Kodak also used digital technology to enhance the services offered by photofinishers. Thus, the Kodak I.Lab system offered a digital infrastructure to photofinishers that digitized every film negative and offered better pictures by fixing common problems in consumer photographs. Kodak's Picture Center was introduced to improve the process of customer drop-off and pick-up, allowing fast self-service ordering of processing and print ordering.

Central to Kodak's digital strategy has been using the World Wide Web to allow consumers to post their photographs and order prints online. Picture Vision's PhotoNet system replaced Kodak's own Picture Network (first introduced in 1997). This allowed consumers to drop off film at retail locations and view their digitized images on Kodak's PhotoNet website from which prints could be ordered. In addition, Kodak partnered with AOL to offer *You've Got Pictures* which allowed AOL members to send photographic images to one another.

Kodak's hybrid approach was also evident in introducing digital enhancement of connectional film. In February 1996, Kodak unveiled its Advantix brand of advanced photo system films. Advanced photo system was the result of agreement between Kodak and Fuji on technical standards for cameras and film that store both chemical film images and data that can be downloaded electronically. The system combined the resolution of conventional film with the versatility and communicability of digital imaging.

In addition, Kodak introduced a wide range of purely digital photographic products that extended from image capote to image printing. From 1995, these were launched under the Kodak Digital Science brand name, to help bring attention to Kodak's positioning and strengths in digital imaging technology.

- Image capture. Kodak developed digital cameras for both the top end and the bottom end of the market. In January 1994, Kodak launched a Professional Digital Camera (the camera alone costing $8,500) and the Apple Quicktake computer camera (manufactured by Kodak, marketed by Apple Computer), which, at $75, was the cheapest digital camera available at the time. In March 1995, Kodak introduced the first full-featured digital camera priced at under $1,000. During the subsequent six years, Kodak continued to bring out new, more sophisticated digital cameras, including professional cameras developed in conjunction with Canon. By 2000, Kodak offered a wide range of digital cameras. At the top end was its DC4800 camera with 3.1 megapixel resolution, at the other a PalmPix camera that allowed a Palm personal digital assistant to be used as a digital camera.
- Image scanning. During the late 1990s, Kodak introduced a range of high-resolution image scanners designed for photographic-quality digital imaging. By the end of 2001, Kodak's focus was almost entirely upon scanners for the business and professional market.
- Image storage and editing. After the failure of its initial launch of the Photo CD system, based upon a Photo CD player that could store digital images on

compact disks, in February 1995 Kodak introduced the next-generation Photo CD imaging workstation, which targeted commercial laboratories, photo processors, and PC users. The system consisted of a CD-player capable of reading high-resolution digital images, viewing them on a TV or computer monitor, and uploading images for editing and subsequent printing.

- During the 1990s, Kodak introduced a broad range of printers including thermal printers for the professional market, laser printers for the professional and medical markets, and inkjet printers (manufactured by Lexmark) for the consumer market.

- These products were supported by a range of software products. These included: DSL software that allowed the editing and printing of digital images in retail photofinishing labs, Access software that permitted the reading and display of PhotoCD disks, PhotoCD Player software that allowed photographic images to be merged with text, graphics and sound, and Kodak's Color Management System for color reproduction.

- Finally, digital imaging created a growing market for one of Kodak's traditional product areas: specialty papers for printing photographic images. During 2000, sales of Kodak's inkjet papers and media business increased by 30 percent. Kodak's new products for photographic printing included its Ultima range of picture paper.

DISTINCT STRATEGIES FOR CONSUMER AND PROFESSIONAL MARKETS

Kodak's approaches to consumer and professional markets were different. Kodak's incremental strategy – providing a pathway for customers from traditional to digital photography – was most evident in the consumer market. Here Kodak focused upon the mass market rather than leading-edge users and sought to exploit the strengths of the Kodak brand and Kodak's huge retail presence to provide consumers with the security and reliability they needed to voyage into the uncharted waters of digital photography.

Four years ago, when we talked about the possibilities of digital photography, people laughed. Today, the high-tech world is stampeding to get a piece of the action, calling digital imaging perhaps the greatest growth opportunity in the computer world. And it may be. We surely see it as the greatest future enabler for people to truly "Take Pictures. Further."

We start at retail, our distribution stronghold. Here consumers are at the peak moment of satisfaction, when they open their photofinishing envelopes. We believe the widespread photo-retailing infrastructure will continue to be the principal avenue by which people obtain their pictures. Our strategy is to build on and extend this existing market strength which is available to us, and at the same time be prepared to serve the rapidly growing, but relatively small, pure digital market that is developing. Kodak will network its rapidly expanding installed base of *Image Magic* stations and kiosks, essentially turning these into nodes on a massive, global network. The company will allow retailers to use these work stations to bring digital capability to the average snapshooter, extending the value of these images for the consumers and retailers alike, while creating a lucrative consumable business for Kodak.[12]

It was in the professional market where Kodak launched its major innovations in digital imaging. The sophisticated needs of the government in satellite imaging, planning military campaigns, weather forecasting, and surveillance activities favored digital technologies for transforming, transmitting and storing images; medical imaging (especially CT, MRI and ultrasound) required digital technologies for 3D imaging, diagnosis, and image storage; while publishers and printers needed digital imaging to complement the new generation of computerized publishing and printing systems for newspapers and magazines. For professional applications ranging from journalism, to highway safety, to real estate, digital imaging provided the linkage to the internet and sophisticated IT management systems.

The role of the professional segment as the lead market for Kodak's new digital products was reinforced by the huge price premium for professional products as compared with mass-market consumer products. The divide in the digital imaging industry between the professional and the consumer segments remained wide, despite the continuous trickle-down of advanced digital technologies and product features from the professional to the consumer market. Most manufacturers – including Kodak – maintained clearly differentiated product ranges for each segment, which was reflected in clear price differentials. During 1999, price multiples between professional and consumer models were as much as 150 times for cameras ($30,000 vs. $200), 100 times for scanners ($10,000 vs. $100), and 15 times for color laser printers ($30,000 vs. $2,000).

In addition to the sophisticated digital cameras that Kodak released first to the professional market, Kodak established a leading position in digital imaging systems for medical diagnosis and commercial printing. For example:

- In the medical field, Kodak's Ektascan Imagelink system, which included the capability of converting medical images to digital images which could then be transmitted via phone lines to local hospitals, was launched in 1995. Kodak established world leadership in medical laser imaging through its Ektascan laser printer, introduced in 1996. This leadership was extended with the acquisition of Imation's Dry View laser imaging business in 1998. By the end of the 1990s, Kodak had built a powerful position in digital health imaging based upon both laser imaging and digital radiography. In 2000, Kodak launched its Application Service Provider business to the medical community allowing images to be captured and managed via Kodak's digital systems to Intel Online Services' data center.
- In the US space program, Kodak cameras and imaging equipment accompanied a number of missions, including the Mars probe and the IKONOS Earth-orbiting satellite.
- Elsewhere in the public sector, Kodak's digital scanning and document management systems were used in national censuses in the US, UK, France, Australia, and Brazil. At a unit of the German post office, a Kodak team achieved a world record, creating digitized copies of 1.7 million documents in 24 hours.
- In commercial printing and publishing, Kodak held a strong position in high-quality, high-speed digital printing systems. Kodak's involvement in this market was increasingly through NexPress, a joint venture between Kodak

and Heidelberger which developed and supplied a range of printing and copying machines.

- In moving pictures, Kodak's traditional role as a supplier of cinematography was extended into the digital field through Kodak's services for digitizing conventional movie films, providing digital formats for cinema and TV film, and generating visual effects.

ALLIANCES

In its traditional photographic business, Kodak had been exceptionally vertically integrated. It had dominated the photographic value chain from basic research through to the processing of customers' photographic film. In digital imaging such dominance was impossible. Unlike silver halide imaging where Kodak had pioneered the development of the film, the cameras, and the chemicals and paper for film processing, the digital imaging field was already populated by some dominant companies. In computers there were Dell, Compaq, Toshiba, and many others; in operating systems and browsers Microsoft dominated; in image formatting software Adobe Systems was the key player; in printers Canon and HP led the field. If Kodak was to provide an integrated solution for its customers, it would need to partner with companies that were already well established in key digital technologies and in key markets for component software and hardware. Under Fisher's leadership, Kodak forged a series of joint ventures and strategic alliances. The partnerships with Canon, Lexmark, AOL, and Heidelberger have already been mentioned; in addition, Kodak established the following alliances:

- Kodak's Picture CD was developed with and co-marketed with Intel Corporation. Kodak's longstanding alliance with Intel also extended to the development of an ASP system for archiving and downloading medical images on a pay-per-use basis.
- Hewlett-Packard played a key role as a source of inkjet technology for Kodak. Phogenix Imaging, a joint venture between Kodak and HP, was established to develop high-quality inkjet solutions for micro and mini photofinishing labs. The systems utilize Kodak's DLS software.[13] In addition, HP had collaborated with Kodak (as well as Microsoft and Live Picture Inc.) in developing the FlashPix image storage system for digital cameras.
- Kodak's collaboration with Microsoft also included cooperation to establish standards for Windows-based Picture Transfer Protocols and cooperation in the development of PhotoCDs.
- A cross-licensing agreement with Olympus to share digital camera technology and to join forces in developing a common approach to web-based storage and printing of photographs. The press release accompanying the announcement noted that Kodak had over a thousand patents related to digital cameras and digital photographic systems, while Olympus also possessed over a thousand patents with particular strengths in high-resolution digital cameras. A similar cross-licensing deal was agreed with Sanyo.

- Several of Kodak's alliances were primarily oriented towards opening Kodak's worldwide distribution system to partner companies. For example, in 2001, Kodak agreed to distribute Better Light Inc.'s top-of-the-line digital cameras (offering up to $12,000 \times 16,000$ resolution) as part of its professional range.

A key element of George Fisher's legacy was the recognition that, in every segment of the digital imaging market – consumer, professional, entertainment, and commercial, Kodak could only achieve a prominent market position if it forged partnerships with those companies that already possessed leadership at particular stages of the digital imaging value chain, whether it was Intel in semiconductors, AOL in consumer internet services, HP in inkjet printers, or Heidelberger in commercial printing systems. Willy Shih, head of Kodak's digital imaging division, observed: "We have to pick where we add value and commoditize where we can't."[14] The difficult decision was identifying the activities and product areas where it could add value, and those that were best left to other companies.

■ THE SITUATION IN APRIL 2001 ■

Much of Pat Russo's first week at Kodak was spent reviewing Kodak's digital strategy in relation to its current situation and future market prospects. Her review focused upon two main areas: the market for digital imaging and Kodak's potential for competitive advantage within it.

THE MARKET

By the time Russo arrived at Kodak, a much clearer consensus had developed around what digital imaging was and what the size of the market was. Increasingly the term *infoimaging* was used to describe the imaging products and services that used electronic technologies to capture, store, transform, edit and display picture images. Broadly defined, the infoimaging market comprised hardware ("devices"), software ("services and media"), and infrastructure. The total infoimaging market was estimated to be in the region of $44 billion (see table 6.1).

For over a decade, a key uncertainty facing Kodak concerned the rate of penetration of digital imaging, and with it the rate of decline of sales of traditional photographic products – film in particular. The transition to digital was slowed by the fact that digital imaging was not unambiguously superior to conventional film-based photography. In particular, with the exception of the most sophisticated (and expensive) professional cameras, digital cameras did not offer such fine resolution as conventional film. And, while digital images could be electronically stored and transmitted, these sizes of image files meant that storage was highly memory intensive and transmission was slow. Hence, market acceptance of digital imaging was dependent upon the development of high-capacity memory devices and software for compressing image files. The overall result was a gradual shift to digital imaging and, in the consumer market, a slow transition from early adopters to mass market. With greater ease of use and more integrated

Table 6.1   The worldwide infoimaging market in 2001

Category	Product	$ billion
Devices ($44.5 billion)	General-use digital cameras	3.5
	"Toy" digital cameras	0.2
	Mass-market flatbed scanners	3.4
	Inkjet printers	11.7
	Flatpanel displays	25.7
Services & Media ($136.5 billion)	All consumer & professional photography	54.6
	Inkjet cartridges & inks	25.7
	Document imaging	22.9
	Health imaging	28.0
	Inkjet papers and media	5.3
Infrastructure ($44.2 billion)	Photofinishing systems & networks	38.1
	Photoprocessing equipment	3.0
	Entertainment imaging	2.2
	Consumer kiosks	0.9

Source: Eastman-Kodak.

solutions, Kodak believed that market penetration would accelerate. Yet, despite a sharp increase in the sales of digital imaging products during 1999 and 2000 (Kodak's sales of digital cameras increased by about 90 percent during 2000), by the end of 2000, the consumer photographic market remained dominated by conventional imaging. For example, digital cameras in use represented only 20 million out of a total of about 830 million (including single-use) cameras. In 2001, most industry observers expected the rate of growth of digital cameras to decline, with an annual growth of unit sales of around 50 percent. In the US, sales of 4.2 million digital cameras in 2000 were expected to increase to 6.5 million in 2001.[15]

While unit sales of digital products and digital services showed strong volume growth, revenues told a different story. During 2000, Kodak's revenues from digital products and services increased by a mere 5 percent, most of the growth coming from consumer digital (where sales revenues rose by 16 percent). The failure to convert strong unit sales growth into revenue growth was a consequence of falling prices. In common with electronic products generally, digital imaging products were subject to steeply declining prices and unit costs. During 2000, prices of digital cameras fell by an average of 18 percent. During the first quarter of 2001, price cuts continued, with many manufacturers reducing prices by between 10 and 15 percent.

Steep price declines were an indication of the intensity of competition in the digital imaging business. While Kodak had long enjoyed market dominance in conventional photography (until the emergence of Fuji as a global competitor), in digital it was forced to compete against a diversity of rivals:

- *Digital cameras.* Casio had been the early leader, with over half the world market during the early 1990s. By 1998, 45 companies had entered the market, with Sony emerging as market leader, and HP, Olympus, Kodak, and Fuji some way behind (see table 6.2).

Table 6.2 Brand shares of the US market for digital still cameras (by units)

Brand	2000 (%)	Jan. 2001 (%)
Sony	26	41
Olympus	18	11
Kodak	17	12
Hewlett-Packard	9	17
Fujifilm	8	5
Polaroid	6	4
Canon	3	4

Source: "Eastman Kodak in 2001," a Georgetown University class paper prepared for Professor Rob Grant by Zhenyu Shen, Xiaotong Jia, Eddy Rasoanaivo, and Joo-Hyung Lee, 2001, using data from IDC and other sources.

- *Printers*. Kodak positioned itself at the high end, producing commercial and professional printing equipment and high-quality inkjet printers for the consumer market. In medical imaging, Kodak was the leading supplier of laser printers. For its consumer range, Kodak increasingly relied upon Lexmark to source inkjet printers. A reassuring feature of digital imaging for Kodak was the continued preference of both professional and amateur users for printed images. The problem for Kodak was that, as standard inkjet printers increased their quality and sharpness of resolution, so the market for dedicated photographic printers became squeezed. Throughout 2000 and early 2001, the prices of both inkjet and laser printers continued to fall, reflecting the intense competition in this field.
- *Scanners*. As with printers, in photograph image scanners, Kodak focused upon the high-price, high-quality segments. It supplied high-resolution, sophisticated scanners for professional and commercial use and scanning modules for retail photo kiosks. In 1999, Kodak's Digital Science 3500 commercial scanner was named product of the year by *Imaging and Document Solutions*. Kodak had also entered into the consumer market. However, the consumer market, especially the lower end, was fiercely competitive and as mass-market consumer machines increased their resolution, so Kodak's position at the upper end was increasingly squeezed.
- *Software*. Software for digital imaging comprised editing software for manipulating images, color control software, file format and storage software, and software for transferring image files between computers through the internet. Editing software ranged from programs to fulfill basic image manipulation, such as Microsoft's Picture It, to more comprehensive editing software where Adobe's Photoshop dominated the market. In software to keep the color consistent from the point of capture, through manipulation, up until the point of display, Kodak's color management software held a strong market position. The other area where Kodak holds a significant position is in its DLS System

Management and Enhanced Services Software for managing retail processing and printing operations. This software allows for manipulation of images (e.g., red-eye elimination) for both film and digital images, printing across a variety of formats and media, order processing, and work flow management.

- *Online photographic services.* Kodak strengthened its position with the acquisition of Picture Vision's PhotoNet business; however, in providing services to upload digital images, post photographs on the web, and order prints, Kodak's PhotoNet lagged behind Zing and competed strongly with PhotoPoint, ClubPhoto, Hewlett-Packard's Cartogra, Fuji.net, and many others.

Kodak's Resources and Capabilities

The fundamental issue for Kodak's digital imaging business was that its competitive position was totally different from that in traditional photography. In silver-halide photography Kodak had been the pioneer, and in pioneering roll film and the cameras, chemicals, and photographic papers that used that roll film, Kodak had gone on to dominate the photographic industry. In digital imaging, Kodak was but one of many companies that had entered digital imaging as a result of the convergence of imaging and electronics. Kodak, like Fuji, had entered digital imaging to protect itself against the threat that digital technologies offered to photographic film (already in Japan film sales had stagnated by 2000, and Europe and North America were believed to be about two years behind). Olympus and Minolta had entered from their positions in cameras. Canon, Ricoh, and Hewlett-Packard came to digital imaging armed primarily with their expertise in microelectronics and printing. Sony entered digital imaging as an extension of its consumer electronics business. All these companies possessed different sets of resources and capabilities with strengths and weaknesses in different areas. Russo recognized that for Kodak to establish leadership in the new world of digital imaging it would need to marshal its considerable base of resources and organizational capabilities, while building the additional capabilities needed to succeed in this technologically fast-moving field.

BRAND AND DISTRIBUTION

Foremost among Kodak's resource strengths were its brand equity and distribution channel presence. After almost a century of global leadership in the photographic industry, Kodak possessed brand recognition and worldwide distribution reach that was unrivalled in the photographic industry. Russo saw Kodak's ability to bring new products to consumers' attention and to support these products with one of the world's best known and most widely respected brand names as a huge advantage in a market where technological change created uncertainty for consumers. Kodak's brand reputation was supported by its massive, worldwide distribution presence – primarily through retail photography stores, film processors, and professional photographers. This retail presence was critical to Kodak's entire digital strategy which was built around providing consumers with a pathway to digital imaging using services offered through retail stores and photofinishers.

To what extent would Kodak's strengths in distribution and brand equity be a source of competitive advantage in digital imaging? Once consumers possessed the computing power, the printing capacity, and the internet linkage to enable them to download digital images directly from their cameras to their PCs and edit, communicate, and print these images, then traditional distributional channels for photographic products and services would be irrelevant to their needs. Nor was it clear that the Kodak brand would carry the same weight in digital as in traditional photography – especially when it was competing against brands such as Canon, Hewlett-Packard, and Sony. In relation to professional, commercial, medical, and government markets, Russo believed that Kodak's market presence might be more secure. The long-established relationship between Kodak and its corporate and institutional customers and the range of support services that Kodak was able to supply provided a greater barrier to consumer electronics companies and high-tech upstarts.

TECHNOLOGY

In technology too, Kodak came to digital imaging with some well-established strengths. Its huge R&D investments in digital imaging since the early 1980s had created proprietary technologies across a broad front. Despite R&D cutbacks during the late 1990s, Kodak maintained one of the world's biggest research efforts in imaging. At its research labs in the US, UK, France, Japan, China and Australia, Kodak employed more than 5,000 engineers and scientists, including more than 600 PhDs.

Moreover, its century of innovation and development of photographic images gave Kodak tremendous depth of understanding of recording and processing images that was not negated by the transition from chemical to digital imaging. C. K. Prahalad, the guru of competence-based strategy, who played a key role in shaping Kodak's digital strategy during the early 1990s, viewed Kodak's imaging capabilities as transcending specific imaging technologies. Fundamental to Kodak's ability to make the transition from chemical to digital imaging was its color management capability. In the transfer of digital images to paper, Kodak possessed a powerful technology base, especially in color management and thermal printing. As *Business Week* observed when Fisher joined Kodak: "The basic know-how of combining electronic image capture and color management has been Kodak's for years. Kodak is a world-beater in electronic sensors, devices that see and capture an image, and has a raft of patents in color thermal printing. It also has the best understanding of color management software, which matches the colors you see on the screen with what's on the printed page."[16] By the late 1990s, Kodak was a world leader in color science, which studied the production, control, measurement, specification, and visual perception of color. In particular, Kodak pioneered the field of *colorimetry* which it used to measure and quantify the initial visual response to a stimulus of light.

At the image capture stage, Kodak developed a leading position in sensors. In CCD image sensors for digital cameras, Kodak held a market share of 25 percent in 2000. Kodak also pioneered CMOS sensors and possessed deep knowledge of megapixel camera architectures. Kodak's image sensing technology provided the heart of its digital image scanners. Using a combined color and monochrome sensor, the i800

Series scanners launched in early 2001 were the first to produce simultaneous capture of bitonal and color information, allowing a document that included both text and photos to produce images that were bitonal, color, or both in a single pass.

In the field of image processing, Kodak deployed complex statistical methods and artificial intelligence to develop algorithms for processing digital images. These were used for automatic color balancing, object and text recognition, and image enhancement and manipulation across a wide range of digital imaging applications, including systems for digital photofinishing where electronically scanned film images or direct-capture digital images could automatically adjust for scene reflectance and lighting conditions, noise, and sharpness – while operating at thousands of frames per hour. Kodak's image processing technology also included algorithms for image compression. In commercial imaging satellites, such proprietary algorithms were used to transmit richly detailed image files back to earth more efficiently than would be possible with non-compressed files.

In image storage, Kodak had a long history of pioneering research and product development, including floppy disks for PCs (1984), 14-inch optical disks (1986), and compact disks (Photo CD was first announced in 1990). Kodak was a leading member of the consortium of firms (which also included Microsoft, Intel, Adobe, Canon, Fuji, HP, and IBM) that developed and promoted FlashPix for digital camera image storage.

In document and image management, Kodak had led the way in developing systems that store, retrieve, edit, and print text and graphics for organizations such as government departments, banks, and insurance companies that handle thousands of documents a day. The capabilities that Kodak developed in designing these complex, large-scale document and image management systems for its commercial and institutional customers have also been relevant to the creation of digital imaging systems for the consumer market. In creating digital imaging systems for retailers and photofinishers, Kodak has been involved in integrating various types of hardware and software in systems that must combine quality, versatility, and reliability. A key feature of such systems is that they require Kodak to partner and cooperate with other hardware and software companies whose products either form part of the Kodak system or with which the Kodak system must be compatible. As Kodak has increasingly used the internet as an infrastructure for linking itself with customers and photofinishers, so Kodak's capabilities in creating and integrating complex systems for editing, processing, storing, and communicating images are extended to a new dimension.

At the root of Kodak's capabilities in designing and managing digital imaging systems was its predictive system modeling that allowed it to measure the characteristics of imaging systems and predict the performance of entire systems of digital and hybrid imaging that included optics, image sensors, scanners, image processing operations, printers, display media, and human visual responses. Such modeling allowed developers to evaluate quickly competing design proposals and select product features delivering the highest value to the customer. Some of Kodak's traditional capabilities were also relevant to the new world of digital imaging. Even if digital imaging displaced most conventional photography, Kodak believed that consumers would still want to have printed copies of their photographic images. In print media, particularly specialty papers, Kodak was world leader. During 2001, sales of Kodak's inkjet papers were expected to grow at about 40 percent.

NEW PRODUCT DEVELOPMENT

Despite Kodak's strengths in basic and applied research and its long history of successful new product development, Russo was acutely aware of the criticisms that had been leveled at Kodak for its weaknesses in bringing new products to market. Most of Kodak's most significant innovations in digital photography had been high-priced products for the professional market. In the consumer market, Kodak was viewed as being handicapped by marketers who had little understanding of the digital world.

Kodak's product development process still reflected the company's origins in chemistry. Product development traditionally began with basic research where innovations were exploited through a long and meticulous product development process before being rolled out on to the world market. One of George Fisher's major initiatives as Kodak chairman and CEO had been to streamline and speed Kodak's cumbersome product development process. In place of Kodak's sequential "phases and gates" development process, Fisher transferred approaches that had worked well at Motorola – greater decentralization of new product development and the use of cross-functional development teams to accelerate cycle times.

Despite these changes, adapting to the new product development methods that characterized the microelectronics sector remained a challenge for Kodak. The Silicon Valley model was based not simply upon speed, but also collaboration with other companies from the outset of the product development process. Kodak had no problem in establishing collaborative agreements with other companies – its size, brand name, and technological strength were sufficient to make it a highly attractive partner for small, technology-intensive firms in digital imaging. The real challenge was for Kodak to overcome a long history of insularity and hierarchical control in order to make its newfound alliances fruitful. A key issue for Kodak was whether its history and location three thousand miles from California's Silicon Valley could permit it to develop the organizational capabilities needed to thrive in a hyper-competitive environment. Russo was reminded of the current woes of Xerox Corporation. Despite Xerox's remarkable success in IT research, its long history of market dominance, bureaucratic culture, and east-coast location had combined to preventing its successful adjustment to the fast-moving world of digital document processing.

FINANCES

One of Kodak's key advantages in withstanding the uncertainties and rapid technological changes of the market for digital imaging was its size and financial security. In contrast to the many start-up companies that sought to establish themselves in the sector, Kodak was independent of venture capitalists and the vagaries of the IPO market. In addition, Kodak could rely upon the cash flow from its traditional photographic products to finance its investments in digital imaging.

Throughout the 1990s, Kodak used its cash flow from conventional imaging to finance its R&D, capital investment, and operating losses in digital. The problem was that the cash flows from its traditional business were being continually squeezed by competition – most notably by Fuji Film which continued to gain market share at Kodak's expense and squeeze margins by aggressive price cutting. The crunch came in 1997. After an average return on equity of 27.6 percent during 1995 and 1996, net income (after restructuring costs and losses on digital imaging of about $400 million) collapsed to almost nothing in 1997. In November 1997, chairman George Fisher announced a turnaround strategy that involved aggressive cost reduction and greater selectivity in digital imaging investments. The resulting cost reductions and parsimony in capital investments did much to restore Kodak's bottom line: in 1999 and 2000 return on equity averaged 40 percent. Despite this recovery, Kodak's top management team remained acutely aware of the risks of disappointing Wall Street – a fear that was reinforced by the dismal performance of Kodak's stock. During 2000, Kodak's return to shareholders was a negative 39 percent; during the first four months of 2001 the share price was largely stagnant, hovering around the low 40 s.

Evidence of Kodak's increasing bottom-line sensitivity was its willingness to divest parts of its digital imaging business and withdraw from particular markets if it felt that the potential returns could not justify the investments being made. In 1998, Kodak sold Fox Photo and its investment in Gretag Imaging (a manufacturer of film processing equipment). In 1999, Kodak folded its digital printer and copier-duplicator business into a joint venture with Heidelberger, sold The Image Bank (which marketed and licensed image reproduction rights), and sold its Motion Analysis Systems Division (which manufactured digital cameras and digital video cameras for the automotive and industrial markets).

Tables 6.3 and 6.4 summarize Kodak's recent financial results.

■ LOOKING FORWARD ■

As Patricia Russo prepared to leave the office after her first week in her new position, she was struck by the sheer magnitude of the challenge that Kodak faced not just in building a strong market position in digital imaging, but also in turning that market position into solid profit returns. Despite all the focusing efforts of George Fisher during his six years of leadership, Kodak continued to compete across a remarkably broad front. In digital imaging, Kodak was supplying products that extended from digital cameras to capture images, right through to printing papers for the printing of these images. Despite Kodak's network of partnerships that permitted it to access other companies' technical capabilities and products, Kodak continued to develop digital capabilities across a wide range. In basic research, its efforts embraced sensors, image processing algorithms, color management systems, image system modeling and simulation, and many other areas.

Given the extent of competition in virtually every area of digital imaging and the technological resources of companies such as Hewlett-Packard, Canon, Fuji, and Sony, Russo wondered whether Kodak had the technological, financial and managerial capacity to support its ambitious digital strategy.

But, if Kodak was to focus its digital strategy, what would that focus look like? Kodak's strengths in different parts of its value chain tended to pull its digital strategy in different directions. At the research end, Kodak had built strengths in a number of

Table 6.3 Eastman Kodak: Selected financial data, 1996–2001 ($ million)

	2001	2000	1999	1998	1997	1996
From income statement						
Sales	13,234	13,994	14,089	13,406	14,713	16,244
Costs:						
Cost of goods sold	8,670	8,019	7,987	7,293	7,979	8,326
Selling, general, and admin.	2,627	2,977	3,295	3,303	3,912	4,410
R&D costs	779	784	817	922	1,044	1,028
Operating earnings	345	2,214	1,990	1,888	1,778	2,480
Interest expense	219	178	142	110	98	83
Other income (charges)	(18)	96	261	328	(1,441)	(564)
Restructuring and other costs (credits)	659	(44)	350	—	1,441	841
Provision for income taxes	32	725	717	716	48	545
Net earnings	76	1,407	1,392	1,390	5	1,288
From balance sheet						
Total current assets	4,683	5,491	5,373	—	5,475	6,965
Including:						
Cash and cash equivalents	448	246	20	—	728	1,777
Receivables	2,337	2,653	2,537	—	2,271	2,738
Inventories	1,137	1,718	1,519	—	1,252	1,575
Property, plant, and equipment (net)	5,659	5,919	6,189	—	5,509	5,422
Other noncurrent assets (excluding goodwill)	2,072	1,767	1,801	—	1,231	1,238
Total assets	13,362	14,212	14,370	—	13,145	14,438
Total current liabilities	5,354	3,275	3,832	—	5,177	5,417
Including:						
Payables	3,276	3,403	1,163	—	3,832	4,116
Short-term borrowings	1,378	2,058	612	—	611	541
Other liabilities:						
Long-term borrowings	1,666	1,166	936	—	585	559
Post employment liabilities	2,728	2,610	2,776	—	3,075	2,967
Other long-term liabilities	720	671	859	—	1,019	557
Total liabilities	10,468	10,784	10,458	—	9,984	9,704
Shareholders' equity	2,894	3,428	3,912	—	3,161	4,734
Total liabilities and shareholders' equity	13,362	14,212	14,370	—	13,145	14,438
From cash flow statement						
Cash flows from operating activities:						
Earnings from continuing operations	76	1,407	1,392	1,390	5	1,011
Adjustments for non-cash items	1,989	(425)	541	93	2,075	1,473
Net cash provided by operating activities	2,065	982	1,933	1,483	2,080	2,484
Cash flows from investing activities:						
Additions to properties	(743)	(945)	(1,127)	(1,108)	(1,485)	(1,341)
Proceeds from sale of properties	—	276	468	297	109	124
Cash flows related to sales of businesses	—	1	(46)	(59)	(194)	681
Acquisitions, net of cash acquired	(306)	(130)	(3)	(949)	(341)	(128)
Net cash used in investing activities	(1,074)	(783)	(685)	(1,839)	(1,896)	(636)
Net cash flows from financing activities	(804)	(314)	(1,327)	77	(1,198)	(1,833)

Source: Eastman Kodak *Annual Reports 2000 and 1997*.

Table 6.4 Eastman Kodak: Results by Business Segments, 1998–2001

(A) Segment results for 1999–2001 (from Annual Report 2001) (in $, millions)

	2001	2000	1999
Net sales:			
Photography	9,403	10,231	10,265
Health Imaging	2,262	2,220	2,159
Commercial Imaging	1,459	1,417	1,479
All Other	110	126	186
Consolidated total	13,234	13,994	14,089
Earnings from operations:			
Photography	787	1,430	1,709
Health Imaging	323	518	483
Commercial Imaging	165	233	257
All Other	(60)	(11)	(109)
Total of segments	1,215	2,170	2,340
Net earnings:			
Photography	535	1,034	1,261
Health Imaging	221	356	324
Commercial Imaging	80	90	178
All Other	(38)	(2)	(61)
Total of segments	798	1,478	1,702
Operating net assets:			
Photography	6,288	7,100	6,875
Health Imaging	1,426	1,491	1,229
Commercial Imaging	1,085	1,045	963
All Other	(219)	(92)	(123)
Total of segments	8,580	9,544	8,944

(B) Segment results for 1998–2000 (from Annual Report 2000) ($ millions)

	2000	1999	1998
Net sales			
Consumer Imaging	7,406	7,411	7,164
Kodak Professional	1,706	1,910	1,840
Health Imaging	2,185	2,120	1,526
Other Imaging	2,697	2,648	2,876
Consolidated total	13,994	14,089	13,406
Earnings from operations			
Consumer Imaging	1,179	1,299	1,080
Kodak Professional	261	374	330
Health Imaging	503	470	321
Other Imaging	227	197	157
Total of segments	2,170	2,340	1,888
Consolidated total	2,214	1,990	1,888
Net earnings			
Consumer Imaging	860	900	785
Kodak Professional	111	265	237
Health Imaging	346	315	205
Other Imaging	161	222	162
Total of segments	1,478	1,702	1,389
Consolidated total	1,407	1,392	1,390

key technologies. However, to turn these technological strengths into top-line revenues, Kodak would need to embody these technologies into world-beating products and collaborate with others to establish technical standards that were compatible with, if not based upon, Kodak's technologies. At the opposite end of the value chain, Kodak's key strengths were its well-known and trusted brand and its powerful, extensive distribution network. If Kodak were to view its key strengths as located in these downstream activities, then Kodak's strategy should be to focus upon providing customer solutions in the form of integrated systems embodying both hardware and software. Whether the technologies or the individual products came from Kodak or from other companies was a secondary issue. Under this latter approach, the key task for Kodak was to use its brand and its systems integration capability to provide customers with a total solution to their imaging needs, whether chemical or digital.

Whichever end Kodak's digital imaging strategy started from – its technological strengths or the creating of customer solutions under the umbrella of the Kodak brand – it was clear to Russo that Kodak must draw upon the resources and capabilities of other companies. To this end, Kodak would need to continue establishing collaborative relationships with companies that were leaders in microelectronics, consumer electronics, and computer software, as well as acquiring smaller companies whose innovative technologies and products could be leveraged by Kodak's brand and global reach. Yet, given Kodak's heritage vertical integration and internal focus, establishing close and fruitful collaboration with other companies required managerial capabilities that were still relatively new within Kodak.

The role of networks of alliances and collaborative relationships was one factor that distinguished the new world of electronic imaging from Kodak's traditional photographic industry. Another was the sheer pace of change. Traditionally, Kodak had been a technological leader, and, because it had dominated the market for photographic products so effectively, it had been able to choose the pace at which it developed new technologies and the time when they would be embodied in new products. Moreover, the pattern of new product development had been a systematic one that began in the lab and worked through engineering and marketing into new products. The field of microelectronics was altogether a faster-moving field, where no company could expect or hope to dominate any substantial area of technology. The implications for the speed of new product development, for cross-functional integration, and for initiatives unbounded by organizational structure or formalized procedures were far-reaching.

The transition from a world of chemical imaging where technology developed gradually along clearly defined trajectories and where Kodak could control the pace of technological and market development to the chaotic, competitive, fast-moving world of digital imaging meant changing values, norms, behaviors, and attitudes within Kodak. If cultural change was the key, then shaking up the Kodak culture required leadership from the top. The 1997 refocusing and cost-cutting initiatives were accompanied by major changes among the top management team. A key feature of these changes was bringing in managers whose thinking was not dominated by the Rochester culture. Although Dan Carp (appointed as COO in January 1997), Robert Keegan (new head of the Consumer division), and Patrick Siewart (new head of the Professional division) were Kodak insiders, all had spent the major part of their careers outside of Rochester. Other top managers were brought from outside the company: Daniel Palumbo, head of

Marketing, came from Procter & Gamble; Willy Shih, head of the Digital Imaging division, had previously worked at Silicon Graphics, DEC, and IBM. As Figure 6.1 shows, Pat Russo was distinguished only by the fact that she was the latest and most senior of a major influx of new managerial talent into Kodak.

As she looked once more at the salutary first quarter results for 2001, Pat Russo recognized that the next 12 months would be critical for Kodak. The evidence from the past was not encouraging. When market leaders were challenged with a radically new technology – whether it was Digital Equipment with the microcomputer revolution, RCA with microelectronics, Bethlehem Steel with minimills, Sears Roebuck with discount stores and "category killers," or Xerox with new printing technologies – the result was a failure either to recognize the disruptive potential of the new technologies or to respond effectively to them. In Kodak's case, top management had long recognized that the future of the picture business was digital imaging. The key question was whether it could develop the capabilities needed for success and to deploy these capabilities through an effective, far-sighted strategy.

NOTES

1. Eastman Kodak Press Release, "Kodak names Patricia F. Russo as President, Chief Operating Officer; will intensify focus on growth in traditional and emerging businesses" (Rochester, NY, April 11, 2001).
2. Eastman Kodak Press Release, op. cit., April 11, 2001.
3. Eastman Kodak Press Release, op. cit., April 11, 2001.
4. Eastman Kodak Press Release, op. cit., April 11, 2001.
5. Andrew Hill, "Digital key to Kodak," www.ft.com (April 11, 2001).
6. These data on digital imaging revenues and earnings are based upon Kodak's 2000 definition of its digital imaging business which excludes some commercial and governmental digital sales.
7. S. C. Wheelwright and K. B. Clark, *Revolutionizing Product Development: Quantum Leaps in Speed, Efficiency and Quality*, New York: The Free Press (1992), pp. 151–5.
8. Paul Ericson, "Struggling with success," *Rochester Business Journal*, July 2, 1990.
9. Linda Grant, "Can Fisher focus Kodak?" *Fortune Magazine*, January 13, 1997.
10. Address to the Academy of Management, Boston, August 1997.
11. "Kodak's New Focus," *Business Week*, January 30, 1995, pp. 62–8.
12. Eastman Kodak Company, "Kodak leaders outline road ahead to get Kodak 'back on track'", Kodak Press Release, November 11, 1997.
13. Eastman Kodak Company, "Kodak and HP joint venture to be named Phogenix Imaging" (Press Release, August 1, 2000).
14. "Why Kodak still isn't fixed," *Fortune*, May 11, 1998.
15. Salomon Smith Barnety, Eastman Kodak, March 5, 2001.
16. "Kodak's New Focus," *Business Week*, January 30, 1995, pp. 62–8.

Organizational Restructuring within the Royal Dutch/Shell Group

Robert M. Grant

At the beginning of 2000, the Royal Dutch/Shell Group of Companies (Shell) was emerging from one of the most ambitious and far-reaching organizational restructurings of its 93-year history. The restructuring had involved the shift from a geographically-based to a primarily business sector-based structure, the elimination of over 1,000 corporate positions, the sale of much of its London headquarters, and the redesign of its systems of coordination and control. The restructuring had been precipitated by the realization that Shell would need to change the way it did business if it was to retain its position as the world's largest energy and chemicals company and offer an adequate return to shareholders in an increasingly turbulent industry environment.

By the end of 1999, it was clear that the changes were bearing fruit. Head office costs had been reduced and the increased coordination and control that the new sector-based organization permitted were helping Shell to control costs, focus capital expenditure, and prune the business portfolio. Return on capital employed (ROCE) and return on equity (ROE) for 1999 were their highest for ten years. However, much of the improvement in bottom-line performance was the result of the recovery in oil prices during the year. Once the benefits of higher oil prices were stripped out, Shell's improvements in financial performance looked much more modest.

At the same time, Shell's competitors were not standing still. BP, once government-owned and highly bureaucratized, had become one of the world's most dynamic, profitable, and widely admired oil majors. Its merger with Amoco quickly followed by its acquisition of Atlantic Richfield had created an international giant of almost identical size to Shell. In the meantime, Shell's longtime archrival, Exxon, was merging with

Mobil. Shell was no longer the world's biggest energy company – its sales revenues lagged some way behind those of Exxon Mobil. Other oil and gas majors were also getting caught up in the wave of mergers and restructurings. In particular, Shell's once-sluggish European rivals were undergoing extensive revitalization. The merger of Total, Fina, and Elf Aquitaine in September 1999 had created the world's fourth "super-major" (after Exxon Mobil, Shell, and BP Amoco). Also asserting itself on the world stage was Italy's privatized and revitalized ENI S.p.A.

The reorganization that had begun in 1994 under chairman of the Committee of Managing Directors, Cor Herkstroter, and continued under his successor, Mark Moody-Stuart, had transformed the organizational structure of Shell. From a decentralized confederation of over 200 operating companies spread throughout the world, a divisionalized group with clear lines of authority and more effective executive leadership had been created. Yet, Shell remained a highly complex organization that was a prisoner of its own illustrious history and where corporate authority remained divided between The Hague, London, and Houston. Had enough been done to turn a sprawling multinational empire into an enterprise capable of deploying its huge resources with the speed and decisiveness necessary to cope with an ever more volatile international environment?

■ HISTORY OF THE ROYAL DUTCH/SHELL GROUP ■

The Royal Dutch/Shell Group is unique among the world's oil majors. It was formed from the 1907 merger of the assets and operations of the Netherlands-based Royal Dutch Petroleum Company and the British-based Shell Transport and Trading Company. It is the world's biggest and oldest joint venture. Both parent companies trace their origins to the Far East in the 1890s.

Marcus Samuel inherited a half share in his father's seashell trading business. His business visits to the Far East made him aware of the potential for supplying kerosene from the newly developing Russian oilfields around Baku to the large markets in China and the Far East for oil suitable for lighting and cooking. Seeing the opportunity for exporting kerosene from the Black Sea coast through the recently opened Suez Canal to the Far East, Samuel invested in a new tanker, the *Murex*. In 1892, the *Murex* delivered 4,000 tons of Russian kerosene to Bangkok and Singapore. In 1897, Samuel formed the Shell Transport and Trading Company, with a pecten shell as its trademark, to take over his growing oil business.

At the same time, August Kessler was leading a Dutch company to develop an oilfield in Sumatra in the Dutch East Indies. In 1896 Henri Deterding joined Kessler and the two began building storage and transportation facilities and a distribution network in order to bring their oil to market.

The expansion of both companies was supported by the growing demand for oil resulting from the introduction of the automobile and oil-fuelled ships. In 1901 Shell began purchasing Texas crude, and soon both companies were engaged in fierce competition with John D. Rockefeller's Standard Oil. Faced with the might of Standard Oil, Samuel and Deterding (who had succeeded Kessler as chairman of Royal Dutch) began cooperating, and in 1907 the business interests of the two companies were combined into a single group, with Royal Dutch owning a 60 percent share and Shell a 40 percent share (a ratio that has remained constant to this day).

The group grew rapidly, expanding East Indies production and acquiring producing interests in Romania (1906), Russia (1910), Egypt (1911), the US (1912), Venezuela (1913), and Trinidad (1914). In 1929 Shell entered the chemicals business, and in 1933 Shell's interests in the US were consolidated into the Shell Union Oil Corporation. By 1938, Shell crude oil production stood at almost 580,000 barrels per day out of a world total of 5,720,000.

The post-war period began with rebuilding the war-devastated refineries and tanker fleet, and continued with the development of new oilfields in Venezuela, Iraq, the Sahara, Canada, Colombia, Nigeria, Gabon, Brunei, and Oman. In 1959, a joint Shell/Exxon venture discovered one of the world's largest natural gas fields at Groningen in the Netherlands. This was followed by several gas finds in the southern North Sea; and then between 1971 and 1976 Shell made a series of major North Sea oil and gas finds.

During the 1970s, Shell, like the other majors, began diversifying outside of petroleum:

- In 1970 it acquired Billiton, an international metals mining company, for $123 million.
- In 1973 it formed a joint venture with Gulf to build nuclear reactors.
- In 1976–7 it acquired US and Canadian coal companies.
- In 1977 it acquired Witco Chemical's polybutylene division.

By the beginning of the 1980s, Shell had built global metals and coal businesses and established several smaller ventures including forestry in Chile and New Zealand, flower growing in the Netherlands, and biotechnology in Europe and the US.

The 1980s saw a reversal of Shell's diversification strategy, with several divestments of "non-core businesses" and a concentration on oil and gas – especially upstream. One of Shell's major thrusts was to increase its presence within the US. After acquiring Belridge Oil of California, it made its biggest investment of the period when it acquired the minority interests in its US subsidiary Shell Oil for $5.4 billion.

■ SHELL'S ORGANIZATION STRUCTURE PRIOR TO 1995 ■

Shell's uniqueness stems from its structure as a joint venture and from its internationality – it has been described as one of the world's three most international organizations, the other two being the Roman Catholic Church and the United Nations. However, its organizational structure is more complex than either of the other two organizations. The structure of the Group may be looked at in terms of the different companies which comprise Royal Dutch/Shell and their links of ownership and control, which Shell refers to as *governance responsibilities*. The Group's structure may also be viewed from a management perspective – how is Royal Dutch/Shell actually managed? The day-to-day management activities of the Group, which Shell refers to as *executive responsibilities*, are complex, and the structure through which the Group is actually managed does not correspond very closely to the formal structure.

The Formal Structure

From an ownership and legal perspective, the Royal Dutch/Shell Group of Companies comprised four types of company:

- *The parent companies*. Royal Dutch Petroleum Company N.V. of the Netherlands and the Shell Transport and Trading Company plc of the UK owned the shares of the group holding companies (from which they received dividends) in the proportions 60 percent and 40 percent. Each company had its shares separately listed on the stock exchanges of Europe and the US, and each had a separate Board of Directors.
- *The group holding companies*. Shell Petroleum N.V. of the Netherlands and The Shell Petroleum Company Ltd of the UK held shares in both the service companies and the operating companies of the Group. In addition, Shell Petroleum N.V. also owned the shares of Shell Petroleum Inc. of the US – the parent of the US operating company, Shell Oil Company.
- *The service companies*. During the early 1990s, there were nine service companies located either in London or The Hague. They were:
  - Shell Internationale Petroleum Maatschappij B.V.
  - Shell Internationale Chemie Maatschappij B.V.
  - Shell International Petroleum Company Limited
  - Shell International Chemical Company Limited
  - Billiton International Metals B.V.
  - Shell International Marine Limited
  - Shell Internationale Research Maatschappij B.V.
  - Shell International Gas Limited
  - Shell Coal International Limited

The service companies provided advice and services to the operating companies but were not responsible for operations.

- *The operating companies* (or "opcos") comprised more than 200 companies in over 100 countries (the 1993 annual report listed 244 companies in which Shell held 50 percent or more ownership). They varied in size from Shell Oil Company, one of the largest petroleum companies in the US in its own right, to small marketing companies such as Shell Bahamas and Shell Cambodia. Almost all of the operating companies operated within a single country. Some had activities within a single sector (exploration and production (E&P), refining, marketing, coal, or gas); others (such as Shell UK, Shell Canada, and Norske Shell) operated across multiple sectors. Figure 7.1 shows the formal structure of the Group.

Figure 7.1 The formal structure of the Royal Dutch/Shell Group

Coordination and Control

Managerial control of the Group was vested in the Committee of Managing Directors (CMD), which forms the Group's top management team. The Committee comprised five Managing Directors. These were the three-member Management Board of Royal Dutch Petroleum and the Chairman and Vice Chairman of Shell Transport and Trading. The chairmanship of CMD rotated between the President of Royal Dutch Petroleum and the Managing Director of Shell Transport and Trading. Thus, in 1993, Cor Herkstroter (President of Royal Dutch) took over from J. S. Jennings (Managing Director of Shell Transport and Trading) as Chairman of CMD, and Jennings became Vice Chairman of CMD. Because executive power was vested in a committee rather than a single chief executive, Shell lacked the strong individual leadership that characterized other majors (e.g., Lee Raymond at Exxon and John Browne at BP).

The CMD provided the primary linkage between the formal (or *governance*) structure and the management (or *executive*) structure of the Group. The CMD also linked together the two parent companies and the group holding companies.

The combination of diffused executive power at the top together with operating authority and financial responsibility dispersed through nearly 250 operating companies meant that, compared with every other oil major, Shell was highly decentralized. However, the technical and economic realities of the oil business limited the autonomy of each operating company – interdependence resulted from linkages between upstream and downstream, between refining and chemicals, and from common financial and technological needs. It was the job of the service companies to provide the necessary coordination. During the early 1960s, Shell created, with the help of McKinsey & Company, a matrix structure within its service companies to manage its operating companies. This structure was viewed as a critical ingredient of Shell's ability to reconcile the independence of its operating companies with effective coordination of

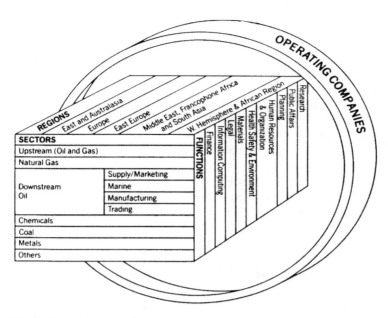

Figure 7.2 The Shell Matrix (pre-1996)

business, regional, and functional commonalties. This matrix organization continued into the 1990s (see figure 7.2).

The three dimensions of this matrix were represented by the principal executives of the service companies, who were designated "coordinators." Thus, the senior management team at the beginning of 1995 included the following:

Committee of Managing Directors

- Chairman
- Vice Chairman
- three other Managing Directors

Principal executives of the service companies

- Regional coordinators:
  - Europe
  - Western Hemisphere and Africa
  - Middle East, Francophone Africa, and South Asia
  - East and Australasia
- Sector coordinators:
  - E&P Coordinator
  - Chemicals Coordinator
  - Coal/Natural Gas Coordinator

- – Metals Coordinator
- – President – Shell International Trading
- – Marine Coordinator
- – Supply and Marketing Coordinator
- Functional coordinators:
  - – Director of Finance
  - – Group Treasurer
  - – Group Planning Coordinator
  - – Manufacturing Coordinator
  - – Group HR and Organization Coordinator
  - – Legal Coordinator
  - – Group Public Affairs Coordinator
  - – Group Research Coordinator
  - – Director of the Hague Office
  - – Director of the London Office

Strategic Planning at Shell

Within this three-way matrix, the geographical dimension was traditionally the most important. The fact that the operating companies were national subsidiaries provided the basis for the geographical emphasis of operational and financial decision making. This was reinforced through the strategic planning process, which put its main emphasis on planning at the national and regional levels.

Shell's planning system lay at the heart of its management system. It was viewed as one of the most sophisticated and effective of any large multinational. It was much discussed and widely imitated. Its main features were the following:

- A strong emphasis upon long-term strategic thinking. Shell's planning horizon extended 20 years into the future – much further than the four- or five-year planning that most companies engage in. Unlike most other companies, the basis for these strategic plans was not *forecasts* but *scenarios* – alternative views of the future which allowed managers to consider strategic responses to the different ways in which the future might unfold.
- A breadth of vision, and emphasis on the generation and application of ideas rather than a narrow focus on financial performance. Shell's planning department was receptive to concepts and ideas drawn from economics, psychology, biochemistry, biology, mathematics, anthropology, and ecology. As a consequence, Shell pioneered many new management techniques, including multiple scenario analysis, business portfolio planning, cognitive mapping, and the application of organizational learning concepts to planning processes.
- More generally, Shell was in the vanguard of the transition from the role of the strategy function as *planning* towards one where the primary roles of strategy were encouraging *thinking about the future*, developing the capacity for *organizational learning*, promoting *organizational dialogue*, and facilitating organizational *adaptation* to a changing world.

Planning at Shell was primarily bottom-up. The CMD identified key issues, set strategic direction, and approved major projects, and the planning department formulated the scenarios. However, most strategic decisions and initiatives originated among the operating companies. The role of the planning staff and the regional and sector coordinators was to coordinate the operating company strategic plans.

■ FORCES FOR CHANGE ■

Between the early 1970s and the early 1990s, the world petroleum industry was transformed by a number of fundamental changes.[1] The growing power of the producer countries was seen not just in the sharp rise in crude oil prices during the first oil shock of 1974, but even more fundamentally in the nationalization of the oil reserves of the international majors. By the 1990s, the list of the world's top 20 oil and gas producers was dominated by state-owned companies such as Saudi Aramco, Petroleos de Venezuela, Kuwait Oil, Iran National Oil Company, Pemex (Mexico), and Russia's Gasprom and Lukoil. In addition, the old-established majors faced competition from other sources. The "new majors," integrated oil companies such as Elf Aquitaine (France), Total (France), ENI (Italy), Nippon Oil (Japan), Neste (Finland), and Respol (Spain), were expanding rapidly, while in North America and the North Sea independent E&P companies such as Enterprise Oil, Triton, and Apache were becoming significant global players. Between 1970 and 1990, the share of world oil production of the "Seven Sisters" fell from 31 percent to 7 percent.[2] The loss of control over their sources of crude oil was a devastating blow for the majors – their whole strategy of vertical integration had been based around the concept of controlling risk through owning the downstream facilities needed to provide secure outlets for their crude oil. As market transactions for crude oil and refinery outputs became increasingly important, so prices became much more volatile. Between 1981 and 1986, crude prices fell from $42 a barrel to $9 before briefly recovering to $38 in the wake of the Iraqi invasion of Kuwait, and then resuming their downward direction.

Between 1985 and 1993, almost all the world's oil majors underwent far-reaching restructuring. Restructuring involved radical simultaneous changes in strategy and organizational structure in a compressed time-frame. Key features of restructuring by the oil majors were:

- Reorienting their goals around shareholder value maximization.
- Greater selectivity in their strategies, involving the divestment of unprofitable businesses, refocusing around core petroleum and gas businesses, withdrawing from countries where investments were not justified by the returns being earned, and outsourcing those activities that could be performed more efficiently by outside suppliers.
- Cutting back on staff, especially at the corporate level. (Table 7.1 shows changes in numbers of employees among the majors.)
- Reducing excess capacity through refinery closures and sales and scrapping of ocean-going tankers.

Table 7.1 Employment among the oil majors ('000)

	1999	1996	1993	1990	1985
Shell	99	101	117	136	142
Elf Aquitaine[c]	81	85	94	92	78
ENI	79	83	106	128	125
Exxon[a]	79	79	91	101	147
Total[c]	57	57	50	43	41
BP[b]	99	53	73	118	132
Mobil[a]	—	43	62	68	72
Amoco[b]	—	42	46	53	48
Chevron	39	41	48	50	62
Texaco	25	29	33	40	57
Arco[b]	17	23	25	28	31

Notes:
[a] Exxon merged with Mobil in 1998.
[b] Amoco merged with BP in 1997. BP acquired Arco in 1999.
[c] Total merged with Fina in 1998 and with Elf Aquitaine in 1999.
Source: *Fortune Global 500*, 2000, 1997, 1994, 1991, and 1996.

- Decentralization of decision making from corporate to divisional levels and from divisional to business unit levels at the same time as giving divisions and business units full profit and loss responsibility.
- Shifting the basis of organizational structure from geographical organization around countries and regions to worldwide product divisions (many of the majors formed worldwide divisions for upstream activities, downstream activities, and chemicals).
- "Delayering" through eliminating administrative layers within hierarchical structures. For example, Amoco broke up its three major divisions (upstream, downstream, and chemicals) and had 17 business groups reporting direct to the corporate center. Mobil also broke up its divisional structure, and created 13 business groups. (The Appendix shows the organization structure of several of the majors.)

■ SHELL IN THE EARLY 1990s ■

Shell was the only major oil company that did not undergo radical restructuring between 1985 and 1993. The absence of restructuring at Shell appeared to reflect two factors:

- Shell's flexibility had meant that Shell had been able to adjust to a changing oil industry environment without the need for discontinuous change. For example, Shell had been a leader in rationalizing excess capacity in refining and shipping, in upgrading its refineries with catalytic crackers, in establishing arm's-length relationships between its production units and its refineries, in moving into natural gas, and in taking advantage of opportunities for deep-water exploration.

- Because of Shell's management structure, in particular the absence of a CEO with autocratic powers, Shell was much less able to initiate the kind of top-down restructuring driven by powerful CEOs such as Larry Rawl at Exxon, Jim Kinnear at Texaco, Serge Tchuruk at Total, or Franco Bernabe at ENI.

Nevertheless, during the early 1990s, a combination of forces was pushing the CMD towards more radical top-down change. The most influential of these pressures was dissatisfaction over financial performance. The early 1990s were difficult years for the industry. The fall in oil prices to the mid-teens meant that returns from the traditional fount of profit – upstream – were meager. At the same time, refining and chemicals suffered from widespread excess capacity and price wars. Meanwhile, investors and the financial community were putting increased pressure on companies for improved return to shareholders. The CMD was forced to shift its attention from long-term development to short-term financial results. Against a variety of benchmarks, Shell's profit performance looked less than adequate:

- Cost of capital was the most fundamental of these – during the early 1990s Shell was earning a return on equity that barely covered the cost of equity.
- Long-term stability was a further goal. Top management asked, "What rate of return is needed to provide the cash flow needed to pay dividends and replace assets and reserves?" The returns of 1990–4 were somewhat below this figure.
- Shell's rates of return, margins, and productivity ratios were below those of several leading competitors.

Table 7.2 shows Shell's financial performance during the 1990s.

Evidence of the potential for performance improvement through restructuring was available from inside as well as from outside the Group. During the late 1980s and early 1990s, several Shell operating companies – notably those in Canada, the US, UK, South Africa, Germany, Malaysia, and France – showed the potential for organizational restructuring, process redesign, and outsourcing to yield substantial cost savings and productivity improvements.

The operating company executives that had been in the vanguard of cost cutting were increasingly resentful of the corporate structure. By 1994, Shell employed 6,800 people in its central organization (in London and The Hague) and in its corporate research and support functions. Even allowing for the differences in organizational structure between Shell and its competitors, this was bigger than the corporate and divisional administration of any other oil and gas major. As the operating companies struggled to reduce their own costs and improve their bottom-line performance, so they became antagonistic towards what they saw as a bloated corporate center whose support and services offered little discernable value. A major gripe was the failure of Shell's elaborate matrix structure to provide effective coordination of the operating

Table 7.2 Royal Dutch/Shell Group: performance data, 1992–9

	1999	1998	1997	1996	1995	1994	1993	1992
Gross sales ($ bill.)	149.7	138.3	171.7	172.0	150.7	129.1	125.8	128.4
Operating profit ($ bill.)	15.2	3.1	15.3	17.1	12.5	9.6	8.9	9.2
Net income ($ bill.)	8.6	0.4	7.8	8.9	6.9	6.2	4.5	5.4
Cash flow from operations ($ bill.)	11.1	14.7	16.7	16.6	14.9			
ROCE (%)	12.1	2.8	12.0	12.0	10.7	10.4	7.9	9.0
ROE (%)	15.4	0.7	12.8	15.1	11.8	11.5	8.7	9.7
Capital expenditure ($ bill.)	7.4	12.9	13.4	12.1	11.8	10.5	9.5	10.4
Employees ('000)	99	102	105	104	106	107	117	127

(The data are for continuing operations only. Hence, Shell's numbers of employees shown in Table 7.1 differ from those here because of acquisitions and disposals.)

companies. Lack of coordination in Europe resulted in UK refineries selling into Spain and Portugal, the Marseilles refinery supplying Belgium, natural geographical units such as Scandinavia split between different operating companies, and difficulties in launching Europe-wide initiatives such as the Shell credit card.

As Chairman Cor Herkstroter noted:

Many Operating Companies are sending us clear signals that they feel constrained by the management processes of the Service Companies, that the support and guidance from them is ineffective or inefficient, and that the services are too costly. They do not see the eagerness for cost reductions in the Operating Companies sufficiently mirrored in the center.[3]

The essential issue, however, was to prepare Shell for an increasingly difficult business environment:

While our current organization and practices have served us very well for many years, they were designed for a different era, for a different world. Over the years significant duplication and confusion of roles at various levels in the organization have developed. Many of you notice this on a day-to-day basis.

We anticipate increasingly dynamic competition. We see the business conditions of today, with flat margins and low oil prices continuing into the future. In addition, there will be no let up on all players in the industry to strive for higher productivity, innovation quality and effectiveness.

Our vision of the future is one of increasing competitive surprise and discontinuity, of increasing change and differentiation in skills required to succeed; and of increasing demands by our people at the front line for accountability within a framework of clear business objectives, and with access to a global source of specialist expertise.[4]

The Change Process

Within Shell, proponents of organizational change, including the heads of several of the operating companies, the finance function, and Group Planning, had had little success in persuading the Committee of Managing Directors of the need for large-scale change. In May 1993, Cor Herkstroter took over as Chairman of the CMD. A Dutch accountant, who had spent his entire career at Shell, Herkstroter was an unlikely pioneer of change. Fellow executives described him as a private, Old World personality without much charisma, and with a preference for written communication. Nevertheless, Herkstroter was widely respected for his intelligence and courage. "He's Shell's Gorbachev," said Philip Mirvis, a consultant working with Noel Tichy at Shell.[5]

Faced with growing evidence of suboptimal financial performance and an over-complex, inward-looking organizational structure, Herkstroter called a meeting of Shell's 50 top managers at Hartwell House, an English country manor, in May 1994. The meeting was a shock for the CMD. The request for frank discussions of the reasons for Shell's lagging return on capital provided a series of barbed attacks on top management and sharp criticism of the service company organization. The corporate center was castigated for taking months to approve operating company budgets and for the general laxness of financial controls. E&P coordinator Robert Sprague tossed a blank transparency onto the overhead projector and commented, "I don't know what to report, this issue is really a mess." The meeting had a powerful impact on the CMD: "We were bureaucratic, inward looking, complacent, self-satisfied, arrogant," observed then-Vice Chairman John Jennings. "We tolerated our own underperformance. We were technocratic and insufficiently entrepreneurial."[6] The outcome was the appointment of a high-level team to study Shell's internal organization and come up with options for redesign.

The team, set up in July 1994, was headed by Ernst van Mourik-Broekman, the head of HR, together with Basil South from Group Planning, Group Treasurer Stephen Hodge, an executive from Shell France, and the head of Shell's gas business in the Netherlands. The internal team was joined by three senior consultants from McKinsey & Company: two from the Amsterdam office and one from the London office.

The starting point for the internal team was a program of interviews with 40–50 managers at different levels within the company. This provided a basis both for assessing the existing structure and for generating ideas for change. The role of the McKinsey consultants was to provide perspective, to challenge the ideas of the Shell team, to introduce the experiences of other large multinationals (ABB for instance), to provide the backup research needed to refine and test out ideas and concepts, and to organize the program of work and consultation.

By October 1994, the group had prepared a diagnosis of the existing Shell structure together with a suite of options for reorganization. During October and November, a series of workshops were conducted, mainly in London, to explore in greater detail the specific dimensions of change and to clarify and evaluate the available options. Each workshop team provided input on a specific area of change. The results of this exercise were written up towards the end of November, and a report was submitted to CMD which identified the areas for change and the options.

During December 1994, the team spent two "away days" with the CMD to identify the objects of change and how the different options related to these. The result was a blueprint which the team wrote up mid-December. After six or seven drafts, the report was approved by CMD during the weekend of Christmas. At the beginning of January, the report was circulated to the chief executives of the main opcos and the coordinators within the service companies with a request for reactions by the end of January. In the meantime, Chairman Herkstroter gave a speech, directed to all company employees, to prepare them for change by indicating the need for change and the likelihood of job losses, but without any specifics as to the organizational changes that were likely to occur.

The driving force behind the redesign was the desire to have a simpler structure in which the reporting relationships would be clearer and thus to allow the corporate center to exert more effective influence and control over the operating companies. A simpler structure would help eliminate some of the cost and inertia of the head office bureaucracies that had built up around Shell's elaborate committee system. There was also a need to improve coordination between the operating companies. This coordination, it was felt, should be based upon the business sectors rather than geographical regions. Globalization of the world economy and the breakdown of vertical integration within the oil majors had meant that most of the majors had reorganized around worldwide business divisions. As was noted above, most of the majors formed upstream, downstream, and chemicals divisions with worldwide responsibility. For Shell, achieving integration between the different businesses within a country or within a region was less important than achieving integration within a business across different countries and regions. For example, in exploration and production, critical issues related to the development and application of new technologies and sharing of best practices. In downstream, the critical issues related to the rationalization of capacity, the pursuit of operational efficiency, and the promotion of the Shell brand.

By the end of January, a broad endorsement had been received. In February a two-day meeting was held with the same group of Shell's 50 senior managers that had initiated the whole process some ten months earlier. The result was a high level of support and surprisingly little dissent. The final approval came from the two parent company Boards. On March 29, 1995, Cor Herkstroter, Chairman of the Committee of Managing Directors, gave a speech to Shell employees worldwide outlining the principal aspects of a radical reorganization of the Group, which were to be implemented at the beginning of 1996.

In the meantime, two totally unexpected events only increased the internal momentum for change. While Shell faulted itself on its ability to produce a return on capital to meet the levels of its most efficient competitors, in managing health, safety, and the environment and in responding to the broader expectations of society, it considered itself the leader of the pack. Then came the Brent Spar incident. A carefully evaluated plan to dispose of a giant North Sea oil platform in the depths of the Atlantic produced outcry from environmental groups, including Greenpeace. Consumer boycotts of Shell products resulted in massive sales losses, especially in Germany. Within a few months, Shell was forced into an embarrassing reversal of its decision.

A few months later the Nigerian military regime executed Ken Saro-Wiwa, a prominent Nigerian author who had protested Shell's poor environmental record in his country. Again, Shell was found to be flat-footed and inept at managing its public relations over the incident. The handling of the Brent Spar and Nigerian incidents convinced many that Shell's top management was both unresponsive and out of touch. "We had to take a good look at ourselves and say, 'Have we got it right?'" said Mark Moody-Stuart, then a Managing Director. "Previously if you went to your golf club or church and said, 'I work for Shell,' you'd get a warm glow. In some parts of the world that changed a bit."[7]

■ THE NEW SHELL STRUCTURE ■

The central feature of the reorganization plan of 1995 was the dismantling of the three-way matrix through which the operating companies had been coordinated since the 1960s. In its place, four business organizations were created to achieve closer integration within each business sector across all countries. It was intended that the new structure would allow more effective planning and control within each of the businesses, remove much of the top-heavy bureaucracy that had imposed a costly burden on the Group, and eliminate the power of the regional fiefdoms. The new structure would strengthen the executive authority of the Committee of Managing Directors by providing a clearer line of command to the business organizations and subsequently to the operating companies, and by splitting central staff functions into a Corporate Center and a Professional Services Organization. The former would support the executive role of the CMD; the latter would produce professional services to companies within the Group. Figure 7.3 shows the new structure.

At the same time, the underlying principles of Shell's organizational structure were reaffirmed:

- The decentralized structure based on the autonomy of the Shell operating companies vis-à-vis the Group was to be maintained.
- The new structure continued the distinction between *governance* and *executive responsibility* which was described above. Thus, the formal structure of parent companies, holding companies, operating companies, and service companies was continued without significant changes. The Boards of these companies discharged the governance functions of the Group, including exercise of shareholder rights, the fulfillment of the legal obligations of the companies, and the appointment and supervision of the managers who fulfill executive responsibilities. It was the management structure where the major changes occurred, especially within the service companies.

The Formal Structure

As noted, the formal corporate structure shown in figure 7.1 was little changed. The principal changes in the formal structure were changes involving the identities and roles of the service companies to create a closer alignment with the new management structure. Thus, the new Corporate Center and Professional Services Organization were

FORMAL STRUCTURE

MANAGEMENT STRUCTURE

N = Netherlands

Figure 7.3 The service companies in 1996: links between the formal structure and the management structure

housed within Shell International Ltd (in London) and Shell International B.V. (in The Hague). Other service companies housed the new Business Organizations. Figure 7.4 shows the relationship between the new management structure and Shell's formal legal structure.

The Management Structure

The new organizational structure can be described in terms of the four new organizational elements – the Business Organizations, the Corporate Center, Professional Services, and the Operating Units – together with the two organizational units that continued from the previous structure, the operating companies and the Committee of Managing Directors.

THE BUSINESS ORGANIZATIONS

The central features of the new organization structure were the new Business Organizations. The CMD was supported by four Business Organizations: E&P ("upstream"), oil products ("downstream"), chemicals, and gas and coal. The Business Organizations were headed by Business Committees made up of a number of Business Directors appointed by the CMD. These Business Directors included:

Figure 7.4   Shell's management structure, 1996

- Business Directors with responsibility for particular business segments. For example, among the members of the E&P Business Committee in 1998 were J. Colligan, Regional E&P Business Director for Asia-Pacific and South America, H. Roels, Regional E&P Business Director for Middle East and Africa, and R. Sprague, Regional E&P Business Director for Europe.
- Certain of the operating companies were so important that their Chief Executives were also Business Directors. For example, in 1998, the E&P Business Committee included A. Parsley, Managing Director of Shell E&P International Venture B.V., while the Oil Products Business Committee included M. Warwick, President of Shell International Trading and Shipping Co. Ltd, and P. Turberville, President of Shell Europe Oil Products B.V.
- A Business Director for Research and Technical Services.
- A Business Director for Strategy and Business Services.

The Business Committees were accountable to CMD for:

- the strategy of their business area;
- endorsing the capital expenditure and financial plans of the operating companies and business segments within their business area;
- appraising operating company and business segment performance; and
- the availability of technical, functional, and business services to the operating companies within their business sector.

Chairing each of the Business Committees was a member of the CMD. Thus, in early 1998, E&P reported to Managing Director P. B. Watts, Oil Products to Managing

Director S. L. Miller, Chemicals to Vice Chairman M. Moody-Stuart, and Gas and Coal to Managing Director M. van den Bergh.

THE CORPORATE CENTER

This supported the CMD in its role in:

- setting the direction and strategy of the Group;
- growing and shaping the Group's portfolio of investments and resources;
- enhancing the performance of Group assets;
- acting as custodian of the Group's reputation, policies, and processes; and
- providing internal and external communication.

Apart from supporting the work of the CMD, the Corporate Center assisted the parent companies and the group holding companies in managing their financial, tax, and corporate affairs. The Corporate Center represented the other two dimensions of Shell's former matrix organization. For example, the Director for Planning, Environment and External Affairs chaired the meetings of Shell's Technology Council and Health, Safety and Environment Council. Also, the Corporate Advice Director undertook ad hoc country reviews.

The Corporate Center comprised six directorates:

- Planning, Environment and External Affairs
- Corporate Advice (supporting each of the Managing Directors in their regional roles as well as responsibility for IT, security, contracting and procurement)
- Group Treasurer
- Group Controller
- Human Resources
- Legal

In addition to these directorates, the Corporate Center also included the Head of Group Taxation, the Chief Information Officer, the Head of Intellectual Property, the Head of Contracting and Procurement, the Head of Group Security, the Head of Learning, and the Secretary to the CMD.

PROFESSIONAL SERVICES

These new units provided functional support for the operating companies and service companies within the Group. They offered their services on an arm's-length basis and competed with external service providers for the business of the operating companies. They were also able to provide services to third-party customers outside the Group. The services provided included:

- Finance (e.g., treasury services, accounting, tax advice)
- HR (e.g., recruitment, training)
- Legal
- Intellectual property (intellectual property protection, licensing)
- Contracting and procurement
- Group Security (security advice)
- Shell Aircraft Ltd (corporate jets)
- Office services (e.g., accommodation, personnel services)
- Health (medical services, environmental and occupational health advice)

Each Professional Services unit was headed by the relevant director from the Corporate Center. For example, HR was headed by the HR Director; legal and intellectual property services were headed by the Legal Director.

THE OPERATING COMPANIES

In the new organizational structure, the operating companies retained their role as the primary business entities within Shell. Each operating company was managed by a Board of Directors and a Chief Executive. The Chief Executive of an operating company was responsible to his/her Board and to his/her Business Director for the effective management of the operating company. The Chief Executive's responsibilities included the following:

- setting the company's strategic aims against the backdrop of any guidelines established by the Business Committee;
- providing leadership to put the strategic aims into effect and instill an entrepreneurial company culture;
- setting internal financial and operating targets and overseeing their achievement;
- supervising the management of the business and setting priorities;
- effective reporting on the company's activities and results to the Group.[8]

OPERATING UNITS

The superimposition of the Business Organizations on top of the operating companies created a problem for Shell because the operating companies were defined by country rather than by business sector and included activities which crossed business sectors. Hence, to achieve alignment between the new Business Organizations and the operational activities of the Group, Operating Units were created:

In the context of the Group organizational structure, Operating Unit refers to the activities in one of the Group Businesses which are operated as a single economic entity. An Operating Unit can coincide with an Operating Company, be a part of an Operating Company or straddle part or all of several Operating Companies.[9]

Thus, where an operating company was in one business only, the operating company was the relevant Operating Unit. However, multi-business operating companies, such as Shell UK and Shell Australia, which included upstream, downstream, chemical, and gas businesses, were divided into separate Operating Units in order to align operating activities with the new Business Organizations. Each of these Operating Units was headed by a manager with executive responsibilities who reported to the relevant Business Director. Where several Operating Units operated in a country under different Chief Executives, the Managing Director with responsibilities for that particular region appointed one of them as a "country chairman" to fulfill country-level responsibilities (with regard to matters of taxation, conformity with national legislation, national government relations, and the like).

In addition, some Operating Units spanned several operating countries. In order to achieve more effective integration across countries and to save on administrative and operating costs, the trend was to form Operating Units which combined businesses in several countries. Thus, in Europe there was a desire to run chemicals and oil products as single business entities.

Changing Culture and Behavior

Changes to the formal organizational structure were only one dimension of the organizational changes of this period. If Shell was to improve its operational and financial performance and improve its responsiveness to the multitude of external forces that impacted its many businesses, then change needed to go beyond formal structures. The criticisms leveled at Shell for being bureaucratic, inward looking, slow, and unresponsive were not about organizational structure, they were about behavior and attitudes. In any organizational change, a new structure may provide the right context, but ultimately it is the effects on individual and group behavior that are critical.

During 1996 and 1997, the Shell management development function moved into a higher gear. Organizational development and change consultants included Noel Tichy from Michigan Business School, Larry Selden from Columbia, McKinsey & Company, Boston Consulting Group, and Coopers & Lybrand. These were in addition to Shell's internal change management team, known as LEAP (Leadership and Performance Operations). The result was a substantial increase in Shell's management development and organizational development activities. *Fortune* magazine reported:

> This army has been putting Shell managers through a slew of workshops. In early February, teams from the gasoline retailing business in Thailand, China, Scandinavia and France spent six hours in a bitter Dutch downpour building rope bridges, dragging one another through spider webs of rope, and helping one another climb over 20-foot walls.
> The Shell managers especially liked Larry Selden. He teaches people to track their time and figure out whether what they're doing contributes directly to growth of both returns and gross margins. Selden calls this "dot movement," a phrase he has trademarked and which means moving the dot on a graph of growth and returns to the north-east. "The

model is very powerful," says Luc Minguet, Shell's retail manager in France. "It's the first time I've seen such a link between the conceptual and the practical. And I realized I was using my time very poorly."

In a particularly revealing exercise, the top 100 Shell executives in May took the Myers–Briggs personality test, a widely-used management tool that classifies people according to 16 psychological types. Interestingly, of its top 100 managers, 86% are "thinkers," people who make decisions based on logic and objective analysis. Of the six-man CMD, 60% are on the opposite scale. They are "feelers" who make decisions based on values and subjective evaluation. No wonder all those "thinkers" had such a hard time understanding the emotion behind Nigeria and Brent Spar. And no wonder the CMD gets frustrated with the inability of the lower ranks to grasp the need for change.[10]

■ FURTHER DEVELOPMENTS, 1996–9 ■

Cost Cutting and Restructuring

The most evident short-tem impact of the reorganization was a substantial reduction in Service Company staffs. Towards the end of 1995, Shell began shrinking its head offices in London and The Hague in anticipation of the introduction of the new organizational structure at the beginning of 1996. During 1996, the downsizing of central services and administrative functions within the Service Companies accelerated. During 1996, one of the two towers at the London Shell Centre was sold and was converted into residential apartments.

The quest for cost reductions did not stop at the Service Companies but extended to the operating companies as well. Between 1995 and 1997, unit costs were reduced by 17 percent in real terms, and between 1994 and 1997, savings in procurement costs amounted to $600 million each year. A priority for the Group was rationalization of capacity and reductions in operating costs in its downstream business. To facilitate this, Shell embarked upon three major joint ventures:

- The amalgamation of Shell Oil's downstream assets in the western US with those of Texaco
- The amalgamation of Shell's European downstream businesses with those of Texaco
- The merging of Shell's Australian downstream business with that of Mobil

Restructuring in Shell's other businesses included a swap of oil and gas properties with Occidental and the creation of a single global chemicals business. The chemicals business has demonstrated particularly clearly the benefits of global integration. In addition to cost savings of around 7 percent each year, investment decisions became better coordinated. "The Center's full control over chemicals, for instance, led Shell to put a new polymer plant closer to customers in Geismar, Louisiana, instead of near the existing plant in Britain. Two years ago that plant automatically would have been added to the UK fiefdom."[11]

Further Organizational Changes under Moody-Stuart

In June 1998, Mark Moody-Stuart succeeded Cor Herkstroter as Chairman of the CMD against a background of declining oil and gas prices and weakening margins in refining and chemicals. With Shell's operating profit and ROCE falling well below the projections for 1998, it was clear that further organizational change and cost reduction would be essential. In September he announced a series of restructuring measures aimed at reducing Shell's cost base while reaffirming Shell's commitment to the target of 15 percent ROACE (return on average capital employed) by 2001. Refinery cutbacks included the closure of Shellhaven refinery and partial closure of Berre refinery in France. The national head offices in the UK, Netherlands, Germany, and France would be closed.[12]

A key element of the organizational changes pushed by Moody-Stuart was the desire to replace Shell's traditional consensus-based decision making with greater individual leadership and individual accountability. To this end, the Business Committees that had been set up to manage the new business sectors were replaced by Chief Executives:

> From today we have CEO's and executive committees running each of our businesses. We have entered a new period where executive decisions have to be made rapidly and business accountability must be absolutely clear. So we have changed our structures.
>
> The major change we announced is establishing executive structures, with CEO's, in Oil Products and Exploration and Production. CEO's already run our other businesses: Gas and Coal, Chemicals and Renewables, as well as Shell Services International. Now we are structured to make rapid progress to our objective in each of our businesses.
>
> Business Committees served us in good stead in a period of transition but as from today they are a thing of the past. We will still have discussion, but we will make business decisions rapidly.[13]

The trend towards executive power and personal accountability was also apparent in the Committee of Managing Directors. In place of the traditional "committee of equals," Moody-Stuart reformed the CMD more as an executive committee where individual members had clearly defined executive responsibilities.

Moody-Stuart also accelerated the integration of Shell's US subsidiary, Shell Oil Inc., into its global structure. By the end of 1998, the chemicals sector was a truly global division and by early 1999 upstream operations in the US had been integrated into the global exploration and production sector. During 1999, the historically separate Shell Oil corporate office in Houston became integrated within Shell's Corporate Center and Professional Services organization. Thus, Shell Oil's Human Resource function staff became part of a new global Shell People Services organization, while Finance, Tax, Legal, and Corporate Affairs also integrated with their counterparts in London. The President and CEO of Shell Oil, Inc. became a de facto member of the CMD.

Figure 7.5 shows Shell's management structure under Mark Moody-Stuart's leadership.

Figure 7.5 Shell's management structure, 2000

■ TOWARDS A SECOND CENTURY ■

As Royal Dutch/Shell approached the second century of its corporate life, there was a clear consensus within the company that the organizational changes made during 1995–9 had created a structure that was much better able to respond to the uncertainties and discontinuous changes that affected the oil industry. Outside the company, Shell-watchers both in the investment community and in other oil companies had little doubt that the 1996 reorganization had contributed substantially to the efficient and effective management of the Group. The stripping away of much of the administrative structure in the Group head offices in London and The Hague, the elimination of the regional coordinating staffs, and the closure of some of Shell's biggest national headquarters not only reduced cost, but seemed to be moving Shell towards a swifter, more direct style of management. The restructuring of chemicals and downstream businesses revealed both a tough-mindedness and a decisiveness that few had associated with the Shell-of-old.

The former Vice-Chairman of the CMD outlined the way in which the changes in organization had impacted Shell's business portfolio and its strategic management:

> We used to have a complex regional matrix system – with multiple reporting lines. In compensation relatively modest annual raises were awarded – and more often than not expected – without being strictly tied to performance. Our businesses were tightly linked

to national markets and then to regions. Accountability was, through the matrix system, diffuse. It wasn't a bad system. When it was launched – in 1958 – it was an excellent system. But, by the early 90s, it had definitely reached its 'use by' date. Hurdle rates were used – good guides – but they allowed unbridled investment growth, which tended to exacerbate portfolio weaknesses. Jobs were for life in the old Shell and virtually all recruitment was internal.

By the early 90s we had a problem. There was no crisis – which in some ways was part of the problem. But ROACE was not good enough and it was obvious that something needed to be done. In the middle of the 90s we instituted something we called 'transformation'. As you can see here there were results, things were improving, but not really as quickly as they should have been. Then, in 1999 we had a particularly difficult environment, which galvanized us to rapidly complete the transformation process. Tough decisions were made, write-downs taken and the whole process accelerated.

As a consequence, today we have global businesses, headed by personally accountable CEOs. Reporting lines are direct, uncomplicated. Incentive pay and stock options are the norm. Every project has to compete globally for capital. Everyone in the organization can compete for any job – and we also actively hire from outside.

This has resulted in a significantly improved profile. Earnings are up on basically stable net revenues. Oil production is up, as are gas, chemical and oil product sales. The number of employees required has declined.

Capital has moved away from the poor performers and declining areas to new opportunities.[14]

The new organization had permitted far-reaching restructuring of Shell's downstream and chemicals businesses:

In the early 1990's we operated refineries in all parts of the world and our refining cover was over 80%. We have been closing or selling refineries . . . Our goal in this effort is two-fold – one is to reduce our refinery cover to a range of 65%–70% by 2001. The other is to achieve a return on average capital employed of 15% by 2001 . . .

At the beginning of the nineties we had [chemical] plants scattered across the globe with 30 plants in Europe, 7 in Asia Pacific, and 17 in America. The plants produced products that were sold through some 22 different product groups, each having profit and loss responsibility. Today we are concentrating on a few, world-scale plants and a much more limited product line. We will have 7 plants in Europe, 6 in Asia Pacific and 4 in America and products will be sold through 12 product groups.[15]

The question in most people's minds was whether Shell was moving ahead of the pack or playing catch up. For all Shell's pride in being a pioneer of modern management ideas – from scenario analysis to organization learning – Shell had created by Year 2000 a business-sector-based organization of a kind that most other diversified multinationals had created decades before. Moreover, some of Shell's leading competitors were moving away from such structures. BP – hailed by many to be the most dynamic and responsive of any of the petroleum majors – had abandoned its traditional divisional structure in favor of a flatter structure in which individual business units reported directly to the corporate center.

Moreover, Shell still retained some relics of the old structure that could compromise the new philosophy of responsiveness and single-point accountability. For example, Shell was still a joint venture rather than a single corporation. Its Committee of Managing Directors was still composed of board members from its dual parent companies. The principle of rotating leadership between the two parents with fixed single terms of office for the CMD Chairman was still intact. While Shell had been consumed with its internal restructuring, other companies had been transforming themselves through mergers and acquisitions. Had Shell missed out on the Great Oil Patch M&A Boom? Probably, but if Royal Dutch/Shell was to get serious about mergers, its first priority should be to merge with itself, noted the *Financial Times'* Lex column.

APPENDIX
The Organizational Structures of Other Oil Majors

Mobil (prior to merger with Exxon)

BP

Business Units are responsible directly to the corporate center. Their relationship to corporate is defined by their annual performance contracts. Larger Business Units are divided into separate Performance Units.
For example, within E&P, there are 30 Business Unites and 110 Performance Units

Peer Groups are functional groupings comprising functional specialists from the Business Units

Elf Aquitaine (prior to merger with Total-Fina)

NOTES

1. This section draws from R. Cibin and R. M. Grant, "Restructuring among the world's largest oil majors," *British Journal of Management*, December 1996.
2. The "Seven Sisters" were the original international oil majors: Shell, Exxon, Mobil, BP, Chevron, Texaco, and Gulf. (Gulf was acquired by Chevron in 1984.)
3. C. A. J. Herkstroter, "Right for the times and right for Shell," Speech delivered in London, March 29, 1995.
4. Ibid.
5. "Why is the world's most profitable company turning itself inside out?" *Fortune*, August 4, 1997, pp. 121–5.
6. Ibid.
7. Ibid.
8. *Reference Guide to Group Organizational Structure,* Shell International Ltd, August 1996.
9. Ibid., p. 17.
10. "Why is the world's most profitable company turning itself inside out?" *Fortune*, August 4, 1997, pp. 121–5.
11. Ibid.
12. "Shell shapes up for future," Speech by M. Moody-Stuart, San Francisco, September 18, 1998 (www.shell.com).
13. M. Moody-Stuart, Changes in Shell's organization: comments to the Shell Global Leadership Conference, London December 10, 1998.
14. Marten van den Bergh; "Strengthening the Portfolio," Shell Press Release, April 3, 2000.
15. Ibid.

case eight

Harley-Davidson, Inc., January 2001

Robert M. Grant

You've shown us how to be the best. You've been leaders in new technology. You've stuck by the basic American values of hard work and fair play . . . Most of all, you've worked smarter, you've worked better, and you've worked together . . . as you've shown again, America is someplace special. We're on the road to unprecedented prosperity . . . and we'll get there on a Harley.

President Ronald Reagan, speech at Harley-Davidson plant, York, Pennsylvania, May 6, 1987

The recovery of this company since the 1980s has been truly remarkable. When you were down in the dumps, people were saying American industry was finished, that we couldn't compete in the global economy, that the next century would belong to other countries and other places. Today, you're not just surviving – you're flourishing, with record sales and earnings; and one of the best-managed companies in America. According to management and labor, one of the reasons you're the best-managed company in America is that you have a genuine partnership between labor and management, where all employees are valuable and expected to make good decisions on their own for the benefit of the common enterprise. And I thank you for setting that example. I wish every manufacturer in America would model it.

President Bill Clinton, speech at Harley-Davidson plant, York, Pennsylvania, November 10, 1999

It's one thing to have people buy your products. It's another for them to tattoo your name on their bodies.

Harley-Davidson website

Rob Grant prepared this case assisted by Teseo Bergoglio, Mark Jeffreys, Matias Mayor, Karolis Pocius, Steve Tansey, Edwin Tockman, and Alexander Wellsteed.

■ DECEMBER 2000 ■

"What a start to the new decade!" thought chairman and CEO Jeff Bluestein as he reviewed Harley-Davidson's full year financial results for Year 2000. He had known for some time that Year 2000 would be another record year for the company – the 15th in succession – but these results not only beat the company's own projections, but also those of most Wall Street analysts. Revenue for the full year was $2.91 billion, 18.5 percent up on 1999. Earnings-per-share were $1.13, a 31.1 percent increase on 1999. And, for the first time in its history, Harley-Davidson (H-D) had produced over 200,000 bikes. What a contrast to the dark days of the early 1980s when H-D emerged as a fragile, run-down, debt-laden management buyout.

The start of the new decade had been marked by a number of significant developments in H-D's continued development. In terms of product development, the new single-cylinder Buell Blast had been successfully launched – H-D's first venture into smaller motorcycles in three decades. In operations and supply-chain management, H-D had continued to invest in state-of-the-art manufacturing systems, information systems, quality management, and supplier relationships. H-D had continued to develop its dealer network with new services, such as Rent-a-Harley, and internet linkages between the company, its dealers, and its customers. Year 2000 also saw H-D increasing its overseas presence, notably in Europe, Latin America, and Asia.

Yet, as Bluestein looked ahead to Harley's centenary celebrations to be held in a mere two years' time, he recognized that his primary task was to combat complacency within the company. H-D's succession of record-breaking results had coincided with America's longest-ever peacetime expansion. As the economic storm clouds gathered in January 2001, Bluestein wondered what the impact would be on the demand for leisure products priced in the $6,000 to $20,000 range. As for competition, Harley had demonstrated its ability to hold its own against similarly-styled V-twins produced by the Japanese and by the smaller upstarts such as Polaris, Big Dog, and Excelsior – they might be able to replicate the look of the Harley Hog, but none could replicate the "Harley Experience." But what if motorcycle riders began to look for a different type of experience? H-D's share of the heavyweight market fell slightly in 2000. Could it be that the appeal of the heavyweight cruiser was declining, and buyers were moving more towards the European-styled sports models produced by Ducati, Aprilia, Triumph, and BMW, or towards the high-performance Japanese machines? Longer term, there were the demographic trends. Harley's popularity was closely associated with the baby-boom generation. As this generation aged, so did Harley's customers. How would Harley appeal to younger generations?

■ THE HISTORY OF HARLEY-DAVIDSON ■

1903–45: From Garden Shed to Mass Production

Harley-Davidson, Inc. was founded in 1903 by William Harley and brothers William Davidson, Arthur Davidson, and Walter Davidson. At the time of the company's

Table 8.1 Annual production of motorcycles by Harley-Davidson

1901	1903	1913	1920	1933	1936	1948	1953	1966	1975
3	150	12,904	28,189	3,700	9,812	31,163	14,050	36,310	75,403

1981	1986	1987	1988	1989	1990	1991	1992	1993	1994
41,586	36,700	43,300	50,500	58,900	62,500	68,600	76,500	81,700	95,811

1995	1996	1997	1998	1999	2000
105,104	118,771	132,285	150,818	177,187	204,592

Source: www.harley-davidson.com.

founding, a motorcycle was no more than a bicycle with a small motor attached. Harley's 1903 model was made in the Davidson family shed and had a three-horse-power engine. In 1909 Harley introduced its first two-cylinder, V-twin engine, featuring the deep, rumbling sound for which Harley motorcycles are known today. Henry Ford's assembly-line concept (1913) and wartime orders pushed Harley out of the small-scale craft shed and into an era of mass production. In 1921 a Harley motorcycle won the first race in which machines reached speeds of over 100 miles per hour. This same year, H-D's new model featured a front brake and the distinctive Harley tear-drop gas tank. Large-scale production and continued technical development caused the industry to consolidate: in 1910 there were some 150 US motorcycle producers, by 1929, Indian, Excelsior, and Harley accounted for the majority of US motorcycle sales. The Great Depression killed Excelsior, and Indian closed in 1953, leaving Harley the sole American manufacturer of motorcycles. Table 8.1 shows H-D's production over the century.

1945–80s: Cycle of Growth and Decline

The post-war era was one of opportunity and problems. Post-war affluence and the rise of youth culture created a growing demand for motorcycles. However, this was satisfied primarily by imports. By 1959, Harley was still market leader with sales of $16.6 million, but British imports amounted to about 30,000 bikes a year with BSA, Triumph, and Norton taking 49 % of the US market.[1] In 1959, Honda entered the US market. The result was the rebirth of motorcycling in the US. Although H-D initially benefited from the rapid expansion of the market, soon Honda and the other Japanese producers moved upmarket into the heavyweight sector. In 1969 Honda introduced its four-cylinder CB750, a huge technical advance on anything produced by H-D or the British. In the same year, H-D was acquired by AMF, which proceeded to expand production capacity with the building of the York, Pennsylvania assembly plant. Boosting capacity to 75,000 units annually had disastrous consequences for product quality. A company audit in the mid-1970s revealed that more than half the cycles coming off the line were missing parts.[2] By the end of the 1970s, Honda had replaced H-D as market leader in heavyweight motorcycles in the US.

1980s–Present: From Buyout to Boom

In 1981 H-D's senior managers, led by Vaughn Beals, organized a leveraged buyout. Harley emerged as an independent, privately owned company, but heavily laden with debt. The buyout coincided with one of the most severe recessions of the post-war US economy and, especially troublesome for a highly leveraged business, a soaring of interest rates under the Fed's tight monetary policies. Registrations of heavyweight motorcycles fell during 1981 and 1982 while Harley's own sales plummeted. By 1982 its sales of bikes were down by more than a third from 1979. During 1981 and 1982, Harley-Davidson lost a total of $60 million. Redundancies came thick and fast with 30 percent of the office staff dismissed and similar cutbacks among hourly workers.

The company's first priority after the buyout was to systematically rebuild production methods and working practices with a view to cutting costs and improving quality. The new Harley management team had visited several Japanese auto-manufacturing plants and carefully studied Toyota's just-in-time (JIT) system. The first few years after the buyout also saw a revolution in Harley's production methods. Less than four months after the buyout, Harley management began a pilot JIT inventory and production-scheduling program called "MAN" (Materials As Needed) in its Milwaukee engine plant. The objective was to reduce inventories and costs and improve quality control. Within a year, all H-D's manufacturing operations were being converted to JIT: components and sub-assemblies were "pulled" through the production system in response to final demand.

During these dark days of the early 1980s, H-D sought sanctuary from Japanese competition. In 1983, President Ronald Reagan increased tariffs on large Japanese motorcycles from 4.4 percent to 49.4 percent, an increase that was to be in effect for five years and declined each year. Even with protection, H-D flirted with bankruptcy between 1984 and 1986. By 1987, the restructuring measures and operational improvements began to pay off. With stronger sales and a successful round of $49 million in debt financing, H-D's financial condition stabilized. Between 1986 and 1990, Harley's share of the heavyweight market expanded steadily from about 30 percent to over 60 percent, with demand outstripping production. During this time, management improved the quality and reliability of its product, and began to explore growth opportunities in retail clothing and international sales.

The 1990s saw year-on-year uninterrupted growth in the heavyweight motorcycle market and continued increase in H-D's market share. The company's biggest challenge continued to be balancing production capacity with surging demand for its product. In order to overcome this constraint, in 1996, the company announced the ambitious Plan 2003. Plan 2003 was a vision to dramatically increase production capacity over eight years by the company's 100th anniversary. By implementing Plan 2003, Harley hoped to capture some of the surging international demand in the heavyweight motorcycle market.

■ THE HEAVYWEIGHT MOTORCYCLE MARKET ■

The heavyweight segment (650 cc and over) has been the strongest-growing part of the world motorcycle market during the decade up to 2001, with the US accounting for a

Table 8.2 Harley-Davidson's motorcycle registrations (1993–2000)*

	1993	1994	1995	1996	1997	1998	1999	2000
United States/Canada	132,800	150,400	163,100	178,500	205,400	246,200	297,800	363,400
Harley-Davidson	63,400	69,700	77,800	86,800	101,200	119,400	146,000	168,300
Market share (650 cc)	47.7%	46.4%	47.7%	48.6%	49.3%	48.5%	49.0%	46.3%
Europe	218,600	201,900	207,200	224,700	250,300	270,200	306,700	293,400
Harley-Davidson	13,200	14,400	15,400	15,300	16,100	17,300	19,900	21,800
Market share (650 cc)	6.1%	7.1%	7.4%	6.8%	6.4%	6.4%	6.5%	7.4%
Japan/Australia	35,700	39,100	39,400	37,417	58,880	69,200	63,100	62,700
Harley-Davidson	6,700	7,600	7,900	8,400	10,100	10,800	12,300	12,900
Market share (650 cc)	18.7%	19.4%	20.1%	22.4%	17.2%	15.6%	19.6%	20.5%

*Includes Buell.
Source: www.harley-davidson.com.

major part of this growth. The total volume of heavyweight motorcycles sold increased from 322,400 units in 1991 to 719,506 in year 2000. The US is the largest market for 650+cc motorcycles, representing 51 percent of the total volume in four major markets. During the period the rate of expansion accelerated from 8.4 percent in 1995 to 22 percent in 2000.

Apart from North America, Europe, Japan and Australia account for the majority of the remaining worldwide market for 650+cc motorcycles. Europe is the second largest heavyweight market, representing 40 percent of the market outside of the US. It grew at an annual rate of over 8 percent during 1995–9, but experienced a decline in year 2000.

H-D gained market share up until 1998. However, during 1999 and 2000, Harley's ability to grow market share was hampered by its inability to meet demand. H-D is the clear leader in the US market, where it held 46.3 percent of the heavyweight market in 2000. In Europe, H-D has grown it market share from 5.6 percent in the early 1990s to 7.4 percent. (See tables 8.2 and 8.3.)

The heavyweight motorcycle market comprises three segments:

- *Cruiser motorcycles* are "big, noisy, low riding, unapologetically macho cycles,"[3] typically with V-twin engines and an upright riding position. Their design reflects the dominance of styling over either comfort or speed. For the urban males (and some females) in Los Angeles, New York, Paris, and Tokyo, the cruiser motorcycle is practical transportation in congested metropolises, but is primarily a statement of style. The cruiser segment was practically created by Harley and is the most prevalent in the US market, representing 56.6 percent of total 650 cc units. Other market sales are comprised of 21.1 percent of sales in the Touring segment and 20.4 percent of the Performance market. Most of the bikes in this segment feature V-twin engines, many with cylinder capacities that exceed those of a small family car. Harley's major

Table 8.3 Market shares in heavyweight motorcycles, 1999 and 2000 (%)

	North America		Europe		Japan/Australia	
	1999	2000	1999	2000	1999	2000
Harley-Davidson	49.0	46.3	6.5	7.4	16.5	20.5
Honda	17.0	19.1	22.2	21.8	30.1	21.8
Kawasaki	10.4	9.1	11.6	9.4	20.2	18.9
Suzuki	9.4	9.5	15.4	14.3	8.7	10.4
Yamaha	7.6	9.0	18.0	17.3	13.9	17.0
BMW	3.5	3.2	13.0	13.0	4.0	4.0
Ducati	—	1.9	5.4	6.3	3.2	4.6
Triumph	—	—	4.2	4.2	—	—
Aprilla	—	—	—	2.1	—	—
Other	3.1	1.9	3.7	4.2	3.1	4.2

Source: Harley-Davidson *Annual Report*, 1999, 2000.

competitors in the cruiser segment include Japanese companies with models based upon traditional Harley design (Honda's Shadow range, Yamaha's Virago, the Suzuki Intruder, and Kawasaki's Vulcan).

- *Touring bikes* include cruisers specially equipped for longer-distance riding and bikes specially designed for comfort over long distance (including the Honda Goldwing and the bigger BMWs). These tourers feature luxuries such as audio systems, two-way intercoms, and heaters. Competitive threats exist for Harley-Davidson in the touring bike segment; Honda and BMW have engineered their motorcycles for greater smoothness and comfort through the use of multi-cylinder, shaft-drive engines.

- *Performance models* are based upon racing bikes. These are high-technology, high-revving engines with a heavy emphasis on speed, acceleration, and race-track styling; minimal concessions are provided to rider comfort. The segment is the most important in the European and the Asian/Pacific market, representing 61.7 percent and 66.2 percent of total 650 cc units respectively. The segment is dominated by Japanese motorcycle companies, with a significant representation of European specialists such as Ducati and Triumph. H-D entered the performance segment in 1993 through its involvement in the formation of Buell Motorcycles, a company it fully acquired in 1998.

In North America, H-D dominates the cruiser and touring segments of the heavyweight market, but internationally it is Honda that leads in the heavyweight market – as it does in most other segments of the motorcycle market. However, the conventional segmentation into lightweight, middleweight, and heavyweight does not clearly define H-D's market. H-D's strength lies not in the heavyweight motorcycle market, but in just one part of this: the *super-heavyweight* segment, comprising bikes with cylinder displacement of more than 850 cc. In the 650–850 cc range, the Japanese dominance is nearly as great as in the lightweight and middleweight markets.

■ HARLEY-DAVIDSON IN 2001 ■

The Brand

The Harley-Davidson image and the loyalty it engenders among its consumer base are undoubtedly the company's strongest assets. Harley-Davidson is one of the archetypes of American style. The famed spread eagle signifies not just the brand of one of the world's oldest motorcycle companies, but an entire lifestyle with which it is associated. Harley has been described as "the ultimate biker status symbol . . . a quasi religion, an institution, a way of life."[4] Like Walt Disney, H-D has a unique relationship with American culture. The values that Harley represents – individuality, honesty, freedom – can be traced back to the cowboy and frontiersman of yesteryear, and before that to the motives that brought people to America in the first place. As the sole surviving American motorcycle company from the pioneering days of the industry, H-D represents a tradition of US engineering and manufacturing.

This appeal of the Harley image and tradition has been central, not just to H-D's marketing, but to its strategy as a whole. The central thrust of the strategy has been reinforcing and extending the relationship between the company and its consumers. H-D has long recognized that it is not selling motorcycles, it is selling the Harley experience. Prominent in H-D's annual reports of recent years have been pictures and prose depicting the Harley Experience:

> A chill sweeps though your body, created by a spontaneous outburst of pure, unadulterated joy. You are surrounded by people from all walks of life and every corner of the globe. They are complete strangers, but you know them like your own family. They were drawn to this place by the same passion – the same dream. And they came here on the same machine. This is one place you can truly be yourself. Because you don't just fit in. You belong.[5]

If the appeal of the Harley motorcycle is the image it conveys and the lifestyle it represents, then the company must ensure that the experience matches the image. To increase H-D's involvement in its consumers' riding experience it formed the Harley Owners' Group in 1983. Through HOG, H-D became involved in organizing social and charity events, and employees, from the CEO down, were encouraged to take an active role in HOG activities. HOG's website describes the kind of emotion and atmosphere that the company is trying to deliver to customers through its HOG organization: "the feeling of being out there on a Harley-Davidson motorcycle links us like no other experience can. It's made HOG like no other organization in the world . . . The atmosphere is more family reunion than organized meeting."[6] By becoming a HOG member, riders get a company pin and patch, a membership card, and a HOG atlas as well as a host of membership benefits, including the *Hog Tales Magazine*, a bimonthly newsletter. The continued growth of the Harley Owners' Group throughout the 1990s was particularly important encouraging repurchase and upgrading by Harley owners. In 1999, 49 percent of Harley purchasers had owned a Harley previously, 30 percent were switching from other motorcycles, while 21 percent were first-time motorcycle buyers.

Throughout the 1980s and 1990s a key challenge for Harley was to extend the loyalty and passion of traditional Harley owners, typically blue-collar men in their 20s and 30s, to a more affluent, upmarket consumer group with the spending power to buy top-of-the-line, ready-customized Harleys. By the mid-1990s, the H-D's customer base had shifted substantially towards this older, more affluent segment and was beginning to bear fruit. In 1999, the median income of a Harley owner was $73,800, up from $38,400 in 1987. The average age grew to 44.6 in 1999, up from 34.7 in 1987, as aging baby-boomers became the loyal H-D consumer base. Meanwhile, by 1999, 9 percent of Harley consumers were female, up from 2 percent in 1987.

The Products

Broadening Harley's market appeal had major implication for product policy and design. The Harley image is linked closely to its big, throaty, V-twins. Ever since its disastrous foray into small bikes during the AMF years, Harley had recognized that its competitive advantage lies in the super-heavyweight segment. Here it has stuck resolutely to the classic styling that has characterized Harleys since its early years. At the heart of the H-D motorcycle is the air-cooled V-twin engine that has been Harley's distinctive feature since 1909. Harley's frames, handlebars, fuel tanks, and seats also reflect traditional designs.

H-D's commitment to traditional design features may be seen as making a virtue out of necessity. H-D's smaller size and scale compared to its competitors limited its ability to invest in technology and new products. As a result, H-D lags far behind its competitors in the application of motor vehicle technology: its motorcycles not only look old-style, the technology is old-style. This can be seen especially in engine technology. When H-D introduced its new Twin Cam 88 engine in 1998, *Motorcycle* magazine reported:

> Honda comes out with an average of two new (or reworked) motors every year. The other Japanese manufacturers are good for about one. Count on Ducati and BMW to do something every few years. That leaves only Moto Guzzi and Harley. So it goes to say that when either of these two old farts gets off the pot, they really raise a stink, so to speak.
>
> The Twin Cam 88 is Harley's first new engine since the Evolution Sportster motor of 1986, and their first new Big Twin motor since the original Evolution, released in 1984. Fifteen years between engines is not really that long a span for Harley. The Evo's predecessor, the Shovelhead lasted 19 years (with a revision after five), and the Panhead lasted nearly as long.[7]

Yet, despite the fanfare, Harley's Twin Cam 88 engine was hardly innovative. It was a 1,450 cc traditional V-twin with push rods and was air-cooled, a decade after Japanese manufacturers had introduced multi-valve, liquid-cooled, overhead camshaft engines. BMW's R1200C cruiser model, launched in 1997 with a star role in the James Bond movie *Tomorrow Never Dies*, featured shaft drive; a multi-valve, fuel-injected engine; triple-disc, anti-lock brakes; and "road-hugging" cornering from its advanced suspension system. While BMW and the Japanese manufacturers apply the latest automotive technology to their new models, H-D has concentrated upon incremental refinements to its engines, frames, and gearboxes aimed at improving power delivery, reliability, increasing braking power, and reducing vibration. This continual upgrading of its technology and its quality has been an essential requirement of H-D shifting its customer base from blue-collar enthusiasts to older professionals who lack the time, inclination, and expertise to reassemble and tune their bikes on a weekend and need "luxuries" such as electric starters and vibration control.

H-D has sought out alliances as a means of accessing advanced automotive technologies. In 1997, it established a joint venture with Porsche AG to source and assemble motorcycle components and to access Porsche's expertise in engine emission compliance. For its VF1000 Superbike race team, H-D collaborates with Cosworth Racing, Ford, and Gemini Racing Technologies.

Low output volumes present another design challenge: reconciling product differentiation with scale economies. Personalization is an essential requirement for the Harley owner. Hence, H-D must offer a wide model range, and a broad set of options regarding paint, accessories, and trim. At the same time, economies in engineering, manufacturing, and purchasing require standardizing components across the model range. The result is that H-D has continually broadened its range of models (its 2001 lineup offered 30 separate models) and for each model offers a range of options. At the same time, it bases this range of product offerings upon two engine types (Evolution and Twin Cam 88), four basic frames, four styles of gas tank, and so on.

The Harley product line also covers a wide price range. The Sportster model is intended as an entry level bike, priced at a mere $5,595, less than one third of the price of the Ultra Classic Electra Glide at $18,980 (see table 8.4).

Buell

H-D's involvement in Buell represented a significant strategic shift for the company. Founded by ex-Harley engineer Erik Buell in the 1980s, Buell Motor Company developed bikes that synthesized the comfort and style of a Harley cruiser with the high-performance attributes of a sports bike. Harley purchased a 49 percent stake in Buell in 1993, and in 1998 acquired complete ownership and control. Buell bikes use Harley engines and other components, but mount them on a lighter, stiffer frame. The lighter weight and superior handling and acceleration of Buell models were seen as appealing to younger motorcyclists and also to the European market, where customers put greater value on sporty performance and a cheaper price tag. In the US, the typical Buell customer was seven years younger that that of Harley buyers and the price tag about $10,000 compared to an average Harley price of $16,000. To appeal to this younger segment, H-D used slogans such as "Pull Some Gs" and "Different in Every Sense" to advertise Buell bikes. As with Harley, Buell has attempted to foster close relations with its customers. The Buell Riders Adventure Group (BRAG) was modeled after HOG.

Buell's production rose from 4,462 units in 1997 to 6,876 in 2000, boosted, in part, by the introduction of the Buell Blast, an entirely new model with a single cylinder engine of under 500 cc and a price tag of $4,395 (see table 8.5). H-D's first entry into the middleweight market and its only departure from its V-twin engines in almost three decades was a significant strategic move for H-D. It followed concern over the rising

Table 8.4 Heavyweight motorcycles: price comparisons, 2000

Manufacturer and model	Engine	Price ($)
H-D XLH 800 Sportster	V-twin, air-cooled, 883 cc	5,595
H-D XL 1200S Sportster	V-twin, air-cooled, 1,203 cc	8,595
H-D Dyna Wide Glide	V-twin, air-cooled, 1,340 cc	15,595
H-D FLSTS	V-twin, air-cooled, 1,340 cc	15,690
H-D Heritage Softail Classic	V-twin, air/c, 1,340 cc carburetor or injection	16,235
H-D Fat Boy	V-twin 1,450 cc, carburetor or injection	15,495
H-D Road King Classic	V-twin carburetor or injection	16,695
H-D Heritage Springer	V-twin 1,450 cc, carburetor or injection	17,545
H-D Ultra Classic Electra Glide	V-twin 1,450 cc, injection	18,980
Honda Shadow ACE 750	V-twin, OHC, 745 cc	6,299
Honda Pacific Coast	V-twin, liquid-cooled, 800 cc	8,699
Honda Shadow Aero	V-twin, liquid-cooled, 1,099 cc	9,695
Honda Shadow ACE Tourer	V-twin, liquid-cooled, 1,099 cc	10,999
Suzuki Marauder	V-twin, liquid-cooled, OHC, 805 cc	5,999
Suzuki Intruder	V-twin, air-cooled, 1,462 cc	9,899
Kawasaki Vulcan 800	V-twin, 8-valve, OHC	7,999
Kawasaki Vulcan Classic	V-twin, air-cooled, 1,470 cc	11,590
Yamaha 750 Virago	V-twin, OHC, 749 cc	6,499
BMW F650	Liquid-cooled, double OHC, injection	8,100
BMW R1200C Cruiser	1,170 cc, ABS, injection, liquid-cooled	14,500
BMW K1200LT Tourer	1,171 cc, ABS, injection, liquid-cooled	16,700
Polaris Victory V92C	V-twin, 4-valve OHC, 1,507 cc	13,595

Source: www.harley-davidson.com; www.motorcycle.com.

average age of Harley owners (44 years old in 2000, up from 34 years old in 1985) as compared to an average of 38 for motorcycle owners generally (up from 27.6 in 1975). In 1997, H-D set up a working group to explore ways of attracting new, younger motorcycle riders. Market research found that many potential riders were put off by motorcycles being "hard to learn," and big cruisers and touring bikes viewed as "intimidating" or "something an old guy would ride." Following one group meeting, CEO Jeff Bluestein was at home thinking about the type of motorcycle to attract new riders to the sport: "I looked over at a picture of the first motorcycle we ever built in 1903 and thought, why don't we go back to our roots and develop a single-cylinder that would be light, yet powerful, easy to ride, and still deliver a genuine riding experience," said Bluestein. The result was the Buell Blast.

Harley-Davidson has promoted the "Blast" in several non-traditional ways. First, in an effort to help novices overcome any fear of the unknown, the company offers a Riders Edge schooling program to these users. The Riders Edge is part of a consumer education campaign targeted at these new users. Second, advertisements are being targeted through consumer publications and cable TV. Buell has been a significant backer of ENFL, the entertainment-oriented football league.

Table 8.5 Harley-Davidson shipments 1997–2000 (units)

	1997	1998	1999	2000
Motorcycle shipments				
United States	96,216	110,902	135,614	158,817
Export	36,069	39,916	41,573	45,775
Motorcycle product mix				
Sportster	23.8%	22.5%	23.6%	22.6%
Custom	53.5%	51.3%	49.6%	49.3%
Touring	22.8%	26.2%	26.8%	28.1%
Buell motorcycle shipments				
United States	1,912	3,333	4,022	4,306
Export	1,197	2,132	2,780	2,570

Source: Harley-Davidson quarterly results (www.harley-davidson.com).

Distribution

Upgrading H-D's distribution network was a key aspect of Harley's development strategy during the 1980s and 1990s. Many of Harley's 620 US dealerships were poorly managed shops, operated by enthusiasts, with erratic opening hours, a poor stock of bikes and spares, and indifferent customer service. If H-D was in the business of selling a lifestyle and an experience, then dealers were the primary point of contact between the company and its customers. Moreover, if H-D's future lay with professionals who possessed the disposal income to lay out $15,000 on a motorcycle for occasional leisure rides – then the retail environment had to be appropriate to the requirements of this customer group.

Harley's dealer development program increased support for dealers while imposing higher standards of pre- and after-sales service, and requiring better dealer facilities. The dealers were obliged to carry a full line of Harley replacement parts and accessories, and to perform service on Harley bikes. Training programs helped dealers to meet the higher service requirements, and encouraged them to recognize and meet the needs of the professional, middle-class clientele that H-D was now courting. Unlike any other motorcycle company, H-D required exclusivity of its dealers – if they were Harley dealers, they couldn't sell any other brand.

The dealers played a central role in Harley's repositioning, growth, and fostering of customer loyalty. Under pressure and guidance from H-D, over 90 percent of the 600 dealers in the United States rebuilt, renovated, or substantially upgraded their stores. Dealers' showrooms moved locations and went from being gritty motorcycle shops to airy boutiques that featured, not just motorcycles, but a wide range of apparel and accessories as well. H-D partnered with its dealers in local advertising and promotion. For instance, the "Genuine Deal" campaign – which offered dealers TV and radio spots and promotional materials – was designed to build the Harley brand image, dealership loyalty, and to develop the sales of the accessory business – which, during the first year of Harley ownership, amounted to an average of $3,500 in incremental retail sales.

Table 8.6   Harley-Davidson's sales of parts, accessories, and general merchandise, 1990–2000 ($ million)

	1990	1991	1992	1993	1994	1995	1996	1997	1998	1999	2000
Parts and accessories	80.2	94.3	103.6	127.8	162.0	192.1	210.2	241.9	297.1	362.6	447.9
General merchandise	29.8	36.0	52.1	71.2	94.3	100.2	90.7	95.1	114.5	132.7	151.4

Source: Harley-Davidson financial statements (www.harley-davidson.com).

H-D believed that its dealer strategy was an important explanation for the fact that, despite a fourfold increase in production capacity since the beginning of the 1990s, demand for Harley motorcycles continued to outstrip supply. Every motorcycle that H-D made in year 2000 had already been sold long before it came off the production line. For many models, would-be buyers must join a waiting list. One result is that used bikes frequently sell at higher prices than new bikes. More generally, the rate of price depreciation of used Harleys is very low. Hence, the high price of the original purchase is mitigated by high resale values.

Other Products

Sales of parts, accessories, and "general merchandise" (clothing and collectibles) represented over 20 percent of total sales in 2000 – much higher than for any other motorcycle company (see table 8.6). Clothing sales include not just traditional riding apparel, but a wide range of men's, women's, and children's apparel.

Only a small proportion of the clothing, collectibles, and other products bearing the Harley-Davidson trademark are sold through the H-D dealership network. Most of the "general merchandising" business represented licensing of the H-D name and trademarks to third-party manufacturers. For example, Nice Man Merchandising supplied Harley-Davidson children's clothes; a giftware company supplied Harley holiday bulb ornaments, music boxes, and a Road King pewter motorcycle replica; L'Oréal offered a line of Harley-Davidson cologne; Harley-Davidson Cafés operated in Manhattan and Las Vegas.

Harley-Davidson Financial Services was established to supply credit, insurance, and extended warranties to H-D dealers and customers. It earned $37.3 million in operating income in 2000, plus an after-tax gain of $6.9 million from the sale of the Harley-Davidson Chrome VISA card business.

International Expansion

A key part of H-D's growth strategy is expanding its sales outside of the US. "A few years ago," says Harley CEO Bleustein, "our prime focus was the domestic market, and the rest was gravy. That view had to change. If our growth is to continue, Europe will have to play a significant part." A critical issue for international marketing is the extent to which the products and the Harley image need to be adjusted to meet the needs of overseas markets. Harley's image is rooted in American culture, and thus seems central to their appeal to European and Asian customers. "The US and Harley are tied together," says Hugo Wilson of Britain's *Bike* magazine, "the guy who's into Harleys here is also the guy who owns cowboy boots. You get a Harley and you're buying into the US mystique."[8] At the same time, the composition of demand and the customer profile is different in overseas markets.

Europe is the focal point of H-D's overseas ambitions, simply because it is the largest heavyweight motorcycle market in the world. Europe is also a huge challenge for H-D. Unlike in the US, H-D has never had a major position in Europe and it must fight to take market share from the established leaders in the heavy bike segment: BMW, Honda, Kawasaki, and Yamaha. The European motorcycle market differs significantly from the American market in that 70 percent of the heavy motorcycle market is for performance bikes (such as the popular Japanese high-power, lightweight, racing-style bikes), while the touring/cruiser bikes such as those Harley makes account for only 30 percent. European buyers tend to be knowledgeable and highly style conscious. Also, European roads and riding style are different from the US. As a result, Harley has modified some of its models to better meet the needs and tastes of its European customers. The US Sportster, for example, has a straight handlebar instead of curled buckhorns and a new suspension system to improve cornering. The name has also changed to the "Custom 53." The Harley Softail has also received a new look, becoming the "Night Train." As in the US, Harley management regards the after-sale value of biker clubs and events as a critical differentiator for its product. The biggest Harley gathering ever planned was for June 20, 1998 in Austria, when some 10,000 European Harley owners gathered in celebration of the company's 95th anniversary.

The European heavyweight market grew strongly during the mid- to late 1990s, especially in Italy, where a new customer base of Italian youth has driven sales. "Sales to those 25 and younger are about 3 percent among the world's motorcycle manufacturers," says Carlo Talamo, owner of 40 Numero Uno Harley Stores scattered around Italy. "In Italy [the youth market] is 37 percent."[9] By 2000, H-D's European Region (Europe/Middle East/Africa) had 349 independent Harley-Davidson dealerships serving 32 country markets. This included 181 combined Harley-Davidson and Buell dealerships. Buell was further represented by 22 dealerships that did not sell Harley-Davidson motorcycles. The European Region, headquartered in Windsor, England, oversees wholly-owned sales and marketing subsidiaries in France, Germany, the Netherlands and the United Kingdom.

However, despite growing sales, Harley has found it difficult to increase its market share significantly in Europe. The high price of Harleys and the rising value of the US dollar during the late 1990s gave Japanese and European manufacturers a competitive edge.

In the Asia/Pacific Region, there were 241 Harley-Davidson outlets serving 8 country markets. This includes 48 Harley-Davidson dealerships, 79 combined Harley-Davidson/Buell dealerships, 5 Buell only dealerships, 81 Harley-Shops, and 28 service shops. Two major markets remained Australia and Japan. The Japan HOG has its own web page and a downtown Tokyo clubhouse available to its members. H-D only sells about 9,000 machines a year in Japan but has been very successful in sales of brand-

Table 8.7 Harley-Davidson facilities, 1999

Location	Function	Total employment
Wisconsin		2,400
Milwaukee sales, R&D	Corporate headquarters, parts/accessories	
Wauwatosa Development Center	XL Engine/Transmission production	
Menomonee Falls	FL Engine/Transmission production	
Franklin	Parts/Accessories Distribution Center	
Tomahawk	Fiberglass parts production/painting	
Pennsylvania		2,600
York	Final assembly plant, parts and painting	
Missouri		350
Kansas City	Manufacturing, painting	
Brazil		
Manaus	Manufacturing	not available

Source: Harley-Davidson *Annual Report*, 1999.

named merchandise, spare parts, and related goods. The potential of the Japanese market has also caught the attention of H-D's competitors: Triumph of the UK announced at the end of 2000 plans to set up a nationwide network of 40 dealerships appealing to those in search of a "more distinctive riding experience."

In Latin America, H-D sells into 16 countries. These sales are managed from Milwaukee, Wisconsin. H-D's market penetration is limited by its sparse distribution network: just 26 Harley dealerships and 10 authorized retail outlets and mall stores focused on selling general merchandise. The two major markets are Brazil and Mexico. In Brazil, H-D opened an assembly plant in Manaus towards the end of 1999.

Operations

Since emerging as an independent company in 1981, H-D has been continuously upgrading its manufacturing operations. This has involved continuous investment in plant and equipment, both to introduce advanced process technologies and to expand capacity. Even more important has been the development of manufacturing capabilities through total quality management, just-in-time scheduling, CAD/CAM, and the devolution of responsibility and decision making to the shopfloor.

At the beginning of 2001, H-D's engine and component manufacturing was clustered around its Milwaukee headquarters, with assembly concentrated at York, Pennsylvania. In addition, H-D had two new plants, Sportster production at Kansas and its Brazilian assembly plant. (See table 8.7.)

Despite the enormous strides in implementing state-of-the-art manufacturing methods and expanding production to offset the problems of small-scale production, H-D low production volumes relative to Honda and the other Japanese manufacturers imposed significant cost disadvantages. A key factor in this volume-related cost disadvantage was in the purchasing components. Bought-in, customized components account for a large proportion of manufacturing costs and H-D does not possess the same buying power as Honda or even some of the smaller manufacturers. Thus, despite its smaller volume of motorcycle production, BMW is able to leverage the buying power of its automobile business.

To meet this challenge, H-D placed purchasing managers at senior levels within its management structure and fostered close relations with its key suppliers. In 1992, Harley extended its program of quality improvement to encompass its suppliers. It established a supplier advisory council (SAC) to expose supplier executives to the best practices of other suppliers in the Harley network.[10] Harley's director of purchasing, Garry Berryman, commented: "Through the SAC, we're able to take some of the entrepreneurial aspects of our smaller, privately held suppliers and inject that enthusiasm, spirit, and energy into those that may be larger, publicly held companies. In this way, the SAC serves not only to improve purchasing efficiency, but also provides a forum to share information, ideas, and strategy." The SAC, says Berryman, is a way "to leverage the successes that occur in one area across the broader organization."[11] The SAC comprised 16 suppliers out of H-D's 400+ OEM suppliers. Each SAC member was encouraged to contact 9–12 other first-tier suppliers on issues of costs, quality, scheduling, and strategy, the goal being to spread best practices within Harley's supplier base and to improve the quality of Harley's own practices. Berryman observed: "The knowledge, leadership, and intelligence represented in our supplier council brings our capabilities well beyond what we could do with internal resources."

Suppliers were also included in Harley's new product development process. Leroy Zimdars, Harley's director of purchasing development, noted: "We want suppliers to be deeply involved, at an early stage, in new product development. We'll use the SAC as a sounding board for how the supply base accepts the new structure, and we can react to it."[12]

People and Management Processes

A key feature of H-D's turnaround during the 1980s was the quest for a new relationship between management and employees. Following the management buyout, H-D's new management team systematically rethought management–employee relationships, employee responsibilities, and organizational structure. The result was a transformation in employee commitment and job satisfaction. "What other company has employees who tattoo the company name on their bodies? Or offers not just a job but a lifestyle?" observed an assembly-line worker at Harley's Milwaukee plant. Harley has a no lay-off policy, 12 weeks of paid maternity leave, and unlimited sick days for staffers.

The process of management innovation is a continuing one. When Harley's new Northland Plant went on-line in Kansas City in January 1998, the plant's management structure and working methods reflected the company's desire to make further advances in employee commitment and self-management. "I'm not aware of anybody anywhere doing anything that emulates this," says plant chief Karl Eberle.[13] In contrast to the traditional layout of Harley's other plants, the Northland Plant does not have a management space that oversees floor production from a glassed-in office upstairs. Instead, the plant manager and other administrators work in a "bullpen area" on the floor and in the center of the 330,000 square-foot building.

In an effort to engage and motivate the entire plant workforce, management developed a novel operating structure different from anything else within the company. The structure comprised three types of teams:

- *natural work groups* – every worker belongs to a work group, with 8–15 people per group
- *process operating groups* – comprised of representatives from each work group, there are four process operating groups; each oversees the plant's four operating divisions: paint, assembly, fabrication, and engine production
- *plant leadership group* – a 14-member committee, responsible for governing the facility; comprised of the plant manager, the presidents of both unions representing the plant workforce, four elected representatives from the process groups, an elected representative from maintenance, and six administrators

Harley's belief is that a less hierarchical, more team-based structure can improve employee motivation and accelerate the learning process at its plants.

Headquarters Organization

The movement toward a flatter, more team-based organizational structure was extended to H-D's corporate structure. "In our new organization," explained Clyde Fessler, VP for business development, "the Harley-Davidson Motor Company has been divided into three broad, functional areas called Circles. They are: the Create Demand Circle (CDC), the Produce Product Circle (PPC), and the Provide Support Circle (PSC). Each Circle is composed of the leaders representing the functions within it. The flexibility of the organization extends even to the decision of which functional areas are identified within a given circle. It is quite possible that Circle definitions may shift from time to time, depending on the demands of the business."[14] Like the team structure developed for the Kansas City plant, each Circle operated as a team with leadership moving from person to person, depending on the issue being addressed. Individual Circles met once a month with all three Circles meeting together quarterly.

Overall coordination was provided by the Strategic Leadership Council (SLC) comprising individuals nominated by each of the three Circles. Explained Fessler:

> The role of the SLC is to resolve issues that have not been settled previously by consensus in Circle meetings. Leadership of the Council also rotates, shifting to Circle representative who "owns" the topic being discussed . . . The Circle format is especially valuable in that it facilitates systems thinking in our strategy implementation. If the marketing function

plans to focus on a specific product, the Circles provide an opportunity to get feedback from manufacturing about timing and availability. If the Manufacturing function needs to shut down its operations to upgrade equipment, the Circle structure allows all the affected functions to be involved in the decision. We have now been working with this organizational design for three and a half years. And we would probably all agree that the shift from hierarchy to Circles has not been easy – practicing consensus decision-making never is. However, defining the roles and responsibilities of each functional Circle and each Circle member has brought clarity, which in turn stimulates dialogue, trust, and eventually, non-threatening confrontation . . . Collaborative interdependent teams may not be able to move as quickly as the single decisive leader in a hierarchy, but they can be more innovative and resourceful and, ultimately, more effective in today's complex business climate.[15]

■ COMPETITION ■

Despite H-D's own insistence that it was supplying a unique Harley experience rather than competing with other motorcycle manufacturers, the more H-D took market share from other manufacturers, the more it was engaged in a brutally competitive market. By broadening its market, H-D came into closer competition with its Japanese and European rivals – Bell's mission was to compete directly with them. And the more successful was the Harley brand, the more it could expect its bigger competitors to target its own market niche. Honda, Suzuki, Yamaha, and Kawasaki had long been offering V-twin cruisers styled closely along the lines of the classic Harleys – but at lower prices, with more advanced technologies, and in some dimensions, superior performance. In competing against H-D, the Japanese manufacturers' key advantage was their sales volume. H-D's single-segment focus and concentration on the US market meant that it produced a much smaller volume of bikes than any of the Japanese producers. The most striking comparison was between H-D and Honda: H-D's total of 204,592 bikes in 2000 was dwarfed by Honda's 5.16 million bikes in the same year. These volume differences have important implications for H-D's ability to access economies of scale. In addition, H-D's greater product and geographic focus meant that it was also more vulnerable to a downturn in demand in its specific segment or in the US economy.

In addition, H-D was also diversified. Honda, BMW, and Suzuki are important producers of automobiles and more than one-third of Yamaha's turnover comes from boats and snowmobiles. These companies could benefit from sharing technology, engineering capabilities, and marketing and distribution know-how between their automobile and motorcycle divisions. In addition, sheer size conferred greater bargaining power with suppliers.

Also, H-D was facing competition from other specialists producing retro-styled cruiser bikes. In recent years Excelsior, Polaris, and Big Dog had all entered Harley's markets during the late 1990s, but with only limited success to date.

Appendix 2 gives profiles of several competitors of H-D in the heavyweight motorcycle market, table 8.3 compares market shares, and table 8.4 shows price comparisons.

■ MEETING THE CHALLENGES OF TOMORROW ■

As Jeff Bluestein thought ahead to H-D's centenary celebrations in 2003, his mind focused upon the possible potholes that the company might encounter on the road forward. H-D had shown that it could build its owner base and extend it overseas without undermining the fervent loyalty of its customers. But how far could H-D go in expanding its production capacity? H-D's ability to run its plants at full capacity was central to its strong profitability and its ability to fund its continued development. The most obvious threat to demand was the risk of a significant recession in the US. Of greater concern to Bleustein was the potential for Harley's big cruiser motorcycles to lose their appeal to its core customer group – middle and upper income American males in their late 30s to early 50s willing to pay $15,000 for a motorcycle. While H-D's marketing emphasized the experience of motorcycling, Bleustein was acutely aware that purchasing a Harley was, for many of its owners, more a statement of style than a desire to ride the great American wilderness. Ultimately all lifestyle products are vulnerable to shifts in fashion ad lifestyle. Even with its Buell division, H-D might be vulnerable to a shift of style away from the heavyweight cruisers towards the sports machines offered by Ducati, Triumph, Aprilia, and of course the Japanese producers.

As H-D grew and expanded its model range, so it needed to be more concerned over the overall health of the US motorcycle market. Although the heavyweight segments had seen strong growth, the market as a whole had been in steady decline – in 1973, 1.2 million new motorcycles were registered, compared to the 416,000 registered in 1998.

If the market for big bikes declined, this would greatly increase the intensity of competition between manufacturers. In such an environment H-D would need to work even harder to create value for its customers through enhancing the differentiation of its products and managing and communicating the Harley Experience. This must involve both the provision of explicit services – training, insurance, repair, service, and customization for its owners – and also activities that built the Harley family through HOG and the variety of company-sponsored rides and events.

The quest to recruit new riders represented a particular challenge for H-D. Bluestein believed that H-D's attributes of independence and ruggedness were particularly appealing to a younger user – a segment it considered as adrenalin-seeking, outdoors-loving, and physically active. Within this younger segment, two groups showed potential. First, friends and families of current motorcyclists. Second, new users who had no connection to the motorcycling industry. According to H-D president John Atwood at the introduction of the Buell Blast, "the first group sells itself and needs no preaching to the choir. The second group, the inexperienced novice and non-riders needed to be oriented, educated and informed."

In terms of product policy, appealing to this new segment meant emphasizing the traditional Harley style, but improving the products to meet the needs of buyers who had neither the time nor the skill nor the inclination to maintain, rebuild, and upgrade their own bikes. It also meant introducing new models. Here, a critical issue was whether H-D reputation and image could extend to radically new products such as the

Buell Blast without damaging that reputation and, even if successful, whether the new riders would remain loyal Harley customers.

Overseas markets provided some of the most significant challenges. Establishing distribution and dealership networks and supporting them with advertising and promotion involved substantial investment. At the same time, H-D's image and competitive position would inevitably differ between countries. How far should H-D seek to adapt its products and their marketing and distribution to the idiosyncrasies of different overseas markets, and did the market potential of these countries for Harleys justify these efforts? The quest for sales growth overseas posed a similar risk as expanding H-D's market base at home: how far could H-D go in expanding its appeal to younger consumers and overseas customers without undermining or losing sight of Harley-Davidson's core identity?

APPENDIX 1

Harley-Davidson, Summary of Financial Statements, 1994–8

Table 8.A1   Harley-Davidson: Selected items from financial statements, 1994–2000 ($ million, except per-share data)

	1994	1995	1996	1997	1998	1999	2000
Net sales	1,159	1,350	1,531	1,762	2,064	2,453	2,906
Gross profit	358	411	490	586	691	836	991
R&D	28.1	30.3	37.3	53.3	58.7	70.3	75.8
Selling, admin., engineering	(204)	(234)	(269)	(329)	(377)	(448)	(513.0)
Operating income	153.6	180.8	228.4	270.0	333.6	415.8	515.0
Of which:							
Financial services	—	3.6	7.8	12.4	20.0	28.0	37.2
Interest income	1.7	0.1	3.3	7.9	3.8	8.0	17.6
Other income/(expense)	1.2	(4.9)	(4.1)	(1.6)	(1.2)	(3.1)	16.0
Income before taxes	156.4	176.0	227.6	276.3	336.2	420.8	548.6
Provision for income taxes	60.2	64.9	84.2	102.2	122.7	153.6	n.a.
Net Income	104.3	112.5	166.0	174.1	213.5	267.2	347.7
Earnings per share (diluted)	$0.62	$0.73	$0.94	$1.13	$1.38	$1.73	$1.13
Balance sheets Assets	*1994*	*1995*	*1996*	*1997*	*1998*	*1999*	*2000*
Current assets							
Cash and cash equivalents	59.3	31.5	142.5	147.5	165.1	183.4	419.7
Finance receivable, net	—	169.6	183.8	249.3	319.4	354.9	580.9

Table 8.A1 *continued*

	1994	1995	1996	1997	1998	1999	2000
Accounts receivable, net	143.4	134.2	141.3	102.8	113.4	101.7	98.3
Inventories	173.4	84.4	101.4	117.5	155.6	168.6	191.9
Other	20.1	20.3	44.0	43.0	50.4	54.3	56.4
Total current assets	405.6	337.2	613.1	704.0	845.0	949.0	1,297.3
Property, plant, equipment	262.8	284.8	409.4	528.9	627.8	681.7	—
Total assets	739.2	1,000.7	1,230.0	1,598.9	1,920.2	2,112.1	2,436.4
Liabilities & stockholder's equity Current liabilities							
Current portion of finance debt	18.2	2.7	8.6	90.6	146.7	181.2	89.5
Accounts payable	64.0	102.6	100.7	106.1	122.7	137.7	—
Total current liabilities	216.3	233.2	251.1	361.7	468.5	518.2	497.7
Non-current liabilities							
Finance debt	0	164.3	258.1	280.0	280.0	280.0	355.0
Other long-term liabilities	89.7	108.6	70.3	62.1	67.4	65.1	97.3
Post-retirement benefits	n.a.	n.a.	65.8	68.4	72.1	75.7	80.7
Total stockholders' equity	433.2	494.6	662.7	826.7	1,029.9	1,161.1	1,405.7
Total liabilities & stockholders' equity	739.2	1,000.7	1,230.0	1,598.9	1,920.2	2,112.1	2,436.4
Cash flows	*1994*	*1995*	*1996*	*1997*	*1998*	*1999*	*2000*
Operating activities	80.8	169.1	228.3	309.7	318.1	416.1	565.5
Capital expenditures	(94.7)	(113.0)	(178.8)	(186.2)	182.8	165.8	(203.6)
Total investing activities	(96.6)	(187.8)	(213.8)	(406.5)	(340.2)	(299.6)	(171.0)
Financing activities	(2.6)	(10.5)	96.5	101.8	39.8	(98.3)	(158.1)
Net increase in cash	(18.4)	(26.4)	(111.0)	5.0	(17.6)	18.2	236.3

*Balance sheet information does not include current portion of finance receivables, net in current assets (1998 = 360.3 / 1999 = 441.0)

Source: Harley-Davidson financial statements (www.harley-davidson.com).

APPENDIX 2
Harley-Davidson's Competitors

Table 8.A2 Comparative financial data for Harley-Davidson, Polaris, Excelsior, Honda and BMW ($ million, except per-share data)

	Harley-Davidson			Polaris			Excelsior*			Honda			BMW		
	1997	1998	1999	1997	1998	1999	1997	1998	1999	1997	1998	1999	1997	1998	1999
Assets															
Current assets															
Cash	147.50	165.1	183.4	1.2	1.5	6.2	24.2	4.7		2,035	2,553	3,132	451	713	356
Trade receivables	102.79	113.4	101.7	42.6	43.0	53.3	0.0	0.0		2,525	1,463	1,609	443	475	503
Finance subsidiary receivables	293.33	360.3	441.0	0.0	0.0	0.0	0.0	0.0		11,261	6,524	7,175	—	3,112	2,588
Inventories	117.48	155.6	168.6	139.4	107.4	118.1	0.0	1.9		4,395	4,549	4,970	1,186	1,463	1,747
Other	42.96	50.4	54.3	34.1	31.9	37.1	0.1	0.5		5,458	2,303	2,773	2,900	642	—
Finance receivables (net)	249.35	319.4	354.9	0.0	0.0	0.0	0.0	0.0		—	—	—	—	—	—
Property and equipment (net)	528.87	627.8	681.7	98.0	229.5	275.6	13.4	30.3		8,387	8,811	9,518	2,662	2,623	2,576
Intangible assets (net)	38.70	n.a	n.a.	23.5	23.0	22.1	0.2	0.0		—	—	—	41	165	335
Other	77.96	n.a.	n.a.	45.8	26.6	38.3	10.2	10.6		536	—	—	3,041	3,117	1,751
Liabilities															
Current liabilities	361.69	468.5	18.2	91.0	204.9	233.8	3.3	10.2		14,516	16,751	18,791	4,816	2,849	2,031
Long-term debt	280.00	280.0	280.0	24.4	20.5	40.0	13.7	20.6		6,153	5,131	5,583.4	35	6	1

Other	130.54	139.5	140.8	0.0	0.0	0.0	0.0	0.0	1,956	2,198	2,546	2,146	4,191	4,375
Shareholders' equity	826.67	1,029.9	1,161.1	169.2	153.2	168.2	31.2	17.2	11,971	12,172	14,632	3,727	5,264	5,102
Sales	1,762.60	2,064	2,453	1,048.3	1,175.5	1,321.1	0.0	0.4	45,383	45,418	51,688	20,200	22,405	21,857
COGS	1,176.40	1,373	1,617	785.8	897.2	992.7	0.0	0.0	31,336	31,362	35,004	12,966	20,028	19,221
Gross profit	586.20	691.0	836.0	262.5	278.3	328.3	0.0	0.1	14,047	14,056	16,685	7,234	2,376	2,637
SG&A	262.91	291.1	337.9	142.7	149.8	183.4	3.9	23.3	8,119	10,556	12,133	7,725	2,846	3,015
R&D	53.30	65.9	82.1	26.7	28.4	31.3	2.6	—	2,211	n.a.	n.a.	n.a.	n.a.	n.a.
Operating income	323.29	399.5	497.9	93.1	100.1	113.6	(6.5)	(23.3)	3,717	3,500	4,532	506	508	489
Non-operating expenses:														
Interest expense (income)	(7.87)	(3.8)	(8.0)	2.8	3.0	4.3	0.0	0.0	194	n.a.	n.a.	—	106	282
Taxes	102.20	122.7	153.6	36.8	17.3	42.0	0.0	0.0	1,760	1,524	1,905	351	290	12
Other expenses (income)	1.57	1.2	3.1	(11.80)	(12.6)	(8.8)	(0.6)	0.7	(212)	3	116.4	(105)	5	-489
Net income	174.1	213.5	267.2	65.3	31.0	76.3	(5.8)	(23.9)	1,975	1,973	2,530	260	329	270
Net income per share	$1.15	$1.38	$1.73	$2.45	$1.19	$3.07	$(0.65)	(1.83)	n.a.	4.05	5.20	n.a.	n.a.	n.a.

* Excelsior does not have information for 1999 as a result of bankruptcy Chapter 11.

Accounts for Honda and BMW are company-wide accounts and includes car building and some other operations.

Exchange rates used: Yen/Dollar 1996: 124.08 yen/$; Yen/Dollar 1997: 130.10 yen/$; DM/Dollar 1996 and 1997: 1.77 DM/$; Euro/Dollar 1998: End-Y 1.77 DM/$; Euro/Dollar 1998: End-Y 0.885 Euro/$; Average 0.899 Euro/$; Euro/Dollar 1999: End-Y 0.996 Euro/$: Average 0.938 Euro/$.

Sources: www.harley-davidson.com; www.polarisindustries.com; http://sec.gov; www.honda.com; www.bmw.com.

■ EXCELSIOR HENDERSON MOTORCYCLE MANUFACTURING COMPANY (EXCELSIOR) ■

In the early 1990s two brothers, Dave and Dan Hanlon, bought the trademarks to a pre-war motorcycle manufacturer, Excelsior and Henderson. Formed in 1876, Excelsior Supply Co. was one of the top three US motorcycle manufacturers at the turn of the century along with Indian Motorcycle and Harley-Davidson. Its motorcycle was the first to break the 100 mph barrier. The company was liquidated during the Depression in 1931 and ever since the Hanlon brothers have been trying to resuscitate its image by manufacturing, marketing, and selling cruisers and touring bikes under the Excelsior brand name evoking "an authentic American motorcycling heritage and lifestyle".[16]

The Hanlons have developed a prototype of a retro-style cruiser with the latest technology and accessories, such as electronic fuel injection, a four-valve cylinder, and an overhead cam engine, named The Super X, to be sold at a sticker price between $17,000 and $20,000.

With no revenue generation and with reported losses of $5.9 million and $2.5 million in 1997 and 1996 respectively, the firm went public in 1997, raising $28 million in proceeds. These IPO funds, together with a $1.7 million State of Minnesota equipment financing bond, financed the construction of the company's new administrative and manufacturing facility in Belle Plain, Minnesota. Production started in 1998 (with 5,500 units of backorders), to be stopped in late 1999 when the firm filed Chapter 11 bankruptcy protection.

E. H. Partners, Inc. acquired the firm from Chapter 11 in September 2000 (the firm's public stockholders and founders did not retain an equity interest) and announced a reorganization plan that consisted in its restructuring, no manufacturing during 2001, and resuming motorcycle production for the 2002 year with the complete re-launch of the firm. Moreover, its dealership networks, owing to lack of support from the firm, have lost huge amounts in warranty repairs not reimbursed and the current availability of parts is almost terminated.

■ POLARIS ■

A leading snowmobile (world's largest manufacturer), ATV (all-terrain vehicle), and personal watercraft maker since the 1950s, and currently one of the largest US manufacturers, the firm has past success with taking on Japanese competitors. In the early 1990s, Polaris entered the personal watercraft and the ATV markets, both dominated by Japanese competitors – Kawasaki and Honda respectively. Since then, Polaris has gained the number two market share in ATV sales (37 percent of revenue), and challenged Kawasaki's dominance of the personal watercraft market by gaining significant market share and brand recognition.

Polaris launched a new cruiser, the Polaris Victory, in the spring of 1998 with a retro look and new technology, and targeting the high-margin, high-growth cruiser market dominated by Harley. High-tech engineering has "eliminated some of the noise and vibration associated with a Harley."[17] The Victory was positioned to compete with technologically advanced Honda, Suzuki, Kawasaki, and Yamaha cruisers on a price level above Japanese models. Polaris "competes with Japanese on price, quality, and technology." The company stresses its "made in the USA" appeal to attract customers away from these foreign competitors and is counting on its previous experience making personal watercraft and ATVs to beat the competition. According to CEO Wendel, "We met these guys in snowmobiles and ATVs and we beat their asses off."[18]

Polaris is a very efficient and aggressive company with high-tech manufacturing capabilities and a wide distribution network of 2,000 dealers (Victory Motorcycles are available at 300 dealers in the US, Canada and the UK). It reported a twelfth consecutive year of record net income. Net income for 2000 totaled $82.8 million (8 percent increase) and sales totaled a record $1,425.7 million (7 percent increase).

The firm entered the motorcycle industry leveraging its resources and capabilities: large distribution network, cross-selling opportunities, engineering and manufacturing capabilities, and low production costs. Engineering of the new cruiser was performed in-house, lowering development costs. Production and assembly takes place at two plants that had extra capacity, and the firm reaches break-even at 4,000 motorcycles per year (3 percent of the current cruiser market). Victory motorcycles sales more than tripled in 1999 and grew by 50 percent in year 2000.

Polaris anticipates becoming a significant player in the motorcycle market, developing a line of touring, cruiser, and performance bikes with projected sales of $500 million by 2003 and expanded capacity of 40,000–50,000 per year.[19] Polaris is known as an efficient, low-cost manufacturer.

■ TRIUMPH ■

Triumph,[20] a British manufacturer, began motorcycle production in 1902. By 1909 the company was producing 3,000 bikes per year and by the 1950s became one of the world's most renowned motorcycle brands (in part thanks to its appearance as Marlon Brando's bike in the classic movie *The Wild One*).

However, by the 1970s the company faced financial problems and was forced to liquidate in 1983. Primarily due to the efforts of its current head, John Bloor, the company revived in the early 1990s and began development and production of new models. In 1996 the company surpassed the 50,000 bikes production level (touring, cruisers) and unveiled plans to introduce a new performance motorcycle.

"Triumph is the greatest name, and only survivor, of the once internationally dominant British motorcycle industry." Triumph is about glamour and rebellion, about speed and performance. The company's most popular model (25 percent of production capacity) is a cruiser, Thunderbird. Thunderbird's styling is similar to that of the 1960s Triumph model with the same name and the bike is positioned to capture a part of the lucrative heavyweight cruiser market.

■ BMW ■

Even though motorcycles made only about 2.6 percent of total BMW sales income in 2000,[21] the company is committed to supporting and developing its line of bikes. With annual 2000 sales of 74,614 bikes, the company exported 69 percent of its motorcycles abroad, comparing to the 66 percent in 1999.

BMW Motorcycles celebrated its 75th anniversary in 1998 and its bikes have led the way to technical innovation, pioneering such things as advanced suspension systems, anti-lock brakes, and fuel injection.[22] Because of these technological innovations, BMW motorcycles have lower operating costs than the competition. In a comparison of Kawasaki and BMW touring bikes, the California Police Department estimated an operating cost of 1.9 cents per mile for the Kawasaki model tested, compared to an operating cost of 1.7 cents per mile for the BMW model tested.[23] The company has always been associated with a high technical and quality standard, and its motorcycles are also known for reliability, safety, and comfort.

BMW offers a full line of performance, touring, and cruiser bikes. Recently it has introduced its new concept model C1, which is designed to unite the mobility of the bike with safety of the car. The first cruiser, BMW R1200C, was introduced in 1997 as part of the latest James Bond movie,

Tomorrow Never Dies,[24] and became BMW's best-selling bike in its first model year.[25] R1200C includes the latest technological innovations and safety features; however, it departs from the retro look favored by other producers. In creating the bike, BMW assumed that in the future "high performance cruisers will replace retro-look customs with a sportier look and feel."[26] The R1200C was the first in this category. At a price of $14,500, the cruiser is priced about $1,000 below the range of comparable Harley models providing superior features such as anti-lock disk brakes, superior acceleration technology, and liquid-cooled engine.[27] Half of R1200C buyers are those who already own a Harley, and the other half are those who own a Japanese motorcycle.

BMW introduced the new luxury touring model K1200LT in 1999. This model also represents the "new" design concept of the modern look. Comparing to the competing models it offers superior comfort and user friendliness.

BMW motorcycles are positioned as a source of "undeniable pleasure and excitement of riding". The underlying idea is that BMW should provide the functionality of the bike with improved comfort and reliability features. In order to achieve this goal the company leverages the innovative car-building technologies of its 70,000 sq. feet R&D campus in Munich. As a result, BMW motorbikes have anti-block braking system (ABS), close-to-car comfort seats as well as enhanced cooling and battery systems to increase reliability of the engine during various riding conditions. Most of the BMW motorcycles are manufactured in the single plant located in the vicinity of Berlin. During the last year the plant was expanded to 2,400 workers (additional 320) to achieve the capacity of 400 items per day. A new C1 model is currently being built in the Carrozzeria Bertone factory.

■ HONDA ■

Honda Motor Co. has been manufacturing motorcycles since 1947 as a second tier player in an expansion cycle of the Japanese motorcycle industry given the need for cheap transportation means after World War II. The company entered the US market in 1959, first with cheaper, light-weight bikes, before quickly moving into the higher-priced segments such as performance and touring bikes. The company leveraged the experience obtained in its domestic market in advertising and distribution in its entrance to the US. Given its initial dependency on an exclusive dealership network in Japan, it decided to go directly to retailers. Moreover, it invested heavily in advertising directly to consumers, which gave Honda excellent results in its domestic market.[28] It achieved an extraordinary growth in the US market, increasing sales from $500 million in 1960 to $77 million in 1965 and shared with Yamaha and Suzuki 85 percent of the US market by 1966.[29] Honda has been the world's largest motorcycle manufacturer since 1959, with 5,190,000 bikes produced in 2000 (vs. 54,000 made by BMW and 204,592 made by Harley).[30] The company holds 26.5 percent of the total US motorcycle market, and enjoys the number one market share position. The firm's motorcycle sales have grown by 20 percent in 1999, reached 296,479 American Honda units sold in the US in 1999 (20 percent increase) compared to 158,817 sold by Harley, and 174,376 motorcycles in year 2000 (a record 34.5 percent increase) in an industry in which sales grew 27.3 percent.

Honda Motor's worldwide sales reached 5.16 million motorcycles in year 2000 and the company has the objective of achieving the 7 million mark by March 2004.[31] Worldwide sales have increased by approximately 20 percent and the decline in unit sales in Japan and Europe has been more than offset by the volume growth in Asian countries (specially India, Indonesia, and Thailand), as well as in North America.[32] Honda is the Japanese car and motorcycle manufacturer most dependent on the US market. Above 50 percent of its consolidated revenues in year 1999 derived from its US operations.

Honda is a superior engineering company and its motorcycles have traditionally been "on the leading edge of technology."[33] "Honda is, above all, an engine company,"[34] and the world's leader in four-stroke technology. The firm was capable of transferring these capabilities into a broad product offering (motorcycle, automobiles, and power products). Its performance bikes have dominated motorcycle racing for decades and are associated with the world's greatest racers. The innovations achieved from racing were adapted to its motorcycle products. In the early 1970s the company also had great success with street and touring bikes with the introduction of the style-setting CB750K0 in 1969 and the Goldwing, the world's first long-distance touring bike, in 1975.[35] Honda's capabilities of product innovation together with heavy investment in R&D, economies of scale, and efficient distribution enable it to develop technical superiority at a lower price. The firm has also committed the largest advertising budget in the industry and established, from early on, the largest dealership network in the US.[36] Its scale advantage together with high growth rates resulted in superior productivity that was translated into lower prices. Honda has experienced steep learning curves of 75–87 percent that enable the company to achieve real price reductions of around 50 percent or more over time.[37]

■ SMALLER COMPETITORS ■

Ducati,[38] a "highly regarded but underfunded [Italian] company," attracts customers by leveraging its legendary reputation for high-performance stylish motorcycles. Traditionally, the company has concentrated on the performance segment of the market and sells about 4,000 of these motorcycles in the US each year. However, in 1998 Ducati expanded into the touring bike market in an effort to double its sales.

Big Dog Motorcycles[39] produces high-end, customized cruisers for prices that often exceed those of comparable Harleys (between $18,000 and $26,000). The company produces 300 bikes per year and primarily sells to customers who do not want to "buy a Harley and put thousands of dollars in it to get it up to real world standards."

■ OTHER JAPANESE COMPETITORS ■

Several Japanese companies followed Honda's example and entered the US motorcycle market in the 1970s. Yamaha, Suzuki, and Kawasaki began with sales of small, lightweight motorcycles and moved into the "heavyweight" segments of cruisers and touring bikes. Most compete on technological innovation and low price driven by the economies of scale of these large companies. However, while these companies had great success in gaining share in the overall motorcycle market (see table 8.3), they have captured only 25 percent of the cruiser market, where the Japanese product competes less effectively against the "Made in the USA" Harley mystique.

NOTES

1. Boston Consulting Group, "Strategy alternatives for the British motorcycle industry," Her Majesty's Stationery Office, London, July 30, 1975; quoted in Richard T. Pascale, "Perspectives on strategy: the real story behind Honda's success," *California Management Review*, March 23 (Spring 1984), 47–72.
2. Peter Reid, "How Harley beat back the Japanese," *Fortune*, September 25, 1989.

3. Gary Strauss, "Born to be bikers," *USA Today*, November 5, 1997.
4. Marc Ballon, "Born to be wild," *Inc*, November 1997, p. 42.
5. Harley-Davidson, Inc. Annual Report, 2000.
6. http://www.harley-davidson.com/experience/family/hog.
7. *Motorcycle* magazine, 1998.
8. Marco R. della Cava, "Motorcycle maker caters to the continent," *USA Today*, April 22, 1998.
9. Ibid.
10. Kevin R. Fitzgerald, "Harley's supplier council helps deliver full value," *Purchasing*, September 5, 1996.
11. Ann Millen Porter, "One focus, one supply base," *Purchasing*, June 5, 1997.
12. Kevin R. Fitzgerald, "Harley's supplier council helps deliver full value," *Purchasing*, September 5, 1996.
13. Stephen Roth, "Harley's goal: unify union and management," *Kansas City Business Journal*, May 16, 1997.
14. Clyde Fessler (H-D VP for Business Development), "Rotating leadership at Harley-Davidson: from hierarchy to interdependence," *Strategy & Leadership*, July 17, 1997.
15. Ibid.
16. "Excelsior Henderson selects J. D. Edwards to provide smooth ride to growth," *Business Wire*, March 24, 1998.
17. Macario Juarez, "City business to help debut American Harley rival," *Albuquerque Tribune*, December 18, 1997.
18. Paul Klebnikov, "Clear the roads, here comes Victory," *Forbes*, October 20, 1997.
19. Strauss, "Born to be bikers."
20. http://www.georgian.net/rally/triumph.
21. http://www.bmw.com.
22. Richard Truett, "Motorcycling has long run in the BMW family," *The Orlando Sentinel*, March 5, 1998.
23. John O'Dell, "Giving chase: BMW wants to break Kawasaki's and Harley's hold on the police market," *Los Angeles Times*, September 21, 1997.
24. "BMW in control with Bond bike cruiser," *The San Diego Union Tribune*, March 14, 1998.
25. Truett, "Motorcycling has long run in the BMW family."
26. Adrian Blake, "Two motorcycle giants celebrate anniversaries," *The Toronto Star*, April 11, 1998.
27. Comparison of dealer suggested retail prices in the table 8.4.
28. Honda (B) Harvard Business School.
29. Honda (A) Harvard Business School.
30. http://www.honda.com; http://www.bmw.com; and table 8.1.
31. American Honda Reports Record Motorcycle Sales For 2000, February 2, 2001 (www.americanmotor.com).
32. Honda's Q2 2000 Motorcycle Sales Up-Overall Net Income Down November 16, 2000 (www.americanmotor.com).
33. Blake, "Two motorcycle giants."
34. American Honda Reports Record Motorcycle Sales For 2000, February 2, 2001 (www.americanmotor.com).
35. Ibid.
36. Honda (A) Harvard Business School.
37. Ibid.
38. Valerie Morris, "Ducati's market challenge," *Business Unusual*, CNN, April 17, 1998.
39. http://www.bigdogmotorcycles.com.

case nine

Online Broking Strategies: Merrill Lynch, Charles Schwab, and E*Trade

Anjali Bakhru and Ann Brown

The downturn of 2001 plunged the online brokerage industry into its first major crisis. The industry's previous five years of phenomenal growth, in volume of online accounts and stock trades, came to an abrupt halt. As the decade-long bull market stalled, order volumes plummeted, causing competition to intensify. The transition from boom to bust had especially dire implications for the new online brokerage firms. In the early years of the internet, from 1996 to 1998, internet share trading posed a major threat to the incumbent brokerage firms. The internet offered a new channel for individuals to trade stocks and shares with the obvious attractions of transaction efficiency, 24-hour trading and real-time provision of stock market information. The very survival of the existing broking firms was brought into question and massive upheavals seemed likely in the traditional broking industry. Yet, despite the influx of new internet brokerage firms – especially in the US where more than 150 had entered by the year 2000 – few traditional brokers disappeared. Instead the market expanded as new customers appeared and private clients increased the frequency of their trading. Incumbent broking firms began to adapt to the new channel provided by technology and exploit the changing market, with some success. By the start of the downturn, the industry looked very different from that of the mid-1990s. It also faced very different challenges: survival not growth was now the key issue.

By 2001, there were three major categories of player competing in the brokerage industry – all of which had entered into internet trading, though using different strategies. Among the traditional full-services brokers, Merrill Lynch ("Merrill") was pre-eminent. For over a century, Merrill operated as a successful full-service brokerage firm, offering a high-class service that includes advice on investment choices to seriously rich clients. Merrill added an online service in 1999. During the 1970s, a new

This case was prepared by Anjali Bakhru and Ann Brown of City University Business School, London. Copyright © 2002 A. Bakhru and A. Brown type of brokerage company, the discount brokers, emerged to challenge the traditional full-service firms. Charles Schwab ("Schwab") was the pioneer of the discount brokerage model and by far the most successful of the discount brokers. Investors were left to manage their own investments, with Schwab offering various customer services like stock market information and a cut-price trading service. Schwab was greatly experienced in developing new channels to its clients and advisors, introducing PC-based online trading in 1984, and in 1996 starting a range of telephone-based services and internet online trading. During the 1990s, the revolution in communications technology created a new type of broker. E*Trade was the pioneer of internet online broking – a mode of securities trading that offered massive cost savings as well as convenience for investors. By 2001, E*Trade and other internet brokers had gained a major share of the retail brokerage business, primarily in the US, but increasingly in Europe, Japan, and other advanced economies too.

The weakening economy and stock market correction of 2001 was a shock to the industry. For Merrill, which added its online service late, as an add-on trading and communications channel for existing clients, the drop in volume sales was likely to be less of a threat than for Schwab and E*Trade, which had embraced internet share dealing more fully. For Schwab and E*Trade, the reduction in trading volumes was serious. Their future profitability was closely linked to continued transactions growth. The downturn would adversely affect both revenues and their relative costs. If the downturn of 2001 marked an end to the long-running bull market, it remained to be seen whether a strategy that was successful in the golden years of 1991 to 2000 could weather hard times. During 2001, all three companies were forced to reassess their strategies in the light of the changing industry environment. Underlying these reconsiderations was the fundamental issue of which business model was likely to be most successful within the brokerage industry in the future, and whether all three business models could co-exist through focusing upon different customer segments.

■ THE IMPACT OF THE INTERNET ON THE BROKERAGE INDUSTRY ■

It is not difficult to understand the optimism of the early forecasts for online share dealing. Many of the key characteristics of the internet made this channel look attractive for share trading. It offered many new ways to communicate and provide information – a key element of brokers' service offerings. Since securities broking involved no shipment of physical goods – it was even possible to dispense with paper documents – the internet provided an ideal medium for the industry. The ability to reach anyone with access to the web made trading available to a vastly expanded set of potential customers. The ability to simplify transactions through electronic capture and transmission of transaction data offered cheaper administrative costs and hence lower fees for execution of trades. Lower transaction costs made it possible for brokerage companies to make money from investors with low levels of net worth and small securities portfolios. The greatest virtue of the internet – its ability to disseminate information to any number of individuals simultaneously and almost instantaneously – proved of great value. Real-time stock market information, for example, previously only available to professionals, could be made available to everyone. The growth in the range and scope of information provided both by online brokers to clients and by investors to other investors was one of the most extraordinary phenomena of the online broking sector. The distributive power of the internet was also a source of new investor benefits – they could download software tools, like portfolio management packages, that help them manage their own investments.

During the late 1990s it seemed that this new channel would create major upheavals in the brokerage industry. It was destined to alter the balance of power in favor of the customer and challenge the traditional giant broking firms like Merrill. However, by mid-2001, the brokerage industry had evolved in some unexpected and intriguing ways.

Emerging Customer Segments and Business Models

After more than five years' experience of online trading, a number of new customer segments had emerged to join the original group of high net worth investors. The mass affluent – generally defined as those households with at least $100,000 (£70,000) to invest – became identified in the late 1990s as a potentially lucrative market. More than 10 percent of all households in developed economies fall into this category. In the US, rapid growth in the number of individuals opening brokerage accounts resulted in at least half the population having investments in the stock market. The growth in the number of small investors was accompanied by the development of websites such as www.fool.com, www.stockhouse.com, www.moneyextra.com, which not only offered stock market information and comment but also created chat rooms for their registered visitors. The ordinary investor could now talk to others, exchange experiences, and access up-to-the-minute company information and expert analysis. The result was growing fragmentation of the brokerage market. Customers could be segmented not just by net worth, but also by their investment styles and investment needs in terms of information and support services. How best to service each of these segments to meet their needs and generate profits for the broker was an open question.

The changes in the market – in particular, the rapid growth in the number and types of individual investors – was partly a result of the economic expansion and political changes during the 1990s[1] and partly a result of the strategies adopted by the broker-age firms. Until the 1990s, the industry had been dominated by a single business model associated with "full service" provision through brokers located in retail offices. The customers were primarily affluent individuals who were supplied with tailored services that comprised personalized advice on investment strategies and individual invest-ments. This advice drew upon sophisticated, in-house analysis of companies and their securities. Clients were assigned to individual brokers who were responsible for man-aging their clients' portfolios, executing their instructions, and providing investment advice. The basic service differs little between brokerage companies. The main differ-ences lie in clients' perceptions of their credibility and expertise. For these "full service" firms, retail broking is only one component of their business. Most are investment banks offering multiple services to corporate clients. Private client broking can be valu-able as a distribution channel for new stock and bond issues underwritten by the bank.

Retail clients are charged fees that tend to be based on accounts rather than trades. Revenues come from the yearly commission per account based on asset value, interest earned on cash kept in accounts, and other commissions from executing trades.

The online brokers adopted a very different strategy which involved offering the basic support services that their customers needed to manage their own investments and execute trades as specified by the client. This was, essentially, a "do-it-yourself" model of investing. Contact with the company was mainly online. Customer support included information and software investment tools. The foundation of this model was technology – for the online brokers to succeed required customer confidence in the reliability and security of the IT systems that executed trades and delivered customer support.

In between these two distinct approaches lay a spectrum of alternatives with levels of personal service that varied from web-based support and telephone advisors to face-to-face contact with brokers. The discount brokers have led the way in developing these models. Discount brokers that emerged during the 1970s and 1980s offering a variant on the traditional model – fewer research and advice services in return for lower commissions. However, like the full-service brokers, they provided their services through brokers located in local retail offices. The emergence of internet and digital telephone services allowed the discount brokers the opportunity to diversify their communication and transactions media through the addition of internet links and automated telephone service. Figure 9.1 depicts the different business models.

While the major traditional brokers were also investment banks, discount and online brokers were essentially distributors of financial products. For these companies, income derived from three main sources: commission on trades, interest income derived from the difference between interest payments to clients on their cash balances and the interest earned on margin loans, and a portion of the market-makers bid–ask spread. Total income, therefore, was significantly affected by trading volumes and size of clients' investment assets. For discount brokers total income was also affected by commission rates which varied between their different service channels and service levels.

Technological advance tended to increase the cost efficiency advantages of the online model over the traditional model. The online brokers were pioneering the integration of client transactions with market execution. Direct Access Trading ("DAT") represented the next generation of online trading, which allowed for direct and instant market access. DAT allowed a client to trade directly with an exchange such as NASDAQ or through an Electronic Communication Network ("ECN"), where the latter were essentially private trading systems that potentially could provide the platform for global access to 24 hours-a-day, real-time trading.[2] ECNs already competed with the traditional exchanges, where they accounted for approximately one-third of total share volume and 40 percent of the dollar volume traded in NASDAQ securities and around 3 percent of total share and dollar volume in listed securities.[3]

Successful Strategies for Online Internet Brokers?

By 1998, the future of online trading looked assured. The volume of online securities trading was growing rapidly and a broad measure of consensus existed regarding the conditions for success for an internet brokerage firm.

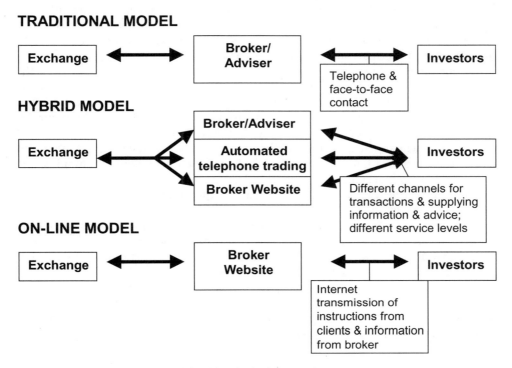

Figure 9.1 Alternative business models within the brokerage industry

Like other dot.com companies of that period, the early internet online broker entrants were obsessed with the critical need for rapid growth in customer accounts. The argument for this strategy was based on solid grounds. The automation of transaction processing resulted in high fixed costs but relatively low marginal costs; hence economies of scale were substantial. As the volume of transactions increased, so these fixed costs were spread over a larger volume of business, hence marginal costs also fell. In addition, there was the critical mass argument. Online brokers derived substantial revenue from sources other than trading fees. These non-commission revenues grew with the number of accounts, admittedly at a diminishing rate. However, marginal costs were also decreasing – usually at a faster rate. Various estimates attempted to find the critical number at which revenue/account exactly balanced cost/account. At this point the broker could be profitable with zero commissions, i.e., free trading. It was thought that the firms that achieved this first would be in a dominant position. This led to further speculation that only a small number of online brokers would survive when this point was reached. These considerations fueled a battle for market share in which all the online brokers spent hugely on marketing to obtain brand recognition and build market share. Evidence suggested that spending on marketing did yield results in terms of growth of customer accounts.

Price competition was fierce in the early years. For example, E*Trade cut commissions seven times in the four years up to 1998. The lower costs of transactions online made this possible but the strong belief in the need to maximize volume growth fueled the entrant firms' commitment to this policy.

Despite the intensity of competition in both advertising and commission rates, the potentially disastrous effects of this competition was offset by the rapid growth of the market. Most of the accounts opened by the online brokers were to new investors – but how long could this growth continue? Most forecasts of the growth of online securities trading were based upon projections of the number of internet users. The exponential growth of internet use during the latter half of the 1990s resulted in expectations that internet securities transactions would also follow an exponential growth trend for the foreseeable future (taken to be around 2002).

The critical role that technology played in supporting online transactions was recognized early by the online brokerage firms. Customers valued security, reliability, speed, ease of use, and integrity of data records. System failure for any reason could be a major factor in losing clients. The choice between building systems in-house or working with an IT vendor could affect success in two ways – performance and capital cost. This was a resource that received much attention.

In the same way that quality of service was a key success factor for full-service brokers, online brokers also accepted the need to compete on added value services like provision of information, new products, and software tools to help portfolio management. The only difference was that these services were web-based.

■ THE THREE COMPANIES ■

Until the downturn of the global equity market at the beginning of 2001, the three companies, Merrill, Schwab and E*Trade, prospered. The threat to the traditional broking industry had not developed as expected; instead new online business models appear to co-exist successfully with full-service broker models. In the following section, we describe recent developments at each of the three brokers.

Merrill Lynch

The investment banking giant, Merrill Lynch & Co., Inc., traced its origins back to 1820. It had offices in 44 countries and total client assets of around $1.6 trillion. Merrill was a late convert to the internet. For several years it seemed trapped on the horns of a dilemma. If it did not offer online trading it would continue to lose clients to the online brokers. If it did offer online trading, what would become of its army of 17,000 brokers, and how could it hope to maintain its client fee structure for its traditional broker service? It was not until the hiring of Michael Packer, a former senior executive at Bankers Trust, as a technology consultant that the firm overcame its paralysis and began to embrace the internet. A group was formed with the mission of developing a technology-based system for retail broking to be in place by the end of 1999.[4] The group was led by another new hire, John McKinley from GE. Momentum gathered and

Table 9.1 Comparison of broking fees

	Online	Telephone
Merrill Lynch	For fee-based, full-service customers, trading is free; for anyone else, $29.95 per trade	
Charles Schwab	(Schwab.com) $29.95 up to 1,000 shares or $0.03 per share for trades over 1,000 shares	TeleBroker® and VoiceBroker® start at $30 + 1.7% of principal for trades up to $2,499
E*Trade	$14.95 per trade for listed stocks & $19.95 for NASDAQ stocks for the first 29 trades	

Source: Casewriters' research.

progress was helped along by the acquisition of D.E. Shaw's discount brokerage in early 1999. By December 1999, the new web-based product was complete.

For Merrill, the opportunity provided by the internet was two-fold. Development of online services enabled it to retain its existing client base as well as attract new clients from the fast-growing affluent customer segment and, additionally, the spill-over effects of embracing internet technology were significant for Merrill's institutional business. Merrill offered two main online services: Merrill Lynch On Line® and Merrill Lynch Direct™. The former service offered clients, by its own admission, the best of both worlds – the convenience of online account access and the advice of a Merrill Lynch Financial Advisor. The latter service offered online transactions, but without the advisory service. Product pricing was simple: for fee-based, full-service customers using Merrill Lynch On Line, trading was free; while for clients of Merrill Lynch Direct, the cost was $29.95 per trade for US equities. Table 9.1 compares the fees of the three brokerage firms. Clients could also have online access to cash management services and Merrill's research. For Merrill's full-service customers, a fee was charged at a rate of 1 percent of equity and mutual fund assets and 0.3 percent of cash and fixed income assets. The rates declined with increasing asset size. The minimum annual fee was $1,500. In return, clients received a personalized service from a Merrill financial advisor as well as unlimited broking transactions at no additional charge, where orders can be placed via a consultant, the telephone or internet.

TECHNOLOGY

Merrill offered a variety of sophisticated tools, such as personalized Watch Lists and securities trackers. Clients could also consolidate information from all their financial service providers on My Financial Picture, which provided an easy way of sharing this information with their advisor to enhance the level of advice and guidance received. Research and information could also be received as a wireless service from Merrill

Mobile. Given that new customers were likely to be drawn to the Merrill Lynch Direct service, Merrill offered the Merrill Lynch Educational Channel on its website, to afford investors the opportunity to learn the basics of financial planning and investing.

PARTNERSHIPS

Given that Merrill was already a full-service broker, which was part of a larger investment banking group, its online services were developed internally for the most part. However, at the end of 2000, Merrill outsourced its mortgage origination and servicing operations to Cendant on a private label basis to provide an enhanced array of services to its clients nationwide. May 2001 further saw a new UK online banking and stockbroking joint venture between Merrill Lynch and HSBC – one of the world's biggest banks.[5] This service was targeted at the mass affluent, self-directed investor, with a minimum investment amount of £10,000 in cash and securities. Clients were offered access to their accounts online and by telephone, as well as through a physical network of investment centers. Merrill aimed to become a broad-based provider of financial services to its retail clients. To this end it worked with a variety of partners to encourage cross-selling of its own financial services and offerings from partners. The rewards program linked to its Visa Signature card offered discounts on goods and services from its partner companies together with the added benefit of reward points. Similarly, through its online service, Merrill offered clients similar partner offers.

RESPONDING TO THE MARKET DOWNTURN

Merrill was one of the most successful and largest securities houses, with group net earnings of nearly $4 billion in 2000 (table 9.2). The market downturn of 2001 soon forced Merrill to downgrade its earnings forecasts. At the end of June it announced that its second quarter revenues would be approximately 15 percent lower than those of its previous 2001.[6] However, Merrill was not as vulnerable to a fall in trading volume as other brokers since its pricing system was based on fees linked to portfolio value rather than charges for specific transactions.

However, the likelihood of prolonged market weakness encouraged Merrill to question its online strategy. Online broking had been offered as part of a market segmentation approach: Merrill was offering internet-based enhancements to its traditional customers while targeting Merrill Lynch Direct at a new customer segment where it competed directly with other deep-discount, online brokers. What were the strategic options facing Merrill? Should it continue with a market segmentation approach targeting both affluent and mass-market customers, even if its discounted online service threatened its traditional advisory business? Or should it refocus on its wealthiest clients, those with $1 million or more to invest, and offer online broking simply as an add-on transaction channel for these clients? According to a report published by the firm in May, the wealth of high net worth individuals around the world rose 6 percent to $27 trillion in 2000, despite declines in global equity markets.[7]

Table 9.2 Merrill Lynch: Consolidated statement of earnings (in $ millions, except per share amounts)

	2000	1999	1998
Revenues:			
Commissions	$6,977	$6,355	$5,814
Principal transactions	5,995	4,752	2,850
Investment banking	4,049	3,614	3,265
Asset management	5,688	4,753	4,202
Other	967	746	650
	23,676	20,220	16,781
Net Interest	3,111	2,101	1,018
Net revenues	26,787	22,321	17,799
Non-interest expenses:			
Compensation & benefits	13,730	11,337	9,308
Communications & technology	2,320	2,053	1,758
Occupancy	1,006	953	881
Advertising & market development	939	783	690
Brokerage, clearing & exchange fees	893	779	764
Professional fees	637	571	559
Goodwill amortization	217	227	227
Provisions for staff reductions costs	—	—	430
Other	1,328	1,412	1,062
	21,070	18,115	15,679
Earnings before income taxes & dividends	5,717	4,206	2,120
Income tax expense	1,738	1,319	725
Net earnings	3,784	2,693	1,271
Net earnings (common stockholders)	3,745	2,654	1,233
Diluted net earnings per common share	$4.11	$3.11	$1.49

Source: Company financial statements.

Charles Schwab

Charles Schwab was incorporated in 1971 and entered the discount brokerage business in 1974 prior to the SEC's (US regulatory body) abolition of fixed commissions in 1975. Always a leader rather than a follower, Schwab began online trading in 1984, although it didn't go live with internet trading until 1996. By 2001, Schwab held more than 7.2 million active customer accounts with total assets worth $805.8 billion at the end of March 2001, and of these, around 4.1 million accounts are online with 81 percent of total trades conducted online. With a US branch network of 398 offices, Schwab has continued to expand both its product range and geographical coverage – it launched its Australian subsidiary at the end of 2000.

Schwab pursued a multi-channel strategy, aimed at providing a wide selection of choices for its clients' investment needs through online and telephone broking as well as a personal broker service provided by its network of offices. Telephone access was in two forms: automated telephone channels or through a service that allowed customers to talk to a firm representative. The latter was organized through five regional client telephone service centers and two online client support centers that operated both during and after market hours. Automated services include Telebroker®, which was Schwab's touch-tone telephone quote and trading system, and Schwab by Phone™, which was Schwab's voice recognition quote and trading service. Online broking services for retail clients were via www.schwab.com, although there was also Cyber Trader's integrated software-based trading platforms for highly active investors as well as a wireless service, Pocket Broker™.

The launch of internet technology provided Schwab with an opportunity to tap into new customer markets while maintaining telephone and branch-based service. The effectiveness of its "bricks-and-clicks" strategy is indicated by the fact that over 70 percent of new accounts were opened at its individual retail branches. Customer education was a key component of Schwab's online offering. Web Shops, which were introduced in 1999, were the first in a series of educational workshops designed to help investors increase their skills in using Schwab's online services. In mid-2001, Schwab had offered approximately 2,700 WebShops, teaching investors how to invest online. A recent variation on this theme was the Schwab Gift Package, which combined an educational toolkit with a low-minimum balance brokerage account designed for young people.

However, while continuing to attract new investors, Schwab was reorienting its customer focus increasingly on the growing numbers of "mass affluent" individuals both in the US and overseas, where surveys showed that up to a quarter of mass affluent investors were prepared to make their own financial decisions with little or no advice, with almost half of these wired to the internet[8]. Since the launch of its Signature Services program in 1999, targeted at mass affluent investors, Schwab had designed a new annuity product, which was intended as a retirement supplement for clients who had maximized contributions to individual retirement accounts (IRAs) or 401K accounts. Schwab Advisor Source was also launched, which refers customers with more investable assets who seek a higher level of investment advice. In this case, clients needed a minimum of $100,000 to use the service, which offered referral to over 400 advisors. More than 16,000 new and existing clients were referred in 1999 alone. Schwab's upmarket movement was reinforced with its acquisition of US Trust, America's leading specialist private bank. However, this acquisition also created overlap between US Trust's private banking services and Schwab's investment advisory services to affluent individuals. Schwab's investment advisory services included custodial, trading, and support services that were offered to about 5,700 independent investment managers who together guided the investments of around a million Schwab accounts containing $224.2 billion in assets at the end of March 2001. Schwab's ability to appeal to affluent investors remained an issue. A recent survey by Siegelgale, a New York branding and marketing strategy agency, showed that Schwab's appeal dropped off among the wealthiest clients – it ranks first in households with income between $35,000 and $74,000, but only ninth in households with incomes of $75,000 and over.

TECHNOLOGY STRATEGY

Technology was at the core of Schwab's online strategy: it provided the basis for Schwab's extension and improvement of its service offerings such as Mutual Fund One Source, which made available nearly 1,300 funds with no-load, no-transaction fees from around 250 fund families. The Analyst Center connected customers to proprietary and third-party investment research and decision-making tools, while the Mutual Fund Performance Profile allowed customers to analyze the performance of their entire mutual fund portfolio. A new strategy called Core & Explore further enabled customers to build a core portfolio of index mutual funds and, as they became more knowledgeable, they could explore actively managed funds. A recent development during the first quarter of 2001 was Stock Explorer, an online screening tool which enabled clients to identify equities that met certain screening criteria according to the investment strategy selected. This tool mimicked the advisory function of a personal broker.

At the same time, systems had to respond to the challenge of varying capacity demands. 1999 was a major growth year for Schwab, with total customer assets up 48 percent on the previous year to $725 billion and with the number of new accounts expanding by 1.5 million to reach a total of 6.6 million accounts at year end. This growth necessitated a $126 million investment in information and communication systems which doubled transaction-processing capacity as well as enabling the website to cope with a single-day record of 78 million website hits in December of that year.

It is not surprising that, given Schwab's focus on multi-channel delivery, the company tended to focus on internal development of its technology to ensure high levels of control and integration. Its recent move to collaborate with outside providers was justified by Schwab's need to enhance existing services, such as its My Accounts service which utilized technology from Yodlee Inc. to aggregate online financial information for clients and enable them to analyze and manage that information within one password-protected site. Similarly, Phrase, a provider of the first dynamic website navigation and precise search platform, was selected by Schwab to be used on the company's websites in an attempt to make the information provided by Schwab easier to access by its customers. Most importantly, Schwab entered into a technology alliance with Ericsson in 2000 to develop wireless trading applications. In fact, Schwab has led the way in committing to the development of wireless broking, believing that wireless services will take off once devices can be "always on" with GPRS (General Packet Radio Service) instead of users having to dial up for access. "We don't think there will be such a thing as a wireless investor. It will not be the only channel. It will be part of an integrated channel concept – people want to be able to access services when, where and how they want" (Robert Sofman, senior VP of global wireless at Charles Schwab).[9]

STRATEGIC ALLIANCES

Between 1999 and 2001, Schwab became more active in forming partnerships and alliances with other companies. Myschwab.com was created in collaboration with the leading portal, Excite, in 1999 to offer a free personal web page service, where

Table 9.3 Schwab's trading volume, 2001 versus 2000

(All figures in 000s)	3 months ended	
	31 March 2001	31 March 2000
Daily average trades:		
Online	204.3	304.0
Telebroker and Schwab by phone	9.5	13.5
Regional client telephone service centers, branch offices and other	<u>39.7</u>	<u>69.1</u>
	253.5	386.6
Active online accounts (millions)	4.3	3.7
Online Schwab client assets ($ billions)	327.9	417.7
Daily average trades (000s)	195.8	310.0
Mutual Fund One*Source*® trades (000s)	57.7	76.6
Total daily average trades	253.5	386.6

Source: www.schwab.com.

customers could create a customized website. This was followed in October 2000 with Schwab forming a global alliance in October 2000 with AOL: Schwab offered investment tools and information to several AOL brands, while Schwab sought to attract new clients from among AOL's 28 million members using special offers, incentive awards, and promotions. Schwab further formed a strategic alliance with E-LOAN Inc. to provide mortgage products to its online clients. Earlier in 2001, it also entered into a joint venture with rival broker, TD Waterhouse, to engage in securities market-making in the UK through the acquisition of a mid-sized UK market-maker, the Glasgow-based Aitken Campbell, for £60 million.

RESPONSES TO THE MARKET DOWNTURN

Weakness in equity markets tends to negatively impact mass-market retail brokers that focus on wealthier private clients. Small investors tend to have less diversified investment portfolios and are more likely to withdraw from equity markets in a downturn. Schwab, whose success was based heavily upon the huge expansion in the number of small investors during the last two decades of the twentieth century, was particularly vulnerable to declining equity markets. Falling trading volumes during 2001 hit Schwab financial performance heavily: trading revenues in the first quarter of 2001 were down 51 percent year-on-year, with total revenues down 30 percent. (See tables 9.3 and 9.4.)

Table 9.4 Charles Schwab Corporation: Consolidated Statement of Income (in thousands, except per share amounts)

	Year Ended December 31		
	2000	1999	1998
Revenues:			
Commissions	2,294,145	1,874,594	1,318,103
Asset management & admin fees	1,583,098	1,220,346	936,796
Interest revenue, net of interest expense[1]	1,237,100	819,790	577,643
Principal transactions	570,207	500,496	286,754
Other	103,101	71,193	58,574
Total	5,787,651	4,486,419	3,177,870
Expenses excluding interest:			
Compensation & benefits	2,414,480	1,888,414	1,374,436
Other compensation	38,703		
Occupancy & equipment	415,356	306,900	236,232
Communications	353,044	278,509	216,389
Advertising & market development	332,311	247,808	159,784
Depreciation & amortization	261,732	174,651	152,107
Professional services	254,549	184,470	114,097
Commissions, clearance & floor brokerage	138,038	100,132	87,273
Merger-related	68,986		
Goodwill amortization	45,544	6,419	6,443
Other	233,435	200,201	153,471
Total	4,556,178	3,387,504	2,500,232
Income before income taxes	1,231,473	1,098,915	677,638
Income taxes	513,336	432,469	267,129
Net income	718,137	666,446	410,129
Weighted average common shares outstanding*	1,403,763	1,373,030	1,342,895
Diluted earnings per share ($)	0.51	0.49	0.31
Dividends per share ($)	0.0407	0.0373	0.0360

[1] $1,351,776 in 2000, $898,219 in 1999, and $773,998 in 1998.
* All periods have been restated to reflect merger of The Charles Schwab Corp. with US Trust Corp., as well as the May 2000 three-for-two stock split.
Source: Company financial statements.

In February 2001, Schwab began encouraging its employees to take time off in an attempt to avoid layoffs. Fridays were abolished for three weeks, with half of Schwab's 26,000 employees told to start their weekends early with days off taken as holiday or unpaid leave.[10] By March, however, the trading situation had worsened and Schwab announced that it was going to fire 13 percent of its employees and, through layoffs and attrition, the workforce was cut by 14 percent to 22,597 during the first half of 2001, the biggest layoffs occurring in the call centers. Schwab also announced proposals for reducing lease commitments for office space, as well as removing from service certain systems hardware. Charles Schwab and 750 of his top managers were not exempt from the cutbacks: all received salary cuts of between 5 and 50 percent for January and February. The one exception to all this was the marketing budget; it was reported that Schwab was still going to spend the same amount on marketing in 2001 – around $330 million – as in the previous year.[11] Given that client daily average trades continued to go down, with trading volume in the first eight days of June down 21 percent from May, the company was forced to consider the need for a more radical and permanent downsizing of its operations.

The severity of the downturn in Schwab's business brought into question the robustness of its strategy. Schwab had pursued a successful multi-channel strategy, where the use of technology has been central to its strategy of enhancing its offering to a broad segment of investors. Its current positioning towards the mass affluent investor did, however, carry risks. Could Schwab differentiate its service offering further and obtain higher fees from a more select and stable investor base, or would it get "stuck in the middle" in between Merrill Lynch (and other full-service brokers) at one end of the investor spectrum and E*Trade and the deep-discount brokers at the other, where price competition was ferocious?

E*Trade

E*Trade was the pioneer of internet trading and a "pure play" entrant. Its success had been rapid: transaction revenues were over $739 million in 2000 (table 9.5) and the company had enhanced its respectability by transferring its listing from the NASDAQ to the New York Stock Exchange early in 2001, less than five years since its IPO on August 16, 1996. From a mere 91,000 customer accounts at the time of listing, in March 2001, E*Trade reported over 3.7 million active customer accounts, total customer assets of $47.9 billion, and 3,800 employees. Growth had been explosive – the number of customer accounts had almost doubled during 2000.

The company launched its new financial portal site, Destination E*Trade, in late 1998 along with a "state-of-the-art" new customer support center. Convenience of access had always been a priority of E*Trade, where customers could access the system through the internet, CompuServe, Prodigy internet, Microsoft Investor, WebTV, direct modem connection, and TELE*MASTER® – their proprietary touchtone and speech recognition telephone investing system. With the opening of the E*Trade Knowledge Center in 1999, E*Trade directed its attention to younger customers who were new to investing. There were two types of accounts: an E*Trade account or a Power E*Trade account, the latter designed for more active investors where commissions per trade declined with the frequency of transactions down to $4.95 per trade for 75 trades or more per calendar quarter. However, like Schwab, E*Trade sought to extend its money management services. It acquired Private Accounts to provide low-cost, direct access to nationally recognized money managers and timely access to portfolio information. It also launched E*Trade Personal Money Management, an online investment resource that allowed investors to search for, compare, and hire professional money managers via the internet. It was available at a low cost to customers with a minimum of $100,000. The OptionsLink service was also launched in early 2001. This provided employees with a means to exercise stock options through activating a margin account and conducting cash exercises on margin, thus helping those who do not have the required funds to exercise their stock options without any cash outlay.

E*Trade was heavily dependent on revenues from brokerage commissions, and vulnerable to any downturn in trading volume since its low commissions implied a high "critical mass" – the point at which a firm is profitable while charging no commissions at all. E*Trade's vulnerability to a market downturn was exacerbated by the fact that a decline in trading volumes typically results in increased price competition among internet brokers. June 2001 saw the launch of www.brokerageamerica.com, which offered investors a rebate on every equity transaction plus commission-free trading for all US equity market orders. It was able to do this by combining brokerage and market-making operations under one roof. It would be a "no-frills" approach, with neither equity research nor other add-ons. E*Trade's response was to diversify its revenues. It developed E*Trade Bank which, with $11 bn in assets and $5 bn in deposits, was the largest pure-play internet bank and the US's 19th largest savings bank. Not only did the bank offer fully integrated banking and broking services, but customer convenience was further enhanced with E*Trade Access, the third largest ATM network in the USA with around 9,600 ATMs. The success of the bank was owed, in part, to gains from cross-selling efforts to the broking customer base, with around 63 percent of net new accounts representing brokerage customers. At year end 2000, the bank's growth rate in deposits was 116 percent over the previous 12 months, with customer acquisition costs down to under $117 per account from $190 a year previously. The acquisition of Loans Direct, the mortgage origination platform, was also successful – during first quarter 2001, the company tripled its volume of loans and generated a volume increase of more than $600 million compared to the same quarter in 2000. The low interest rate environment had expanded the demand for home loans, and the mortgage banking business provided a source of assets for E*Trade Bank.[12] In early 2001, E*Trade Bank further entered into the first virtual banking partnership customized for employees of Oracle Corp. An E*Trade Access ATM was set up on Oracle's Redwood Shores campus, and Oracle employees were targeted by customized internet banking products. Through a co-branded website, employees were able to research and access the products and services created exclusively for them. At the same time, E*Trade Bank aimed to target many of the 3,600 corporate clients of E*Trade Business Solutions, while more than one million employees participated in the options administration program of E*Trade Business Solutions.

The company also expanded geographically: as of May 2001, E*Trade served customers in Australia, Canada, Denmark, Hong Kong, Israel, Korea, Japan, Norway,

South Africa, Sweden, the UK, and the US through branded websites. Recent overseas expansion included joint ventures such as that with Softbank Corp. in Japan (October 1999) and Korea (February 2000), as well as new operations in South Africa and Sweden. During 2001 E*Trade launched in Hong Kong after initially entering the Hong Kong market in 1999 with the acquisition of TIR Securities, an institutional broker with seats on multiple global exchanges. E* Trade also inaugurated its expansion into the Middle East with a subsidiary in Israel – an attractive market for E*Trade in view of Israel's high rate of internet usage (nearly 20 percent of Israel's population was online in 2001). The Hebrew and English language site offered online trading of US stocks with plans to add trading on the Tel Aviv Stock Exchange later in 2001.[13] Orders were processed in real time using the company's proprietary technology with customers able to use a multi-currency (Shekel and/or US dollar) trading account.

Through its business diversification and geographical expansion, E*Trade increased its physical presence. In addition, the company announced in 2001 that it would become the exclusive ATM network for all Target stores through its E*Trade Access subsidiary, with the aim of installing over 1,000 units during 2001 and 2002. In addition, the company agreed to open E*Trade Zones (400 square foot E*Trade stores) in 20 Super Target stores in 2001. It also planned to open a new "super store" in New York City, where visitors would have access to their accounts through 200 computers and via three ATMs on-site. The center would include a café, gift shop, bookshop, and access to E*Trade On Air's daily broadcasts on market conditions. Financial advisors would be available for high net worth clients, and educational seminars would be held on-site.[14] As Chairman and CEO, Christos Cotsakos, explained:

> In the changing market environment, it's important for investors to know they have both electronic and physical access to information, products and services to meet their individual investment needs.

TECHNOLOGY

E*Trade's success as an online broker was based upon its development of proprietary transaction-processing technology and an IT infrastructure based on a modular architecture that was scaleable to handle increasing transaction volumes. Recent development included the enhancement of E*Trade Account Express (the first real-time account opening and funding service that allowed customers to open and fund an account electronically) by increasing the cash amount that new customers could initially invest as well as enabling faster and easier transfer of additional funds to E*Trade. New customers could begin investing within minutes with their buying power increased from $2,000 to $5,000. Market Caster, a new applet product, provided brokerage customers with free, streaming, real-time stock quotes. Customers were able to set up one or more customized watch lists and monitor the performance of stocks without having to refresh their computer screen. Market Trader was also a new tool, aiming to provide all *Power E*Trade* customers with streaming NASDAQ Level II quotes, integrated trading and personal account information in a single screen. It was offered to E*Trade's most active traders – those who traded more than 30 (Power E*Trade) and

75 times (Platinum Level) per quarter respectively. Later in 2001, E*Trade intended to launch E*Trade Pro, which featured direct access to ECNs (Electronic Communication Network), streaming market data, and dynamic order status in a customizable desktop application. Integrated wireless banking and brokerage was launched in October 2000. Since early 2001, its wholly-owned subsidiary, Clear Station, a leading investment website and community, offered wireless services to mobile phone users, giving them access to content and tools via web-enabled phones. Its offerings were compatible with all web-enabled phones, and it expected to offer wireless access through personal digital assistant (PDA) devices in the second quarter of 2001.[15] As Pam Kramer, E*Trade's Chief Global Content and Product Officer, announced:

> Our continuing commitment to on-the-go investors is to provide access to our services and content anytime, anywhere, on any device.

PARTNERSHIPS AND ALLIANCES

As part of its strategy, E*Trade continued to develop content, technology, and distribution alliances, including *Bond Exchange* (Bond Trading), *Instinct* (after-hours trading), *Briefing.com* (research), *Inset* (insurance), *Critical Path* (e-mail services), and *Every Path* (wireless application provider). At the same time, E*Trade acquired a number of companies, including *Private Accounts* (providing low-cost, direct access to nationally recognized money managers), *VERSUS Technologies* (software for global cross-border trading), *Card Capture Services* (to expand the array of financial transactions and ultimately online brokerage via ATMs), *Taliban* (the nation's largest pure-play internet bank), and *Clear Station* (a financial media site that integrates technical and fundamental analysis with community discussion to offer investors ideas, analysis and opinion). Also, E*Trade together with Ernst and Young announced a joint venture in 2000 to provide a personal electronic advisory service to help prepare clients for major financial events such as buying a home, tax and estate planning, educational funding, and retirement planning.

RESPONSES TO THE MARKET DOWNTURN

Revenue diversification was important for pure-play internet companies, particularly for E*Trade whose average customer balance was $17,500 versus $106,000 for Schwab and $180,000 for Merrill.[16] E*Trade's transaction revenues at the end of the first quarter 2001 were down 48 percent year-on-year, with commission revenues down 51 percent. The company's 10-Q report dated May 2001 reported unrealized losses of $11.6 million in its own equity investments; however, E*Trade was financially liquid for at least the next twelve months, although funds may have to be raised thereafter. Tables 9.5 and 9.6 show E*Trade's performance during 2000 and early 2001.

What did the future hold for a pure-play entrant like E*Trade? The events of 2001 highlighted to E*Trade the financial vulnerability of its business model in a market downturn. Given the criticality of trading volumes for the success of the online, deep-

Table 9.5 E*Trade: Consolidated statement of operations (in $ thousands, except per share amounts)

	Year Ended September 30		
	2000	1999	1998
Revenues:			
Transaction revenues	739,078	355,830	162,097
Net Interest	359,496	153,622	65,789
International	166,061	124,233	105,851
Other	107,686	40,546	28,173
Provision for loan losses	(4,003)	(2,783)	(905)
Net revenues	1,368,318	671,448	361,005
Cost of services	515,571	302,342	151,329
Operating expenses:			
Sales and marketing	521,532	325,449	126,141
Technology development	142,914	79,935	36,203
General & administrative	209,436	102,826	51,346
Amortization of intangible assets	22,764	2,915	2,480
Merger related expenses	36,427	7,174	1,167
Total operating expenses	933,073	518,299	217,337
Total cost of services & operating expenses	1,448,644	820,641	368,666
Non-operating income	184,775	65,787	10,504
Income (loss) before income taxes	104,449	(83,406)	2,843
Provision (benefit) for income taxes	85,478	(31,288)	1,883
Net income (loss)	19,152	(56,769)	(402)
Diluted net income (loss) per share ($)	0.06	(0.21)	(0.01)
Shares used in per share calculation	319,336	272,832	195,051

Source: Company financial statements.

Table 9.6 Operating data for E*Trade, 1st quarter 2001 versus 2000

	Three months ended	
	31 March 2001	31 March 2000
Daily average domestic trades (000's)	130.4	226.1
Active brokerage accounts (millions)	3.2	2.4
Domestic brokerage client assets ($000)	39,995	61,569
Average domestic brokerage commission ($)	13.62	15.85

Source: E*Trade (www.etrade.com).

discount, business model, E*Trade had attempted to diversify revenues, while creating a bricks-and-mortar presence. But this quest for new sources of revenue was also raising costs, while compromising the simplicity of E*Trade's strategy.

■ FUTURE PROSPECTS ■

The application of internet technologies to traditional markets led to the emergence of new, online markets, where new customer segments emerged from the application of new business models. Nowhere was this more apparent than in the retail securities brokerage industry. Powerful, long-established incumbents such as Merrill Lynch were challenged by an entirely new type of player. Established discount brokers, such as Charles Schwab, were even more threatened, since their competitive advantage – low costs and low prices – was dramatically undermined by E*Trade and the other new players. During the late 1990s, all the established players – both full-service like Merrill and discount like Schwab – hurried to embrace the new web-based technologies and add new online services to their existing offerings.

The market downturn of 2001 dramatically changed the competitive environment for all the players. While established brokers such as Merrill had been converging towards the discount and online brokers such as Schwab and E*Trade, now the convergence was the other way round: Schwab was moving upmarket to attract high net worth investors, while E*Trade was diversifying its product and service offering and establishing bricks-and-mortar outlets. But despite the security offered by high net worth clients and diversified revenue sources, things were not entirely going Merrill's way. Increasingly, the investment banks were being criticized for allowing their investment advice to their brokerage clients to be subordinated to their investment banking relationships with their corporate clients. During spring 2001, Merrill was hit by a series of lawsuits alleging that its stock recommendations were biased by the company's investment banking relations. Several of these lawsuits related to Merrill's top internet analyst, Henry Bloget, whose recommendations tended to be skewed towards companies for which Merrill acted as an underwriter or advisor.

In the changed economic climate of 2001, all three companies needed to consider how they should continue to adapt their strategies to the new market circumstances and, even more fundamentally, which business model of the brokerage business was likely to be most successful in the future.[17]

NOTES

1. In Western Europe and in the former socialist countries of Eastern Europe, the privatization of state-owned enterprises provided a huge boost in share ownership.
2. http://www.tradefreedom.com/features/freedom.html.
3. http://www.sec.gov/news/studies/ecnafter.htm.
4. *The Economist*, June 9, 2001.
5. www.mlhsbc.co.uk.
6. Merrill Lynch Press Release, June 26, 2001.

7. Merrill Press Release, May 14, 2001.
8. *Financial Times*, June 22, 2001.
9. *Financial Times*, February 7, 2001.
10. *The Independent*, February 3, 2001.
11. *Financial Times*, March 28, 2001.
12. *Canada Newswire*, April 19, 2001.
13. *Canada Newswire*, May 8, 2001.
14. *Funds International*, April 30, 2001.
15. *Canada Newswire*, April 24, 2001.
16. *Forbes Global*, October 1, 2001.
17. For additional information on the industry and the companies, see the following websites: US Securities and Exchange Commission (www.sec.gov/cgi-bin/srch-edgar) and company websites (www.ml.com, www.schwab.com, www.etrade.com)

EMI and the CT Scanner [A] and [B]

Christopher A. Bartlett

■ CASE A ■

In early 1972 there was considerable disagreement among top management at EMI Ltd, the UK-based music, electronics, and leisure company. The subject of the controversy was the CT scanner, a new medical diagnostic imaging device that had been developed by the group's Central Research Laboratory (CRL). At issue was the decision to enter this new business, thereby launching a diversification move that many felt was necessary if the company was to continue to prosper.

Complicating the problem was the fact that this revolutionary new product would not only take EMI into the fast-changing and highly competitive medical equipment business, but would also require the company to establish operations in North America, a market in which it had no prior experience. In March 1972 EMI's board was considering an investment proposal for £6 million to build CT scanner manufacturing facilities in the United Kingdom.

Assistant Professor Christopher A. Bartlett prepared this case as a basis for class discussion rather than to illustrate either effective or ineffective handling of an administrative situation. Information was obtained from public sources and third parties. Although employees of the subject company discussed with the researcher events referred to in the case, they did not participate in the preparation of the document. The analysis, conclusions, and opinions stated do not necessarily represent those of the company, its employees or agents, or employees or agents of its subsidiaries. Thorn EMI PLC, on its own behalf and on behalf of all or any of its present or former subsidiaries, disclaims any responsibility for the matters included or referred to in the study.

Development of the CT Scanner

COMPANY BACKGROUND AND HISTORY

EMI Ltd traces its origins back to 1898, when the Gramophone Company was founded to import records and gramophones from the United States. It soon established its own manufacturing and recording capabilities, and after a 1931 merger with its major rival, the Columbia Gramophone Company, emerged as the Electric and Musical Industries, Ltd. EMI Ltd quickly earned a reputation as an aggressive technological innovator, developing the automatic record changer, stereophonic records, magnetic recording tape, and the pioneer commercial television system adopted by the BBC in 1937.

Beginning in 1939, EMI's R&D capabilities were redirected by the war effort toward the development of fuses, airborne radar, and other sophisticated electronic devices.

The company emerged from the war with an electronics business, largely geared to defense-related products, as well as its traditional entertainment businesses. The transition to peacetime was particularly difficult for the electronics division, and its poor performance led to attempts to pursue new industrial and consumer applications. EMI did some exciting pioneering work, and for a while held hopes of being Britain's leading computer company.

Market leadership in major electronics applications remained elusive, however, while the music business boomed. The 1955 acquisition of Capitol Records in the United States, and the subsequent success of the Beatles and other recording groups under contract to EMI, put the company in a very strong financial position as it entered the 1970s. In 1970 the company had earned £21 million before tax on sales of £215 million, and although extraordinary losses halved those profits in 1971, the company was optimistic for a return to previous profit levels in 1972 (see exhibits 10.1 to 10.3 for EMI's financial performance).

Exhibit 10.1: EMI Limited: Profit and Loss Statement, 1969–71 (£ Thousands)

Years Ended June 30	1969	1970	1971
Sales			
Music	£110,554	£129,439	£128,359
Leisure	20,960	32,651	35,798
Television	4,640	10,625	13,593
Electronics	40,170	42,571	52,819
Total	176,324	215,286	230,569
Profit (loss) before Interest and Taxation			
Music	13,293	16,427	1,970
Leisure	1,691	3,875	4,146
Television	733	992	3,833
Electronics	3,741	3,283	3,090
Subtotal	19,458	24,577	13,039
Property	—	(20)	939
Total	19,458	24,557	13,978

Exhibit 10.1: *continued*

Years Ended June 30	1969	1970	1971
Sales			
United Kingdom	63,144	89,069	103,824
Europe	25,987	27,017	39,673
North America	65,528	74,622	58,989
Other countries	21,665	24,578	28,083
Total	176,324	215,286	230,569
Profit (loss) before Interest and Taxation			
United Kingdom	8,301	10,465	13,113
Europe	3,176	3,230	3,113
North America	5,525	7,627	(5,754)
Other countries	2,456	3,235	3,506
Subtotal	19,458	24,557	13,978
Net interest payable	(1,857)	(3,599)	(5,010)
Total	£17,601	£20,958	£8,968
As a percentage of net assets	15.8%	17.3%	7.4%
Taxation	£8,407	£10,443	£3,541
As a percentage of profit	47.8%	49.8%	39.5%
Profit after Taxation	£9,194	£10,515	£5,427
As a percentage of net assets	8.3%	8.7%	4.5%

Exhibit 10.2: EMI Group Consolidated Balance Sheet, 1972

Employment of Capital		
Goodwill		80,814
Fixed assets		104,174
Other investments		14,354
Current assets		
Inventories	45,508	
Films, programs, and rights	7,712	
Accounts receivable	82,483	
Liquid funds	20,086	
	155,789	
Less		
Current liabilities		
Accounts payable	96,942	
Bank borrowings	14,168	
Taxes payable	17,174	
Dividends declared	4,202	
	132,486	
Net current assets		23,303
Total		222,645
Capital Employed		
Share capital		40,937
Reserves		90,239
Minority shareholders' interests		14,992
Loan capital		76,011
Deferred taxes		466
Total		222,645

Exhibit 10.3: EMI Group Projected Funds Flow, 1972 (£ Thousands)

Sources of Funds	
Profit before tax	18.3
Depreciation	6.7
Sale of fixed assets	5.5
Sale of investments	5.4
Loan capital	0.3
Decrease in working capital	4.5
Total	40.7
Uses of Funds	
Tax payments	5.9
Dividends paid	5.6
Fixed asset additions	13.0
Repayment of loan capital	3.4
Reduction in short-term borrowings	12.8
Total	40.7

Around that time, a change in top management signaled a change in corporate strategy. John Read, an accountant by training and previously sales director for Ford of Great Britain, was appointed chief executive officer after only four years in the company. Read recognized the risky, even fickle, nature of the music business, which accounted for two-thirds of EMI's sales and profits. In an effort to change the company's strategic balance, he began to divert some of its substantial cash flow into numerous acquisitions and internal developments.

To encourage internal innovation, Read established a research fund that was to be used to finance innovative developments outside the company's immediate interests. Among the first projects financed was one proposed by Godfrey Hounsfield, a research scientist in EMI's Central Research Laboratories (CRL). Hounsfield's proposal opened up an opportunity for the company to diversify in the fast-growing medical electronics field.

CT SCANNING: THE CONCEPT

In simple terms, Hounsfield's research proposal was to study the possibility of creating a three-dimensional image of an object by taking multiple X-ray measurements of the object from different angles, then using a computer to reconstruct a picture from the data contained in hundreds of overlapping and intersecting X-ray slices. The concept became known as computerized tomography (CT).

Although computerized tomography represented a conceptual breakthrough, the technologies it harnessed were quite well known and understood. Essentially, it linked X-ray, data processing, and cathode ray tube display technologies in a complex and precise manner. The real development challenge consisted of integrating the mechanical, electronic, and radiographic components into an accurate, reliable, and sensitive system. Figure 10.1 provides a schematic representation of the EMI scanner, illustrat-

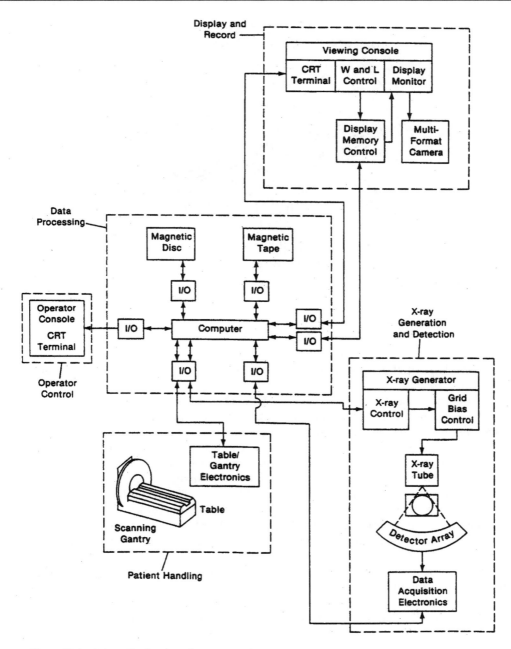

Figure 10.1 Schematic drawing of scanner system

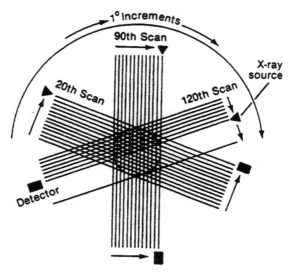

Figure 10.2   Translate-rotate CT scanning

ing the linkage of the three technologies, as well as the patient handling table and X-ray gantry.

Progress was rapid, and clinical trials of the CT scanner were under way by late 1970. To capture the image of multiple slices of the brain, the scanner went through a translate-rotate sequence, as illustrated in figure 10.2. The X-ray source and detector, located on opposite sides of the patient's head, were mounted on a gantry. After each scan, or "translation," had generated an X-ray image comprising 160 data points, the gantry would rotate 1° and another scan would be made.

This procedure would continue through 180 translations and rotations, storing a total of almost 30,000 data points. Since the detected intensity of an X-ray varies with the material through which it passes, the data could be reconstructed by the computer into a three-dimensional image of the object that distinguished bone, tissue, water, fat, and so on.

At about the time of the CT clinical trials, John Powell, formerly managing director of Texas Instrument's English subsidiary, joined EMI as technical director. He soon became convinced that the poor profitability of the nonmilitary electronics business was due to the diffusion of the company's 2,500-person R&D capability over too many diverse small-volume lines. In his words, "EMI was devoted to too many products and dedicated to too few."

Because the CT scanner project built on the company's substantial and well-established electronics capability, Powell believed it gave EMI an important opportunity to enter an exciting new field. He felt that this was exactly the type of effort in which the company should be prepared to invest several million pounds.

Diagnostic Imaging Industry

During the first half of the twentieth century, diagnostic information about internal organs and functions was provided almost exclusively by conventional X-ray examination, but in the 1960s and 1970s, several new imaging techniques emerged. When the CT scanner was announced, three other important technologies existed: X-ray, nuclear, and ultrasound.

EMI management believed its CT scanner would displace existing diagnostic imaging equipment in only a few applications, specifically head and brain imaging.

X-RAY

In 1895 Wilhelm Roentgen discovered that rays generated by a cathode ray tube could penetrate solid objects and create an image on film. Over the next 40 to 50 years, X-ray equipment was installed in almost every healthcare facility in the world. Despite its several limitations (primarily due to the fact that detail was obscured when three-dimensional features were superimposed on a two-dimensional image), X-rays were universally used. In 1966 a Surgeon General's report estimated that between one-third and one-half of all crucial medical decisions in the United States depended on interpretation of X-ray films. That country alone had more than 80,000 X-ray installations in operation, performing almost 150 million procedures in 1970.

The X-ray market was dominated by five major global companies. Siemens of West Germany was estimated to have 22 percent of the world market, N.V. Philips of the Netherlands had 18 percent, and Compagnie Generale de Radiologie (CGE), subsidiary of the French giant Thomson Brandt, held 16 percent. Although General Electric had an estimated 30 percent of the large US market, its weak position abroad gave it only 15 percent of the world market. The fifth largest company was Picker, with 20 percent of the US market, but less than 12 percent worldwide.

The size of the US market for X-ray equipment was estimated at $350 million in 1972, with an additional $350 million in X-ray supplies. The United States was thought to represent 35–40% of the world market. Despite the maturity of the product, the X-ray market was growing by almost 10% annually in dollar terms during the early 1970s.

A conventional X-ray system represented a major capital expenditure for a hospital, with the average system costing more than $100,000 in 1973.

NUCLEAR IMAGING

In the mid-1960s a nuclear diagnostic imaging procedure was developed. Radioisotopes with a short radioactive life were projected into the body, detected and monitored on a screen, then recorded on film or stored on a tape. Still in an early stage of development, this technology was used to complement or, in some instances, replace a conventional X-ray diagnosis. Both static and dynamic images could be obtained.

Table 10.1 Numbers of hospitals in the United States, 1972

Number of beds	Short-term	Long-term (chronic)	Total
Less than 100	3,110	375	3,485
100–299	1,904	385	2,289
300–499	574	141	715
More than 500	537	91	628
Total	6,125	992	7,117

Following the pioneering development of this field by Nuclear-Chicago, which sold the first nuclear gamma camera in 1962, several other small competitors had entered the field, notably Ohio Nuclear. By the late 1960s larger companies such as Picker were getting involved, and in 1971 GE's Medical Systems Division announced plans to enter the nuclear medicine field.

As new competitors, large and small, entered the market, competition became more aggressive. The average nuclear camera and data processing system sold for about $75,000. By 1973, shipments of nuclear imaging equipment into the US market were estimated to be over $50 million.

ULTRASOUND

Ultrasound had been used in medical diagnosis since the 1950s, and the technology advanced significantly in the early 1970s, permitting better-defined images. The technique involves transmitting sonic waves and picking up the echoes, which when converted to electric energy could create images. Air and bone often provide an acoustic barrier, limiting the use of this technique. But because the patient was not exposed to radiation, it was widely used as a diagnostic tool in obstetrics and gynecology.

In 1973 the ultrasound market was very small, and only a few small companies were reported in the field. Picker, however, was rumored to be doing research in the area. The cost of the equipment was expected to be less than half that of a nuclear camera and support system, and perhaps a third to a quarter that of an X-ray machine.

US MARKET POTENTIAL

Because of its size, sophistication, progressiveness, and access to funds, the US medical market clearly represented the major opportunity for a new device such as the CT scanner. EMI management was uncertain about the sales potential for their new product, however.

As of 1972, there were around 7,000 hospitals in the United States, ranging from tiny rural hospitals with fewer than 10 beds to giant teaching institutions with 1,000 beds or more (see table 10.1).

Since the price of the EMI Scanner was expected to be around $400,000, only the largest and financially strongest short-term institutions would be able to afford one. But the company was encouraged by the enthusiasm of the physicians who had seen and worked with the scanner. In the opinion of one leading American neurologist, at least 170 machines would be required by major US hospitals. Indeed, he speculated, the time might come when a neurologist would feel ethically compelled to order a CT scan before making a diagnosis.

During the 1960s the radiology departments in many hospitals were recognized as important money-making operations. Increasingly, radiologists were able to commission equipment manufacturers to build specially designed (often esoteric) X-ray systems and applications. As their budgets expanded, the size of the US X-ray market grew from $50 million in 1958 to $350 million in 1972.

Of the 15,000 radiologists in the United States, 60 percent were primarily based in offices and 40 percent in hospitals. Little penetration of private clinics was foreseen for the CT scanner. Apart from these broad statistics, EMI had little ability to forecast the potential of the US market for scanners.

EMI's Investment Decision

CONFLICTING MANAGEMENT VIEWS

By late 1971 it was clear that the clinical trials were successful and EMI management had to decide whether to make the investment required to develop the CT scanner business. One group of senior managers felt that direct EMI participation was undesirable for three reasons. First, EMI lacked medical product experience. In the early 1970s EMI offered only two very small medical products, a patient-monitoring device and an infrared thermography device, which together represented less than 0.5 percent of the company's sales.

Second, they argued that the manufacturing process would be quite different from EMI's experience. Most of its electronics work had been in the job shop mode required in producing small numbers of highly specialized defense products on cost-plus government contracts. In scanner production, most of the components were purchased from subcontractors and had to be integrated into a functioning system.

Finally, many believed that without a working knowledge of the North American market, where most of the demand for scanners was expected to be, EMI might find it very difficult to build an effective operation from scratch.

Among the strongest opponents of EMI's self-development of this new business was one of the scanner's earliest sponsors, Dr Broadway, head of the Central Research Laboratory. He emphasized that EMI's potential competitors in the field had considerably greater technical capabilities and resources. As the major proponent, John Powell needed convincing market information to counter the critics. In early 1972 he asked some of the senior managers how many scanners they thought the company would sell in its first 12 months. Their first estimate was five. Powell told them to think again. They came back with a figure of 12, and were again sent back to reconsider. Finally, with an estimate of 50, Powell felt he could go to bat for the £6 million investment, since at this sales level he could project handsome profits from year one. He then prepared an argument that justified the scanner's fit with EMI's overall objectives, and outlined a basic strategy for the business.

Powell argued that self-development of the CT scanner represented just the sort of vehicle EMI had been seeking to provide some focus to its development effort. By definition, diversification away from existing product-market areas would move the company into somewhat unfamiliar territory, but he firmly believed that the financial and strategic payoffs would be huge. The product offered access to global markets and an entry into the lucrative medical equipment field. He felt the company's objective should be to achieve a substantial share of the world medical electronics business not only in diagnostic imaging, but also through the extension of its technologies into computerized patient planning and radiation therapy.

Powell claimed that the expertise developed by Hounsfield and his team, coupled with protection from patents, would give EMI three or four years, and maybe many more, to establish a solid market position. He argued that investments should be made quickly and boldly to maximize the market share of the EMI scanner before competitors entered. Other options, such as licensing, would impede the development of the scanner. If the licensees were the major X-ray equipment suppliers, they might not promote the scanner aggressively since it would cannibalize their sales of X-ray equipment and consumables. Smaller companies would lack EMI's sense of commitment and urgency. Besides, licensing would not provide EMI with the major strategic diversification it was seeking. It would be, in Powell's words, "selling our birthright."

THE PROPOSED STRATEGY

Because the CT scanner incorporated a complex integration of some technologies in which EMI had only limited expertise, Powell proposed that the manufacturing strategy should rely heavily on outside sources of those components rather than trying to develop the expertise internally. This approach would not only minimize risk, but would also make it possible to implement a manufacturing program rapidly.

He proposed the concept of developing various "centers of excellence" both inside and outside the company, making each responsible for the continued superiority of the subsystem it manufactured. For example, within the EMI UK organization a unit called SE Labs, which manufactured instruments and displays, would become the center of excellence for the scanner's viewing console and display control. Pantak, an EMI unit with a capability in X-ray tube assembly, would become the center of excellence for the X-ray generation and detection subsystem. An outside vendor with which the company had worked in developing the scanner would be the center of excellence for data processing. Finally, a newly created division would be responsible for coordinating these subsystem manufacturers, integrating the various components, and assembling the final scanner at a company facility in the town of Hayes, not far from the CRL site.

Powell emphasized that the low initial investment was possible because most of the components and subsystems were purchased from contractors and vendors. Even internal centers of excellence such as SE Labs and Pantak assembled their subsystems from purchased components. Overall, outside vendors accounted for 75–80 percent of the scanner's manufacturing cost. Although Powell felt his arrangement greatly reduced EMI's risk, the £6 million investment was a substantial one for the company, representing about half the funds available for capital investment over the coming year. (See exhibit 10.2 for a balance sheet and exhibit 10.3 for a projected funds flow.)

The technology strategy was to keep CRL as the company's center of excellence for design and software expertise, and to use the substantial profits Powell was projecting from even the earliest sales to maintain technological leadership position.

Powell would personally head up a team to develop a marketing strategy. Clearly, the United States had to be the main focus of EMI's marketing activity. Its neuroradiologists were regarded as world leaders and tended to welcome technological innovation. Furthermore, its institutions were more commercial in their outlook than those in other countries and tended to have more available funds. Powell planned to set up a US sales subsidiary as soon as possible, recruiting sales and service personnel familiar with the North American healthcare market. Given the interest shown to date in the EMI scanner, he did not think there would be much difficulty in gaining the attention and interest of the medical community.

Getting the $400,000 orders, however, would be more of a challenge. In simple terms, Powell's sales strategy was to get machines into a few prestigious reference hospitals, then build from that base.

THE DECISION

In March 1972 EMI's chief executive, John Read, considered Powell's proposal in preparation for a board meeting. Was this the diversification opportunity he had been hoping for? What were the risks? Could they be managed? How? If he decided to back the proposal, what kind of an implementation program would be necessary to ensure its eventual success?

■ CASE B ■

The year 1977 looked like it would be a very good one for EMI Medical Inc., a North American subsidiary of EMI Ltd. EMI's CT scanner had met with enormous success in the American market. In the three years since the scanner's introduction, EMI medical electronics sales had grown to £42 million. Although this represented only 6 percent of total sales, this new business contributed pretax profits of £12.5 million, almost 20 percent of the corporate total (exhibit 10.4). EMI Medical Inc. was thought to be responsible for about 80 percent of total scanner volume. And with an order backlog of more than 300 units, the future seemed rosy.

Exhibit 10.4: EMI Limited: P&L Statement, 1969–76

Years ended 30 June	1969 £'000	1970 £'000	1971 £'000	1972 £'000	1973 £'000	1974 £'000	1975 £'000	1976 £'000
Sales								
Music	110,554	129,439	128,359	137,755	169,898	213,569	258,343	344,743
Leisure	20,960	32,651	35,798	37,917	45,226	53,591	66,566	81,428
Television	4,640	10,625	13,593	17,165	22,011	22,814	29,107	38,224
Electronics – Other than Medical	40,170	42,571	52,819	58,215	83,516	104,811	128,644	164,943
Medical Electronics	—	—	—	—	321	5,076	20,406	42,104
	176,324	215,286	230,569	251,052	320,972	399,861	503,066	671,442
Profit (loss) before interest and taxation								
Music	13,293	16,427	1,970	9,333	16,606	26,199	19,762	27,251
Leisure	1,691	3,875	4,146	4,983	4,255	2,639	5,981	5,619
Television	733	992	3,833	5,001	6,104	4,465	2,982	5,646
Electronics – Other than Medical	3,741	3,283	3,090	1,353	5,264	5,835	5,378	13,937
Medical Electronics	—	—	—	—	(67)	1,242	9,230	12,502
	19,458	24,577	13,039	20,670	32,162	40,380	43,333	64,955
Property	—	(20)	939	2,118	1,842	402	(103)	—
	19,458	24,557	13,978	22,788	34,004	40,782	43,230	64,955
Sales								
United Kingdom	63,144	89,069	103,824	113,925	142,945	165,641	198,153	241,972
Europe	25,987	27,017	39,673	52,541	82,405	105,251	134,450	170,385
North America	65,528	74,622	58,989	53,151	55,143	67,141	78,154	128,798
Other countries	21,665	24,578	28,083	31,435	40,479	61,828	92,309	130,287
	176,324	215,286	230,569	251,052	320,972	399,861	503,066	671,442
Profit (loss) before interest and taxation								
United Kingdom	8,301	10,465	13,113	15,447	19,287	16,784	16,494	21,802
Europe	3,176	3,230	3,113	3,133	6,133	9,043	9,679	14,521
North America	5,525	7,627	(5,754)	1,091	3,555	6,412	7,065	13,067
Other countries	2,456	3,235	3,506	3,117	5,029	8,543	9,992	15,565
	19,458	24,557	13,978	22,788	34,004	40,782	43,230	64,955
Net interest payable	1,857	3,599	5,010	4,452	6,386	5,690	8,258	5,604
Profit before taxation	17,601	20,958	8,968	18,336	27,618	35,092	34,972	59,351
As a percentage of net assets	15.8	17.3	7.4	14.4	18.9	22.8	21.2	31.2
Taxation	8,407	10,443	3,541	8,575	13,227	18,666	19,549	31,224
As a percentage of profit	47.8	49.8	39.5	46.8	47.9	53.2	55.9	52.6
Profit after taxation	9,194	10,515	5,427	9,761	14,391	16,426	15,423	28,127
As a percentage of net assets	8.3	8.7	4.5	7.7	9.8	10.7	9.3	14.8
Extraordinary items	—	—	—	—	843	264	(14,472)	(146)
Profit attributable to ordinary stockholders	7,259	8,736	4,562	7,297	10,864	13,327	13,124	24,399

Despite this formidable success, senior management in both the subsidiary and the parent company were concerned about several developments. First, this fast-growth field had attracted more than a dozen new entrants in the past two years, and technological advances were occurring rapidly. At the same time, the growing political debate over hospital cost containment often focused on $500,000 CT scanners as an example of questionable hospital spending. Finally, EMI was beginning to feel some internal organizational strains.

Entry Decision

PRODUCT LAUNCH

Following months of debate among EMI's top management, the decision to go ahead with the EMI Scanner project was assured when John Read, the company CEO, gave his support to Dr Powell's proposal. In April 1972 a formal press announcement was greeted by a response that could only be described as overwhelming. EMI was flooded with inquiries from the medical and financial communities, and from most of the large diagnostic imaging companies wanting to license the technology, enter into joint ventures, or at least distribute the product. The response was that the company had decided to enter the business directly itself.

Immediately action was implemented to put Dr Powell's manufacturing strategy into operation. Manufacturing facilities were developed and supply contracts drawn up with the objective of beginning shipments within 12 months.

In May, Godfrey Hounsfield, the brilliant EMI scientist who had developed the scanner, was dispatched to the US accompanied by a leading English neurologist. The American specialists with whom they spoke confirmed that the scanner had great medical importance. Interest was running high in the medical community.

In December, EMI mounted a display at the annual meeting of the Radiological Society of North America (RSNA). The exhibit was the highlight of the show, and boosted management's confidence to establish a US sales company to penetrate the American medical market.

US MARKET ENTRY

In June 1973, with an impressive pile of sales leads and inquiries, a small sales office was established in Reston, Virginia, home of the newly appointed US sales branch manager, Mr Gus Pyber. Earlier that month the first North American head scanner had been installed at the prestigious Mayo Clinic, with a second machine promised to the Massachusetts General Hospital for trials. Interest was high, and the new sales force had little difficulty getting into the offices of leading radiologists and neurologists.

By the end of the year, however, Mr Pyber had been fired in a dispute over appropriate expense levels, and James Gallagher, a former marketing manager with a major drug company, was hired to replace him. One of Gallagher's first steps was to convince the company that the Chicago area was a far better location for the US office. It allowed better servicing of a national market, was a major center for medical electronics companies, and had more convenient linkages with London. This last point was important since all major strategic and policy decisions were being made directly by Dr Powell in London.

During 1974, Gallagher concentrated on recruiting and developing his three-man sales force and two-man service organization. The cost of maintaining each salesman on the road was estimated at $50,000, while a serviceman's salary and expenses at that time were around $35,000 annually. The production rate for the scanner was running at a rate of only three or four machines a month, and Gallagher saw little point in developing a huge sales force to sell a product for which supply was limited, and interest seemingly boundless.

In this seller's market the company developed some policies that were new to the industry. Most notably, they required that the customer deposit one-third of the purchase price with the order to guarantee a place in the production schedule. Sales leads and enquiries were followed up when the sales force could get to them, and the general attitude of the company seemed to have somewhat of a "take it or leave it" tone. It was in this period that EMI developed a reputation for arrogance in some parts of the medical profession.

Nonetheless, by June 1974 the company had delivered 35 scanners at $390,000 each, and had another 60 orders in hand.

Developing Challenges

COMPETITIVE CHALLENGE

Toward the end of 1974, the first competitive scanners were announced. Unlike the EMI scanner, the new machines were designed to scan the body rather than the head. The Acta-Scanner had been developed at Georgetown University's Medical Center and was manufactured by a small Maryland company called Digital Information Sciences Corporation (DISCO). Technologically, it offered little advance over the EMI scanner except for one important feature. Its gantry design would accommodate a body rather than a head. While specifications on scan time and image composition were identical to those of the EMI scanner, the $298,000 price tag gave the Acta-Scanner a big advantage, particularly with smaller hospitals and private practitioners.

The DeltaScan offered by Ohio Nuclear (ON) represented an even more formidable challenge. This head and body scanner had 256×256 pixels compared with EMI's 160×160, and promised a $2\frac{1}{2}$-minute scan rather than the $4\frac{1}{2}$-minute scan time offered by EMI. ON offered these superior features on a unit priced $5,000 below the EMI scanner at $385,000.

Many managers at EMI were surprised by the speed with which these products had appeared, barely two years after the EMI scanner was exhibited at the RSNA meeting in Chicago, and 18 months after the first machine was installed in the Mayo Clinic. The source of the challenge was also interesting. DISCO was a tiny private company, and ON contributed about 20 percent of its parent Technicare's 1974 sales of $50 million.

To some, the biggest surprise was how closely these competitive machines resembled EMI's own scanner. The complex wall of patents had not provided a very enduring defense. ON tackled the issue directly in its 1975 annual report. After announcing that $882,200 had been spent in Technicare's R&D Center to develop DeltaScan, the report stated:

> Patents have not played a significant role in the development of Ohio Nuclear's product line, and it is not believed that the validity or invalidity of any patents known to exist is material to its current market position. However, the technologies on which its products are based are sufficiently complex and application of patent law sufficiently indefinite that this belief is not free from all doubt.

The challenge represented by these new competitive products caused EMI to speed up the announcement of the body scanner Dr Hounsfield had been working on. The new CT 5000 model incorporated a second-generation technology in which multiple beams of radiation were shot at multiple detectors, rather than the single pencil beam and the single detector of the original scanner (see exhibit 10.5). This technique allowed the gantry to rotate $10°$ rather than $1°$ after each translation, cutting scan time from $4^1/_2$ minutes to 20 seconds. In addition, the multiple-beam emission also permitted a finer image resolution by increasing the number of pixels from 160×160 to 320×320. Priced over $500,000, the CT 5000 received a standing ovation when Hounsfield demonstrated it at the radiological meetings held in Bermuda in May 1975.

Despite EMI's reassertion of its leadership position, aggressive competitive activity continued. In March 1975, Pfizer Inc., the $1.5 billion drug giant, announced it had acquired the manufacturing and marketing rights for the Acta-Scanner.

By June 1975, managers at EMI estimated competitors' cumulative orders as follows:

	Total shipped	*On order*
EMI	122	110
Ohio Nuclear	2	50 (est.)
Pfizer	0	20 (est.)

EMI was then operating at an annual production rate of 150 units, and ON had announced plans to double capacity to 12 units per month by early 1976. Pfizer's capacity plans were unknown. The most dramatic competitive revelation came at the annual RSNA meeting in December 1975, when six new competitors displayed CT scanners. Although none of the newcomers offered immediate delivery, all were booking orders with delivery dates up to 12 months out on the basis of their spec sheets and prototype or mock-up equipment exhibits.

Some of the new entrants (Syntex, Artronix, and Neuroscan) were smaller companies, but others (General Electric, Picker, and Varian) were major medical electronics competitors. Perhaps most impressive was the General Electric CT/T scanner, which took the infant technology into its third generation (see exhibit 10.6). By using a $30°$-wide pulsed fan X-ray beam, the GE scanner could avoid the time-consuming

Exhibit 3
EMI AND THE CT SCANNER (B)

Three Generations of CT Scanning Technology

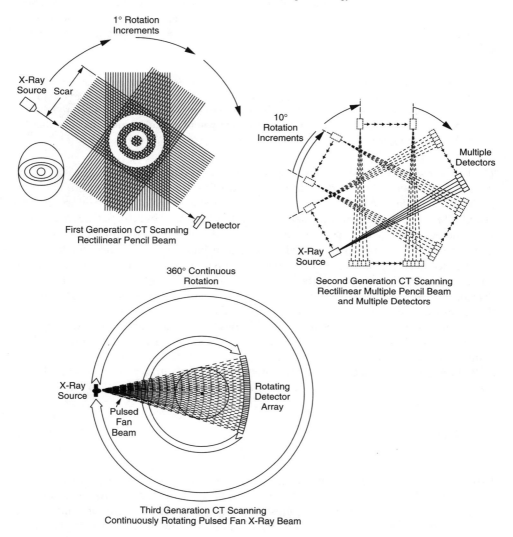

1° Rotation
Increments

X-Ray
Source   Scar

First Generation CT Scanning
Rectilinear Pencil Beam

Detector

10°
Rotation
Increments

Multiple
Detectors

X-Ray
Source

Second Generation CT Scanning
Rectilinear Multiple Pencil Beam
and Multiple Detectors

360° Continuous
Rotation

X-Ray
Source

Pulsed
Fan
Beam

Rotating
Detector
Array

Third Genaration CT Scanning
Continuously Rotating Pulsed Fan X-Ray Beam

"translate-rotate" sequence of the first- and second-generation scanners. A single continuous 360° sweep could be completed in 4.8 seconds, and the resulting image was reconstructed by the computer in a 320 × 320 pixel matrix on a cathode ray tube. The unit was priced at $615,000. Clinical trials were scheduled for January, and shipment of production units was being quoted for mid-1976.

The arrival of GE on the horizon signaled the beginning of a new competitive game. With a 300-person sales force and a service network of 1,200, GE clearly had marketing muscle. They had reputedly spent $15 million developing their third-generation scanner, and were continuing to spend at a rate of $5 million annually to keep ahead technologically.

During 1975, one industry source estimated, about 150 new scanners were installed in the US, and more than twice as many orders entered. (Orders were firm, since most were secured with hefty front-end deposits.) Overall, orders were split fairly evenly between brain and body scanners. EMI was thought to have accounted for more than 50 percent of orders taken in 1975, ON for almost 30 percent.

MARKET SIZE AND GROWTH

Accurate assessments of market size, growth rate, and competitors' shares were difficult to obtain. The following represents a sample of the widely varying forecasts made in late 1975:

- Wall Street was clearly enamored with the industry prospects (Technicare's stock price rose from 5 to 22 in six months) and analysts were predicting an annual market potential of $500 million to $1 billion by 1980.
- Frost and Sullivan, however, saw a US market of only $120 million by 1980, with ten years of cumulative sales only reaching $1 billion by 1984 (2,500 units at $400,000).
- Some leading radiologists suggested that CT scanners could be standard equipment in all short-term hospitals with 200 beds or more by 1985.
- Technicare's president, Mr R. T. Grimm, forecast a worldwide market of over $700 million by 1980, of which $400 million would be in the US.
- Despite the technical limitations of its first-generation product, Pfizer said it expected to sell more than 1,500 units of its Acta-Scanner over the next five years.

Within EMI, market forecasts had changed considerably. By late 1975, the estimate of the US market had been boosted to 350 units a year, of which EMI hoped to retain a 50 percent share. Management was acutely aware of the difficulty of forecasting in such a turbulent environment, however.

INTERNATIONAL EXPANSION

New competitors also challenged EMI's positions in markets outside the US. Siemens, the $7 billion West German company, became ON's international distributor. The distribution agreement appeared to be one of short-term convenience for both parties, since Siemens acknowledged that it was developing its own CT scanner. Philips, too, had announced its intention to enter the field.

Internationally, EMI had maintained its basic strategy of going direct to the national market rather than working through local partners or distributors. Although all

European sales had originally been handled out of the UK office, it quickly became evident that local servicing staffs were required in most countries. Soon separate subsidiaries were established in most continental European countries, typically with a couple of salesmen, and three or four servicemen. Elsewhere in the world, salesmen were often attached to EMI's existing music organization in that country (e.g., in South Africa, Australia, and Latin America). In Japan, however, EMI signed a distribution agreement with Toshiba which, in October 1975, submitted the largest single order to date: a request for 33 scanners.

EMI in 1976: Strategy and Challenges

EMI'S SITUATION IN 1976

By 1976 the CT scanner business was evolving rapidly, but, as the results indicated, EMI had done extremely well financially (exhibit 10.5). In reviewing developments since the US market entry, the following was clear:

- While smaller competitors had challenged EMI somewhat earlier than might have been expected, none of the big diagnostic imaging companies had brought its scanner to market, even four years after the original EMI scanner announcement.
- While technology was evolving rapidly, the expertise of Hounsfield and his CRL group, and the aggressive reinvestment of much of the early profits in R&D, gave EMI a strong technological position.
- While market size and growth were highly uncertain, the potential was unquestionably much larger than EMI had forecast in their early plans.
- In all, EMI was well established, with a strong and growing sales volume and a good technical reputation. The company was unquestionably the industry leader.

Nonetheless, in the light of all the developments, the strategic tasks facing EMI in 1976 differed considerably from those of earlier years. The following paragraphs outline the most important challenges and problems facing the company in this period.

STRATEGIC PRIORITIES

EMI's first sales priority was to protect its existing highly visible and prestigious customer base from competitors. When its second-generation scanner was introduced in mid-1975, EMI promised to upgrade without charge the first-generation equipment already purchased by its established customers. Although each of these 120 upgrades was estimated to cost EMI $60,000 in components and installation costs, the US sales organization felt that the expense was essential to maintain the confidence and good faith of this important core group of customers.

To maintain its leadership image, the US company also expanded its service organization substantially. Beginning in early 1976, new regional and district sales and service offices were opened with the objective of providing customers with the best service in the industry. A typical annual service contract cost the hospital $40,000 per scanner. By year's end, the company boasted 20 service centers with 150 service engineers – a ratio that represented one serviceman for every two or three machines installed. The sales force by this time had grown to 20, and was much more customer oriented.

Another important task was to improve delivery performance. The interval between order and promised delivery had been lengthening; at the same time, promised delivery dates were often missed. By late 1975, it was not unusual for a 6-month promise to convert into a 12- or 15-month actual delivery time. Fortunately for EMI, all CT manufacturers were in backorder and were offering extended delivery dates. However, EMI's poor performance in meeting promised dates was hurting its reputation. The company responded by substantially expanding its production facilities. By mid-1976 there were six manufacturing locations in the UK, yet because of continuing problems with component suppliers, combined capacity for head and body scanners was estimated at less than 20 units a month.

ORGANIZATIONAL AND PERSONNEL ISSUES

As the US sales organization became increasingly frustrated, they began urging top management to manufacture scanners in North America. Believing that the product had reached the necessary level of maturity, Dr Powell judged that the time was ripe to establish a US plant to handle at least final assembly and test operations. A Northbrook, Illinois site was chosen.

Powell had become EMI's managing director and was more determined than ever to make the new medical electronics business a success. A capable manager was desperately needed to head the business, particularly in view of the rapid developments in the critical North American market. Consequently, Powell was delighted when Normand Provost, who had been his boss at Texas Instruments, contacted him at the Bermuda radiological meeting in March 1975. He was hired with the hope that he could build a stronger, more integrated US company.

With the Northbrook plant scheduled to begin operations by mid-1976, Normand Provost began hiring skilled production personnel. A Northbrook product development center was also a vision of Provost's to allow EMI to draw on US technical expertise and experience in solid state electronics and data processing, and the company began seeking people with strong technological and scientific backgrounds.

Having hired Provost, Dr Powell made several important organizational changes aimed at facilitating the medical electronics business's growth and development. In the UK, he announced the creation of a separate medical electronics group. This allowed the separate operating companies, EMI Medical Ltd (previously known as the X-Ray Systems Division), Pantak (EMI) Ltd, SE Labs (EMI) Lt., and EMI Meterflow Ltd, to be grouped together under a single group executive, John Willsher. (See exhibit 10.6.) At last, a more integrated scanner business seemed to be emerging organizationally.

Exhibit 4
EMI AND THE CT SCANNER (B)
EMI Medical Electronics Organization, 1976

*Only the medical business responsibilities reporting to Dr. Powell are shown. In addiction, he had overall
responsibility for EMI's other business (music, industrial electronics, etc.).

The US sales subsidiary was folded into a new company, EMI Medical Inc., but continued to operate as a separate entity. The intention was to develop this company as an integrated diversified medical electronics operation. Jim Gallagher, the general manager of the US operations, was fired and Bob Hagglund became president of EMI Medical Inc. While Gallagher had been an effective salesman, Powell thought the company needed a more rounded general manager in its next phase of expansion. Hagglund, previously executive vice president of G.D. Searle's diagnostic business, seemed to have the broader background and outlook required to manage a larger integrated operation. He reported through Provost back to Dr Powell in the UK.

While Provost's initial assignment was to establish the new manufacturing and research facilities in the US, it was widely assumed within EMI that he was being groomed to take responsibility for the company's medical electronics businesses worldwide. However, in April 1976, while visiting London to discuss progress, Provost died of a heart attack. As a result, the US and UK organizations reported separately to Dr Powell.

PRODUCT DIVERSIFICATION

Since EMI wished to use the scanner as a means to become a major force in medical electronics, Powell argued that some bold external moves were needed to protect the company's leadership position. In March 1976, EMI acquired for $2 million (£1.1 million) SHM Nuclear Corporation, a California-based company that had developed linear accelerators for cancer therapy and computerized radiotherapy planning systems. Although the SHM product line needed substantial further development, the hope was that linking such systems to the CT scanner would permit a synchronized location and treatment of cancer.

Six months later EMI paid £6.5 million to acquire an additional 60 percent of Nuclear Enterprises Ltd, an Edinburgh-based supplier of ultrasound equipment. In the 1976 annual report, Sir John Read, now EMI's chairman, reaffirmed his support for Dr Powell's strategy:

> We have every reason to believe that this new grouping of scientific and technological resources will prove of national benefit in securing a growing share of worldwide markets for high-technology products . . .

Future Prospects

At the close of 1976, EMI's medical electronics business was exceeding all expectations. In just three years, sales of electronics products had risen from £84 million to £207 million; a large part of this increase was due to the scanner. Even more impressive, profits of the electronics line had risen from £5.2 million in 1972/73 to £26.4 million in 1975/76, jumping from 16 to 40 percent of the corporate total.

Rather than dwindling, interest in scanners seemed to be increasing. Although the company had sold around 450 scanners over the past three years (over 300 in the US alone), its order backlog was estimated to be 300 units. At the December 1976 RSNA meeting, 120 of the 280 papers presented were related to CT scanning.

As he reviewed the medical electronics business he had built, Dr Powell was generally pleased with the way in which the company had met the challenges of being a pioneer in a new industry segment. However, there were several developments that he felt would need considerable attention over the next few years. First, Powell felt that competitive activity would continue to present a challenge; second, some changes in the US regulatory environment concerned him; and finally, he was aware that the recent organization changes had created some strains.

COMPETITIVE PROBLEMS

By the end of 1976, EMI had delivered 450 of the 650-odd scanners installed worldwide, yet its market share had dropped to 56 percent in 1975/76 (198 of 352 scanners sold that June-to-June period were EMI's). The company gained some consolation from the fact that despite their premium pricing strategy and their delivery problems, they had conceded less than half the total market to the combined competitive field. They also felt some sense of security in the 300 orders they held awaiting delivery. Nonetheless, Sir John Read was clearly concerned:

[We are well aware of the developing competition. Our research program is being fully sustained to ensure our continued leadership . . .

In mid-1976, the company announced its intention "to protect its inventions and assert its patent strength," and subsequently filed suit against Ohio Nuclear claiming patent infringement. However, at the same time, EMI issued a statement proclaiming that "it was the company's wish to make its pioneering scanner patents available to all under suitable licensing arrangements."

At the annual RSNA meeting in December 1976, sixteen competitors exhibited scanners. The year's new entrants (including CGR, the French X-ray giant; Hitachi from Japan; and G.D. Searle, the US drug and hospital equipment company) were not yet making deliveries, however. The industry's potential production capacity was now estimated to be over 900 units annually.

GE's much-publicized entry was already six months behind their announced delivery date, but it was strongly rumored that production shipments of GE's third-generation scanner were about to begin. EMI Medical Inc. awaited that event with some trepidation. (A summary of major competitors and their situations as of 1976 is presented in table 10.2.)

REGULATORY PROBLEMS

By mid-1976 there were indications that government might try to exert a tighter control over hospital spending in general, and purchase of CT scanners in particular.

The rapidly escalating cost of healthcare had been a political issue for years, and the National Health Planning and Resources Development Act of 1974 required states to control the development of costly or unnecessary health services through a mechanism known as the Certificate of Need (CON) procedure. If they wished to qualify for Medicare or Medicaid reimbursements, healthcare facilities were required to submit documentation to their state's department of health to justify major capital expenditures (typically in excess of $100,000).

Before 1976, the CON procedures had generally been merely an administrative impediment to the process of selling a scanner, delaying but not preventing the authorization of funds. However, by 1976, the cost of medical care represented 8 percent of the gross national product and Jimmy Carter made control of the "skyrocketing costs of healthcare" a major campaign issue. One of the most frequently cited examples of waste was the proliferation of CT scanners. It was argued that this $500,000 device had become a symbol of prestige and sophistication in the medical community, so that every institution wanted its own scanner, even if a neighboring facility had one that was grossly underutilized.

Table 10.2 Selected competitive data

Company	Product line	Price	Delivery (months)	Company strengths/weaknesses
EMI	2nd generation Head and body 20 second scan Multiple models for various applications 320 × 320 pixels 2nd generation	$395 K (head) $550 K (body) 20% deposit $385 K (head)	10 10	Original innovator – some base in ultrasound $10 million per annum in R&D $1.2 B sales: $85 M in medical Strong service base Modular product line Strong customer base Rapid follower
Ohio Nuclear	Head and body 20 second scan 256 × 256 pixels 1st generation	$525 K (body) 20% deposit $295 K (head)	 9	R&D increased to $8–10 M per annum Technicare sales $100 M; scanners 50% Had nuclear; acquired ultrasound co. Strong marketing Acquired technology – slow developing
Pfizer	(announced 2nd generation) Head and body 30+ second scan 3rd generation	$475 K (body) $25 K deposit $315 K (head)	15	Company sales $1.6 bn; scanners 2% No other diagnostic imaging Strong R&D capability
General Electric	Head and body 3 second scan 320 × 320 pixels	$595 K (body) $15 K with order $75 K on mfg. start	10–12	Leader in diagnostic imaging (X-ray, nuclear, entering ultrasound) $16 bn sales: Medical Systems $400 M Very strong sales and service base Good design and development skills
Picker	Hybrid 3rd generation (announced) Body only 20 second (est.) Expected on market mid-1977	$550 K		Late entrant – but strong performance expected Leader in X-ray, nuclear, and ultrasound Strong marketing and service base $300 M sales

217

In response to heightened public awareness of the issue, five states declared a moratorium on the purchase of new scanners, including California, which had accounted for over 20 percent of total US scanner placements to date. In November, Jimmy Carter was elected president.

ORGANIZATIONAL PROBLEMS

Perhaps most troublesome to Dr Powell were the organizational problems. Tensions within the EMI organization had been developing for some time, centering on the issues of manufacturing and product design. Managers in the US company felt that they had little control over manufacturing schedules and little input into product design, despite the fact that they were responsible for 80 percent of corporate scanner sales. In their view, the company's current market position was being eroded by the worsening manufacturing delivery performance from the UK, while its longer-term prospects were threatened by the competitive challenges to EMI's technological leadership.

Although the Northbrook plant had been completed in late 1976, US managers were still not satisfied they had the necessary control over production. Arguing that the quality of subassemblies and components shipped from the UK was deteriorating and delivery promises were becoming even more unreliable, they began investigating alternate supply sources in the US.

UK-based manufacturing managers felt that much of the responsibility for backlogs lay with the product engineers and the sales organizations. Their unreliable sales forecasts and constantly changing design specifications had severely disrupted production schedules. The worst bottlenecks involved outside suppliers and subcontractors that were unable to gear up and down overnight. Complete systems could be held up for weeks or months awaiting a single simple component.

As the Northbrook plant became increasingly independent, US managers sensed that the UK plants felt less responsibility for them. In tight supply situations they felt there was a tendency to ship to European or other export customers first. Some US managers also believed that components were increasingly shipped from UK plants without the same rigid final checks they normally received. The assumption was that the US could do their own QC checking, it was asserted. Both these assertions were strongly denied by the English group.

Nonetheless, Bob Hagglund soon began urging Dr Powell to let EMI Medical Inc. become a more independent manufacturing operation rather than simply a final assembly plant for UK components. This prospect disturbed John Willsher, managing director of EMI Medical Ltd, who argued that dividing manufacturing operations could mean duplicating overhead and spreading existing expertise too thin. Others felt that the "bootleg development" of alternate supply sources showed a disrespect for the "center of excellence" concept, and could easily compromise the ability of Pantak (X-ray technology) and SE Labs (displays) to remain at the forefront of technology.

Product development issues also created some organizational tension. The US sales organization knew that GE's impressive new third-generation "fan beam" scanner would soon be ready for delivery, and found customers hesitant to commit to EMI's new CT 5005 until the GE product came out. For months telexes had been flowing from

Northbrook to EMI's Central Research Laboratories asking if drastic reductions in scan time might be possible to meet the GE threat.

Meanwhile, scientists at CRL felt that US CT competition was developing into a specifications war based on the wrong issue, scan time. Shorter elapsed times meant less image blurring, but in the trade-off between scan time and picture resolution, EMI engineers had preferred to concentrate on better-quality images. They felt that the 20-second scan offered by EMI scanners made practical sense since a patient could typically hold his breath that long while being diagnosed.

CRL staff were exploring some entirely new imaging concepts and hoped to have a completely new scanning technology ready to market in three or four years. Dr Hounsfield had conducted experiments with the fan beam concept in the early 1970s and was skeptical of its ability to produce good-quality images. To use sodium iodide detectors similar to those in existing scanners would be cost prohibitive in the large numbers necessary to pick up a broad scan; to use other materials such as xenon gas would lead to quality and stability problems, in Hounsfield's view. Since GE and others offering third-generation equipment had not yet delivered commercial machines, he felt little incentive to redirect his staff to these areas already researched and rejected.

There were many other demands on the time and attention of Hounsfield and his staff, all of which seemed important for the company. They were in constant demand by technicians to deal with major problems that arose that nobody else could solve. Sales people wanted him to talk to their largest and most prestigious customers, since a visit by Dr Hounsfield could often swing an important sale. They were also involved in internal training on all new products. The scientific community wanted them to present papers and give lectures. And increasingly, Dr Hounsfield found himself in a public relations role as he accepted honors from all over the globe. The impact was to greatly enhance EMI's reputation and to reinforce its image as the leader in the field.

When it appeared that CRL was unwilling or unable to make the product changes the US organization felt it needed, Hagglund made the bold proposal that the newly established research laboratories in Northbrook take responsibility for developing a three- to five-second-scan "fan beam"-type scanner. Dr Powell agreed to study the suggestion, but was finding it difficult to evaluate the relative merits of the US subsidiary's views and the CRL scientists' opinions.

By year's end, Dr Powell had still been unable to find anybody to take charge of the worldwide medical electronics business. By default, the main decision-making forum became the Medical Group Review Committee (MGRC), a group of key line and staff managers which met, monthly at first, to help establish and review strategic decisions.

Among the issues discussed by this committee were the manufacturing and product development decisions that had produced tensions between the US and UK managers. Powell had hoped that the MGRC would help build communications and consensus among his managers, but it soon became evident that this goal was unrealistic. In the words of one manager close to the events:

> The problem was there was no mutual respect between managers with similar responsibilities. Medical Ltd was resentful of Medical Inc.'s push for greater independence, and were not going to go out of their way to help the Americans succeed.

As the business grew larger and more complex, Dr Powell's ability to act both as corporate CEO and head of the worldwide medical business diminished. Increasingly, he was forced to rely on the MGRC to address operating problems as well as strategic issues. The coordination problem became so complex that, by early 1977, there were four sub-committees of the MGRC, each with representatives of the US and UK organizations, and each meeting monthly on one side of the Atlantic or the other. Committees included Manufacturing and Operations, Product Planning and Resources, Marketing and Sales Programs, and Service and Spares.

POWELL'S PROBLEMS

As the new year opened, Dr Powell reviewed EMI's medical electronics business. How well was it positioned? Where were the major threats and opportunities? What were the key issues he should deal with in 1977? Which should he tackle first, and how?

These were the issues he turned over in his mind as he prepared to note down his plans for 1977.

Rivalry in Video Games

Robert M. Grant

In May 2002, the video games industry was entering into the growth phase of a new cycle of expansion stimulated by the launch of 128-bit video games consoles. This was fifth such cycle since the late 1970s, each of them associated with a new generation of technology. With each cycle, the industry had surpassed its previous sales peak (see figure 11.1). Industry forecasts suggested that the fifth-generation 128-bit machines would be no exception – worldwide sales of video games consoles were expected to peak at around 45 million in 2003. However, the major part of the industry's revenues – and virtually all of its profit – was generated by software. The production of video games software had emerged as one of the most important and profitable aspects of the entertainment industry, and with retail sales increasing from about $15 billion in 2001 to $19 billion in 2003, the games software industry was comparable in revenues to the motion picture industry.

For the three main players in the industry, the key issue was how revenues and profits would be split among them. Sony had taken an early lead in new generation of 128-bit consoles, and its PlayStation2 was well positioned to repeat the dominance that its original PlayStation had achieved in the previous generation of 32- and 64-bit machines. However, by the summer of 2002 its continued market dominance was far from assured. Nintendo, with its powerful reputation among younger video games enthusiasts and its proven ability to create blockbuster games (*Super Mario Brothers*, *Zelda*, *Gran Turismo*, and *Pokémon*) was competing ferociously to take market share from Sony. In the meantime, newcomer Microsoft had launched the world's most powerful games console – the Xbox with massive computing power and graphics capability and equipped with broadband connections to allow fully interactive games playing.

The intensity of competition between the players was strongly influenced by the history of the industry. In every previous generation of machines, one company had successfully dominated the world market and had scooped the major part of the industry profit pool – the only exception being the third-generation 16-bit machines in which Sega and Nintendo had split the world market. Escalating development costs for both hardware and software would reinforce this tendency for video games to be a "winner-take-all" industry. Already Sega had exited the hardware market, its Saturn and Dreamcast machines having failed to establish viable market shares.

Yet, despite all the advantages of market leadership, the technological and creative dynamism of the industry had resulted in transitions of market leadership. Nintendo had taken over from Atari, Sony had displaced Sega and Nintendo. The key issue for Nintendo and Microsoft was to understand how to harness the forces of change – new technology, consumers' desire for novel games, and the complementarities between hardware and software – in strategies that would confer competitive advantage in the new product cycle. For Sony, the critical issue was how it could best exploit the advantages of incumbency – a vast installed base and massive library of games titles – to thwart the ambitions of the old challenger, Nintendo, and the new warrior, Microsoft.

■ ATARI AND THE 4-BIT GAMES MACHINES: 1972–85 ■

The home video games market emerged during the late 1970s. Its origins lay in the video games machines designed for amusement arcades. The first of these electronic arcade video games was *Pong*, created by Nolan Bushnell in 1972. With $500, Bushnell and a friend formed Atari to market the game. This simple coin-operated table-tennis game caught on in bars and arcades, but Atari's failure to establish effective patent and trademark protection resulted in a flood of imitators. By 1973, Atari held 10 percent of the new video game industry, and the rest of the market was shared among the followers.

Meanwhile, several companies, including Magnavox, had developed home video game consoles with a few preprogrammed games, but these dedicated machines attracted little consumer interest. Atari itself introduced a home version of its *Pong* machine in 1975. The key innovation that permitted the development of the home video market was Fairfield's release of Channel F, the first home video game system to accept interchangeable cartridges. Interchangeable cartridges allowed games consoles to become versatile machines capable of playing a variety of games. Nolan Bushnell saw the potential of games consoles with interchangeable cartridges. Two months after the release of Channel F, he sold Atari to Warner Communications for $27 million to give him the financial backing required to develop and launch a new home games machine. In 1977, Atari (now a division of Warner) released its 2600 home video games console at a retail price of $200. The release of *Space Invaders* (1979) and *Pac-Man* (1981) unleashed a craze for video games. In 1982, both games were transferred from arcades to the Atari 2600: sales skyrocketed. During 1982 Atari held almost 80 percent share of the video game market.

However, competition in both hardware and software intensified in 1982. Mattel had entered the industry with its Intellivision system in late 1979, Coleco introduced ColecoVision, and former Atari employees set up Activision. Like the Atari 2600, all these competing consoles were 4-bit machines. During 1982, 20 new suppliers of Atari-compatible cartridges entered the market and 350 new game titles were released in that year. Atari was unable to prevent independent software developers from marketing games for the Atari 2600, though Atari was able to collect a royalty. The market became oversupplied, forcing software manufacturers with slow-selling game titles to liquidate their inventories at closeout prices during 1983 and 1984: on some games, prices were slashed from $40 to $4. Meanwhile, consumer interest was shifting from video games to personal computers. The collapse of sales forced Atari into burying truckloads of unsold video game cartridges in the Arizona desert, forcing parent Warner Communications to report a $539 million loss on its consumer electronics business in 1983. In 1984 Warner Communications and Mattel were driven to the brink of bankruptcy by the losses of their video game subsidiaries. Warner sold its Atari division that year, and in 1985 both Mattel and Coleco announced they were exiting the video game business. Industry sales of video games collapsed from $3 billion in 1982 to $100 million in 1985.

■ NINTENDO AND THE 8-BIT ERA: 1986–91 ■

Nintendo was established in 1889 in Kyoto, Japan as a playing card manufacturer. In 1922, Hiroshi Yamauchi, the great-grandson of Nintendo's founder, became the company's president at the age of 22 and led Nintendo's expansion into the toy business. In 1975, Yamauchi encouraged Nintendo's entry into video games, initially through licensing Magnavox's system. In 1983, Nintendo released the 8-bit Famicom home video system that used interchangeable cartridges. The ¥24,000 ($100) machine sold 500,000 units in Japan during its first two months.

In 1980, Nintendo established Nintendo of America to enter the $8 billion-a-year US arcade business. After a slow start, Nintendo had a hit in 1981 with *Donkey Kong*, created by Nintendo's legendary game developer, Sigeru Miyamota. In the fall of 1985, Nintendo test-marketed Famicom, which was renamed the Nintendo Entertainment System (NES), in New York. Despite the widespread belief that home video game systems were a fad that had seen its day, Nintendo sold over a million units in the US during its first year. By the end of 1987, three million games had been sold. *Legend of Zelda* became the first game to sell over a million copies and in 1986, *Super Mario Brothers* was launched; the game would eventually sell 40 million copies worldwide. Miyamota developed both games. By 1988, Nintendo had an 80 percent market share of the $2.3 billion US video game industry. In 1989, Nintendo expanded its market with the launch of GameBoy, a portable video game system.

However, Nintendo learned a valuable lesson from Atari's failure: it was important to control the supply of the game cartridges to ensure quality and prevent fierce price competition. To this end, Nintendo required its game developers to follow strict rules regarding the creation and release of new games for its NES game players. Prior to release, Nintendo had to approve the content of a game. Every games cartridge incorporated a "security chip" that permitted it to operate on the Nintendo console. Nintendo controlled all manufacturing of cartridges and charged its independent games developers a 20 percent royalty and a manufacturing fee of $14 per cartridge (the subcontracted cost of manufacture to Nintendo was $7). The minimum order was 10,000 cartridges for the Japanese market and 50,000 for the US market – paid in advance. Licensees were charged about twice the cost of manufacturing. Cartridges were delivered to licensees at the shipping dock at Kobe, Japan, and then distribution became the licensees' responsibility. Licensees were also limited to developing five NES games a year and could not release an NES game on a competing system for a period of two years.

By 1983 only 30 percent of the NES cartridges sold were games developed by Nintendo; the rest were from licensed third-party developers.

Nintendo's stranglehold over its software developers resulted in the huge success of its NES console, but also reflected its massive marketing and distribution effort. Its advertising, which amounted to 2 percent of sales, was closely linked to new game releases. Its monthly magazine, *Nintendo Power*, had a readership of 6 million. Its retail presence was huge – in 1989, Nintendo products amounted to 20 percent of total US spending on toys and games. Retail distribution was tightly controlled. New games were released according to a carefully designed schedule and were quickly withdrawn once interest began to wane. Nintendo typically restricted shipments of its most popular games, and discouraged its retailers from carrying competitive products.

Between 1984 and 1992, Nintendo's sales rose from $286 million to $4,417 million. By 1990, one-third of US and Japanese households owned an NES and in both countries its share of the home video console market exceeded 90 percent. Nintendo's return on equity over the period was 23.1 percent – far above the average for large Japanese companies, while its stock market value exceeded that of both Sony and Nissan during most of 1990–1. Table 11.1 shows the sales of Nintendo and other manufacturers since 1990.

■ SEGA AND THE 16-BIT ERA: 1992–5 ■

Sega Enterprises, Ltd (Sega) is a Japanese company founded by Americans. In 1951, two Americans in Tokyo, Raymond Lemaire and Richard Stewart, began importing jukeboxes to supply American military bases in Japan. In 1965, their company merged with Rosen Enterprises, founded by David Rosen, a former US airman who had been stationed in Japan. Not happy with the game machines available from US manufacturers, Rosen decided to make his own. The company's first hit was a submarine warfare arcade game called Periscope. Sega was acquired by Gulf & Western in 1969 and went public in 1974. Hayao Nakayama, a Japanese entrepreneur and former Sega distributor, was recruited to head Sega's Japanese operation; Rosen headed the US operation. Through the 1970s and early 1980s, the video game industry went through a boom period. Sega's revenues reached $214 million in 1982. The overall game industry hit $3 billion in 1982, but collapsed three years later with sales of $100 million. With the video game slump, Gulf & Western were keen to sell, and Nakayama and Rosen bought Sega's assets for $38 million in 1984, thus forming Sega Enterprises Ltd. The deal was backed by CSK, a large Japanese software company that in 1998 owned 20 percent of Sega. Nakayama became the chief executive, and Rosen headed the US subsidiary. Sega went public in 1986. Rosen had since become a director of Sega and co-chairman of its American subsidiary.

Like Nintendo, Sega had migrated from arcade games to home games; however, in Japan, Sega's 8-bit Master System lagged well behind Nintendo's Famicom. The US story was similar. Sega launched Master System in the US in 1986, but despite better graphics than Nintendo's NES, Sega achieved only a 15 percent market share. In Europe, where Nintendo sales had been slow to take off, Sega did better and Sega of Europe accounted for a large share of Sega's revenues.

Table 11.1 US retail sales of hardware and software by console type, 1990–2001 ($, millions)

	1990	1991	1992	1993	1994	1995	1996	1997	1998	1999	2000	2001
Nintendo												
NintendoES	2,904	1,833	720	370	102	34	15	—	—	—	—	—
Super NES	—	560	1,733	1,890	1,471	823	514	243	137	20	0	—
N64	—	—	—	—	—	—	490	1,690	2,032	1,887	1,532	804
GameCube	—	—	—	—	—	—	—	—	—	—	—	—
Sega												
Genesis	280	586	1,090	1,706	1,490	719	294	180	0	0	—	—
Game Gear	—	91	162	219	318	135	77	34	13	0	—	—
Sega CD	—	—	61	232	215	30	0	—	—	—	—	—
32-X	—	—	—	—	107	63	0	—	—	—	—	—
Saturn	—	—	—	—	—	140	368	311	148	0	0	—
Dreamcast	—	—	—	—	—	—	—	—	—	1,160	820	182
Sony												
PlayStation	—	—	—	—	—	375	1,254	2,525	3,161	2,882	2,087	1,157
PlayStation2	—	—	—	—	—	—	—	—	—	—	493	3,762
Microsoft												
X-box	—	—	—	—	—	—	—	—	—	—	—	540
Other												
Atari Lynx	32	40	32	13	3	—	—	—	—	—	—	—
Atari Jaguar	—	—	—	7	64	52	0	0	0	0	—	—
3DO-based	—	—	—	29	238	252	24	0	50	50	10	0
Phillips CD-I	—	—	49	78	64	54	138	21	—	—	—	—
Total hardware & software	3,216	3,110	3,847	4,534	4,066	2,686	3,174	5,004	5,541	5,999	4,942	6,445
Sales composition												
Hardware	31%	37%	40%	37%	34%	34%	43%	43%	36%	22%	32%	46%
Software	69%	63%	60%	63%	66%	66%	57%	57%	64%	78%	68%	54%
Total	100%	100%	100%	100%	100%	100%	100%	100%	100%	100%	100%	100%

Sources: IDC, Gerard Klauer Mattison & Co., and case writer estimates.

In October 1988, Sega introduced its 16-bit Mega Drive home video system in Japan. Despite superior graphics and sound to the existing 8-bit systems and support from several of its arcade games, only 200,000 units were sold in the first year. In September 1989, the system, now renamed Genesis, was launched in the US priced at $190 with games selling at between $40 and $70. This was 16 months before Nintendo released its 16-bit Super NES player. In June 1991, Sega launched its *Sonic the Hedgehog* game and began bundling the game with its Genesis player.

The success of *Sonic* together with an advertising campaign built around the slogan "Genesis does what Nintendon't" established Sega's Genesis as the cool alternative to the Nintendo NES. In addition, Sega targeted a broader market than Nintendo, directing its appeal to adults as well as teenagers. The result was a surge of independent software developers who began writing games for Sega. By September 1991 there were 130 software titles available for the Genesis. Sega's licensing terms were similar to those of Nintendo, but there was no exclusivity clause and Sega's royalty charge was higher than Nintendo's – around $20 per cartridge. Support by games developers and retailers for Sega's Genesis was partly a result of the unpopularity that Nintendo had generated through its allegedly monopolistic practices.

Nintendo launched its 16-bit machine, the Nintendo Super-NES, in September 1991. It modified its licensing terms with games developers to mach those of Sega: it raised its fees to $20 a cartridge and abandoned its exclusivity clause.

Despite Nintendo's huge installed base, brand awareness, and extensive distribution, the 16-bit market represented a new competitive arena where Sega was able to offer a wider variety of 16-bit games titles: by January 1993, Sega's library of 16-bit titles totaled 320, compared with 130 for Nintendo. During 1992–6, the two companies split the US market almost evenly. Elsewhere, the picture varied. In Japan, Nintendo held a commanding market position over Sega with the Super NES outselling Genesis by about nine to one. Nintendo maintained its market leadership in Europe – but barely. Sega was a market leader in several European countries and was a close follower in several others.

■ THE SONY PLAYSTATION AND THE 32/64-BIT GENERATION: 1995–8 ■

Established in Japan in May 1946, Sony Corporation emerged during the 1970s and 1980s as one of the world's most successful and innovative consumer electronics companies. In 1990, Sony began developing a 32-bit games machine that utilized software stored on CD-ROMs. Sony introduced its PlayStation in the Japanese market in December 1994 and in the US in September 1995. The European launch did not occur until the spring of 1997.

In the new generation of 32-bit video games using CD-ROM software, Sega was able to beat Sony to market. Sega's Saturn was launched in Japan a month before PlayStation, and in the US it had a three-month lead over PlayStation. Nevertheless, it was Sony that quickly became the market leader in the new generation of machines. Prior to its launch, Sony had built a large library of games titles. It had courted the top games developers, to the point of contributing financially for developing games on the Play-

Station, and offering a broad range of game development tools, designing its hardware to facilitate game development.

Sony's ability to gain the support of both developers and retailers was also a result of Sony's stature and credibility. Despite Sony's lack of history in video game hardware or software, the company was considered a formidable competitor because of its global distribution capability, brand awareness, and the content potential of the movie libraries of Columbia Pictures and Tri-Star Entertainment (both Sony subsidiaries). Sony made few mistakes in launching its PlayStation: it came to market with a wider range of quality games, well-planned distribution, and a massive advertising budget.

By contrast, Sega, despite its solid reputation among video game consumers and its well-known brand, suffered from the ill-coordinated product launch of its Saturn system. Only a handful of game titles were available at the launch, the supply of machines was limited by lack of manufacturing capacity, and distribution was haphazard. Sony's machine attracted such a huge early following that Sega could not recover. Sega's US sales were sluggish throughout 1996 and 1997. At the end of 1997, Saturn had an estimated total installed base of fewer than 2 million units. Almost no third-party licensees published titles exclusively on the Saturn, and very few planned to publish any new titles for the Saturn system. Saturn's market failure was attributed to its comparatively high launch price, its lack of blockbuster exclusive titles, and a development system that many developers felt was inferior to that of the PlayStation. To bolster the declining market share of its Saturn player, Sega instituted rebate and incentive programs. Sega stopped marketing the Saturn in the United States in the spring of 1997.

Meanwhile, Nintendo attempted to recapture market leadership by leapfrogging Sony in technology. The N-64 system launched in Japan in May 1996, in the US in September 1996, and in Europe in the spring of 1997 used a 64-bit processor. One of its launch games – *Super Mario 64* – was acclaimed as one of the best games ever developed, while the James Bond game, *GoldenEye*, was a major draw that attracted customers to the N64. Unlike Sony, Nintendo stuck with cartridges instead of CD-ROMs. Although this permitted cheaper hardware, it resulted in lower margins for developers and made distribution more cumbersome. Nintendo games were priced $15 to $20 above those of PlayStation games.

There was little doubt as to the winner of this competitive battle. Sony achieved market share leadership in Japan, the United States, and Europe. In early 1998, Sony's game division had sold more than 33 million PlayStation game players worldwide, along with 236 million games CDs. PlayStation was one of Sony's greatest product successes in its history.

From a consumer standpoint, Sony PlayStation's most attractive features (compared to those of Nintendo's N-64) were its lower software costs and greater library of titles. The average PlayStation title retailed for fewer than $45, whereas N-64 titles averaged close to $60. Hardware prices were comparable at $150, with some industry participants expecting a possible PlayStation price cut to below $100 sometime in 1998.

From a software developer's point of view, the PlayStation system had both advantages and disadvantages. On the positive side, the manufacturing cost of PlayStation CD-ROMs was far lower than that of N-64 cartridges, and CD-ROMs containing a PlayStation video game could be pressed and shipped to retailers in much less time than

Table 11.2 Relative costs: Playstation and Nintendo 64, 1997

	PlayStation $	Nintendo 64 $
Hardware		
Graphics subsystem	35.83	29.11
Central electronics	51.51	78.16
Audio subsystem	25.71	10.02
Card MVA	16.27	10.98
CD-ROM subsystem	48.50	—
PCB	12.09	2.55
Other	23.54	29.10
Total	213.45	159.92
Software		
Cost to software developer, of which:	12.00	34.00
manufacturing cost	1.50	12.00
royalty fee	7.50	19.00
developer's variable cost	3.00	3.00
Wholesale price	30.00	45.00
Retail price	40.00	60.00

Source: CIBC Oppenheimer.

Nintendo cartridges (which were made in Japan). Furthermore, N-64 cartridges had to be paid for at the time of order placement. The longer lead times for getting N-64 cartridges on retailer shelves also meant greater inventory and sales risks for Nintendo game developers. It was difficult to judge how quickly a title would sell, particularly in the case of newly introduced games. To keep from losing out on sales and from disgruntling both retailers and consumers, publishers of Nintendo games were motivated to order larger quantities in order to avoid retailer stock-outs of what might prove to be a popular-selling title. In contrast, retailers could normally be resupplied with additional copies of hot-selling PlayStation titles within a matter of days (the packaging and booklets took longer to complete than the CD pressing). If a PlayStation's title didn't sell well, no additional discs had to be pressed, and the costs associated with slow-selling inventories were minimized. Table 11.2 shows cost comparisons between PlayStation and the N-64 for both software and hardware.

Most software publishers liked developing PlayStation games because of their lower prices and short production lead times, features which gave them a lower break-even point for recovering development costs – the estimated break-even point for the N-64 was 190,000 units, versus 172,000 units for the PlayStation.

In terms of gaining the support of third-party developers, the competitive disadvantages Nintendo faced from higher cartridge costs and longer lead times to supply retailers had to be balanced against the advantages afforded by Nintendo's strategy of restricting the number of its game titles. Sony's PlayStation had over 300 titles vying for shelf space. It was estimated that the average N64 title sold over 400,000 units in

Table 11.3 Worldwide sales of 32-, 64-, and 128-bit hardware systems, 1994–2000 (millions of units)

	1994	1995	1996	1997	1998	1999	2000
Unit sales							
United States	—	1.0	4.8	11.8	13.5	9.0	7.3
Europe	—	0.6	1.9	4.4	6.4	6.4	4.7
Japan	0.8	3.6	6.6	7.0	6.9	6.6	5.1
Rest of World	0.0	0.3	0.8	1.5	1.9	2.0	1.8
Total	0.8	5.4	14.1	24.7	28.7	23.9	18.9
Cumulative installed base							
United States	—	1.0	5.8	17.6	31.1	40.1	47.5
Europe	—	0.6	2.4	6.9	13.2	19.6	24.3
Japan	0.8	4.4	11.0	18.0	24.9	31.4	36.5
Rest of world	0.0	0.3	1.1	2.6	4.6	6.6	8.4
Total	0.8	6.2	20.3	45.0	73.7	97.6	116.7

Sources: Gerard Klauer Mattison & Co., and IDC.

1997 whereas the average PlayStation game had sales of just over 69,000 copies. Hence, software developers had the potential to make more profit from a successful N-64 game than from a successful PlayStation game. Sony's ability to offer a vast library of titles for the PlayStation, assisted by its high ratio of games sold per console (called the *tie ratio*), was increasing. The PlayStation had a particularly attractive tie ratio (from a game developer's perspective). PlayStation's tie ratio was estimated to be 5.82 : 1 in 1997 and grew to about 6.40 : 1 in 1998. This compared to tie ratios of less than 5 : 1 for older systems during their prime and a 2.55 : 1 ratio for the N-64 titles.

In June 1997, in an effort to combat the cost disadvantage of its cartridges, Nintendo began cutting the prices it charged third-party licensees for N-64 cartridges from over $30 to as low as $21. Nintendo management believed that N-64's rapidly growing installed base and recently reduced software prices would attract more game developers and publishers. The fierce competition between Sony and Nintendo fueled further expansion in the market. During 1997 and 1998, worldwide sales of video games consoles reached unpredicted levels. (See table 11.3.)

■ THE BATTLE FOR THE 128-BIT GENERATION ■

The Sega Dreamcast

The failure of Saturn was a massive blow for Sega. During 1998, Sega began work on its Dreamcast games system which it hoped would give it market leadership in the new generation of 128-bit machines. The key to Sega's strategy was to be first to market with a new 128-bit console, thus leapfrogging Sony and Nintendo in technology. By using PC-based technology for its hardware, Sega aimed to make it easy for game developers to create games for Dreamcast, and facilitate new versions of existing PC-based games. The company also wanted to pioneer internet-based interactivity.

Dreamcast was launched in Japan at the end of 1998. A major feature of Dreamcast was in permitting interactive games playing through the internet. The launch was seen as Sega's last chance: "This is the last roll of the dice for Sega. If it doesn't work it will have to pull out of the sector," said Stuart Dinsey of trade magazine *MCV*. Nick Gibson of stock broking and consulting firm Durlacher added: "Sega has to make this work; it has no contingency plans. It is heavily in debt to fund the marketing." The development and launch of Dreamcast strained Sega's financial resources to the limit. In the year to March, Sega made a net loss of ¥45bn ($490m) and was forced to cut costs, including the elimination of 1,000 jobs.

Sega's president, Shoichiro Irimajiri, set a target for Dreamcast at half the global market. This was seen as an ambitious goal, given Sega's 1998 market share of less than 5 percent of the world market coupled with Sony's brand strength. "PlayStation is an unbelievably strong brand; that's taken a lot of work and a lot of cash. It has done incredibly well and could sell even more this year than last. If Sony does its job properly it can keep PlayStation hot," said Stuart Dinsey. To undermine the impact of the Dreamcast launch, Sony provided advance publicity about its new version of PlayStation (PlayStation2). In particular, it emphasized Playstation2's technologically superiority to Dreamcast (especially its use of DVD technology) and its backward compatibility (allowing consumers to use their existing PlayStation software).

Failure to produce adequate games had tripped up Sega in the past; it was a key factor in Saturn's failure: "The fact that there's a new machine with 128 bits is irrelevant to consumers to a large extent. Sega needs a killer application such as PlayStation's Lara Croft – and Sonic is not so sexy. It needs to woo developers to support the platform, something Sony has worked hard to do," said Jeremy Dale, commercial and marketing Director at Nintendo.

Launched at the end of 1998, Dreamcast achieved sales of 900,000 units by March, just short of its target of a million. During 1999, Dreamcast was launched in both North America and Europe. In both regions, Dreamcast was able to establish a strong market foothold. With Sonic playing a prominent role in Sega's marketing, Sega's US market share of game machines grew to 15% in the fourth quarter of 1999 from just 0.1% a year before. Meanwhile, Nintendo and Sony lost ground: Sony dropped to a 53% market, from 63% a year earlier; Nintendo (excluding GameBoy) slipped to a 32% share from 37%. Sega even exceeded its own expectations: It sold 1.5 million of its $199 Dreamcast machines and 4.5 million games in the US market in the last quarter of 1999 – garnering some $523 million in revenue. In software, Sony had 64% market share, the same as a year before, Nintendo had 29% market share compared with 35% in the previous year, while Sega had 7.1% compared with 0.6% a year earlier.

Yet, despite Dreamcast's successful launch, it was not the savior that Sega had hoped for. Its technical advances were significant; nevertheless, the advantages of 128-bit over 64-bit technology were much less evident than the advantages of 32-bit over 16-bit. As a result, PlayStation continued to sell strongly long after Dreamcast hit the market. In the fourth quarter of 1999, 3.3 million PlayStations were sold in North America compared with 3.9 million in fourth quarter 1998. Moreover, despite its lead in the new generation of machines, Dreamcast was always overshadowed by the hype and expectation that surrounded the forthcoming launch of PlayStation2.

PlayStation2

The launch of PlayStation2 on March 4, 2000 was the most eagerly anticipated event in the history of the Japanese consumer electronics industry. By 7 A.M. in the morning of the launch, lines of eager games enthusiasts formed outside Sony dealers and, in several instances, police had been called to control the games enthusiasts. In 48 hours, all one million PlayStation2s were sold, ten times the number sold when the original PlayStation was made available.

Ken Kutaragi, the maverick engineer who was the driving force behind Sony's entry into video games, had masterminded the design of PlayStation2. In the summer of 1996, Kutargari had assembled a team of engineers from Sony and its manufacturing partner, Toshiba, and asked them to design a games machine with performance that exceeded any PC and with graphics processing power ten times that of the original PlayStation.

At ¥39,800, PlayStation2 was a 128-bit machine offering cinematic-style graphics, a DVD player capable of showing films, and the potential for internet connectivity. Nobuyuki Idei, Sony's president, aimed to make the PlayStation2 the main mechanism for consumers to access the internet, offering online games, e-commerce, e-mail, and the ability to download music, software and video. As Kazuo Hirai, president of Sony US, enthused, "PlayStation 2 is not the future of video games entertainment, it is the future of entertainment, period." However, initially, PlayStation2 did not include a modem, a mistake according to Sega's president Shoichiro Irimajiri. Sony's Idei countered that modem technology was moving so fast that it was better to sell them as add-ons.

PS2 represented a huge investment for Sony. The company invested $1 billion in two plants, one a joint venture with Toshiba to make the main central processing unit (the "Emotion Engine"), and another to manufacture the graphics synthesizer. But the marketing expenses incurred in the global rollout of PS2 would dwarf investment in technology and manufacturing plants. Given these investments, and PS2's low price, analysts were forecasting that it would not be until 2002 that Sony's games division exceeded the ¥136bn record operating profits it achieved in 1998. However, Sony was confident that the business model underlying its original PlayStation remained sound. "The great thing about the games console business is that products last for three years," said Mr. Idei. "In the world of the PC, a product is doing well if it lasts three months. With the PlayStation2 we have lots of time to recoup our investment." The product provided two profit streams: those generated by the sale of the console (the original PlayStation sold 71 million units) and the much bigger profit stream from software (Dresdner Kleinwort Benson estimated that almost half of Sony's ¥255 billion operating profit for 2000 would derive from games software). PS2 also offered the possibility of a third revenue stream: online usage.

Despite massive investments and careful planning, the launch of the PS2 was far from smooth. Shortages of two key components – the graphics synthesizer (made by

Sony) and the "Emotion Engine" central processor – resulted in a shortage of PS2s for the critical US Christmas shopping period. PS2 was also handicapped by a shortage of software. The power and sophistication of PS2, together with a number of technical quirks, meant that it was a difficult machine for which to develop games. Hence, most of the early PS2 games were revisions of earlier titles.

Sega's Response

Despite good sales of Dreamcast in North America and Europe, as the launch of Sony's PlayStation2 approached, Sega's sales in Japan began to decline. Although Sega sold two million Dreamcast consoles in Japan between its launch in November 1998 and the first quarter of 2000, Sony sold 1.8 million PlayStation2s in just two months. During the first half of 2000, pessimism grew over Sega's prospects. Its share price more than halved between February and June 2000 and rumors circulated that Shoichiro Irimajiri, Sega's president, would resign because of the poor performance.

Facing the prospect of becoming an also-ran in the video game machine market, Sega initiated a bold new plan to grab market share: give away the hardware. Starting in August, Sega offered its Dreamcast console at no charge. The offer was available to customers who subscribed to a new Sega web service for two years at $21.95 a month. Customers who already owned a Dreamcast would get a free keyboard and a $200 check if they subscribed. Sega was betting on spurring revenues from software and internet service: "We may give up $400 million in hardware revenue," said Peter Moore, Marketing VP at Sega of America, "but with two-year service contracts we can make $1 billion in internet service-provider revenue." The key issue for Sega was whether sufficient numbers of game players wanted to hook their machines to their television sets and cruise the web. Despite the hype about accessing the web with video games consoles, the primary medium for the internet is still the personal computer.

During summer 2000, Sega established Sega.com, an independent company headed by Brad Huang, a 35-year-old whiz kid and former hedge-fund manager who pitched the strategy to Sega Chairman Isao Okawa a year earlier. Sega's online-gaming website, SegaNet, made its debut in August 2000. The website provided Sega with a portal to the internet and a gathering place for Sega fans, permitting Sega to sell space to other advertisers. Eventually, Sega hoped to provide games for which it would be able to charge a premium monthly fee. Gamers with Dreamcast consoles would be able to use any internet service provider to access the SegaNet site. But Sega hoped to persuade them to sign up for its high-speed service, which would be provided by GTE Corp.'s GTE internetworking unit.

Sega's vision of using internet connectivity as a basis to wrest market share from Sony was never fulfilled. By the fall of 2000, Sega's sales revenues were slipping, losses were mounting, and the company was carrying a debt burden of $500 million. In October 2000, Sega threw in the towel. It announced its withdrawal from video games hardware in order to concentrate upon games software.

Nintendo: the GameCube

Meanwhile, Nintendo saw little option but to continue fighting its corner in the video games market. During 1999 sales of the N64 began to decline. In the fourth quarter, Nintendo sold 1.9 million units, compared with 2.4 million in fourth quarter 1998. Between its launch in 1996 and April 2000, it had sold 29.6 m Nintendo 64 machines, against 70 m PlayStations over the same five-year period. Increasingly, the N64, which used bulkier games cartridges instead of the CD-ROMs or DVDs, was viewed as technologically outdated. However, Nintendo still dominated the hand-held market, and continued to be profitable. Like Sony, Nintendo tried to head-off declining sales by cutting console prices in the US from $129 to $99 in the fall of 1999.

In June 2000, it unveiled a new portable version of its Nintendo 64 console, quickly countering Sony's announcement of a smaller, portable version of its rival PlayStation console, known as the PSone. Both companies were targeting mobile internet users of Japan's NTT DoCoMo's I-mode web phone service. Nintendo was also preparing to launch a new version of the GameBoy, its popular hand-held game machine.

However, Nintendo's major hopes for the future were pinned on the new internet-ready 128-bit machine that was code-named Dolphin, but renamed GameCube prior to its release in 2001. The new system would offer unprecedented graphics capability and would feature state-of-the-art software, much of which would be developed internally by Nintendo's crack developers. The GameCube involved close collaboration with a number of hardware and software companies. The specially designed processor was developed by IBM from its PowerPC processor used in the Apple iMac. The graphics chip was supplied by ArtX – a start-up company founded by ex-Silicon Graphics engineers. To encourage software writers, it improved the financial terms available to third-party developers and made available a full set of development tools well in advance of the launch. Table 11.4 compares the features of GameCube with its rivals.

GameCube went on sale in Japan on September 14, 2001, with its US debut on November 18, occurring just three days after the launch of the Microsoft Xbox. Although its launch generated massive attention in Japan, initial sales of 240,000 during the first week were a far cry from selling out (initial shipments to retailers were 450,000). Despite Nintendo's internal development efforts and its wooing of external developers, only three games were available for GameCube at the time of its Japanese launch. To maximize its US market impact, Nintendo set a US marketing budget of $75 million for the fourth quarter of 2001, and set the retail price at $199 – a full $100 below that of the Microsoft Xbox and PS2. The GameCube's games library expanded during December and January. In addition to Nintendo's well-known characters, great hopes were placed on *Pikmin* – the latest creation of Nintendo's top game developer, Shigeru Miyamoto, whose earlier successes had included *Super Mario Brothers* and *Zelda*.

The Microsoft Xbox

Microsoft's decision to launch a video games console was the greatest bombshell to hit the industry in the new decade. Throughout 2000 and most of 2001, Microsoft's

Table 11.4   Comparison of the 128-bit games consoles

	Sega Dreamcast	Sony PlayStation2	Nintendo GameCube	Microsoft X-Box
CPU	200 Mhz SH4 Hitachi-made RISC processor	294 Mhz 0.18 micron custom CPU manufactured by Toshiba	485 Mhz 0.18 micron IBM "Gecko" processor derived from Power PC	Intel P3 733 Mhz
Polygons per second	3 million; 1 million with curved surfaces, fogging and lighting	66 million; 16 million with curved surfaces; 36 million with fogging and lighting	6 to 12 million real-world polygons	100 million with all effects on
Storage	1 gigabyte GD-ROM (a proprietary double-density CD-ROM)	4.7 gigabyte DVD-ROM	4.7 gigabyte DVD-ROM	DVD-ROM Also, hard drive
Graphics	128-bit 3D graphics	128-bit 3D graphics	128-bit 3D graphics	Nvidia NV-25 running 300 MHz 256-bit graphics pipeline
DVD movie player	No	Yes	No	Yes
Memory bus bandwidth	800+ megabytes/second	3.2 gigabytes/second	3.2 gigabytes/second	6.4 gigabytes/second
Modem	56 kbps	None	None	Broadband modem

Source: Nintendo Next Generation Comparison Chart.

development efforts were the subject of a frenzy of speculation by industry players, outside commentators, and games players. The software giant's entry was seen as symbolizing the emerging potential of video games consoles. As children's toys, games consoles were emerging as the primary tool for electronic entertainment, with a potential to offer movies, music, and many of the communications functions currently performed by PCs.

The Xbox was designed to place Microsoft far ahead of any other games machine in terms of technological capabilities. The *Financial Times* described it as: "Arguably the most powerful games console ever made, developed after consultation with more than 5,000 gamers and games creators, it has a staggering array of features: an internal hard disk with a 733 MHz processor, 64 MB of memory, a DVD player, Dolby Digital 5.1 Surround Sound and an Ethernet port that makes it the only game console that's internet-ready and broadband-enabled."[1]

However, despite its state-of-the-art technology, Xbox's technological advantages did not translate into a clearly superior user experience: "Although the Xbox is very good, it doesn't offer a sufficiently different gaming experience from existing consoles . . . The technological difference between generations of consoles is getting smaller all the time, and all three consoles now on the market in the US (Xbox, GameCube, PS2) have great graphics. It's hard for the average player to tell the difference."[2] The industry had long recognized that blockbuster games generated console sales; this was becoming ever more true. And, as with all newcomers to the video games industry, software availability was Xbox's major weakness. When Xbox was launched in the US in November 2001, 19 games were available. Although this was substantially more than the GameCube, it paled in comparison to PS2's more than 200 titles. Moreover, Xbox also lacked the recognizable characters owned by its established rivals, such as Mario Brothers and Lara Croft. As Nick Gibson, games analyst at Durlacher, observed: "By the time Microsoft and Nintendo complete their global launches in 2002, Sony will have built up an installed base of over 25m units compared to 4m to 5m for the others at best. This momentum, combined with strong developer and publisher support, gives Sony an unassailable lead in this console cycle."[3] Xbox's US launch was successful with 1.5 million sold in the six-week Christmas shopping period.

Xbox's biggest challenge was to make a major dent in PS2's market share in Japan. Microsoft's Japanese launch of Xbox was a major event for Microsoft. Bill Gates was present to sell the first Xbox in Japan, on February 22, 2002, and in the week prior to the launch, Microsoft released 12 new games for Xbox. Priced at ¥34,800 ($259.3), the Xbox cost 17 percent more than PS2 and 39 percent more than GameCube. However, Xbox's reception in Japan was disappointing for Microsoft. In its first three days, 150,000 units were sold of the 250,000 that were shipped (PS2 had sold 720,000 in its first three days). Soon after the launch, a number of consumers began making complaints that the Xbox was scratching their CDs and DVDs. Microsoft's hesitant response to these complaints alienated many Japanese consumers and retailers. Moreover, none of Xbox's initial games releases proved to be major hits with Japanese games players.

■ THE VIDEO GAMES MARKET IN MAY 2002 ■

Market Demand

As summer 2002 approached, the world video games industry was moving into a period of expectancy and uncertainty. Most forecasts showed the market to be on the threshold of its biggest-ever expansion phase. Each generation of games consoles had surpassed its predecessor in terms of unit sales. Despite their hesitant start, the fifth-generation 128-bit machines (PS2, GameCube, and Xbox) would surpass the unit sales of all the 32/64-bit machines (PS1, Saturn, and N64). Industry sales for 2002 were estimated at between $25 billion and $31 billion, although the breakdown between hardware and software sales varied greatly between different market analysts. There was consensus over the importance of the industry within the entertainment sector:

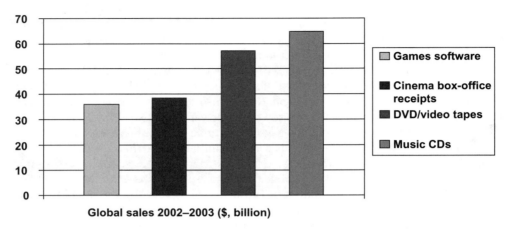

Figure 11.1 Estimated world entertainment sales by media type, 2002 and 2003 *Source*: Goldman Sachs

sales of games software would rival the film industry's box office receipts (see figure 11.1).

The increasing revenues generated by the industry throughout its history were a contrast to most of the high-tech sector, in which increasing unit sales were typically more than offset by declining unit prices. The prices of games consoles fell sharply within each generation of players, but across the generations prices had remained fairly steady. New products were typically introduced at around $200–$300, with prices eventually falling to between $100 and $200. However, by far the greater portion of revenues was generated by software whose unit prices remained around the $50 level.

Market expansion was primarily the result of the success of the hardware and software manufacturers in expanding the industry's user base. From its initial teen and pre-teen customers of Atari, games machines had gradually expanded their demographic penetration:

> Gaming is no longer the province of children and teenagers. According to a survey carried out by the Interactive Digital Software Association, 60 percent of Americans play games, either on consoles, hand-held devices, or PCs. Of those gamers, 61 percent are adults, 43 percent women, and the average age is 28. Figures from Europe and Japan tell a similar story. A generation that grew up with games has simply kept on playing. And as gamers age, their disposable income increases, making gaming an extraordinarily lucrative market.[4]

While children who grew up playing video games continued to do so as adults, game preferences changed greatly with age. Adolescents were more concerned with what was "in" and "hot." The adult market was composed of numerous niches, each with an interest in a different type of game. Adults liked titles that fit in with their lifestyle and interests. Sports-based games were very popular among adult males. Among older players, *The Sim* which simulated family life, those based on TV shows (such as *Who Wants To Be a Millionaire?*), and those based on professional sports were popular.

Despite the breadth of the market, gaining market leadership depended critically upon gaining the support for the core, games-playing enthusiasts. This group numbered about 7 to 12 million individuals within the US. They were mostly males and between the ages of 12 and 30 years old. Many read game magazines like *EGM*, *GamePro*, and *Next Generation*, and were linked by their own websites which communicated news, views, and reviews of new hardware and software.

Software

Video game console makers ("platform providers") each licensed third parties to develop software for use with their respective game-playing systems. Typically, the software developer submitted a prototype for evaluation and approval that included all artwork to be used in connection with packaging and marketing of the product. The platform providers usually retained the right to limit the number of games and approve timing of release under manufacturing and licensing arrangements. Home video game production was based on estimated demand for each specific title, with on-hand inventories depending on seasonal variations in demand during the market life of a specific game title. At the time that a newly developed game was approved for manufacturing, the developer had to provide the platform manufacturer with a purchase order for that product and an irrevocable letter of credit for 100 percent of the purchase price. Initial orders generally required 30 to 75 days to produce, depending on the platform. Reorders of cartridge games had required approximately 50 days for manufacturing. This figure had been reduced to 14 days for CD-ROM-based games. Shipping of orders required an additional 3–10 days, depending on the mode of transport and location of the software producer.

Increasing demand for multi-featured, action-packed game titles has driven up the cost of developing new game titles in the past five years. In the early 1990s, publishers customarily spent around $300,000 to develop a game for PC, Super NES, or Genesis systems. In 1998, the average budget was around $1 million per game, and many complex games, with all kinds of multimedia features, entailed even higher development costs. The development costs for some games had exceeded $10 million (e.g., Origin's *Wing Commander IV* was a high-profile example). The advent of 128-bit consoles had further added to the sophistication and cost of software development. By 2001–2, development costs were typically $2 million to $5 million per game. A successful title could bring in $200 million to $300 million – similar to box office revenues from a blockbuster movie. However, like movies, the success rate was low – a minority of games covered their development costs, while a mere handful provided the money-spinning blockbusters. Games software was almost entirely a sunk-cost business: development costs ran into the millions of dollars, but production costs were between $1 and $2 per copy.

The software side of the video game industry focused on several competitive weapons: product quality and features, compatibility of products with popular platforms, brand-name recognition, access to distribution channels, marketing effectiveness, reliability and ease of use, price, and technical support. Given the substantial cost of product development and of the marketing required to support best-selling titles, significant financial resources were increasingly becoming a major competitive asset.

Competitive forces in the entertainment software and video game marketplace had increased the need for higher-quality, distinctive entertainment software concepts. Competition for titles, themes, and characters from television, movies, and other media as the basis for "hits" resulted in higher development costs for software producers. Substantial non-refundable advance licensing fees and significant advertising expenses also increased the financial risk involved. Moreover, the ability to incorporate compelling story lines or game experiences with full-motion video, digital sound, other lifelike technology, and ease of use presented artistic as well as technical challenges that added to the cost equation.

The profits received by the console manufacturers were also derived – almost exclusively – from sales of software. The billions of dollars spent by each of the manufacturers on their 126-bit consoles were recouped through the sales of software rather than the sales of hardware: the selling price of the consoles failed to cover the cost of manufacture, let alone the cost of development. However, the licensing fees paid by the games publisher to the console manufacturer were typically about $10 per copy. The result was strongly cyclical earnings of the hardware companies. The launch of a new console would result in massive cash outflows. Even after a successful market launch, booming hardware sales would typically generate continuing losses since the manufacturers' revenues from consoles barely covered the cost of goods sold. It was not until a healthy installed base had been established that the manufacturer would begin to recoup the investment made. Thus, Sony's installed base of 30 million PS2s at the end of May 2002 and a similar number of its original PlayStations still in use gave it a huge financial advantage over Nintendo and Microsoft.

The development of video games required a blend of technology and creative talent. The development process included game development and design, prototyping, programming, art, computer graphic design, animation, sound engineering, technical writing, editorial review, and quality assurance. It took 12 to 24 months (occasionally longer) to complete a new title with a new engine, and 6 to 14 months to make existing titles compatible for play on a different platform. Many games were based on characters and themes that were either owned by the game developer or licensed from third parties. Software companies had to grapple with several strategic issues when embarking upon a new development project: (1) what development and distribution agreements to arrange, (2) whether to acquire content from outsiders or create original content with an in-house group, (3) which game-playing platform to develop for, and (4) how to attract and retain their key creative and technical talent.

The most common strategy in creating a new title was for a software publisher to hire a developer. The developer was responsible for creating and programming the game and assuring the quality of the product. The publisher handled manufacturing, packaging, marketing, and distribution issues. The publisher bore the risk of unsold inventory if the title was a failure in the marketplace. Generally, game developers were paid a royalty based on wholesale revenues. Royalty payments varied greatly, but typically ranged from 5 to 15 percent.

Many developers were attempting to publish their own titles. Affiliated label and co-publishing programs had become a popular means for small companies to publish their own titles and maintain their independence. Under an affiliated label program, a developer handled marketing and publishing, while a co-publisher dealt with distribution. In return, the developer received a royalty of up to 75 percent of wholesale revenue. A variation on the affiliated label program was expected to become the distribution method of choice.

The licensing fees paid by software publishers for exclusive rights to the intellectual property of media companies and sports organizations grew substantially between 1998 and 2002. Securing the license to produce a game based on a hit movie (e.g. *Harry Potter*) could cost several millions of dollars. In the sports market, licenses paid to sports leagues (NFL, NHL, MLB, NBA, MLS) typically involved an up-front payment, plus a royalty of 5 to 15 percent of the wholesale price for each unit sold. Many large entertainment conglomerates were setting up interactive divisions to create titles based on their own property.

The Competitive Situation, May 2002

During spring 2002, competition in all three major markets – North America, Japan, and Europe – was intensifying. For Nintendo and Microsoft, the next six months would be critical. If they were to retain the support of software developers and retailers and recoup a significant proportion of their development and launch costs, it was essential that they grabbed a substantial share of new hardware sales in all three major markets. For Sony, the key was to utilize its incumbency advantage of installed base and huge library of titles to thwart its two rivals. In March 2002, Sony cut the US price of its PS2 from $299 to $199 and made similar cuts in other countries. Microsoft responded by cutting the price of its Xbox from $299 to $199, and Nintendo reduced its GameCube from $199 to $149. Despite PS2's problematic launch, it was clearly established as market leader with an installed base of 30 million worldwide as compared to about 4.5 million each for GameCube and Xbox. Estimates for the full year suggested that Sony would maintain its leadership of a very strong worldwide market for games consoles (see table 11.5).

However, it was too early to declare Sony the winner. The advent of network gaming had the potential to upset the competitive situation. Online games playing had become increasingly popular on PCs and most forecasters anticipated that interactivity would be the next big wave for dedicated games consoles. However, as the games have raced ahead in sophistication, dial-up modem links have become increasingly unsatisfactory in providing interactivity. The different manufacturers were pursuing different internet strategies. Sony and Nintendo had developed adapters for their consoles that allowed internet access, while leaving it to service providers, cable companies, and others to provide infrastructure and host games. Microsoft had adopted a more pioneering approach. It had announced the establishment of Xbox Live to support online games through a $2 billion dedicated network. Subscription fees would be paid directly to Microsoft.

While Sony and Nintendo's approach involved less capital outlay and greater flexibility to adjust to the network technologies and billing systems of different countries,

Table 11.5 Estimate of the world video game market in 2002

	$, billions
Total industry sales	31
Of which, hardware	22
software	9
	Millions of units
Cumulative unit sales by model	
PlayStation2	48.4
GameCube	15.1
Xbox	6.9
	$, millions
Sales of PC games	8,500 (down 8.5% on 2001)
Sales of games for mobile phones, PDAs, and interactive TV	873 (100% increase on 2001)

Source: Informa Media Group.

other analysts viewed Microsoft's strategy as a potential winner. Not only would it give Microsoft control over the provision of software, such a network would offer Microsoft a distribution system for a wide array of entertainment products, including movies and music.

APPENDIX
Financial Data on the Leading Hardware Manufacturers

NINTENDO *(Yen, billions)*

	1992	1994	1995	1996	1997	1998	1999	2000	2001	2002
Total sales	562	497	429	401	463	534	573	531	463	555
Consoles								30	99	n.a
Handheld								123	190	n.a
Console software								129	64	n.a
Console software								139	165	n.a
Royalties								14	8	n.a
Operating income	157	104	86	133	115	172	156	145	85	119
Income taxes	94	59	50	74	50	88	165	108	71	77
Net income	87	53	42	60	65	84	86	56	97	106
Cash and cash equivalents	n.a.	343	397	483	542	xxx	639	594	825	895
Total current assets	n.a.	519	498	571	660	xxx	809	810	958	1038
Total assets	517	591	579	650	736	849	893	933	1069	1157

NINTENDO *(Yen, billions)*

	1992	1994	1995	1996	1997	1998	1999	2000	2001	2002
Total current liabilities	n.a.	140	108	136	170	xxx	189	169	225	212
Total liabilities	147	110	137	172	xxx	893	933	231	219	
Total shareholder equity	329	444	465	513	564	633	700	757	835	935
Capital expenditures	n.a.	162	224	252	298	388	354	436	n.a.	n.a.
Return on av. total assets (%)	18.5	10.1	7.2	9.8	9.4	10.6	9.9	6.1	9.7	9.5
Return on av. equity (%)	30.0	13.2	9.2	12.3	12.1	14.0	12.9	7.7	12.2	12.0

SEGA *(Yen, billions)*

	1992	1993	1994	1995	1996	1997	1998	1999	2000	2001	2002
Net sales:	213	347	354	333	346	360	331	226	339	243	206
Consumer products	135	229	236	188	170	164	114	85	186	116	85
Amusement Center operations	41	59	62	74	82	88	95	92	75	79	69
Amusement machine sales	36	58	52	61	85	98	124	91	74	52	53
Royalties on game software	0.4	1	4	9	10	9	4	2	n.a	n.a	n.a
Cost of sales	151	252	270	257	271	285	271	202	290	218	145
Gross profit	62	95	84	76	75	75	60	24	49	25	62
Selling, general and admin. expenses	23	33	37	45	46	44	64	62	89	77	47
Operating income	39	63	47	31	30	31	7	4	(40)	(52)	14
Net income	14	28	23	14	5	6	(36)	(32)	(52)	(418)	(18)
Total assets	226	295	301	426	441	387	369	426	375	284	244
Total shareholders' equity	90	117	165	176	178	179	122	81	81	92	84
Financial ratios											
Return on average assets (%)	8.2	10.8	7.8	3.9	1.2	1.3	(9.7)	(8.1)	(15.7)	(115.2)	(7.5)

SONY

(Yen, billions)

	1993	1994	1995	1996	1997	1998	1999	2000	2001	2002
Return on average equity (%)	16.7	27.1	16.5	8.3	3.0	3.1	(24.0)	(32.0)	(60.1)	(375.0)	(20.5)
Sales and operating revenue	4,001	3,744	3,990	4,592	5,663	6,761	6,804	6,687	7,315	7,578
of which: Games	n.a	n.a	n.a	201	408	700	760	631	661	1,004
Operating income (loss)	131	107	(167)	235	370	526	348	241	225	135
of which: Games	n.a	n.a	n.a	n.a	n.a	117	137	77	(51)	84
Pre-tax income	93	102	(221)	138	312	459	378	264	266	93
Income taxes	50	79	65	77	164	215	178	95	116	65
Net income (loss)	36	15	(293)	54	139	222	179	122	17	15
Capital expenditures	251	196	251	251	298	388	354	436	465	327
R&D expenses	232	230	239	257	283	318	375	394	417	433
Net working capital	367	616	538	816	844	1,151	1,127	974	831	779
Stockholders' equity	1,428	1,330	1,008	1,169	1,459	1,816	1,824	2,183	2,315	2,370
Total assets	4,530	4,270	4,224	5,046	5,680	6,403	6,299	6,807	7,827	8,186

Source: Company annual reports.

NOTES

1. Sathnam Sanghera, "Out of the box at last," *Financial Times*, Creative Business section, November 20, 2001.
2. Ibid.
3. S. Sanghera, "Out of the box at last," *Financial Times*, Creative Business section, November 20, 2001.
4. "Console wars," *The Economist*, June 22, 2002, pp. 71–2.

Birds Eye and the UK Frozen Food Industry

Robert M. Grant

On February 12, 1946, George Muddiman arrived in Liverpool from Canada to take up the job as first chairman of Birds Eye Foods Ltd. "It was raining," he recalled. "There were no lights on the streets; it was seven o'clock at night and dark. As I looked out of the cab window my heart went into my boots and I thought, 'What have I done? Why have I left Canada to come to this?'"

By the early 1950s, after a host of problems with production, raw materials, and distribution, Birds Eye was firmly established. In 1952, it opened the "Empire's largest quick-frozen food factory" in Great Yarmouth and was set to embark upon a period of continuous expansion. By 1964 the food sales for the previous year had grown to £75 million (from a mere £150,000 in 1946), with Birds Eye accounting for 70 percent of the market.

However, from the late 1960s both return on capital and market share declined as competition in the market intensified. By the retirement of Birds Eye's second chairman, James ("Mr Fish Fingers") Parratt in July 1972, the company's fortunes had passed their peak and by 1983, Birds Eye's share of retail frozen food sales had shrunk to 18.5 percent.

■ BEGINNINGS[1] ■

Quick-freezing arrests the process of decay in perishable foods and enables fresh foods to be distributed to the consumer, wherever located and at any season. However, the freezing process must be quick to prevent the formation of large ice crystals that damage the cell structure of the food. By the late 1920s General Foods Corporation was

This case is based upon an early case by Robert M. Grant, subsequently developed by David Collis and published by Harvard Business School (*Birds Eye and the UK Frozen Foods Industry[A]*, Case Number 9-792-074, 1994).

successfully manufacturing and marketing "Birds Eye" frozen foods in the United States using the multi-plate quick-freezers developed by Clarence Birdseye.

The establishment of Birds Eye frozen foods in the UK was the initiative of Robert Ducas, chairman of a Kent engineering company, Winget Ltd, who had tried frozen foods in the US and was impressed by their British potential. In August 1938 Birds Eye Foods Ltd was incorporated, owned by General Foods Corp., Robert Ducas, and Chivers and Sons Ltd (a British canner and jam-maker).

Birds Eye was not alone in pioneering frozen foods in Britain. Commercial quick-freezing had begun in Britain before 1939, initiated by Smedley's (National Canning). In the early years Smedley's was better established than Birds Eye. Among other leading firms striving to establish viable frozen food businesses were several distributors and marketers of fish, notably Smethurst Ltd, Mudd and Son, and Associated Fisheries Ltd (through Eskimo Foods Ltd). A cold storage company launched "Fropax" frozen foods and Manuel's, an importer and wholesaler of frozen foods, obtained the UK concession for importing and distributing Findus frozen foods.

By 1942, Unilever had become strongly interested in the Birds Eye business for its value to its subsidiaries Macfisheries (fish), Batchelors Peas (dried peas), and Poulton & Noel, Ltd (poultry). At a meeting of Unilever's management committee on February 4, 1942, the guidelines for a frozen food business were established.

> They expected to see the business develop in three main groups of produce – fruit and vegetables, fish, and meat. They hoped to see Birds Eye companies in operation all over the world, and they expected to get together a team of people who could go wherever they were needed to give help with setting up these new companies. They could see that some of their products were likely to be expensive, and they were not against running luxury lines, but in the true tradition of a business founded on the demand of the mass market for everyday products, they hoped that, in general, the business would be built on the large-scale development of certain main products.[2]

In March 1943, when World War II was at its height, Unilever acquired Birds Eye Foods. Its task of establishing a frozen food business in the UK was formidable:

> The costs of quick-freezing are high, and it does not pay to freeze any food except the best, that will sell for a price high enough to cover overhead and yield a profit worth having. . . . Next, food must be frozen at the top of its condition or most of the value of the process is lost. That means that something must be done to see that produce is gathered at precisely the right moment and processed, if possible, within hours. For fish, of course, and for some other foods there can be no control over production, but there must be a highly efficient buying organization.
>
> When the produce is frozen, there is the problem of keeping it frozen until it reaches the [consumer]. Since many of the products, such as peas, are seasonal, that means keeping them for months in cold storage. On the journey from factory to shop, there must be insulated vehicles. In the shops themselves, there must be cabinets; the shopkeepers must be persuaded to find room, and somebody must finance them – either the shopkeepers themselves or the freezing firms.[3]

Birds Eye's early history was directed towards establishing an organization that was fully integrated from controlling food production to stocking the retailer's frozen food cabinet. In the absence of a well-developed infrastructure for producing, storing, distributing, and retailing frozen foods, Birds Eye was forced to build its own system.

■ BUILDING MARKET LEADERSHIP ■

Production and Raw Material Supplies

In production, the chief problems arose from the concentration of processing into a short time space, the unreliability of machinery, and the lack of skilled labor. Much of the machinery had to be imported from the US and Canada, and capital costs were high. Over two-thirds of processing costs were fixed, although each plate freezer could be used to freeze almost any food depending on seasonal availability. The location of frozen food processing factories was determined primarily by the source of raw materials. Prepared foods, like desserts or entrees, could be located anywhere. However, for vegetables and fish, production needed to be located on the eastern side of Great Britain, near the vegetable growing areas and the big fishing ports. Peas, for example, needed to be processed within 90 minutes of picking so processing plants were concentrated in Humberside, Lincolnshire, and East Anglia. By 1960, Birds Eye operated six factories and associated cold stores at Great Yarmouth, Lowestoft, Kirkby, Grimsby, Hull, and Eastbourne. Each factory produced a number of different products in order to utilize manpower and equipment efficiently in the face of seasonal availability of raw materials.

Once production facilities had been planned, the next task was to secure supplies of high-quality raw materials. For vegetables, this was usually achieved through annual contracts with farmers who committed a certain acreage to Birds Eye, in return for a fixed price per ton according to quality. Birds Eye exercised close control over the crops, supplying the seed, determining the planting times, and approving the fertilizer and insecticide used. Technicians monitored the moisture level in the produce to determine the optimal harvesting time and radioed the processing plants which coordinated the movement of harvesting equipment from farm to farm and the transportation of produce from farm to factory.

Initially, Birds Eye owned most of the harvesting equipment that growers used. Equipment took the place of manual labor because of the speed with which the crop needed to be harvested before freezing. Over the years, growers bought their own machines under long-term contracts with Birds Eye which agreed to repurchase the equipment if the parties could not agree on an annual acreage contract. Because of the high cost of pea harvesting equipment, farmer cooperatives became the main source of vegetables. By 1974 they were supplying 70 percent of the peas and 60 percent of the beans used for freezing. Many had been supplying Birds Eye continuously for 20 years. As the demand for frozen vegetables grew, the frozen food industry became the single most important customer for green vegetables. In 1975, half of all the peas were grown for freezing, as were three-quarters of green beans.

The fish used for quick-freezing was whitefish, mainly cod, haddock, halibut, plaice, sole, and coley. Most of it was either bought fresh from dockside auctions, or imported from Scandinavia in frozen blocks of fillets for use in fish fingers and other heavily processed items. Some fish, however, was frozen at sea and bought on contract. A typical contract guaranteed to buy a proportion of the catch, provided the catch exceeded a certain size, at a price up to 5 percent below the previous month's auction price. By the late 1960s, one-third of the total whitefish catch went to frozen food companies; as a result, contracts were tending to replace open auction at fish markets. Birds Eye also purchased fish at dockside auctions – mainly at Grimsby.

In some instances, Birds Eye sought direct ownership of its sources of raw material. It entered the broiler chicken industry in 1958 and within a few years had built a capacity for producing 6.5 million birds a year at about twenty farms. It sold the farms to Ross Poultry in 1972 in the face of overproduction in the broiler chicken industry and a belief that it was of suboptimal size. In 1965, Birds Eye acquired a majority stake in a fishing company to secure a regular supply of cod. Operating problems coincided with a drop in world fish prices, and Birds Eye sold the assets of the fishing company in 1969.

As Birds Eye developed a number of innovations in food processing and freezing techniques and developments in quality management, it sought improvements in the production of its raw materials. In horticulture, Birds Eye was responsible for improvements in vegetable cultivation techniques, and harvesting equipment.

Distribution

Production problems were minor in comparison with those of establishing a national system of distribution. Distribution costs were estimated at between 15 and 25 percent of total costs for frozen food.[4] Only a limited capacity existed in public cold stores, which were used primarily for frozen meat, frozen fish, and ice cream. These were concentrated near big cities. Cold stores were also expensive. A minimum efficient scale cold store of 2.4 million cubic feet cost £0.6m in the mid-1960s. It was estimated that each doubling of capacity reduced operating expenses by 20 percent.

Birds Eye's investment in cold storage and refrigerated distribution was primarily through its sister company, SPD (Speedy Prompt Delivery) – also a wholly-owned subsidiary of Unilever:

> SPD was increasingly drawn into the problem. They developed their cold storage capacity and added insulated vehicles to get the goods to shops. . . . Cold storage has increased steadily, with buildings that were more and more advanced in their design. Depots were run in close conjunction with SPD and increased to the point where Birds Eys could store about 50,000 tons of frozen food.[5]

By the end of the 1960s, SPD had built a national system of frozen food distribution for Birds Eye. It operated from 42 depots and enabled Birds Eye to directly serve some 93,000 outlets. Birds Eye treated it as an integral part of its own activities, paying for its services at cost and making an annual profit contribution to cover the capital employed by SPD on Birds Eye's behalf. In the few areas that it could not serve cost-effectively, Birds Eye franchised exclusive wholesalers to distribute its frozen foods to retailers. The coordination of investment between Birds Eye and SPD allowed Birds Eye's tonnage sales to increase at a remarkable 40 percent per annum during the 1950s.

Retailing

The biggest barrier to the development of the frozen foods industry was the state of retail distribution. During the 1940s and early 1950s retail distribution was highly fragmented, with many small shops and with counter service nearly universal. The structure of the retail trade virtually ossified in the early post-war period as a result of food rationing which continued until 1953 and almost eliminated competition among retailers. The chief short-term problem was persuading food retailers to install refrigerated cabinets:

> At an average cost of about £150, a QIF cabinet is a big enough outlay to cause the average retailer to think twice about installing one. However, it can be shown that an average-sized cabinet of 10 cu. ft. can be made – even without proper siting – to yield an annual turnover of anything between £500 and £1,500. On an average retail margin of 20%, a retailer with an annual turnover of, say, £1,000 can net a profit of £200 before servicing and maintenance charges are deducted. Over the 12–15-year life of the cabinet this represents a substantial return on investment.[6]

In the supply of ice cream, the major manufacturers lent cabinets to retailers. The problem of this approach was the enormous capital requirements (equivalent at least to the size of investment in production facilities). In 1953, Birds Eye decided that it would not rent cabinets to retailers. Instead, it persuaded two producers of industrial refrigerators and air-conditioning equipment, Prestcold and Frigidaire, to start the production of "open top" display cabinets suitable for frozen food storage and display. Birds Eye only sought new business with retailers that installed such cabinets.

Market Development and Product Innovation

With the infrastructure in place, demand for frozen foods expanded. In the beginning, frozen foods were regarded as a luxury preferred over canned or dried food for their retention of the appearance and flavor of the fresh product.

As the price of frozen foods fell, growth increased rapidly, though the price elasticity of demand remained very high and seasonal and annual fluctuations in the consumption of frozen foods were strongly influenced by the price and availability of fresh produce. Between 1956 and 1981, sales increased at an average annual rate of about 15 percent. although the rate of growth of tonnage sales tended to decline over time. From 1956 to 1961, average annual growth was 36 percent, falling to 10.5 percent per annum between 1962 and 1973, and 6.9 percent between 1974 and 1980. Table 12.1 shows the growth in UK spending on frozen food sales.

During the 1950s and 1960s, the number of retail outlets supplying frozen foods expanded rapidly. So too did the range of frozen foods available. Beginning with seasonal produce – green vegetables and fruit – a wide variety of processed foods and prepared meals soon appeared.

Once Birds Eye had established its integrated system of production and distribution during the 1950s, its strategy became more marketing oriented. With a national,

Table 12.1 UK Frozen Food Expenditure 1967–82

	Total at constant 1975 prices (£ million)	Freezer owners %	Nonfreezer owners %	Consumption	
				In-home %	Catering %
1967	322	—	—	84	16
1973	510	17	54	71	29
1974	527	20	50	70	30
1975	500	24	48	72	28
1976	515	30	46	76	24
1977	508	32	43	75	25
1978	514	37	40	77	23
1979	539	40	37	77	23
1980	570	47	32	79	21
1981	593	53	28	81	19
1982	621	59	24	84	16
1983	646	63	21	84	16
1984	692	67	18	85	15

Source: Birds Eye.

integrated organization in place, the company's principal task was to expand sales by introducing new products, promoting consumer awareness of the convenience and value for money of frozen foods, and developing consumer recognition of the quality associated with the Birds Eye brand. The introduction of fish fingers in 1955 was followed by beefburgers in 1960 and by a stream of new fish, meat, and dessert products. The five biggest-selling products – peas, beans, chips, fish fingers, and beefburgers – accounted for nearly 40 percent of revenue. The introduction of commercial television in 1955 was vitally important for its marketing strategy by allowing it to engage in mass-market advertising of its brand and new products. The medium also gave Birds Eye a big advantage over smaller producers – until 1958, Birds Eye was the sole industry advertiser.

Birds Eye pioneered frozen foods with a product quality higher than people were used to in processed food and with a personality that combined efficiency, hygiene, confidence, and completeness. Bird Eye added values beyond the physical and functional ones that contributed to a clear and likeable personality for the brand.[7]

■ BIRDS EYE'S MARKET DOMINANCE ■

The result of Birds Eye's pioneering efforts backed by massive investment by the Unilever Group was Bird Eye's dominance of the fast-growing UK frozen food market. Throughout the 1950s and 1960s, Birds Eye accounted for over 60 percent of UK frozen food sales on a tonnage basis. In terms of the retail market, the company estimated its brand market share at over 70 percent by value and around two-thirds by tonnage for most of the

Table 12.2 Brand shares of the UK retail market for frozen foods (% of total volume)

	1966	1970	1974	1978	1982
Birds Eye	62	60	45	29	20
Ross	5	8	6	6	8
Findus	13	13	11	8	4
Own-label	—	6	14	21	28
Other	20	13	21	35	40

Table 12.3 Comparative profitability (pre-tax return on capital employed %)

	1964	1967	1971	1972	1973	1974
Birds Eye	16.2	22.2	19.1	18.4	18.7	15.9
Findus	NA	NA	7.2	5.9	7.2	8.9
Ross	NA	NA	NA	7.6	5.5	4.3
UK manufacturing industry	14.6	12.0	12.5	14.9	17.4	17.4

Source: Monopolies and Mergers Commission.

period. Among the outlets served by Birds Eye, its share of frozen food sales was 75 percent, and some 40,000 retail outlets were served exclusively by Birds Eye. Its top twenty retail customers accounted for nearly a third of total sales.

Birds Eye held a substantial competitive advantage over its closest competitors, Ross and Findus, and consistently achieved higher returns on capital employed (on an historic cost basis) than them. In 1974, for example, while Birds Eye's return on capital stood at 15.9 percent, Findus earned 8.9 percent (frozen food only) and Ross Foods earned 4.3 percent (all food businesses). Both Findus and Ross acted as followers to Birds Eye, while Birds Eye pioneered the development of the market. Findus and Ross followed with similar approaches to production, distribution, product development, and marketing. Because they imitated many of Birds Eye's product and marketing strategies, their advertising expenditures were limited. Ross Foods' parent company, Imperial Foods, told the Monopolies and Mergers Commission that it "considered massive brand support aimed at achieving dramatic increases in sales, to be far beyond the means of its frozen food companies and it never sought to answer Birds Eye's intensive advertising in kind. In 1973, Ross Foods virtually ceased advertising its retail packs since it was not making it more competitive."[8] Tables 12.2 and 12.3 show Birds Eye's brand leadership and superior profitability.

Neither of these leading competitors was prepared to undercut Birds Eye. Birds Eye's brand leadership was evident in the pattern of pricing behavior observed in the industry. Based on the evidence of published list prices, the Monopolies and Mergers Commission concluded: "The recommended retail prices of Birds Eye, Ross Foods, and Findus frozen food have until recently moved broadly in parallel, with Birds Eye more often than not, being the first to change its price."[9] The willingness of smaller producers to follow Birds Eye was explained by Imperial Foods:

In supplying frozen foods to retailers for sale under the Ross name, Ross Foods sets its prices generally at the same level as Birds Eye. Since Ross Foods only advertises and promotes its products on a very limited scale, it cannot hope to win space in retailers' cabinets and charge prices above those charged by Birds Eye. On the other hand it cannot afford to undercut Birds Eye's prices to any significant extent.[10]

Birds Eye's retail dominance was assisted by a system of discounts that encouraged larger retailers to give Birds Eye the major part of their frozen foods business. The company offered discounts to a number of retailers. The size of discounts from its published trade prices depended on the annual turnover of the retailer, the cabinet space allocated to Birds Eye products, and the frequency and size of deliveries. Overall discounts averaged 6 percent of the gross revenues of all retailers. Its "criterion in discount negotiation was to achieve a consistent level of gross profitability from various customers"[11] and the discounts were intended to capture differences in the costs of serving different customers. As a result, "large retailers achieved the highest discount – over 10% of the gross value of their purchases – although these were said to exceed the cost savings in supplying them."[12]

■ THE GROWTH OF COMPETITION ■

During the 1970s and into the 1980s, Birds Eye market share, and its profitability, declined as competition grew in the frozen foods market.

Developments in Retailing

In the 1960s, developments in food retailing began to influence the frozen food industry. First was the move away from counter service towards self-service which increased vastly the marketing opportunities available to the frozen food processors, including introducing new and novel products and packaging. Second was the emergence of supermarkets and large supermarket chains. In 1960 there were only 367 supermarkets (self-service food shops with 2,000 square feet or more floor space). The ability of the supermarket chains to pass on their cost savings to consumers, together with consumers' demand for the wider variety of goods made available by supermarkets, were major factors behind increasing concentration in the grocery trade.

Many of the major supermarket chains operated central or regional warehouses from which they distributed grocery products to their individual supermarkets. They also began to supply their own brands of frozen foods. Following the introduction by Sainsbury of its own brand of frozen peas in 1967, retailer' brands took an increasing share of retail frozen food sales.

The impact of supermarkets in expanding the amount of retail cabinet space available was reinforced towards the end of the 1960s by the introduction of specialist frozen foods stores to serve the increasing number of home freezer owners. To serve this growing market, a new model of frozen food retailing emerged: home freezer centers that combined the sale of home freezers with the sale of large packs of frozen

Table 12.4 Shares of UK packaged grocery sales by type of retailer

	1970	1974	1978	1981
Multiples	49	53	64	70
Cooperatives	19	21	18	17
Voluntary groups	16	14	10	
Independents	18	13	8	6
Four-firm concentration ratio	0.26	0.27	0.34	0.42

Source: C. Baden Fuller, *Rising Concentration: The UK Grocery Trade 1970–82*, London Business School, 1984.

foods (packed for caterers). The retailing of frozen foods by these outlets was characterized by large pack sizes, wide product range, lack of brand consciousness, and low prices. Larger cabinet capacity, usually with backup storage, enabled freezer centers to require fewer deliveries with bigger drops. Their share of frozen food sales was 18 percent in 1978 and 23.5 percent in 1986. Table 12.4 shows the changing structure of UK grocery retailing.

New Entry

While the early development of the industry had seen a consolidation around three major, vertically integrated suppliers, there was a wave of new entries in the 1960s and 1970s. For companies already engaged in food processing, a new technology, blast freezers, could be purchased "off the shelf" for as little as a few thousand pounds for a small unit. These allowed freezing and packing to occur together and eliminated the need for two separate production processes. While large-scale processing and freezing offered opportunities for automation and greater division of labor, the cost savings from increased scale of production tended to be small.

New entrants to the industry were a diverse group. The Monopolies Commission observed in 1976 that:

> A number of new companies have entered the frozen food processing industry during the past twenty years. They include Jus-Roll Ltd and Primecut Foods Ltd (then W. B. Wright Provision Ltd) in 1954, Northray Foods Ltd in 1956, Kraft Foods Ltd in 1963, McCain International Ltd and Potato and Allied Services Ltd in 1968, Frozen Quality Ltd in 1969, Country Range Ltd and King Harry Foods in 1970, White House Foods Ltd and Fife Growers Ltd in 1971, and Wold Growers Ltd in 1974.
>
> Although some of the new entrants have been new enterprises, most have been either established companies or subsidiaries of established companies. In many cases companies already engaged in the production of food have extended production to include frozen foods. Many of the smaller processors of vegetables and fruit, for example, Northray Foods Ltd, Frozen Quality Ltd, Fife Growers Ltd and Wold Pea Growers Ltd originated as agricultural cooperatives. Among the meat companies which have entered frozen food processing are FMC Ltd, Dalgety Ltd (chiefly through Dalgety-Buswell Ltd and Dalgety Frozen Foods Ltd) and Thos Borthwick & Sons Ltd (through Freshbake Foods Ltd). Several fishing

and fish merchanting companies have developed the processing of frozen food, notably Associated Fisheries Ltd, J. Marr (Fish Merchants) Ltd and Chaldur Frozen Fish Co. Ltd.

[Most] companies specialize in one or other of the broad categories of frozen food products, namely vegetables, fish, meat products and fruit and confectionery. Some companies specialize in a single product only – McCain's output is exclusively potato chips and King Harry Foods produces mainly pizzas.[13]

In addition, marketing-only companies, such as W. B. Pellew-Harvey & Co. Ltd and J. Muirhead, emerged. These bought frozen food from other manufacturers and placed their own brand names, "Angelus," "Chef's Garden," and "4F," on the products. Independent companies such as Christian Salvesen handled their physical distribution needs.

Specialist storage, freezing, and transportation providers played a critical role in allowing the entry and viability of these smaller, specialist, frozen food suppliers. Public cold storage companies such as Christian Salvesen, Union Cold Storage, and Frigoscandia doubled their cold storage capacity between 1969 and 1973. These companies came to offer not only storage facilities but a comprehensive range of processing, freezing, and distribution services. By 1974, Christian Salvesen's cold storage capacity was almost one-third of Birds Eye's. In 1978, Christian Salevesen processed three-quarters of the vegetables it stored, up from 20 percent in 1969. Services were made available on medium term, multi-year contracts. Salvesen's fleet of refrigerated trucks operating out of its national network of cold stores was also available for rent, either on long-term contracts or as needed. Sainsbury and Marks & Spencer, two of Britain's largest food retailers each with a wide range of own-brand frozen foods, used Christian Salvesen for some of their refrigerated distribution needs. Other firms specialized in the importing, broking, and distribution of frozen foods. For example, Frionor and Bonduelle began marketing products imported from their overseas parents while companies such as Anglo European foods, Snowking, Frozen Foods, and Flying Goose specialized in distribution (mainly to the catering trade).

The rapid growth of eating away from the home by the British, and the rapid shift of the catering industry from fresh and canned foods to frozen foods, provided a particularly attractive opportunity for new entrants into frozen foods. Catering establishments were served by a separate segment of the market that was more concerned with price than with brand name recognition and sophisticated product packaging. Smaller processors could easily market their products to the catering trade without the need for investing in brands and distribution. From serving the catering industry it was easy to expand into supplies to retail home freezer centers and to supermarket's own-label products.

Decline and Strategic Reappraisal

The retirement of Birds Eye's chairman, James Parratt, in July 1972 marked the highpoint of the company's fortunes. Under his successor, Kenneth Webb, Birds Eye was to face a new era of competitive pressure that led to a fundamental reassessment of its strategy.

Although still far and away the UK market leader in frozen foods, Birds Eye's market dominance existed primarily in sales of small retail packs to independent grocers and to a lesser extent, supermarkets. Birds Eye was poorly represented in some areas: in home freezer centers its share was around 8 percent in 1974 and it had little involvement in retailers' own labels. In the catering sector Birds Eye's market share by value was about 10 percent in 1973. After the early 1970s, the company's share of tonnage sales fell continuously although the market as a whole continued to expand, albeit at a slower rate.

To respond to changes in the market – particularly the rise in bulk buying by consumers with home freezers – and to the competition of recent entrants in this sector, Birds Eye introduced bulk packs to the retail market in 1972 and followed this with the establishment in 1974 of a new business, County Fair Foods, to supply the home freezer centers and other purchasers willing to accept a minimum drop size. County Fair Foods shared production facilities with Birds Eye but had a separate distribution system using Christian Salvesen because of the different requirements of freezer centers with regard to quality, product types, distribution, prices, and promotion. In 1976, Birds Eye established Menumaster Ltd to supply frozen prepared meals to caterers. In the traditional retail market, Birds Eye's main aim was to maintain sales growth, primarily by extending its product range through new product introductions. During the 1970s the company's dependence upon its traditional products – vegetables, fish fingers, and beefburgers – was reduced by a constant flow of new product introductions – especially ready-to-eat meals, desserts, and ethnic dishes (e.g., Chinese, Indian, and Italian dishes).

The widening of Birds Eye's product range and increased range of market segments that it sought to serve posed major difficulties for Birds Eye's marketing strategy and the allocation of its advertising budget. The marketing effort necessary to promote Birds Eye's products in widely different sectors – promoting upmarket prepared dishes while expanding into economy packs of commodity products – was difficult to orchestrate. "We will be walking a tightrope," explained marketing director Keith Jacobs, "the company's advertising will have two jobs to do: to maintain its image as a basic convenience foods company and to make it credible as a purveyor of, for example, pizzas." In relation to advertising, Birds Eye adopted a more targeted approach. It focused its national TV advertising on its lead lines, while new products were introduced with more regionally and segment-focused advertising. Advertising support was largely withdrawn from "support products."

In response to the growing power of large supermarket chains, Birds Eye redirected its marketing efforts. During the 1960s, marketing had been focused almost exclusively on the consumer. During the 1970s, Birds Eye shifted its focus from consumer marketing to trade marketing, with particular emphasis on developing relationships with major supermarket chains, including joint promotion efforts.

On the production side, the mid-1970s witnessed a program of heavy investment in modernization and rationalization that was designed to exploit efficiency from volume production. Between 1977 and 1980 expenditure on this program amounted to some £20 million. A key feature of the program was the focus of production resources for different product groups at specific factories – fish products at Hull and Grimsby, ready meals at Kirkby and Yarmouth, vegetables at Hull and Lowestoft, and cakes and desserts

Table 12.5 Birds Eye Foods Ltd: financial data for 1972–9 (£ 000s)

	1972	1973	1974	1975	1976	1977	1978	1979
Sales	91,838	113,997	132,636	157,142	187,415	212,322	226,308	266,018
Operating profit	2,110	2,875	3,445	4,414	3,453	2,477	6,310	9,352
After-tax profit	1,223	1,465	1,468	1,925	249	(679)	1,094	1,094
Group service charge	n.a.	n.a.	n.a.	n.a.	n.a.	5,305	5,527	8,145
Net current assets	15,164	24,717	31,034	32,069	44,792	53,337	59,141	59,141
Stocks (Inventories)	17,479	26,012	29,263	30,983	40,356	52,431	54,317	54,317
Debtors	5,928	10,677	12,124	13,739	17,483	13,523	21,102	28,522
Creditors	4,863	7,484	8,768	9,481	10,592	14,563	15,350	24,573
Capital employed	33,893	42,947	48,993	52,199	90,383	100,004	122,352	132,801

Source: Robert M. Grant, "Birds Eye and the UK Frozen Food Industry," case study, July 1985, p. 13a.

at Eastbourne – since it was observed that some specialist producers achieved much higher levels of automation.

The quest for lower costs was instrumental in the decision to merge Unilever's two principal frozen product operations, Birds Eye Foods and Walls Ice Cream, into a single company, Birds Eye Walls Ltd. Although the potential for cooperation and the elimination of duplicated functions between Birds Eye and Walls had been identified in the 1960s, the two Unilever subsidiaries had been almost entirely independent prior to the merger. During 1979–81, Birds Eye Walls worked on merging and rationalizing the two companies' distribution networks. On January 1, 1982, the combined refrigerated distribution company, Unicold-Walls, was transferred to Birds Eye Walls with the intention of speeding the reorganization of distribution and improving coordination. The plan was to complete the reorganization of distribution by early 1985 with a streamlined national network of seven regional distribution centers in operation.

Despite Birds Eye's efforts to adjust to new market circumstances, its market and financial performance continued to deteriorate throughout the 1970s. Although, in its 1979 Annual Report, Birds Eye was still able to report that "few brands in the British grocery market can claim the sort of dominance which Birds Eye has in frozen foods," that leadership was no guarantee of growth and prosperity. In the face of rising competition, Birds Eye maintained its advertising budget during the mid-1970s while cutting prices on some major-selling products. Though this approach raised sales volume, in July 1975 Chairman Kenneth Webb complained that profit margins had been halved over the previous two years and were currently one-third of the level consistent with the company's heavy investment in manufacturing and distribution facilities. In 1976, the company barely broke even and in 1977 it registered a post-tax loss. Table 12.5 shows Birds Eye's financial performance.

The appointment of Mr Don Angel to the chairmanship of Birds Eye early in 1979 led to Birds Eye reappraising its strategy in the UK frozen foods market and considering a new phase of internal restructuring. Reflecting on the erosion of the company's dominant market position, Don Angel observed that the model that had served Birds Eye's development and growth during the 1950s and 1960s needed to be reconsidered and "choices must be made about what the company is best at." In particular, there was a widespread realization that the vertically integrated approach to the sourcing, processing, distribution, and marketing of frozen foods through which Birds Eye had developed the UK market for frozen foods may now be a weakness rather than a strength for Birds Eye.

NOTES

1. Birds Eye's history is outlined in Reader, W. J., *Birds Eye Foods Ltd: The Early Days*, Birds Eye Foods Ltd, 1963.
2. W. J. Reader, *Birds Eye Foods Ltd: The Early Days*, Birds Eye Foods Ltd, 1963, p. 9.
3. Ibid., p. 3.
4. K. McClaren, "The effect of range size on distribution costs," *International Journal of Physical Distribution and Materials Management*, Vol. 10, 1980, pp. 445–56.
5. C. Wilson, *Unilever 1945–1965: Challenge and Response in the Post-War Industrial Revolution*, Cassell, London, 1968, pp. 172–3.
6. "Frozen Food: Market Prospects," *Retail Business*, Special Report No. 14, April 1959, p. 83.
7. S. King, *Developing New Brands*, London: Pitman, 1973, p. 13.
8. *Report on the Supply of Frozen Foodstuffs*, Monopoly and Mergers Commission, HMSO, 1976, p. 44.
9. Ibid., p. 53.
10. Ibid., p. 42.
11. Ibid., p. 32.
12. Ibid., p. 32.
13. Ibid., p. 9.

Euro Disney: From Dream to Nightmare, 1987–94

Robert M. Grant

At the press conference announcing Euro Disneyland SCA's financial results for the year ended September 30, 1994, CEO Philippe Bourguignon summed up the year in succinct terms: "The best thing about 1994 is that it's over."

In fact, the results for the year were better than many of Euro Disneyland's long-suffering shareholders had predicted. Although revenues were down 15 percent – the result of falling visitor numbers caused by widespread expectations that the park would be closed down – costs had been cut by 12 percent, resulting in a similar operating profit to that of the previous year. The bottom line still showed a substantial loss (net after-tax loss was FF 1.8 bn); however, this was a big improvement on the previous year (FF 5.33 bn loss). Tables 13.1 and 13.2 show details of the financial performance.

Regarding the future, Bourguignon was decidedly upbeat. Following the FF 13 bn restructuring agreed with creditor banks in June, Euro Disney was now on a much firmer financial footing. As a result of the restructuring, Euro Disneyland S.C.A was left with equity of about FF 5.5 bn and total borrowings of FF 15.9 bn – down by a quarter from the previous year. With the threat of closure lifted, Euro Disney was now in a much better position to attract visitors and corporate partners.

Efforts to boost attendance figures included a new advertising campaign, a new FF 600 m attraction (Space Mountain) which was due to open in June 1996, and changing the park's name from Euro Disneyland to Disneyland Paris.

In addition, Euro Disney had made large numbers of operational improvements. Mr Bourguignon reported that it had cut queuing times by 45 percent during the year through new attractions and the redesign of existing ones; hotel occupancy rates had risen from 55 percent in the previous year to 60 percent; and managers were to be given greater incentives. The net result, claimed Bourguignon, was that the company would reach break-even during 1996.

The stock market responded positively to the results. In London, the shares of Euro Disneyland SCA rose 13 p to 96 p. However, this did not take the shares much above

Table 13.1 Euro Disneyland SCA: financial performance 1990–94. Operating revenue and expenditure (millions of French francs)

	1994	1993
Revenue:		
Theme park	2,212	2,594
Hotels	1,613	1,721
Other	322	559
Construction sales	114	851
Total revenue	4,261	5,725
Direct costs/expenses:		
Park & Hotels	(2,961)	(3,382)
Construction sales	(114)	(846)
Operating income	1,186	1,497
Depreciation	(291)	(227)
Lease rental expense	(889)	(1,712)
Royalties	—	(262)
General & Admin.	(854)	(1,113)
Financial income	538	719
Financial expenses	(972)	(615)
Loss	(1,282)	(1,713)
Exceptional loss, net	(515)	(3,624)
Net loss	(1,797)	(5,337)
Employees (cast members)		
Number	11,865	10,172
Annual Cost (FF, millions)	2,108	1,892

their all-time low. On November 6, 1989, the first day of trading after the Euro Disneyland initial public offering, the shares had traded at 880p. Since then, Euro Disneyland stock had been on a near-continuous downward trend (see figure 13.1). The *Financial Times*' Lex column was also unenthusiastic:

> Still beset by high costs and low attendances, Euro Disney will find it hard to hit its target of break-even by the end of September 1996. Costs in the year were reduced by FF 500 m by introducing more flexible labor agreements (more part-timers, increased job sharing and the use of more students in the peak season) as well as outsourcing contracts in the hotel operation. But the company admits that the lion's share of cost reductions has now been realized. Now it hopes attendances are rising . . . Getting people to spend more once they are at the park might be more difficult. Euro Disney is pinning its hopes on economic recovery in Europe. It'll have to start paying interest, management fees and royalties again in five years' time. Management will not say whether it'll be able to cope then.[1]

Returning to his office at the end of the press conference, Bourgingnon sighed. Since taking over from the previous chief executive, Robert Fitzpatrick, in 1993, the 46-year-old had been engaged in a continuing battle to ensure the survival of Euro Disney. Now

Table 13.2 Euro Disneyland SCA: financial statements 1993–4 (under US GAAP)

Balance sheet

	1994	1993	1992
Cash and investments	289	211	479
Receivables	227	268	459
Fixed assets, net	3,791	3,704	4,346
Other assets	137	214	873
Total assets	4,444	4,397	6,157
Accounts payable & other liabilities	560	647	797
Borrowings	3,051	3,683	3,960
Stockholders' equity	833	67	1,400
Total liabilities & stockholders' equity	4,444	4,397	6,157

Statement of operations

	1994	1993	1992
Revenues	751	873	738
Costs and expenses	1,198	1,114	808
Net interest expense	280	287	95
Loss before income taxes and cumulative effect of accounting change	(727)	(528)	(165)
Income tax benefit	—	—	30
Loss before cumulative effect of accounting change	(727)	(528)	(135)
Cumulative effect of change in accounting for pre-opening costs	—	(578)	—
Net loss	(727)	(1,106)	(135)

Source: Walt Disney Company, 10 K report, 1994.

that survival was no longer an issue, Bourgingnon now faced his next challenge: could Euro Disneyland ever become profitable?

■ DISNEY THEME PARKS ■

Walt Disney pioneered the theme park concept. His goal was to create a unique entertainment experience that combined fantasy and history, adventure, and learning in which the guest would be a participant, as well as a spectator. Current Disney-designed theme parks in California, Florida, Japan, and France are divided into distinct lands. All the parks include a number of similar lands with identical attractions. These include Main Street, Frontierland, Tomorrowland, Fantasyland, and Adventureland. The objective is to immerse the guest in the atmosphere of the particular land. The theme of each land is reflected in the types of rides and attractions, the costumes of employees, the architectural style of the buildings, and even the food and souvenirs sold within the

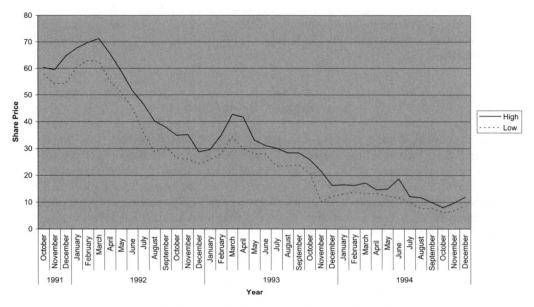

Figure 13.1 Euro Disneyland's share price in Paris, 1991–4 (in French francs)

boundaries of the particular land. Rather than presenting a random collection of roller coasters, merry-go-rounds, and other rides, the Disney parks create an all-embracing experience which envelops the guest in carefully designed, tightly managed fantasy experience such as space flight, a Caribbean pirate attack, a flying ride with Peter Pan, or a race down the Matterhorn in a bob-sleigh.

Disney theme parks benefit from the talent and expertise of the Walt Disney "family" of businesses. Parks are designed by the engineers and architects of a wholly-owned subsidiary – WED Enterprises. The themes for the attractions and characters that are featured in them often have their origins in cartoons and live action movies produced by Disney's studios. The parks also benefit from management and merchandising techniques developed over many years at Disney. These techniques have led to tremendous successes. In merchandising, Disney retail stores achieved some of the highest sales per square foot in the United States.

Disney's success can be traced to the control of the environment to create a unique experience for the visitor. This control is achieved through highly systematized operations management and human resource management. Disney has sophisticated procedures for selecting and training employees to ensure the highest levels of service, safety, and maintenance in the industry. Disney's ability to reconcile a high level of occupancy with high levels of service and customer satisfaction is achieved through sophisticated methods of forecasting visitor levels on a daily basis, and careful design of parks to minimize the frustrations of crowds and waiting. Disney also emphasizes the continual renewal of its theme parks' appeal through investment in new attractions. It then supports these with heavy promotion.

Disney parks have historically had higher attendance levels than other theme and amusement parks throughout the world. During the late 1980s and early 1990s, Disney's theme parks in Anaheim, Orlando, and Tokyo together attracted over 50 million guest visits annually.

Los Angeles Disneyland

Shortly after developing the idea of a theme park, Walt Disney hired the Stanford Research Institute to conduct an economic feasibility study of his amusement park plan and then a follow-up study to analyze demographics and traffic patterns in order to come up with a recommendation for the site. Based on the results of this study, Disney acquired 160 acres of land in Anaheim, California in 1953, and later obtained financing from ABC Television to move forward with the plan. With the financing agreement, ABC owned 34.48 percent of the shares of the new "Disneyland" park, which was the equivalent of the proportion of shares owned by Walt Disney Productions. In order to finance construction, ABC put up half-a-million dollars and guaranteed loans for a further $4.5 million. The Los Angeles Disneyland theme park was finally opened in July of 1955.

Orlando Disney World

The success of Disneyland created a real estate boom in Anaheim, resulting in Disneyland being surrounded by a ring of hotels, motels, restaurants, and other businesses. For his next theme park project, Walt Disney aimed for undiluted control over the business and its revenue stream. Walt Disney World Resort opened in 1971 on a huge track of 29,000 acres that Walt acquired outside of Orlando, Florida. Walt Disney World eventually comprised three separate theme parks: the original Magic Kingdom, the Experimental Prototype Community of Tomorrow (EPCOT) Center that opened in 1982 which in itself hosted two themes: *Future World* and *World Showcase*, and Disney-MGM Studios which opened in 1989.

The experience of creating a theme park as a destination resort represented a major development in Disney's conception of a theme park and was influential in its expansion plans into Europe. The huge 27,000 acre site allowed Disney to broaden the scope of its theme park activities to create themed hotels, golf courses and other sports, convention facilities, night clubs, a range of retail stores, even residential housing. The complementary coupling of a theme park with resort facilities that could even host commercial activities (conferences, a technology park) became central to Disney's theme park strategy.

By 1990, Walt Disney World had become the largest center of hotel capacity in the United States with approximately 70,000 rooms, of which almost 10 percent were owned and operated by Disney. Even though the room rates charged by Disney were considerably higher than other hotels in the vicinity, they achieved a remarkable occupancy rate of 94 percent during the late 1980s.

Tokyo Disneyland

Tokyo Disneyland, which opened in 1983, was a major departure for Walt Disney Company. The Oriental Land Company Limited (OLCL), a Japanese development company, had approached Disney with a proposal to open a Disneyland in Japan. Disney's top management regarded a Disney theme park in another country with a different climate and a different culture as a risky venture. Disney insisted on a deal that would leave OLCL with all the risk: the park would be owned and operated by OLCL while Disney would receive royalties of 10 percent on the admissions revenues and 5 percent on receipts from food, beverages, and souvenirs. These royalties represented licensing fees for Disney's trademarks and intellectual property, engineering designs for rides, and ongoing technical assistance. Despite the challenges of limited space and cold winter weather, Tokyo Disneyland was a huge success. By the late 1980s it was drawing 15 million visits a year – more than any other Disney park.[2]

■ PLANNING AND DEVELOPMENT ■

Beginnings of Euro Disneyland

The success of Tokyo Disneyland was clear evidence to Disney's top management of the international potential for Disney's theme parks. Europe was considered the obvious location for the next Disney park. Europe had always been a strong market for Disney movies, and there was a strong European demand for toys, books, and comics that featured Disney characters – European consumers generated about one-quarter of revenues from Disney licensed consumer products. The popularity of Disney theme parks with Europeans was evident from the 2 million European visitors to Disneyland and Walt Disney World each year. Moreover, Western Europe possessed a population and affluence well capable of supporting a major Disney theme park.

In 1984, Disney management made the decision to commit to development of a European theme park and commenced feasibility planning and site selection. In assessing alternative locations, the following criteria were applied:

- proximity to a high-density population zone with a relatively high level of disposable income;
- ability to draw upon a substantial local tourist population, availability of qualified labor, and readily accessible transportation;
- availability of sufficient land to permit expansion of the project to meet increasing demand;
- economical provision of necessary infrastructure, such as water and electricity.

Two locations quickly emerged as front-runners: Barcelona and Paris. While Barcelona had the advantages of a better year-round climate, Paris offered key economic and infrastructure advantages, together with strong backing from the French government. Disney's interest in a European theme park corresponded with the French government's plans to develop the Marne-la-Vallée area east of Paris. The result was rapid progress of Disney's formal negotiations with the range of local government authorities and public bodies whose cooperation and agreement was essential for a project of this scale. The proposed site's demographic characteristics offered the right set of conditions for a successful theme park. The park rested on a 4,500-acre site 32 kilometers east of Paris, providing proximity to a metropolitan area and room for expansion; the high population of the greater Paris area (over 10 million) and Europe (over 330 million) provided a large consumer market; and existing and planned transportation equipped the park with access to vital infrastructure. Paris was already a major tourist destination with excellent air, road, and rail links with the rest of Europe.

On March 24, 1987, the Walt Disney Company entered into the Agreement on the Creation and the Operation of Euro Disneyland in France (the "Master Agreement") with the Republic of France, the Region of Ile-de-France, the Department of Seine-et-Marne, the Etablissement Public d'Aménagement de la Ville Nouvelle de Marne-la-Vallée, and the Régie Autonome des Transports Parisiens. This was followed by incorporation of Euro Disneyland SCA (the "Company") and the conclusion of an agreement with the SNCF (the French national railway company) to provide TGV (the French high-speed train) service to Euro Disneyland beginning in June 1994. The agreement involved commitments by Disney to establish Euro Disneyland as a French corporation, to develop a major international theme park, and to create 30,000 jobs in the process. The French authorities committed to provide land (at Marne-la-Vallée 32 km east of Paris) and infrastructure over the project's 30-year development period ending in 2017. The real estate deal involved Disney acquiring 1,700 hectares (approximately 4,300 acres[3]) of agricultural land at Marne-la-Vallée. In addition, a further 243 hectares were reserved for public facilities and infrastructure. The purchase price for the land included the raw land price (FF 11.1 per square meter or approximately $8,360 per acre), direct and indirect secondary infrastructure costs, and certain financing and overhead expenses of the French authorities. The area of the total site was equivalent to one-fifth of the area of the city of Paris. The land for the first phase of the development was purchased outright by Euro Disneyland SCA with purchase options on the remaining land. Euro Disneyland SCA also had the right to sell land to third parties, as long as the development plans of any purchasers were approved by the French planning authority.

The agreement provided for motorway links to Paris, Strasbourg, and the two international airports serving Paris – Charles de Gaulle and Orly, while the planned extension of the RER (the express commuter rail network) would allow visitors to reach the Magic Kingdom from the center of Paris within 40 minutes. Euro Disney[4] would also be linked to France's TGV (high-speed rail) system, with its own station serving the park. This would also give rail service from Britain through the Channel Tunnel. In addition to infrastructure, the French government's financial inducements included FF 4.8 billion in loans and a favorable tax rate (34 percent). The total package of incentives added up to roughly FF 6.0 billion.[5]

Table 13.3 Attendance at major theme parks

	Estimated attendance in 1988 (millions of guest visits)
Sea World – *Florida*	4.6
Tivoli Gardens – *Denmark*	4.5
Universal Studios Tour – *California*	4.2
Knott's Berry Farm – *California*	4.0
Busch Gardens – *Florida*	3.7
Sea World – *California*	3.4
Six Flags Magic Mountain – *California*	3.1
King's Island – *Ohio*	3.0
Liseberg – *Sweden*	2.8
Atton Towers – *United Kingdom*	2.3
De Efteling – *The Netherlands*	2.3
Phantasialand – *West Germany*	2.2

Source: Euro Disneyland SCA abridged offering circular.

The Market: Demand and Competition

A key factor attracting Disney to Paris was market potential. The greater Paris metropolis has a population of over 10 million. Sixteen (16) million people lived within a 160 m radius of the proposed site; within a 320 km radius were 41 million people; and within a 480 km radius were 109 million people. Paris' presence as a transportation hub facilitated access to this huge market. As a result, Euro Disneyland would be capable of achieving a high level of capacity utilization, even with much lower market penetration rates than those achieved by Disney's California and Florida theme parks. European vacation patterns were also seen as conducive to visits – Europeans received substantially longer weeks of vacation than US workers and in addition to their summer vacation, European families frequently took shorter vacations throughout the year. Projections of numbers of visitors to Euro Disney and their expenditures were made by consultants Arthur D. Little as part of their financial projections for Euro Disneyland SCA (see Appendix A).

The ability of Euro Disney to achieve its visitor targets would depend not only on the size of the market but also upon the relative attractiveness and number of competing tourist destinations. Although Disney viewed its theme parks as unique in terms of the quality and intensity of the entertainment experience that it offered, the company also recognized that, ultimately, a wide range of family vacation and entertainment experiences compete for household disposable income. Although there were very few large-scale theme parks in Europe to directly compete with Euro Disneyland (most of the world's major theme parks were located in the US), there were a number of family-entertainment destinations within Europe that would be potential competitors (see table 13.3). In addition, European cities – such as London, Paris, Rome, Prague, Barcelona, and many others – offered a richness and variety of cultural and historical experiences that few US cities could match and represented an alternative to Euro Disney for short family vacations. In addition, there were a host of traditional forms of family entertainment in Europe, including fairs, carnivals, and festivals, some of which were small and local while others – such as the Munich Sierfest, the Pamplona bull-running festival, the Edinburgh cultural festival, and the Dutch tulip festivals – were major events attracting large numbers of international visitors.

Of particular concern was the tendency of Euro Disneyland to create its own competition. Within two years of Walt Disney Company's announcement that it planned to build Euro Disney, three French theme parks – Mirapolis, Futuroscope, and Zygofolis – had opened in an attempt to preempt Disney's entry into the market. By the summer of 1989, two more theme parks – Asterix and Big Bang Schtroumph – opened their gates. However, with aggregate annual losses of about $43 million on a total investment of over $600 million, these parks were considered financial disasters.[6]

The Development Plan

Euro Disney's Development Program provided for a theme park based closely upon the themes and concepts of Disney's US theme parks that would be the largest theme park and resort development in Europe. The plan established two stages for the project.

PHASE 1

This, the initial and most significant part of the overall project, was subdivided into two sections. Phase 1A comprised the Magic Kingdom theme park, the Magic Kingdom Hotel (which would serve as the entrance area to the theme park), and a camping ground, which were to be completed at a budgeted cost of FF 14.9 billion. Of the 570 acres allocated for Phase 1, Phase 1A would account for the use of 240 acres to develop the theme park. The rest of the land would be developed in Phase 1B to accommodate five additional hotels; an entertainment, restaurant, and shopping complex; and sports facilities with an 18-hole championship golf course. Phase 1A also provided for the French government to construct two junctions with the nearby motorway, main access roads to the park, a drinking-water supply and distribution system, storm drainage, sewers, solid waste treatment, and telecommunications networks. The cost of the additional infrastructure, including links with the RER and the TGV, were to be constructed by the French authorities and financed by Euro Disneyland SCA.

The Magic Kingdom theme park was to include five themed lands: Main Street USA, the gateway to the park; Frontierland, a reproduction of wooden streets typical of a mid-nineteenth-century frontier town; tropical Adventure Land, the most exotic of the park settings; Fantasyland, with attractions drawn from well-known Disney characters; and Discoveryland, which, through the sophisticated use of technology, illustrates the past and the future. Each offers appropriately themed restaurants and shopping facilities.

To permit year-round operation, Euro Disney included adaptations designed to make attendance less dependent on the weather, with more interconnected covered areas than at other Disney parks. Many modifications to the themes, architecture, and dining facilities were made to tailor the park to the European market. For example, while French is the first language of the park, universal signposting is used wherever possible to aid non-French-speaking visitors, and many attractions are identified by visual cues.

PHASE 2

Phase 2 of the Long Term Development Strategy extended to 2011. It envisioned a second theme park (Disney-MGM Studios) on a site adjacent to the Magic Kingdom; 15 additional hotels, which would increase the number of rooms available by 13,000; a water recreation area and second golf course; and residential and commercial development. This phase was left flexible to accommodate the policies of the French authorities, economic and market conditions, participant needs, and visitor preferences.

CONSTRUCTION

Disney exercised close control over design and construction of Phase 1A of Euro Disney. Lehrer McGovern Bovis Inc. (LMB), an independent construction management firm with international experience in the management of large-scale construction projects, was the main contractor. LMB reported to Euro Disneyland Imagineering SARL (EDLI), a French subsidiary of Disney that had overall responsibility for designing and constructing Phases 1 and 2 of the theme park. Also reporting to EDLI were separate Disney companies responsible for design, conceptual and otherwise; engineering; and the development and equipping of attractions.

PARTICIPANTS

As with other Disney theme parks, at Euro Disneyland Participants played an important role in financial and in marketing terms. Participants are companies or organizations that enter into long-term marketing agreements with the Company. Typically, these relationships represent a 10-year commitment and physically tie the Participant to the Magic Kingdom, where it hosts or presents one or more of the theme park's attractions, restaurants, or other facilities. Relationships with Participants may also involve marketing activities featuring the association between the Participant and the Company. Each Participant pays an individually negotiated annual fee, which may contribute to the financing of a particular attraction or facility. Initial participants at Euro Disneyland included Kodak, Banque Nationale de Paris, Renault, and Europcar.

■ FINANCIAL AND MANAGEMENT STRUCTURE ■

For Euro Disneyland, Disney chose a unique financial and management structure. Rather than a pure franchise operation similar to Tokyo Disneyland, Disney chose to

Figure 13.2 The financial and management relationship between Walt Disney and Euro Disneyland

retain management and operational control of the park while allowing European investors to take majority ownership and European banks to provide most of the debt financing. The relationship between Walt Disney Company and Euro Disneyland is depicted in figure 13.2.

Euro Disneyland SCA

Euro Disneyland SCA was formed to build and own Euro Disneyland. The company was a *société en commandite par actions* – the French equivalent of a limited partnership. The company was governed by a supervisory board elected by the shareholders and chaired by Jean Taittinger, the chairman and chief executive of Societe du Louvre and Banque du Louvre. Disney took a 49 percent stake in Euro Disneyland SCA; the remaining 51 percent of equity was floated through an initial public offering underwritten by three investment banks. The shares were listed on the Paris and London stock markets. Although Disney held 49 percent of Euro Disneyland SCA equity it contributed only 13 percent of its equity book value (FF 273 m net of incentives received). The difference was "granted" to the company, both as a goodwill "gesture" in recognition of Disney's reputation and credibility in the investment community and as compensation for Disney's assumed risk in the undertaking.

The Management Company

Euro Disneyland SCA was managed by a separate management company, Euro Disneyland SA (the "Management Company"), a wholly-owned subsidiary of Disney. The Management Company, or *gerant*, was responsible under French law for managing Euro Disneyland SCA and its affairs in the company's best interests. In turn, the Management Company agreed that the provision of management services to the Company would be its exclusive business. Under the Articles of Association, the Management Company was entitled to annual fees consisting of a base fee and management incentive fees. The base fee in any year was set at 3 percent of the Company's total revenues, and increased to 6 percent after five years of operation, or after the Company had satisfied certain financial targets. On top of the base fee, the Management Company was entitled to incentive fees based on Euro Disneyland SCA's pre-tax cash flow. These incentives increased in stages up to a possible maximum of 50 percent of Euro Disneyland SCA's net profit. The Management Company also received 35 percent of pre-tax gains on the sales of hotels. In addition, Euro Disneyland SCA was obligated to reimburse the Management Company for all its direct and indirect expenses incurred in its management role. The management contract was for five years.

The Shareholding Company and General Partner

Disney's shareholding in Euro Disneyland SCA was held by EDL Holding, a wholly-owned subsidiary of Disney. This shareholding company also owned EDL Participations SA, which held the key role of "general partner" in Euro Disneyland SCA – it assumed unlimited liability for the debts and liabilities of Euro Disneyland SCA. As general partner, EDL Participations SA was entitled to a distribution each year equal to 0.5 percent of Euro Disneyland SCA's net after-tax profits.

The Financing Company

Euro Disneyland SNC was formed to buy the park facilities from Euro Disneyland SCA at book value plus development costs, then lease them back to Euro Disneyland SCA. Euro Disneyland SNC was owned 17 percent by Disney and 83 percent by French corporations. The rationale was to allow French corporations to take advantage of the tax benefits of Euro Disneyland's early years of projected losses. Once again, Euro Disneyland SNC was to be managed by a Disney subsidiary and Disney would act as its general partner with full debt default liability.

The License Agreement

Under the License Agreement, Walt Disney Company granted to Euro Disneyland SCA a license to use any present or future Disney intellectual and industrial property rights incorporated in Disney's attractions and facilities and made available to the Company for Euro Disney. These included the Walt Disney name, the Disney characters, and the proprietary technology in theme park attractions. Disney was to receive royalties as follows:

- 10% of gross revenues (net of TVA, the French value-added tax, and similar taxes) from rides and admissions and certain related fees (such as parking, tour guide, and similar services) at all theme parks and other attractions (including the Magic Kingdom and any future theme park);
- 5% of gross revenues (net of TVA and similar taxes) from merchandise, food, and beverage sales in or adjacent to any theme park or other attraction or in any other facility (other than the Magic Kingdom Hotel) whose overall design concept is based predominantly on a Disney theme;
- 10% of all fees due from Participants;
- 5% of all gross revenues (net of TVA and similar taxes) from room rates and related charges at Disney themed accommodations (excluding the Magic Kingdom Hotel).

■ CULTURAL ISSUES ■

Euro Disneyland presented huge challenges for Disney. Climate was a major problem. The long gray winter of Northern France created complex design problems that were absent from Disney's sun-drenched California and Florida parks. However, the challenges posed by adverse weather conditions were mainly technical and amenable to careful analysis. The issues of culture were much less tractable.

While the success of Tokyo Disneyland was a major factor behind the decision to create Euro Disney, the cultural challenges of France were very different from those of Japan. Tokyo Disneyland had been conceived, built, and operated on a wave of popular Japanese acclaim. As a result, Tokyo Disneyland had made very few concessions to Japanese culture. Although, at first, Disney wanted to adapt some of the attractions to the Japanese context (for example, Samurai-Land instead of Frontierland), their Japanese partners strongly resisted efforts to "localize" Disneyland, arguing that the park would attract more Japanese people if it were built as a perfect replica of US Disneyland. They emphasized that Disney's cartoon characters were very familiar to the Japanese people and that visitors would want "the real thing." As a result, only minor changes were made, such as the addition of Cinderella's Castle and the Mickey Mouse Theater.

After the enthusiasm with which the Japanese greeted Disney's entry, the response of the French could not have been more different. France presented a very different situation. French intellectuals had long shown antagonism towards American popular culture, and they were supported by widespread nationalistic sentiment that saw the French language and French culture as threatened by the global hegemony of the English language. At the political level too, France had been the most independent of the Western European powers in terms of its independent foreign policy and unwillingness to accept US leadership in world affairs. The announcement of the

Euro Disneyland project was greeted by howls of outrage from the French media and from the intelligentsia who viewed the park as a "a cultural Chernobyl," "a horrifying step towards world homogenization," "a horror made of cardboard, plastic, and appalling colors, a construction of hardened chewing gum and idiotic folklore taken straight out of the comics books written for obese Americans."[7] Euro Disney quickly became a focal point for anti-Americanism, fueled by multiple issues. For example, shortly after opening, Euro Disney was blockaded by farmers protesting US farm policies.

The design of the park incorporated many adaptations of French and European culture. Disney emphasized the European heritage of many of Disney's characters and storylines (referred to by chairman Michael Eisner as "European folklore with a Kansas twist"). Some attractions featured European adaptations: Cinderella lived in a French inn and Snow White's home was in a Bavarian village. Other attractions were unique to Euro Disney: Discoveryland featured a Jules Verne attraction, while an Alice-in-Wonderland attraction was surrounded by a 5,000 sq. ft. hedge maze.

Some "American" themed attractions were adapted on the basis of market research findings. For example, the finding that European visitors to Disney's US parks responded positively to themes embodying the American West encouraged Disney to redesign several attractions around a Wild West theme – including a mining town setting for one ride, a "Davy Crockett" themed campground, and hotels named the "Cheyenne," "Santa Fe," and "Sequoia Lodge."

Other adaptations were made to cater to European social behavior and culinary tastes. Concern over European aversion to queuing resulted in the provision of video screens, movies, and other entertainment for guests waiting in line. Disney's no-alcohol policy was adjusted by allowing wine and beer to be served at Feastival Disney, an entertainment complex just outside the theme park. In the restaurant facilities, greater emphasis was placed on sit-down dining and much less on fast food. At a seminar at UCLA in 1990, Robert Fitzpatrick placed a major emphasis on the Company's determination to provide the highest standards of quality at Euro Disney. This was evident both in the cuisine and in the furnishings and service standards of the hotels. In both areas, Fitzpatrick argued, quality was well in excess of the standards at Disney's US parks.

Human relations management posed an even greater cultural challenge. Central to the Disney theme park experience was the way in which "cast members" interacted with the guests. Disney was famous for its meticulous approach to recruitment, its commitment to employee training, and the maintenance of rigorous standards of employee conduct. For example, Disney's employee handbook spelled out a strict code with respect to dress and appearance, including:

- Above average height and below average weight
- Pleasant appearance (straight teeth, no facial blemishes)
- Conservative grooming standards (facial hair or long hair is banned; no mustache; hair length is specified to be no longer than 1 inch above the collar)
- Very modest make-up, very limited jewelry (for example, no more than one ring on each hand; size of the earrings can be no more than $^{1}/_{2}$ inch)
- Employees were required to wear specific types and colors of underwear; only neutral colors of pantyhose were allowed.[8]

Training embraced both general principles and specific knowledge and behaviors. For example, employees were instructed that their behavior on the job should be governed by three major rules: "First, we practice a friendly smile; Second, we use only friendly phrases; Third, we are not stuffy."

To what extent could locally recruited employees provide the level and quality and consistency of service at Euro Disney that would match that of other Disney theme parks, and to what extent could Disney simply transplant its US HRM practices? Euro Disney's selection and training were closely modeled on Disney's US approach. A Euro Disney branch of Disney University was opening and recruitment of 10,000 employees began in September 1991. Selection criteria were "applicant friendliness, warmth, and liking of people." The rules for job applicants were spelled out in a video presentation and in the employee handbook, "The Euro Disney Look." The rules went far beyond weight and height requirements, describing the length of the men's hair, beard and mustache requirements, tattoo coverage requirements, and hair color specifications (for example, hair had to be of a natural-looking color, without frosting or streaking). Only moderate use of cosmetics was allowed.[9] The goal was a nationality mix that would match that of Euro Disney's customers, about 45 percent of whom were French. However, in response to local pressure and the greater availability of local applicants, some 70 percent of employees were French. At the management level, Disney relied on importing about 200 managers from other Disney parks and training 270 locally recruited managers (this involved training at Disney's other theme parks).

Disney's recruiting practices and employee policies produced a storm of protest. French labor unions started protesting right from the moment that Euro Disney started interviewing applicants. Representatives of the General Confederation of Labor handed out leaflets in front of Euro Disney's HQ warning applicants that the Disney hiring practices represented "an attack on individual freedom." Many of Disney's US hiring and employment practices contravened French law. Workforce flexibility was limited by the restrictions on terminating employees with more than two years with the company and the high severance payments involved. There were also legal limits over the recruitment and dismissal of seasonal workers. As for Disney's dress and personal grooming codes, French law prohibited an employer from restricting "individual and collective freedoms" unless the restrictions could be justified by the nature of the objective to be accomplished and were proportional to that end. Since Disney estimated that no more that 700 employees would be involved in "theatrical actions," reasonable dress code limitations could only be imposed on those employees, not on those who would only be "back stage."

■ THE FIRST YEAR ■

Euro Disney's opening on April 12, 1992 combined both fanfare and protest. An extravagant opening ceremony involved some of the world's leading entertainers and was televised in 22 countries. Michael Eisner proclaimed Euro Disney to be "one of the greatest man-made attractions in the world" while the French Prime-Minister described the park as an "incredible achievement which transcends national frontiers . . . We are deeply attached to the links of friendship between our continent and yours. Euro Disney is one of the symbols of this transatlantic friendship". However, the opening was marred by a demonstration of local residents, a train strike affecting lines leading to the park, and a terrorist bomb that attempted to disrupt power to the park.

The park ran into early teething problems. Design problems ranged from insufficient breakfast facilities to an absence of toilet facilities for bus drivers and a shortage of employee accommodation. During the first nine weeks of operation, 1,000 employees left Euro Disney, about one-half voluntarily. Long hours and hectic work pace were the main reasons given for leaving. Nevertheless, visitor reactions were mainly highly positive. Negative comments related to frustration with long periods of waiting in line and the high cost of admission, food, and souvenirs. Some voiced concern over the multinational, multicultural flavor of Euro Disney: "They haven't yet figured out whether it's going to be an American park, a French park, or a European park . . . Differences in waiting line behavior is striking. For instance, Scandinavians appear quite content to wait for rides, whereas some of the southern Europeans seem to have made an Olympic event out of getting to the ticker tape first.[10] Some visitors had difficulty envisaging Disney within a European context: "Disney is very much an American culture. Florida is the true Disney World, the true feeling of Disney, what Disney is trying to project. Americans are part of that, the French aren't."

Start-up difficulties were normal in the theme park business – all major theme parks, including those of Disney, experienced some teething problems during the period of initial operation. Universal Studios in Florida had a disastrous first few months, but subsequently rebounded – certainly its visitor numbers were close to projections. With 30,000 visitors daily during the summer of 1992, it seemed that Euro Disney might reach its projected target of 11 million visitors annually. The concern was that visitor numbers would drop substantially during the winter months. What was very clear was that, despite good visitor numbers during the summer, Euro Disney's profitability would fall far below expectations. There were a larger number of day-visitors and fewer period-visits than had been anticipated. As a result, Euro Disney cut hotel rates by up to 25 percent. Moreover, average visitor expenditure on beverages, food, and gifts was about 12 percent of the $33 per day that had been anticipated. Part of the problem was the economic situation – during 1992, most of Western Europe was mired in one of the worst economic downturns since World War II. The depressed state of the French real estate market also prevented Euro Disney from boosting revenues through land sales.

By the end of Euro Disney's first full financial year, the extent of the financial under-performance was becoming clear. Even with exceptional items, the Company lost over FF 1.7 billion. In terms of US GAAP, Euro Disneyland's pre-tax loss was over half a billion dollars. Top line performance was a key problem. Instead of the 11 million visitors forecast, Euro Disney attracted 9.8 m visitors during its first full year. Equally serious was the fact that average visitor spending was below target, and much lower than at Disney's US and Japanese parks. Fewer visitors than projected were staying in Disney theme hotels, deterred by room rates that were much higher than in comparable hotels in Paris. Hotel occupancy rates were below 50 percent in contrast to the 60 percent figure projected. On the cost side, Disney's emphasis on quality had boosted both construction and operating costs, while higher than anticipated debt together with rising interest rates caused interest charges to spiral upward. Labor costs amounted to a huge 24 percent of sales, rather than the forecasted level of 13 percent of sales. Much of the cost overruns could be attributed to Disney's belief that "Lacoste and Polo loving" Europeans would not tolerate anything unsophisticated or cheap. For example, in the US, "The Walt" restaurant had wallpaper but at Euro Disney the walls were covered in Moroccan leather. When it came to trading-off sophistication for lower prices, most Euro Disney customers opted for the latter.

For Walt Disney Company, the financial returns were better than they were for Euro Disneyland's other shareholders. During 1992 and 1993, Disney's 49 percent share of Euro Disneyland's losses was offset by royalties from its licensing agreement. These amounted to $36.3 million in 1993 and $32.9 million in 1992; however, Disney agreed to defer its base management fees for 1992 and 1993.

■ RESTRUCTURING ■

During the winter of 1993/94, Euro Disney visitor numbers plummeted. Despite a fall of the French franc against the US dollar, many Europeans found that Disneyland Florida was not only a more attractive destination during the winter months, it was also cheaper. "It's cheaper to go on a two-week holiday in Florida than to come to Euro Disney for five days," remarked one British traveler with a family of four. With low transatlantic fares, European visitors to Walt Disney World in Orlando increased sharply during 1992 and 1993. By early 1994, Euro Disney was in crisis. Faced with mounting losses, rising debt, and doubts about the Company's capacity to cover its interest payments, rumors were rife that the park would be forced to close.

Crisis talks between Euro Disneyland, Disney, and creditors resulted in agreement upon a financial restructuring package in June 1994. The financial rescue package that was announced involved:

- A $1.1 billion rights offering of which Disney agreed to take up 41 percent
- The provision by Disney of $255 in lease financing at an interest rate of 1 percent
- The cancellation by Disney of $210 million in receivables from Euro Disneyland
- The agreement by Disney to waive royalties and management fees for five years
- The agreement that Disney would receive warrants for the purchase of 28 million Euro Disneyland shares and would receive a development fee of $225 million once the second phase of the development project was launched. Euro Disneyland's lenders agreed to underwrite 51 percent of the Euro Disney rights offering, to forgive certain interest charges until September 2003, and to defer all principal payments for three years. In return, Euro Disneyland issued the lenders 10-year warrants for the purchase of up to 40 million shares of Euro Disneyland stock.

In a separate agreement, Disney agreed to sell 75 million shares, equivalent to 10 percent of Euro Disneyland's total shareholding, to Prince Alwaleed Bin Talal Bin Abdulaziz Al Saud. The sale reduced Disney's shareholding in Euro Disneyland to 39 percent.

■ LOOKING AHEAD ■

While the restructuring packaging had staved off disaster for the time being, the traumas of the past year made Bourguignon cautious about the future. Despite heavy advertising, the addition of new attractions, and the fine-tuning of Disney's image, customer service, and offering of food, drinks, and souvenirs, Euro Disney had yet to reach the initial forecast of 11 million visitors annually. Significant cost reductions had been achieved; however, the scope for further cost reductions was limited if Euro Disney was to maintain Disney's respectable standards and customer service excellence. While Bourguignon was convinced that the Company would be generating operating profits by 1995, such profits would have been the result of Disney's agreement to forgo its royalties and management fees. Once these were reinstated, Euro Disney's costs would increase by about $500 million annually.

Bourguignon believed that many of the problems that had dogged Euro Disney from the beginning had been resolved. In particular, the renaming of the park as Disneyland Paris had helped alleviate ambiguity and conflict over the park's identity. Euro Disney's top management avoided the early hyperbole about Euro Disney "meshing the cultural traditions of America and Europe." Disneyland Paris was to be a Disney theme park located close to Paris. Dropping the "Euro" prefix released the Company from the public's mistrust of all things Euro, and helped the park to avoid the debate over what European culture and European identity actually meant. Moreover, the new name firmly associated Euro Disney with the romantic connotations of the city of Paris. In terms of the need to differentiate Euro Disney from Disney's other theme parks, the experience of the past two years suggested that Euro Disney's expensive adaptations to meet European tastes and European culture were not greatly appreciated by customers. For the most part, visitors were delighted by the same rides as existed in Disney's US parks and generally preferred fast food over fine dining.

Over the next six months, Bourguignon recognized that key decisions needed to be taken:

- To what extent should Euro Disney cut admission prices in order to boost attendance? An internal study had estimated that a 20 percent reduction in admission prices would boost attendance by about 800,000 visitors; however, the net result would still be a reduction in total revenues of about 5 percent.
- The problems of insufficient demand related primarily to the winter months. In previous winters some senior mangers had argued for the closure of the park. However, so long as most of Euro Disney's employees were permanent staff, such a closure would do little to reduce total costs.
- Bourguignon had already deferred Phase 2 of the development plan – construction of a Disney–MGM Studios theme park. The other members of his senior management team were urging him to go ahead with this phase of development. Only with a second theme park, they believed, would Euro Disney's goal of becoming a major destination resort become realized. However, Bourguignon was acutely aware of Euro Disney's still-precarious financial situation. With net equity of about FF 5.5 bn and total borrowings

of FF 15.9 bn, Euro Disney was not well-placed to begin the large-scale capital expenditures that phase 2 would involve.

As Bourguignon arranged the papers on his desk at the end of a long day, he reflected on his success at pulling off the rescue plan and the continuing uphill struggle to realize the ambitions that had driven the project in the early days. The wartime words of Winston Churchill summed up the situation well: "This is not the end. It is not the beginning of the end. It is the end of the beginning."

APPENDIX A
Euro Disneyland SCA's Financial Model

The Company has prepared a financial model, based on the principal assumptions described below, which projects revenues, expenses, profits, cash flows, and dividends of the Company for 12-month periods beginning 1st April, 1992 and ending 31st March, 2017 as summarized in Table 13.A1. Although the Company's accounting year-end is 30th September, years beginning lst April have been used for the projections in order to represent whole operating years from the projected date of opening of the Magic Kingdom. The projections contained in the model do not constitute a forecast of the actual revenues, expenses, profits, cash flows or dividends of the Company. The model assumes that the Company will complete Phase 1 as described in this document and will develop the remaining elements of Euro Disneyland according to the Long Term Development Strategy. As discussed above, the Company retains the flexibility to change the Long Term Development Strategy and the designs for Phase IB in response to future conditions. Table 13.A2 summarizes the principal components of the development plan.

In addition, the model is based on other assumptions developed by the Company in light of Disney's experience with existing theme parks and resorts, after taking into account analyses of local market conditions and an assessment of likely future economic, market and other factors. The major assumptions have been reviewed by Arthur D. Little International, Inc. ("ADL"), the

Table 13.A1 Summary of Walt Disney Company financial results, 1984–8 (US$ millions)

	1984	1985	1986	1987	1988
Revenue					
Theme parks and resorts	1,097.4	1,257.5	1,523.9	1,834.2	2,042.0
Filmed entertainment	244.5	320.0	511.7	875.6	1,149.2
Consumer products	109.7	122.6	130.2	167.0	247.0
Operating Income					
Theme parks and resorts	185.7	255.7	403.7	548.9	564.8
Filmed entertainment	2.2	33.7	51.6	130.6	186.3
Consumer products	53.9	56.3	72.4	97.3	133.7
Net income	97.8	173.5	247.3	444.7	522.0

Source: The Walt Disney Company annual reports.

Table 13.A2 Planned development of Euro Disneyland

	Phase 1A	Phase 1B	Long Term Development	Total
Theme parks	1	—	1	2
Hotel capacity (rooms)	500	4,700	13,000	18,200
Camping ground (campsite plots)	595	—	1,505	2,100
Entertainment center (sq. meters)	—	22,000	38,000	60,000
Offices (sq. meters)	—	30,000	670,000	700,000
Corporate park (sq. meters)	—	50,000	700,000	750,000
Golf courses		1	1	2
Single-family homes	—	570	1,930	2,500
Retail shopping center (sq. meters)	—	—	95,000	95,000
Water recreation area	—	—	1	1
Multi-family residence	—	—	3,000	3,000
Time-share units	—	—	2,400	2,400

Source: Euro Disneyland SCA abridged offering circular.

independent consultancy firm retained by the Company to test and verify their reasonableness. Set out at the end of "The financial model" is a letter from ADL regarding its reports. While the Company believes that the assumptions underlying the model are reasonable, there is no certainty that the projected performance of the Company outlined below will be achieved.

■ PRINCIPAL ASSUMPTIONS AND RATIONALE UNDERLYING THE FINANCIAL MODEL ■

Theme Park Attendance

In order to project the number of visitors expected to visit the Euro Disneyland theme parks, several internal and external studies were commissioned. The most recent of these studies was undertaken by ADL in 1989 to verify and confirm the methods and assumptions used in the previous studies, and to make its own estimates of attendance.

THE MAGIC KINGDOM

The model assumes that the Magic Kingdom will be constructed as described in this document, and that it will open and be fully operational by April 1992.

Summary figures for assumed attendance at the Magic Kingdom are shown in the table below. Attendance is measured in terms of the total numbers of daily guest visits per annum. For example, a visitor who enters a theme park on three separate days will count as three daily guest visits.

	1992	1996	2001	2011
Magic Kingdom (in millions of persons)	11.0	13.3	15.2	16.2

The assumed attendance of 11 million for the first full year of operation of the Magic Kingdom is in line with the average attendance achieved in the first year of operation of the Magic Kingdom theme parks in Florida and Japan, and is below the range of potential initial attendance estimated to be between 11.7 and 17.8 million in the attendance study conducted by ADL. Depending upon its seasonal distribution, the higher end of the range could require acceleration of the attraction investment program. ADL concluded that the attendance target of 11 million could be achieved if the development program envisaged for Phase 1A is accomplished and a well-conceived marketing campaign tailored to European patterns is carried out to support the opening of the Magic Kingdom.

Attendance at the Magic Kingdom is assumed to grow over the period covered by the financial model at an average compound rate of 2% per annum. This growth rate compares with an average growth rate of 3.8% per annum for the three Magic Kingdom theme parks in California, Florida and Japan.

The assumed growth rate, which is higher in early years, consists of a basic growth rate, adjusted for the effect of the addition of new attractions every two to three years and for the effect of the opening of a second theme park. The overall assumed growth rate is broken down as follows:

Years	2–5	6–10	11–20	20+
Annual growth (%)	4.9	2.7	0.6	0.0

The method used by ADL involved three steps: first, individual target markets were identified by distance and population; secondly, penetration rates (the percentage of the total population in a target market which visits the theme park) were estimated for each target market; and third, the average number of annual visits per guest from each target market was estimated.

ADL noted that a number of factors, including the following, contribute to the high attendance levels at Disney-designed theme parks:

- The design and scope of a Magic Kingdom theme park are such that a complete visit requires more than one full day. This means that visitors are likely either to extend their stay or to return at a future date.
- The quality and capacity available at Disney hotels allow the demand for longer stays to be satisfied.
- The level of recognition of the Disney name and the quality of the experience make Disney theme parks popular holiday destination resorts.

In the opinion of ADL these factors distinguish Disney-designed theme parks from existing theme parks and amusement parks in Europe, which are much smaller and are basically designed for single-day visits. Accordingly, in determining potential penetration rates and the number of annual visits per guest in order to derive projected attendance levels at Euro Disneyland, ADL relied largely on the experience at Disney-designed theme parks.

ADL concluded that because of the large number of people living within a convenient traveling distance of Euro Disneyland, the assumed attendance figures in the model could be achieved with market penetration rates at or below those experienced at other Disney-designed theme parks.

The Company believes that these factors will exist at Euro Disneyland and will support the assumed penetration rates and attendance levels, which are consistent with those experienced at Disney-designed theme parks. The Company also believes that the location of the site at the center of an area of high population density with well-developed transport links will enable Euro Disneyland to draw visitors from both local and more distant markets.

SECOND THEME PARK

The model assumes that a second theme park will be completed and will open to the public in the spring of 1996. Summary figures for assumed attendance at the second theme park are as follows:

	1992	1996	2001	2011
Second theme park (in millions)	–	8.0	8.8	10.1

Attendance at the second theme park is assumed to grow at an average compound rate of 2% per annum over the first ten years, and 1% per annum for the next ten years until 2016. These assumptions are primarily based on Disney's experience of opening a second theme park at Walt Disney World, where EPCOT Center drew attendance of over 11 million guest visits in its first year of operation.

Per Capita Spending

Theme parks derive their revenues principally from admission charges, sales of food and beverages consumed by visitors while at the park, and from sales of merchandise available at the park's shopping facilities. Revenues from these sources are measured in terms of *per capita* expenditure, which is the average sum spent per daily guest visit.

The Company has assumed *per capita* expenditure figures separately for the two theme parks under the four categories below:

	Magic Kingdom		Second theme park	
	Amount in 1988 FF[a]	Annual growth rate	Amount in 1988 FF[a]	Annual growth rate
Admissions	137.6	6.5%	137.6	6.5%
Food and beverage	56.7	5.0%	53.2	5.0%
Merchandise	74.9	5.0%	46.5	5.0%
Parking and other	5.2	5.0%	5.2	5.0%

[a] Excluding Value-Added Tax.

The assumed real growth rate of admission prices of 1.5% per annum is less than the average 2.6% experienced at the Disney theme parks since 1972.

The *per capita* spending assumptions are based upon experience in theme parks designed by Disney, adjusted for local conditions. A separate report on *per capita* spending was undertaken by ADL. In order to evaluate the reasonableness of the assumed admission prices, ADL reviewed the admission prices charged in Paris for major attractions which could be considered competitive in terms of entertainment value and also the prices charged by European theme and amusement parks. These reviews showed that the assumed admission prices for Euro Disneyland, although higher than those charged at other European theme and amusement parks, (i) could be considered low when related to prices charged in the Paris region for quality adult-oriented entertainment, and (ii) appeared in tune with prices charged for other family-oriented attractions. ADL concluded that the Company's assumed admission prices were justified, having regard for the destination resort features of Euro Disneyland and the high quality of its entertainment.

In order to evaluate the reasonableness of the assumed prices for food and beverage at Euro Disneyland, ADL analyzed the prices paid by residents of, and tourists to, Paris in those areas which were particularly attractive to visitors. ADL also examined food and beverage prices at other European theme and amusement parks and reviewed typical food and beverage expenditure patterns in France as compared with the United States. ADL concluded that Euro Disneyland's assumptions concerning food and beverage expenditure were reasonable.

ADL determined, in the case of assumed merchandise sales, that there was no comparable experience in the Paris region of small, high-intensity retail shops, exposed to a high volume of visitor traffic, as are found at Disney-designed theme parks. ADL accordingly concluded that it was reasonable to forecast Euro Disneyland's retail sales revenue on the basis of that at other Disney theme parks.

Revenues

Total revenues projected in the financial model for the two theme parks are summarized in the table below (in FF. millions):

	1992	1996	2001	2011
Magic Kingdom				
Admissions and parking	1,909	2,981	4,664	9,314
Food, beverage and merchandise	1,759	2,692	4,065	7,401
Participant fees and other	229	303	417	421
Second theme park				
Admissions and parking	–	1,788	2,697	5,794
Food, beverage and merchandise	–	1,178	1,660	3,107
Participant fees and other	–	162	208	412

The first two categories of projected revenues are based on the attendance and *per capita* spending assumptions described above. Projected Participant fees are based on the assumption that approximately ten Participant contracts will have been signed by the opening of the Magic Kingdom. Four contracts have been signed, each with a term of at least ten years.

Operating Expenses

The principal operating expense assumptions are based on the following estimates:

Labor costs (including related taxes) have been estimated on the basis of experience at Disney parks, adjusted to the conditions of the French labor market. They include a premium on operating labor rates of approximately 10% over the market average, intended to attract high-quality personnel. On this basis, it has been assumed that gross operating labor costs will be FF 424 million for the Magic Kingdom and FF 232 million for the second theme park (measured in 1988 French francs) in the respective opening years of these parks and that they will increase at the rate of inflation, taking into account increased employment associated with higher attendance levels. Cost of sales has been estimated on the basis of experience at Disney parks, adjusted to reflect factors specific to Euro Disneyland. The assumptions are:

Cost of sales (% of revenue)	
Magic Kingdom	
Merchandise	40–43[1]
Food and beverage	31
Second theme park	
Merchandise	41.5
Food and beverage	31

[1] Declining from 43% in 1992 to 40% in 1996 and thereafter.

Other operating expenses have similarly been based on Disney experience, adjusted to reflect local market conditions. Individually they are assumed to be as follows:
- maintenance expenses:
    - Magic Kingdom: 6% of revenues
    - Second theme park: 6.5% of revenues
- general and administrative expenses (which include marketing, legal, finance and data processing):
    - Magic Kingdom: 14% of revenues
    - Second theme park: 16% of revenues
- property and business taxes, which have been estimated according to the French tax regime
- the base management fee (see "Corporate, management and shareholding structure" below).

Operating Income

Operating income is the difference between revenues and operating expenses, but before royalties, financing costs and interest income, depreciation and amortization, lease expense, management incentive fees, and income taxes. The summary table below shows the operating income projected by the financial model for the two theme parks:

	1992	1996	2001	2011
Magic Kingdom (in FF millions)	1,603	2,773	4,226	8,006
Second theme park (in FF millions)	–	1,334	1,921	4,293
Total	1,603	4,107	6,147	12,299

Cost of Construction

The cost of construction of the Magic Kingdom is assumed to be FF 9.5 billion and the total cost of Phase IA is assumed to be FF 14.9 billion, in accordance with the estimated cost for Phase IA. The construction cost of the second theme park has been assumed to be FF 5.9 billion, with construction and related expenditures being incurred equally in 1994 and 1995. The construction

Table 13.A3 Euro Disneyland SCA: projected revenues and profits (FF, millions)

1992–7

12 months commencing April 1	1992	1993	1994	1995	1996
Revenues					
Magic Kingdom	4,246	4,657	5,384	5,835	6,415
Second theme park	0	0	0	0	3,128
Resort and property development	1,236	2,144	3,520	5,077	6,386
Total revenues	5,482	6,801	8,904	10,930	15,929
Profit before taxation	351	620	870	1,676	1,941
Net profit	204	360	504	972	1,121
Dividends payable	275	425	625	900	1,100
Tax credit or payment	0	138	213	313	450
Total return	275	563	838	1,213	1,550
Per share (FF)	1.6	3.3	4.9	7.1	9.1

Later years

12 months commencing April 1	2001	2006	2011	2016
Revenues				
Magic Kingdom	9,730	13,055	18,181	24,118
Second theme park	4,565	6,656	9,313	12,954
Resort and property development	8,133	9,498	8,979	5,923
Total revenues	22,428	29,209	36,473	42,995
Profit before taxation	3,034	4,375	6,539	9,951
Net Profit	1,760	2,538	3,793	5,771
Dividends payable	1,750	2,524	3,379	5,719
Tax credit or payment	536	865	1,908	2,373
Total return	2,286	3,389	5,287	8,092
Per share (FF)	13.4	19.9	31.1	47.6

Source: Euro Disneyland SCA abridged offering circular.

cost of the second theme park has been estimated on the basis of Disney's direct experience of recent theme park construction, notably in completing the Disney–MGM Studios Theme Park within Walt Disney World. The construction cost of that theme park was then adjusted for capacity considerations, inflation, and the construction cost differential between Florida and the Paris region.

Table 13.A3 summarizes Walt Disney Company's financial results during 1984–8.

APPENDIX B

Excerpt from Walt Disney 1994 Annual Report

■ INVESTMENT IN EURO DISNEY ■

1994 vs. 1993

The Company's investment in Euro Disney resulted in a loss of $110.4 million in 1994. The loss consisted of a $52.8 million charge recognized in the third quarter as a result of the Company's participation in the Euro Disney financial restructuring, and the Company's equity share of fourth quarter operating results. The prior year's loss reflected the Company's equity share of Euro Disney's operating results and a $350.0 million charge to fully reserve receivables and a funding commitment to Euro Disney, partially offset by royalties and gain amortization related to the investment. The funding commitment was intended to help support Euro Disney for a limited period, while Euro Disney pursued a financial restructuring.

A proposed restructuring plan for Euro Disney was announced in March 1994. During the third quarter of 1994, the Company entered into agreements with Euro Disney and the Euro Disney lenders participating in the restructuring (the "Lenders") to provide certain debt, equity and lease financing to Euro Disney.

Under the restructuring agreements, which specify amounts denominated in French francs, the Company committed to increase its equity investment in Euro Disney by subscribing for 49% of a $1.1 billion rights offering of new shares; to provide long-term lease financing at a 1% interest rate for approximately $255 million of theme park assets; and to subscribe, in part through an offset against fully-reserved advances previously made to Euro Disney under the Company's funding commitment, for securities reimbursable in shares with a face value of approximately $180 million and a 1% coupon. In addition, the Company agreed to cancel fully-reserved receivables from Euro Disney of approximately $210 million, to waive royalties and base management fees for a period of five years and to reduce such amounts for specified periods thereafter, and to modify the method by which management incentive fees will be calculated. During the fourth quarter of 1994, the financial restructuring was completed and the Company funded its commitments.

In addition to the commitments described above, the Company agreed to arrange for the provision of a 10-year unsecured standby credit facility of approximately $210 million upon request, bearing interest at PIBOR. As of September 30th, 1994, Euro Disney had not requested that the Company establish this facility.

As part of the restructuring, the Company received 10-year warrants for the purchase of up to 27.8 million shares of Euro Disney at a price of FF 40 per share. The terms of the restructuring also provide that, in the event that Euro Disney decides to launch the second phase of the development of its theme park and resort complex, and commitments for the necessary financing have been obtained, the Company will be entitled to a development fee of approximately $225 million. Upon receipt of the development fee, the Company's entitlement to purchase Euro Disney shares by exercise of the warrants described above will be reduced to 15 million shares.

In connection with the restructuring, Euro Disney Associes SNC ("Disney SNC"), an indirect wholly-owned affiliate of the Company, entered into a lease arrangement (the "Lease") with the entity (the "Park Financing Company") which financed substantially all of the Disneyland Paris theme park assets, and then entered into a sublease agreement (the "Sublease") with Euro Disney. Under the Lease, which replaced an existing lease between Euro Disney and the Park Financing

Company, Disney SNC leased the theme park assets of the Park Financing Company for a non-cancelable term of 12 years. Aggregate lease rentals of FF 10.5 billion ($2.0 billion) receivable from Euro Disney under the Sublease, which has a 12-year term, will approximate the amounts payable by Disney SNC under the Lease.

At the conclusion of the Sublease term, Euro Disney will have the option to assume Disney SNC's rights and obligations under the Lease. If Euro Disney does not exercise its option, Disney SNC may continue to lease the assets, with an ongoing option to purchase them for an amount approximating the balance of the Park Financing Company's outstanding debt. Alternatively, Disney SNC may terminate the Lease, in which case Disney SNC would pay the Park Financing Company an amount equal to 75% of its then-outstanding debt, estimated to be $1.4 billion; Disney SNC could then sell or lease the assets on behalf of the Park Financing Company in order to satisfy the remaining debt, with any excess proceeds payable to Disney SNC.

As part of the overall restructuring, the Lenders agreed to underwrite 51% of the Euro Disney rights offering, to forgive certain interest charges for the period from April 1st 1994 to September 30th 2003, having a present value of approximately $300 million, and to defer all principal payments until three years later than originally scheduled. As consideration for their participation in the financial restructuring, Euro Disney issued to the Lenders 10-year warrants for the purchase of up to 40 million shares of Euro Disney stock at a price of FF 40 per share.

Euro Disney has reported that it expects to incur a loss in 1995, which will have a negative impact on the Company's results. The impact on the Company's earnings, however, will be reduced as a result of the sale by the Company in October, 1994 of approximately 75 million shares, or 20% of its investment in Euro Disney, to Prince Alwaleed Bin Talal Bin Abdulaziz Al Saud. The sale will reduce the Company's ownership interest in Euro Disney to approximately 39%. Beginning in 1995, the Company will record its equity share of Euro Disney's operating results based upon its reduced ownership interest. The Company has agreed, so long as any obligations to the Lenders are outstanding, to maintain ownership of at least 34% of the outstanding common stock of Euro Disney until June 1999, at least 25% for the subsequent five years and at least 16.67% for an additional term thereafter.

1993 vs. 1992

The Company's investment in Euro Disney resulted in a loss of $514.7 million in 1993, including the charge referred to below, after being partially offset by royalties and gain amortization related to the investment. The operating results of Euro Disney were lower than expected, due in part to the European recession which affected Euro Disney's largest markets.

During 1993, Euro Disney, its principal lenders and the Company began exploring a financial restructuring for Euro Disney. The Company agreed to help fund Euro Disney for a limited period, to afford Euro Disney time to pursue the financial restructuring. The operating results for the fourth quarter and the year, and the need for a financial restructuring, created uncertainty regarding the Company's ability to collect its current receivables and to meet the funding commitment to Euro Disney. Consequently, the Company recorded a charge of $350.0 million in the fourth quarter to fully reserve its current receivables and funding commitment.

In 1992, the Company's investment in Euro Disney contributed income of $11.2 million. Although Euro Disney incurred a loss in 1992, the Company's 49% share of the net loss was offset by royalties and gain amortization related to the investment.

Source: Walt Disney Annual Report, 1994.

APPENDIX C
Time Line: Major Events in the Development of Euro Disney

March 24, 1987	The Agreement of March 24, 1987, "for the creation and operation of Euro Disneyland in France," is signed by the French Government, the Walt Disney Company, the Ile-de-France Regional Counsel, the Seine-et-Marne Departmental Counsel, the Parisian public transport authority (RATP) and the Public Planning Board (EPA) for the new town of Marne-la-Vallée.
August 1988	Excavation work begins on-site
November 6, 1989	Stock market floatation (Paris, London and Brussels)
April 1990	The first facades of the Disneyland Hotel are constructed
September 1991	The Casting Center opens in Noisy-le-Grand
March 31, 1992	The Marne-la-Vallée–Chessy RER station is inaugurated
April 12, 1992	The Theme Park opens
June 1993	The "Indiana Jones™, the Temple of Peril" attraction is inaugurated
April 23, 1993	The Disneyland Paris Convention Center welcomes the first joint meeting of the two major international organizations in the tourism industry: the European Tourism Commission and the European Commission of the World Tourism Organization
February 1994	The first European Children's Summit is hosted: over 300 children representing 14 countries reflect on the world of tomorrow
March 1994	Inauguration of two new attractions: "Casey Jr., le Petit Train du Cirque" and "Le Pays des Contes de Fées"
May 19, 1994	Inauguration of the TGV station at the Park entrance
June 8, 1994	Extraordinary General Shareholders Meeting approves resolutions related to the financial restructuring
October 1, 1994	Euro Disneyland becomes Disneyland Paris Euro Disney SCA, remains the company owning and operating Disneyland Paris and its subsidiaries
May 31, 1995	The "Space Mountain – from the Earth to the Moon" Attraction is inaugurated

NOTES

1. "Euro Disney," *Financial Times*' Lex column, 30 October 1996.
2. "Disney Goes to Tokyo," in D. Ancona, T. Kochan, M. Scully, J. Van Maanen, and E. Westney, *Organizational Behavior and Processes*, Cincinnati, OH: Southwestern College Publishing, 1999, pp. M-10, 25.
3. The conversion factors used in the case are: 1 hectare = 2.47 acres, and 1 acre = 4,047 square meters. The US dollar/French franc exchange rates at the beginning of each year were: 1987 6.35, 1988 5.36, 1989 6.03, 1990 5.84, 1991 5.08, 1992 5.22, 1993 5.59, 1994 5.93.
4. "Euro Disney" is used to refer to the Euro Disneyland theme park; "Euro Disneyland SCA" or "the company" refers to the company that owns Euro Disney.

5. "The Euro Disneyland Project" – "Project Financing: Asset-Based Financial Engineering," Case Study: John D. Finnery, © 1996 by John D. Finnery, John Wiley & Sons.

6. "No magic in these kingdoms," *Los Angeles Times*, December 15, 1989.

7. "Disneyland goes to Europe," in Ancona, Kochan, Scully, Van Maanen, and Westney, *Organizational Behavior and Processes*, 1999, pp. 38–9.

8. Ancona, Kochan, Scully, Van Maanen, and Westney, *Organizational Behavior and Processes*, "Disneyland goes to Europe", p. 15.

9. From Jacques, Neher, "France amazed, amused by Disney dress code," *The New York Times*, October 5, 1995.

10. *Euro Disney: the First 100 Days*, Harvard Business School, Case no. 9-693-013, 1993, p. 14.

Richard Branson and the Virgin Group of Companies in 2002

Robert M. Grant

Richard Branson's 50th birthday in July 2000 had no discernible effect either on Sir Richard's energy or on the entrepreneurial vigor of his Virgin group of companies. The new millennium saw Branson's sprawling business empire spawn yet more new ventures. These included new companies within Virgin's existing lines of business – a new airline in Australia, retail ventures in Singapore and Thailand, and wireless telecom ventures in Asia, the US, and Australia – and entirely new enterprises. A number of these new ventures involved internet-based businesses: online sales of cars and motorcycles through Virgin Car and Virgin Bike, online auctions through Virgin Net, Virgin's ISP and portal business. Other initiatives included acquisition of a consortium with a minority stake in Britain's air traffic control system and an (unsuccessful) bid to run Britain's National Lottery. In May 2002, Branson was planning yet more business ventures, including a wireless phone company in Japan, a low-cost airline in the US, a car rental business in Australia, and an online pharmacy in the UK.

Yet despite Branson's unstoppable enthusiasm for launching new business ventures, there was increasing evidence of a rising tide of financial problems within the Virgin group:

- Virgin's Megastores and its Our Price music chains were suffering heavily from the downturn in sales of music CDs.
- All of Virgin's travel businesses – but especially its flagship, Virgin Atlantic – were suffering from the aftermath of September 11, 2001. Even before the terrorist attack, Virgin Atlantic was incurring significant losses. Virgin Blue in Australia was also losing money, though in Europe, Virgin Express made a small profit in 2001.
- Several of Virgin's new ventures of the late 1990s had run into serious difficulty. Victory Corporation, Virgin's clothing and cosmetics company, was incurring losses of around 20 percent of sales. Virgin Cola had failed to make

any significant market impact in Continental Europe and its US launch was regarded as pure bravado by most observers.

• Virgin Trains continued to be a source of adverse publicity for the group. The British passenger rail system had been plagued by problems of safety, inadequate infrastructure, and train delays since its privatization. Virgin Train's profitability was only possible because of government subsidies that were about to be phased out.

For several years press reports had questioned the financial health of the Virgin group. An in-depth inquiry into the fragmented and secretive structure of the Virgin group had painted a far from reassuring picture:

> Virgin Travel is the only one of Mr. Branson's businesses to make a large profit . . . The rest of Mr. Branson's firms, in both groups, lost money in total. Those firms that he controls lost £28 million on a turnover of some £84 million. The firms that are jointly-owned are mostly recent start ups and mostly loss-making. Together they lost £37.5 million.[1]

Further evidence of financial weaknesses in the Virgin group was supplied by the *Financial Times*. Analysis of Virgin's 13 biggest operating companies in the UK over a three-year period ending December 1997 pointed to negative cash flow and economic value added (EVA) during the past two years and a deteriorating interest cover. The *Financial Times* suggested that Branson might have to resort to raising long-term capital through stock market flotation of equity in some of his larger companies – an avenue that Branson was reluctant to go down because of the various irksome restrictions attached to running a publicly quoted company.[2]

London's *Independent* newspaper noted that performance problems of several Virgin companies were adversely affecting the reputation of Branson himself. In an article titled "Is Branson's honeymoon finally over?" the paper observed the slipping halo of a man "once ranked second only to Mother Teresa as a role model for the young."[3]

In its 1998 article, *The Economist* has warned:

> In a recession, an empire founded on such principles may become over-extended. Cash flow could suddenly become inadequate to finance the expansion that is already underway. At that point the only way to raise money would be to borrow more, or to sell stakes in businesses – at a time when valuations might well be falling.[4]

By the spring of 2002, speculation over the financial state of the Virgin group of companies was gathering pace, and some observers thought that the *Economist*'s dire warning was in danger of fulfilling itself. The London newspaper *The Business* reported that the losses that previously had affected a sizable minority of the Virgin business were now widespread. In particular, the group's cash cow, Virgin Atlantic, was now hemorrhaging cash.[5] The article speculated that Branson was planning to float a major part of the Virgin empire on the stock market. This was backed up by a report on May 26, 2002 that Virgin was planning stock market flotations of 20 percent of the shares of Virgin Atlantic together with seven other Virgin companies (including Virgin Blue). Prior to the listings of these companies, Branson would step down as chairman, the report stated.[6]

As ever, Branson was dismissive of claims that his Virgin group was in financial difficulties. He has claimed that most outside analysts and financial journalists have misunderstood his business empire. Each Virgin company, he argued, was financed on a stand-alone basis; hence attempts to consolidate the income and assets of the companies were irrelevant and misleading. Moreover, Branson has little regard for accounting profits, preferring cash flow and capital value as the critical performance indicators. Thus, most of the Virgin companies were growing businesses that were increasing in their real value and long-term cash-generating potential, even if accounting profits were negative. "The approach to running a group of private companies is fundamentally different to that of running public companies. Short-term taxable profits with good dividends are a prerequisite of public life. Avoiding short-term taxable profits and seeking long-term capital growth is the best approach to growing private companies."[7] Regarding the recent speculation that Branson was planning to take eight of his Virgin companies public, Virgin stressed that any initial public offering of its companies would be a result, not of cash flow shortfall, but of the desire to fund new ventures. However, news that Virgin had arranged a bank loan of £75 million secured on its equity in Virgin Atlantic only fueled the rumors of impending financial crisis.

Even if Branson could shrug off attacks upon the profitability and financial stability of his business empire, the widespread speculation over the future of his Virgin group reflected uncertainty over the rationale and strategic direction of this motley collection of over 200 separate companies. By 2002, the Virgin group had expanded from music and airlines into rail transport, soft drinks, cinemas, radio broadcasting, clothing, bridal shops, hotels, insurance, mutual funds, internet services, car sales, and health clubs. In an era of corporate refocusing and the nurturing of core competences, what possible business rationale could explain the structure and composition of the Virgin group? While most external attention had been directed towards the adequacy of Virgin's financial resources, there were concerns over the group's other key resources too. With regard to the brand, what was the range of businesses over which the brand could be applied without damaging its appeal or integrity? With regard to Branson himself, what should his role be in the management of his business empire? To what extent should he attempt to involve himself personally in guiding the various Virgin companies? As the group became bigger and more diverse and Branson became more of a strategic and charismatic leader rather than a hands-on manager, did the group need to establish a more systematic approach to control, exploiting synergies between businesses, and managing risk?

Lying behind these questions was the issue of what Branson wanted to do with his own life. Up until now, Richard Branson and the Virgin companies had been inextricably entwined. Looking ahead, Branson could see the need to establish a management structure that could operate more independently of him. This would give greater freedom to him to pursue his many sporting and social interests, while making the company less vulnerable to his absences or to his possible injury or death in one of his high-profile, high-risk sporting exploits.

■ THE DEVELOPMENT OF VIRGIN ■

Richard Branson's business career began while he was a student at Stowe, a private boarding school. His start-up magazine, *Student*, was first published on January 26, 1968. The early success of the magazine encouraged Branson to leave school at 17 years old, before taking his final exams. Agreeing to the boy's request to leave, the headmaster offered the prophetic statement, "Richard, you will end up in prison or as a millionaire." Both predictions were to be fulfilled.[8]

This early publishing venture displayed features that would characterize many of Branson's subsequent entrepreneurial initiatives. Robert Dick provides an insightful discussion of these:

> Branson's brainchild *Student* magazine was a product of the 1960s, the decade when the post-war "baby-boomers" came of age. Across Western Europe and North America young people enjoyed educational, employment and lifestyle opportunities unknown to their parents, all made possible by rapid economic growth. The decade become known for its promotion of youth culture in which authority was challenged, fashions changed rapidly, and rock stars became global gurus of a new age.

It was in such a climate that Richard Branson, tired of the boring inadequacies of the traditional school magazine and recognizing a "gaping hole in the market," founded his publication. Aimed at people aged 16 to 25, *Student* was to be the "voice of youth" and would "put the world to rights." Its eclectic style reflected its founder's ability to commission articles by celebrities and to identify subjects not touched by many well-established magazines. Norman Mailer, Vanessa Redgrave, and Jean-Paul Sartre contributed pieces which appeared among articles on sex, rock music, interviews with terrorists, and proposals for educational reform.

The success of the magazine (Branson optimistically claimed a circulation of 100,000) promoted favorable notice in the national press. Branson was described in complimentary terms as "The editor, publisher and sole advertising manger . . . a teenage professional whose enthusiasm gets things done to an extent that would shame his elders." Certainly his energy and enthusiasm were needed to keep the organization going. The offices were transient, first in a friend's basement flat, later in a disused church. The staff – a closely organized cooperative of friends, acquaintances and hangers-on – distributed magazines, took copy and, frequently, avoided creditors. As Branson said at the time: "The staff all work for nothing. I supply them with somewhere to sleep and some food. It's not so much they are working for you as working with you."[9]

Virgin Records

Branson's next venture was mail order records. Beginning with a single advertisement in the last issue of *Student* magazine, Branson found that he was able to establish a thriving business with almost no up-front investment and no working capital, and could easily undercut the established retail chains. The name "Virgin" was suggested by one of his associates who saw the name as proclaiming their commercial innocence, while possessing some novelty and modest shock-value. Virgin Records brought together Branson and his childhood friend Nik Powell, who took a 40 percent share in the company and complemented Branson's erratic flamboyance with careful operational and financial management. The start of a national postal strike in 1971 encouraged Branson to open his first retail store – on London's busy Oxford Street.

Expansion into record publishing was the idea of Simon Draper – one of Virgin's record buyers. Draper introduced Branson to Mike Oldfield, who was soon installed at Branson's Oxfordshire home with a fully equipped recording studio. *Tubular Bells*, launched in 1973, was an instant hit, eventually selling over 5 million copies worldwide. The result was the Virgin record label, which went on to sign up bands whose music or lifestyles were unacceptable to the major record companies. Among the most successful (certainly the most outrageous) were the Sex Pistols, who were contracted to Virgin until the band's breakup following the arrest (for murder) and subsequent death of Sid Vicious.

The recession of 1979–82 was a struggle for Virgin. There was disaffection among many of Virgin Records employees, several business ventures were unsuccessful – including *Event* entertainment magazine – and Nik Powell left Virgin, selling his shareholding back to Branson in return for a million pounds and Virgin's cinema and video recording interests. Despite these setbacks, the 1980s saw rapid growth for Virgin Records with the signing of Phil Collins, Human League, Simple Minds, and Boy George's Culture Club. By 1983, the Virgin group was earning pre-tax profits of £2.0 million on total revenues of just under £50 million.

Virgin Atlantic Airways

Virgin Atlantic began with a phone call from Randolph Fields, a Californian lawyer who proposed founding a transatlantic, cut-price airline. To the horror of Branson's executives at Virgin Records, Branson was enthralled with the idea. On June 24, 1984, Branson appeared in a World War I flying outfit to celebrate the inaugural flight of Virgin Atlantic in a second-hand 747 bought from Aerolinas Argentina. With the launch of Virgin Atlantic, Branson had embarked upon a perilous path strewn with the wreckage of earlier entrepreneurs of aviation, including Laker, Braniff, and People's Express. Unlike Branson's other businesses, not only was the airline business highly capital intensive, it also required a completely new set of business skills from Branson, in particular the need to negotiate with governments, regulatory bodies, banks, and aircraft manufacturers.

Private to Public to Private

By 1985, a transatlantic airfares price war and the investment needs of Virgin Atlantic had created a cash squeeze for Virgin. Branson became convinced of the need to expand the equity base of the group. He assigned Don Cruikshank, a Scottish accountant with an MBA from Manchester and Branson's group managing director, the task of organizing an initial public offering for Virgin's music, retail, and vision businesses, which were combined into the Virgin Group plc, a public corporation with 35 percent of its equity listed on the London, and later the NASDAQ, stock market.

Branson was not happy as chairman of a public corporation. He felt that investment analysts misunderstood his business and that the market undervalued his company. A clear conflict existed between the financial community's expectations of the chairman of a public corporation and Branson's personal style. With the October 1987 stock market crash, Branson took the opportunity to raise £200 million to buy out external shareholders.

As a private company, Virgin continued to expand, using both internal cash flows – mainly from Virgin Atlantic Airways – and external financing. The retailing group moved aggressively into new markets around the world. The Virgin Megastore concept provided the basis for new stores in Japan, the United States, Australia, the Netherlands, and Spain. This growth was facilitated by the formation of a joint venture with Block-buster Corporation, the US video-store giant. New ventures launched during the early 1990s included Virgin Lightships, an airship advertiser; Vintage Airtours, an operator of restored DC-3 aircraft between Orlando and Key West; Virgin Games producing video games; West One Television, a TV production company; and Virgin Euromagnetics, a personal computer company. Meanwhile, Virgin Atlantic Airways continued to expand. It gained the right to operate out of London's Heathrow Airport, won a court battle with British Airways requiring BA to transfer some of its Japanese air routes to Virgin, and pursued its plan to fly to 20 cities worldwide. Its transatlantic market share grew and the airline won many awards for its customer service.

1990–2001: Continued Expansion, Selective Divestment

The cash demands of the airline business continued to pressure the group. In particular the Persian Gulf War of 1990–1991 reduced revenues for the airline business as a whole. Increasingly, Branson relied upon joint ventures to finance new business development. The period from 1990 to 1992 was one of major change for the Virgin group. During that time, Branson forged several important joint venture agreements with other companies. The partnering arrangements were primarily in the retailing area and included one with Marui, a leading Japanese retailer, and another with W. H. Smith, a prominent UK retail chain. Branson and his Virgin group have long relied on the joint venture as an impor-tant strategic tool for expanding into new businesses. In 1998, the company's various arrangements with partners continued to play a critical role in Virgin's overall strategy.

By now, the airline had come to dominate Branson's business interest and imagina-tion. As the capital-hungry Virgin Atlantic needed more money, Branson would have to let go of other parts of his empire. In March 1992, Branson sold his most profitable and successful business, Virgin Music, the world's biggest independent record label, to Thorn EMI for £560 million (close to $1.0 billion). Virgin Music's tangible assets had a balance sheet value of only £3 million. The sale marked a dramatic shift in focus for Virgin away from its core entertainment business towards airlines and travel, and pro-vided the capital to support new business ventures.

In the meantime, Branson's long-standing rivalry with British Airways took a nasty turn. Evidence emerged that British Airways had pursued a "dirty tricks" campaign against Virgin. This included breaking into Virgin's computer system, diverting Virgin customers to BA flights, and spreading rumors about Virgin's financial state. These allegations promoted furious denials from the BA chairman Lord King and criticism of both Branson and Virgin. The outcome was a UK court case which resulted in BA paying $1.5 million dollars in damages to Branson and Virgin. The hostility between Virgin and BA continued after the Lord King's early retirement. During the late 1990s, Branson battled tirelessly against the proposed alliance between BA and American Airlines.

The second half of the 1990s saw acceleration in Virgin's business development activities with a host of new ventures in disparate markets. Virgin's new ventures were a response to three types of opportunity:

- *Privatization and deregulation.* The rolling back of the frontiers of state ownership and regulation in Britain (and elsewhere) created business opportunities that Richard Branson was only too eager to seize. Virgin's most important privatization initiative was its successful bids for two passenger rail franchises: the west coast and cross-country rail services. The resulting business – Virgin Rail – was a joint venture with transportation specialist, Stagecoach. Deregulation in the world's airline sector also created opportunities for Virgin. In 1996, Euro-Belgian Airlines was acquired and re-launched as Virgin Express, and in Australia, Virgin Blue began operations during 2000. Branson's bid to operate the British National Lottery was unsuccessful, but in 2001, Virgin Atlantic was part of the consortium that acquired a stake in the British air traffic control system.

- *Direct selling of goods and services to consumers.* Branson was continually on the lookout for business opportunities offering a "new deal" to consumers. Most of these ventures involved direct sales to consumers and passing on the cost savings from bypassing traditional distribution channels. Virgin Direct launched in 1995 as a joint venture with Norwich Union offered telephone-based financial services to consumers. Virgin Car and Virgin Bike challenged the existing dealership system of the automobile and motorcycle manufactures by offering direct sales of cars and motorbikes at discounted prices. Virgin Wine was also launched.

- *TMT.* The "TMT" (Technology, Media, Telecom) boom of 1998–2000 created a tremendous buzz within Virgin. Virgin foundations were in media and the internet offered a new channel for Virgin to reach consumers. In 1997 Virgin Net, an internet service provider and portal, was launched as a joint venture between Virgin and cable operator NTL. The next year Virgin Mobile, a joint venture with Deutsche Telecom's One-to-One wireless telephone service, began business in Britain. The success of Virgin Mobile in Britain – half a million subscribers were signed up within the first year – encouraged Virgin to expand into the US, Australia, and south-east Asia. The ability of Virgin to communicate directly with customers through the telephone and the internet was seen as offering important opportunities to the Virgin group as a whole. Text messaging allowed Virgin Atlantic to sell discounted airline seats to Virgin Mobile customers. *Thetrain.com* was set up as an online reservation service for train passengers. Virgin established a chat room for Virgin Cola consumers. The Virgin.com portal became a shopfront for all of Virgin's consumer offerings.

The launching of so many new ventures provided the impetus for Branson to sell off equity stakes in some of his more established ventures. During this period, sales included: Virgin's stake in the ISP part of Virgin Net that was sold to partner NTL, the Virgin cinema chain (leaving only the Japanese cinemas owned by Virgin), Virgin Megastores in France, and 50 percent of Virgin Blue. However, by far the biggest deal was the sale of 49 percent of Virgin Atlantic to Singapore Airlines for £600 million.

A time line of the development of the Virgin group is given in exhibit 14.2.

Exhibit 14.1: Virgin's Vision

When we started Virgin as a mail order music business in 1970, we chose a brand name that could be applied to other businesses in the future. From that humble beginning a shop in Oxford Street followed in 1971 and a record company with its own recording studio in 1972. Thirty years later the dream of 1970 has become a reality and Virgin has evolved a unique business model as a branded venture capital organization. We invest, along with a range of different institutional and trade partners, in a wide range of businesses that either share or have the prospect of sharing common brand values.

Two important business developments helped create the Virgin brand of today. Firstly, the record company and the Virgin Megastore businesses created a youthful image for Virgin as it challenged the major record companies and was at the heart of the "Indy" revolution in the late 1970s. The Megastore business changed the face of music retailing and brought the concept of a home entertainment superstore to the marketplace for the first time. Secondly, through the launch of Virgin Atlantic, the brand took on the role of consumer champion and built up an enviable reputation by 1990 of quality, value for money, innovation and fun.

Following the sale of Virgin's original music business in 1992 to Thorn EMI Plc for £560 million, we began to build a business model based on the concept of developing discreet businesses with their own investors. These future businesses, if they were to use the Virgin brand, should fulfil or have the potential to fulfil both the emerging public perception of the brand and provide the shareholders with a good return on their equity investment.

The core developments of the last 8 years have been in the fields of travel, leisure, music, entertainment retailing, financial services and mobile telephony. As a result, the brand is now one of the most highly regarded in Europe with a world-wide presence that gives it the opportunity to become a global force in both consumer and business to business markets. We believe that Virgin can now build a number of truly global businesses from a strong consumer base in the UK. Virgin Atlantic has already established a presence in most of the world's major economies and is comfortably but also profitably providing service to the world's business community and independent travelers. We believe that a number of our brands can build on this success. In particular we are planning a global presence in travel, mobile communications, entertainment retailing and music. For example, plans are well under way to develop Virgin Mobile in all the world's major markets.

Virgin also intends to continue to develop the depth of its UK businesses and exploit the opportunities of "convergence marketing" which are emerging from the concurrent convergence of e-commerce and mobile telephony technologies. It is envisaged that these opportunities will provide significant consumer benefits whilst at the same time enhancing shareholder value. For example, by 2005, it is likely that UK consumers will be able to use their mobile phone to bank, buy or book virtually any service. Travel (both rail and air), financial services and content businesses will be particular beneficiaries of these developments with more efficient yield management and lower transaction costs. The complementary UK business development will be the creation of a single branded retail chain, split between our large Megastores and smaller V.Shops coupled to a "clicks and mortar" strategy from Virgin's e-commerce and mobile activities.

During the past ten years, outstanding shareholder value has been created for investors through a number of transactions including the sale of Virgin Interactive Entertainment, Virgin Records, Virgin Radio, Virgin Cinemas and the partial sale of Virgin Atlantic and Virgin Rail. We would envisage continuing this policy of active venture capital over the next decade through growing our branded businesses and taking a number of them public.

The document you are reading comprehensively lays our businesses and their prospects. We are in exciting markets which are set to benefit considerably from technological developments in distribution and fulfillment. I believe that Virgin has the opportunity to be in the top 20 of global brands by 2010.

Welcome to our world.

Source: Virgin.

Exhibit 14.2:   The History of Virgin

1968	First issue of *Student* magazine, January 26.
1970	Start of Virgin mail order operation.
1971	First Virgin record shop opens in Oxford Street, London.
1972	Virgin recording studio opens at The Manor near Oxford, England.
1973	Virgin record label launched with Mike Oldfield's "Tubular Bells."
1977	Virgin Records signs the Sex Pistols.
1978	Virgin opens The Venue night club in London.
1980–2	Virgin Records expands overseas. Signs Phil Collins and Boy George/Culture Club.
1983	Virgin Vision (forerunner of Virgin Communications) formed to distribute films and videos and to operate in television and radio broadcasting.
	Vanson Developments formed as real estate development company.
	Virgin Games (computer games software publisher) launched.
	Virgin Group's combined pre-tax profit climbs to £2.0 million on turnover of just under £50 million.
1984	Virgin Atlantic Airways and Virgin Cargo launched.
	First hotel investment (Deya, Mallorca).
	Virgin Vision launches The Music Channel, a 24-hour satellite-delivered music station and releases its first feature film *1984* with Richard Burton and John Hurt.
1985	Private placement of 7% Convertible Stock completed with 25 English and Scottish institutions.
	Virgin wins Business Enterprise Award for company of the year.
	Virgin Vision extends film and video distribution internationally.
	Virgin Holidays formed.
1986	Virgin Group, comprising the Music, Retail & Property, and Communications divisions, floated on London Stock Exchange. 35% of equity sold to 87,000 shareholders. Airline, clubs, holidays, and aviation services remain part of the privately owned Voyager Group.
1987	Virgin Records subsidiaries in US and Japan launched.
	British Satellite Broadcasting (Virgin a minority partner) awarded satellite broadcasting license. (Virgin sells its shareholding in 1988.)
	Virgin acquires Mastertronics Group, which distributed Sega video games in Europe.
	Virgin Airship & Balloon Company launched to provide aerial marketing services.
1988	Recording studios opened in Barnes, London.
	New international record label, Virgin, launched.
	Virgin Broadcasting formed to further develop Virgin's radio and TV interests.
	Virgin Hotels formed.
	Virgin Megastores opened in Sydney, Paris, and Glasgow.
	Branson takes Virgin private with 248 million pound bid for outstanding shares.
1989	Virgin Music Group sells 25% stake to Fujisankei Communications for $150 million.
	Virgin Vision (video distribution) sold to MCEG of Los Angeles for $83 million.
1990	Virgin Retail Group and Marui form joint venture company to operate Megastores in Japan.
	Virgin Lightships formed to develop helium airships for advertising.

1991   W. H. Allen plc acquired. Merged with Virgin Books to form Virgin Publishing.
        Sale of Virgin Mastertronic to Sega. Remaining part of the business becomes Virgin Games.
        Virgin Retail Group forms 50:50 joint venture with W. H. Smith to develop UK retail business.

1992   Sale of Virgin Music Group to Thorn EMI plc.
        Joint venture with Blockbuster to own and develop Megastores in Europe, Australia and US.
        UK Radio Authority grants Virgin Communications and TV-AM plc the license for Britain's first national commercial rock station (Virgin 1215AM goes on the air in April 1993).
        Virgin acquires Euro-Magnetic Products, a specialist in the personal computer consumable market.
        Vintage Airtours established to fly Orlando–Florida Keys in vintage DC-3s.

1993   Virgin Games floated as Virgin Interactive Entertainment plc with Hasbro and Blockbuster taking minority equity stakes.
        Virgin Euromagnetics launches a range of personal computers.

1994   Virgin Cola Company formed as joint venture with Cott Corp.
        Agreement with W. Grant to launch Virgin Vodka.
        Virgin acquires Our Price retail music chain, owned 75% by W. H. Smith, 25% by Virgin.
        Virgin Retail Group forms joint ventures to develop Megastores in Hong Kong and S. Korea.
        Virgin City Jet service launched between Dublin and London City Airport.

1995   Virgin Direct Personal Financial Service is launched as a joint venture with Norwich Union (whose stake is later acquired by Australian Mutual Provident).
        Acquisition of MGM Cinemas, UK's biggest movie theater chain, to create Virgin Cinemas.

1996   Virgin Travel Group acquires Euro-Belgian Airlines to form Virgin Express.
        V2 record label and music publishing company formed.
        London & Continental Railways (in which Virgin is a major shareholder) wins a £3bn. contract to build the Channel Tunnel Rail Link and operate Eurostar rail services.

1997   Virgin Rail wins bid to operate the InterCity West Coast and is awarded the 15-year rail franchise.
        Virgin Net, an internet Service Provider, formed with NTL.
        Branson acquires a 15% stake in the London Broncos rugby league team.
        Victory Corporation, a joint venture with Rory McCarthy, launches the Virgin Clothing and Virgin Vie toiletry products.
        Majority share in Virgin Radio sold to Chris Evans' Ginger Media Group.
        Virgin Bride, a chain of wedding retailers, formed.
        Virgin One telephone bank account and "one-stop integrated financial service" launched in collaboration with Royal Bank of Scotland.

1998   Virgin Entertainment acquires W. H. Smith's 75% stake in Virgin/Our Price.
        Virgin Cola launched in the US.

1999   Virgin sells it UK cinema chain to UGC for £215 million
        Virgin launches mobile phone service in joint-venture with Deutsche Telecom's One-to-One (November)
        49% of Virgin Atlantic sold to Singapore Airlines for £600 million.
        Restructuring and re-launch of loss-making Our Price record stores.

2000   Virgin Mobile launches US wireless phone service in joint venture with Sprint and announces plan to expand into Europe, Africa and South-East Asia. Virgin Mobile Australia (a joint venture with Cable & Wireless) begins service in October.
        Virgin Net, Virgin's portal and ISP venture closes its content division.
        Virgin announced the closing of its clothing company (February).
        Virgin Cars, online sales of new cars launched.
        Virgin and Bear Stearns set up Lynx New Media, a $130 million internet-focused venture capital fund.
        Inaugural flight of Virgin Blue, Virgin's low-cost Australian airline (August).
        Branson knighted by the Queen.
        Virgin fails to win franchise to run Britain's government-owned National Lottery.

2001   50% of Virgin Blue sold to Patrick Corporation for A$138.
            Virgin expands into Singapore and SE Asia with joint ventures with local companies in radio stations, cosmetic retailing, and wireless phone services.
            Virgin.net merges its ISP and portal businesses.
            16 French Virgin Megastores sold to Lagardere Media for 150 million Euros.
2002   Virgin Bikes (UK) launched. Offers direct sale of new motorcycles at discount prices.

■ THE VIRGIN GROUP OF COMPANIES IN 2002 ■

The Virgin group is not a single corporate entity. The Virgin companies comprise some 20 holding companies (most of which are entirely financial and legal entities, the majority registered in the British Virgin Islands) and over 200 operating companies, most of which are based within Britain. They are owned by Branson, both individually and through a series of Channel Islands-located trusts, the beneficiaries of which are Branson and his family. The linkage between the companies is the common use of the Virgin trademark, Branson's role as shareholder (both directly and indirectly through the trusts), Branson's role as chairman of the companies, and Branson's management role, which is primarily in publicity, public and government relations, and appointing senior executives. The Virgin empire comprises those companies which were wholly or majority owned by Branson and those in which Branson held a minority equity stake. Figure 14.1 shows the structure of the Virgin group of companies, including some major operating companies and the holding companies that own them. Exhibit 14.3 shows the main companies within the group.

Figure 14.1   The Virgin group of companies
Source: Virgin Management Ltd.

Exhibit 14.3: Businesses within the Virgin Group, 2002

Virgin Active	Chain of health and leisure clubs in UK and South Africa.
Virgin Airship & Balloon Company	Commercial hot air balloons for advertising, brand building, and specialist film work.
Virgin Atlantic	London-based airline serving 20 destinations in the US, Caribbean, South Africa, and Asia.
Virgin Atlantic Cargo	Air freight using Virgin Atlantic's network.
Virgin Balloon Flights	Passenger balloon flights in the UK, Holland and Belgium.
Virgin Bikes	Direct motorcycle sales.
Virgin Blue	Low fare airline flying in Australia.
Virgin Books	Publishes books on music, sport, TV, movies, and comedy.
Virgin Brides	Chain of bridal retail stores.
Virgin Cars	Direct sales of new cars in the UK.
Virgin Cinemas	Chain of movie theaters in Japan.
Virgin Cosmetics	Direct sales of specially formulated cosmetics.
Virgin Credit Card	Credit card issued by Virgin Money.
Virgin Drinks	Distributes Virgin-branded soft drinks.
Virgin Energy	Markets gas and electricity in the UK.
Virgin Experience	Offers innovative leisure experiences, from bungee jumping to Ferrari driving.
Virgin Express	Brussels-based airline offering scheduled flights to UK and other European destinations.
Virgin Healthcare	Charity promoting education into current healthcare issues.
Virgin Holidays	UK based tour operator specializing in long haul holidays to America, the Far East, Australia, and South Africa, using Virgin Atlantic flights.
Virgin Incentives	Corporate incentive vouchers exchangeable for Virgin goods and services
The Lightship Group	Rents airships for advertising and promotional purposes.
Virgin Limobike	Motorcycle taxi service in London.
Virgin Limousines	Limos serving Northern California.
Virgin Megastores	80 Megastores in Europe, Japan, and N. America sell music, movies, computer games, and books.
Virgin Mobile	Wireless telephone resellers offering easy-tariff service with no line rental or fixed-term contract.
Virgin Money	Online financial services offering loans, mutual funds, and stock trading.
Virgin.net	UK-based internet service provider.
Radio Free Virgin	UK digital radio broadcaster.
Virgin Space	Chain of internet cafés.
Virgin Student	One-stop shop serving UK's student population.
Virgin Student.com	Student website.
Virgin Trains	Major UK operator of passenger train services and facilities and allows booking of Virgin Train tickets online.
thetrainline.com	Online rail ticket sales and reservations.
Virgin Travelstore	UK-based online travel agency.
Virgin Wines	Direct seller of wines.
V.Shop	UK's High Street stores with off-the-shelf and online sales of music, movies, and wireless phones.
V2 Music	Independent record label (artists include the Stereophonics, Tom Jones, Moby, and Underworld).

Despite the remarkable diversity of the Virgin group, all of the Virgin companies possessed an entrepreneurial culture and a strategy that was based upon novel approaches to creating value for consumers (and, ultimately, for Branson). Consider, for example, some of the leading companies within the Virgin group.

The airline business was the only segment of Virgin's diversified organization directly managed by Richard Branson (he was the Chief Executive Officer).

Virgin Atlantic

The core of the Virgin empire was its travel business which was the major revenue generator and, until recently, the main source of profit for the group. The flagship, Virgin Atlantic, had launched as a cut-price airline, but its success was based upon targeting the lucrative business traveler segment of the North Atlantic market with superior and innovative customer service. The airline has offered business travelers amenities not even offered to first-class passengers on other airlines. Virgin had pioneered state-of-the-art reclining seats, in-flight massages, hair stylists, aromatherapists, and motorcycle and limo home-pick-up service. In 1998 it began a luxury boat service up the Thames from Heathrow to the City of London allowing executives and bankers to dodge London traffic jams. In economy, Virgin was the first to provide passenger-controlled personal video screens in every seat-back. In-flight entertainment has included clowns, London buskers, even Richard Branson serving drinks while dressed as a female flight attendant. The inaugural transatlantic flight was still remembered fondly by travel writers who took the journey to New York. Bands played music in the aisles, Miss World danced with passengers, butlers handed out caviar, brandy, and cigars. Branson's father, who was along for the ride, commented, "When I die, I hope heaven is like this: 35,000 feet up, endless champagne and surrounded by pretty women."[10] What Virgin did was to re-create the mystique of air travel through mixing unique in-flight luxuries with circus side-show.

The airline won numerous awards for its customer service and became one of the most profitable of the world's smaller airlines. Its success in the North Atlantic market encouraged it to extend its routes to Asia (Tokyo, Hong Kong, Delhi), the Caribbean, and South Africa.

A constant theme of Virgin Atlantic's development was its war against the major airlines and against British Airways in particular. This involved Branson in one of his favorite roles: casting his plucky Virgin upstart as David against the corporate Goliaths of big business. BA under Lord King was the ideal foil for Branson – big, stuffy, and establishment. Branson's fight, first against the BA "dirty tricks" campaign and then against the BA-American Airlines alliance, provided Branson and Virgin Atlantic with massive publicity and established them as virtuous underdogs representing entrepreneurship and the spirit of competition.

For all Virgin Atlantic's success, it was competing in a tough industry and defending a difficult strategic position. The international airline industry has been a financial disaster for most of the past decade – none of the major airlines had covered their cost of capital. Virgin Atlantic's dependence on business travelers was a major source of vulnerability when most companies were trimming their travel budgets. Virgin Atlantic's competitive advantage depended critically upon its superior service, yet almost all its service innovations were being imitated by the major airlines.

In the year to April 2001, Virgin Atlantic lost £82.7 million, compared with a £42 million in the previous year.

Virgin Cargo

Air freight business was an important complement to Virgin Atlantic's passenger service. While planning the launch of Virgin Atlantic, Branson asked New York "Air Freight Godfather" Angelo Pusateri to join him on Branson's London houseboat to discuss the start-up of a Virgin Airlines cargo service. "It was sort of strange," remembered Pusateri. "He was a very relaxed guy, continually scribbling in this big notebook. He said he was putting together an airline and it was going to be fun. He told us, 'I don't know much about cargo, but I know it's important to our revenue package, and I'd like you guys to build an air freight operation for us. Go forth and develop.' Anyone who could lay out a plan of this size without a single typed piece of paper – I was impressed."[11] Based at the then-underutilized Newark airport, Virgin Cargo grew to handle close to 100,000 metric tons of cargo by 2000. The company managed freight operations for other carriers such as Lufthansa, America West, and Midwest Express. Pusateri was chief executive of Virgin Aviation Services, the parent company to Virgin Cargo and other smaller Virgin aviation companies. Under Pusateri's leadership, the Virgin management style based upon initiative, entrepreneurship, and a high level of autonomy worked well in the air cargo business. Managers were encouraged to tailor products to customer needs, price service aggressively, and take risks. When a federal regulation required US law enforcement agencies to discard outdated, but still effective bullet-proof vests, Pusateri had the vests collected and shipped free of charge to London's Metropolitan police force: "The bobbies get piece of mind, English taxpayers don't pay a quid, and Virgin gets some great PR."

Virgin Express

In April 1996, Branson purchased Euro-Belgian Airlines SA, a short-haul carrier based in Brussels servicing destinations throughout Europe. After changing the name to Virgin Express plc, 49 percent of its stock was floated on the Brussels and NASDAQ stock markets. Virgin Express took advantage of the liberalization of the European aviation market to expand its range of scheduled services. Virgin Express moved into profit in 1997, but in competing with low-cost airlines such as easyJet and GO, was hampered by a high cost base resulting from its Belgium location. In July 1998, Virgin Express moved the company's registration to the Republic of Ireland to benefit from lower corporate and employment taxes. Its operational base remained in Brussels which meant that its routes did not link with those of Virgin Atlantic.

Virgin Rail

Virgin's biggest, and potentially riskiest, diversification of the 1990s was its entry into rail travel. Early in 1996, Virgin Rail was formed to bid for operating franchises in the partitioned and privatized British Rail system. By 1997 Virgin Rail operated two rail companies: Virgin Cross-Country with train services between the South West, Midlands, and Wales, with Birmingham as a hub; and Virgin West Coast with services between London and Glasgow. In addition, Virgin was also one of the six investors in London and Continental Railway (LCR), which was responsible for running the Eurostar train service between London and Paris through the Channel Tunnel. To promote awareness of the Virgin brand, Branson had all of the trains painted in Virgin's cardinal red. Virgin Rail was profitable to 2001; however, government operating subsidies were scheduled to be phased out in 2002. In addition, the capital investment requirements of operating passenger rail services were substantial, though the sale of 49 percent of Virgin Rail to Stagecoach for £158 million had reduced Virgin's exposure. Of particular concern to Branson was the tide of general dissatisfaction of the British public with the inadequacies of the UK's privatized rail network. Virgin Rail's record of poor punctuality was primarily a result of the poor state of Britain's rail infrastructure; however, limited opportunities for innovative differentiation meant that Virgin Rail could not easily respond to the company's deteriorating relationships with its customers.

Virgin Entertainment Group

Virgin Entertainment Group comprises Virgin's retailing businesses together with Virgin's remaining cinema chains. The retailing companies include Virgin Megastores, with 122 locations around the world, and the UK Our Price chain. The Megastores sold music, music accessories, electronic equipment, clothing, and concert tickets. The Virgin Megastores did not form a single integrated business but were operated as separate businesses with different business partners in different countries. Thus, in Japan, Virgin Megastores were a joint venture with Marui, a Japanese department store, while in France Virgin no longer had an equity stake in the Megastore chain.

The other major retail business was the Virgin/Our Price music retailing chain, 75 percent of which had been sold to the book and newspaper retailer W. H. Smith in 1991 but was reacquired by Branson for £145 million in 1998.[12]

Despite the success of the Virgin stores as leading retailers of recorded music, the format has not developed into a "category killer" in the same way as Home Depot in home improvement supplies, IKEA in home furnishings, or The Gap in casual clothing. Retailing revenues have totaled around half a billion pounds annually. However, profitability has been miserable. The impact of the internet and illegal recording of CDs has been a major problem only partly ameliorated by Virgin's use of its retail network to sell mobile phones. Despite a program of reformatting and refurbishment of the UK Megastores during 2000–1, the chain still appeared to be searching for a viable business model.

Virgin Trading Group Limited

Virgin Trading Group, a wholly-owned Virgin subsidiary, comprised Branson's beverage start-ups – the ventures had been widely viewed as pure follies by most outside marketing experts. Virgin Spirits, a joint venture with Scottish whisky distiller William

Grant, was established to market and distribute Virgin Vodka. The brand failed to gain significant market presence outside of Virgin's own planes and hotels and the venture was wound up in March 1998. The Virgin Cola Company was a joint venture with the Canadian soft drink company Cott & Company, the world's largest supplier of retailer own-brand soda drinks. Virgin Cola was introduced in the UK in 1994 and achieved initial success in the pub and restaurant trade. The drink was packaged in a "Pammy" bottle based upon the body of Pamela Anderson. After gaining a peak of 8 percent share of the UK market, sales declined. In 1997, Virgin Cola lost about £5 million on revenues of £30 million. In 1998, Virgin acquired Cott's share of the business and launched Virgin Cola with a $25 million investment and the goal, according to Branson, of "driving Coke out of the States."[13] Despite gaining massive publicity, there was little evidence of Virgin being able to convert media coverage into sales. By 2002, Virgin Drinks Company was still marketing Virgin Cola in the UK, Continental Europe, and Asia, but no sales figures were available.

Virgin Direct

The Virgin Direct financial services group was launched in the UK in March 1995. It was a joint venture between Virgin, which owned 49.9 percent, and Australian Mutual Provident Society (which acquired Norwich Union's initial stake). Virgin Direct offered retirement plans called "PEPs" (personal equity plans), life insurance, and other financial services. It was organized into several units, including: Virgin Direct Life, which offered life insurance and retirement plans; Virgin Unit Trusts Managers, which managed mutual funds; the Virgin One Bank, a joint venture with the Royal Bank of Scotland; and Virgin Credit Card, issued by MBNA. It direct-marketed several index-linked mutual funds ("unit trusts") that offered lower management costs and better average performance than most actively managed mutual funds. Within three years of the launch, Virgin Direct had some 250,000 customers and its mutual funds had £1.5 billion under management. By 2002, Virgin Direct's financial services were delivered primarily through the internet. Virginmoney.com offered access to the full range of Virgin financial services, including bank accounts, credit cards, ISAs, home and car insurance, life insurance, mutual funds, and share dealing. Virgin's financial services were characterized by two features. First, they were low cost. Virgin's credit card interest rates, fund management charges, and other fees tended to be below those of the major financial institutions. Second, Virgin's product offered several ease-of-use features. For example, the Virgin One bank account allowed a number of products – home loans, savings account, checking account, credit card debt – to be pooled into a single account offering significant administrative and interest cost conveniences. Despite considerable market success, Virgin Direct was still losing money in 2000.

Victory Corporation

Victory Corporation – Virgin's clothing and cosmetics company – had also met with considerable criticism from outside commentators. The company was floated as a start-up on London's Alternative Investment Market in 1996. Its two parts were:

- Virgin Vie, a cosmetics and toiletries company which designed and marketed its own range of products (intended to expand to about 1,000 separate products) to be sold through 3,000 consultants and 100 UK stores, as well as an international launch. By mid-1998, the venture was going badly, with the planned store openings canceled after the pilot stores failed to achieve target sales.
- Virgin Clothing Company, a designer and marketer of men's clothing that sold through UK fashion retailers and through its internet site, www.virgin-clothing.com. The company's advertisements showed a scruffy Richard Branson with the caption, "Giorgio designs. Ralph designs. Calvin designs. Don't worry, Richard doesn't." The clothing range did not sell well. Launches of new ranges were behind schedule because of the need to redesign.

Since flotation, Victory Corporation's share price declined from 55 pence to 3 pence in May 2002, reflecting the company's dismal sales and profit performance – the company turned in operating losses of £8 million for 1997. Finance director, Stephen Murphy, said that a key lesson for Virgin from the Victory Corporation experience was the danger of floating start-up companies: "Thrusting a start-up company into the public arena on day one is not a good thing to do. Because of the public company perspective, we did not grasp control in the way we should have done."[14]

Virgin Net

Virgin Net was both an internet service provider and a portal offering a variety of content and retailing opportunities through partnership arrangements between Virgin Net and a range of partner suppliers. Virgin's monthly subscription rate undercut AOL, BT, and most other major ISPs. Virgin had attempted to dispose of its half share of the business to its partner, NTL; however, the sale ran into difficulties and the service continues as a joint venture.

Virgin Mobile

Virgin Mobile was the most successful of the UK's "mobile virtual network operators" – companies that partnered with major wireless operators to offer service over their partners' networks. Virgin's rapid market penetration may be attributed to its brand recognition; marketing through Virgin retail stores, Virgin.net, and Sainsbury's supermarkets; and Virgin's simple market approach – unlike other telecom companies, Virgin has no line rental, no monthly contract, and a simple tariff: 15p a minute for the first five minutes of each day and 5p a minute after that. It has scored a number of firsts, including being the first operator to scrap peak rate calls, introduce a daily discounting tariff, and was the first company in the world to introduce an integrated MP3 mobile phone. Virgin Mobile (Australia), a partnership with Cable and Wireless Optus, opened for business at the end of October 2000, Virgin Mobile (Asia) a joint-venture with Singapore Telecom was launched in summer 2001, and US entry involved a joint venture with Sprint.

Table 14.1 The financial performance of major Virgin companies, 1999

Company	Revenue ($ million)	Profit (Loss) ($ million)	Ownership (%)
Virgin Travel	1,800	173	51
Virgin Entertainment Group	1,300	12	100
Virgin Direct	900	(25)	50
Virgin Rail	800	42	51
Virgin Express Holdings	300	(6)	58
Virgin Trading	100	(6)	100
V2 Records	53	(55)	66
Victory Corporation	40	(24)	85
Virgin Hotels	40	7	100
Virgin Bride	30	(0.4)	100
Virgin Net	20	(7)	51

Source: *Fortune*, July 2, 2000.

Virgin Bride

Branson's Virgin Bride venture was a classic example of Branson's entrepreneurial opportunism in the face of an underserved consumer market. The idea had come from a Virgin Atlantic employee who was appalled at the inadequacies of bridal shops within the UK. The first Virgin Bride store was launched by Branson wearing a $10,000 bridal gown. The stores offered a full range of wedding goods and services, including apparel and wedding planning services.

■ FINANCIAL STRUCTURE AND PERFORMANCE ■

Financial reporting by the Virgin companies was fragmented, difficult to locate, and awkward to consolidate because of lack of public information and different financial years. Sleuthing by financial journalists has resulted in piecing together financial data for a major part of the Virgin group (see table 14.1 and figure 14.2). Despite the limited information available, it was apparent that, in terms of accounting profitability, cash flow, and economic value added (EVA), the profit performance of the Virgin group as a whole was far from stellar during the period 1995–7. Branson and Virgin executives have dismissed the analysis by both newspapers, claiming that accounting profits are poor indicators of the value and performance of the Virgin companies and that, unlike public companies, private companies have tax-minimizing incentives to minimize rather than maximize reported profits. The primary goal is long-term value creation.

The financial structure of the Virgin group has changed substantially over the years. In terms of financial structure, the primary feature of the group was the stand-alone financing of each company. At the beginning of the 1990s, the group had debts of more than $400 million, most of which were personally guaranteed by Branson or subject to cross-guarantees within the group. This left Virgin highly vulnerable to bad debts in

Figure 14.2 Virgin group cash flow, 1995–9
Source: *Financial Times*, August 13, 1998, p. 24; *Mail on Sunday*, "Revealed: the truth behind Virgin's finances." September 3, 2ooo, p. 5.

one part of the group swiftly infecting the rest. Virgin's near collapse during the 1990–2 recession resulted in a more conservative approach to financing by Branson. Each company was separately financed, often with outside investors taking much of the risk. Lenders to Virgin companies have no recourse to Mr Branson's assets or those of any other part of the group.

However, the recent financial woes of the group have resulted in Branson having to shift finances between companies in order to prop up weaker businesses. While Virgin Atlantic was generating a strong positive cash flow, then the rest of the Virgin group was safe. Virgin Atlantic's transition from profit to loss at a time when other major businesses are doing badly has placed considerable added pressures on the group.

The rapid diversification of the 1990s, together with the cash demands of the railroad companies, retailing, and financial services, encouraged Branson to look increasingly to outside equity financing. This has resulted in Branson attracting investment by venture capital funds, joint venture partners, and initial public offerings. Of the 13 businesses that formed the bulk of Virgin's operations, only three were wholly owned by Branson and his interests: Virgin Atlantic, Virgin Hotels, and the V Entertainment Group. The others all had substantial outside interests:

- Virgin Rail was half-owned by Stagecoach.
- Virgin Direct was half-owned by Australian Mutual Provident, with its direct banking venture with The Royal Bank of Scotland.
- Virgin Retail had different partners and investors. These included Blockbuster and Marui.
- Virgin Trading drinks ventures had been launched with investments from William Grant and Cotts.

- Victory Corporation, the fashion and toiletries companies, was pioneered by entrepreneur and investor Rory McCarthy. In addition, outside investors owned 25 percent of the equity. McCarthy also held one-third of V2 Music.
- Virgin Express was a publicly traded company.
- Apart from the joint venture partners and public stockholders, there were also a number of private investors – often major equity and venture capital funds.

A central role for Branson was his ability to attract outside investors through his high profile, personality, and network of connections. Typically, by offering the Virgin brand and his own celebrity status to promote new ventures, Branson was able to negotiate some very attractive deals. For example, Branson put up only £2,000 initially for minority stakes in Virgin Clothing and Virgin Vie. The attractiveness of Virgin to The Royal Bank of Scotland and Australian Mutual was that it permitted these companies to develop a novel approach to marketing and distribution using one of the best-known and highly regarded personalities in Britain, without putting their own names at risk. The Virgin name together with the image and entrepreneurial drive of Branson were also major considerations in encouraging Stagecoach to acquire a major stake in Virgin Rail. Branson's willingness to extend the Virgin brand to a wide range of new enterprises, many of them with minor equity stakes by Virgin, has stimulated the observation that Virgin was increasingly a brand-franchising operation.

■ ORGANIZATIONAL STRUCTURE AND CORPORATE CULTURE ■

As noted earlier, the Virgin group was an unusual organization. It comprised a loose alliance of companies linked primarily by the Virgin trademark and Branson's role as shareholder, chairman, and public relations supremo.[15] The group's financial and legal structure was partly a reflection of Branson's unconventional ideas about business and his wariness of the financial community. To some extent, the intricate structure of offshore-owned private companies was a deliberate attempt by Branson to cloak the Virgin empire in a thick veil of secrecy. This was apparent from the use of "bearer shares" by several of the Virgin holding companies through which minority shareholders (venture capitalists and other investors) could not be identified. However, there was more to the Virgin structure than opaqueness and tax efficiency. Branson viewed the loosely knit structure as consistent with his vision of people-oriented capitalism:

> We're structured as if we are 150 small companies. Each has to stand on its own two feet, as if they are their own companies. Employees have a stake in their success. They feel – and are – crucial to their company because they are one-in-fifty or one-in-a-hundred instead of one-in-tens-of-thousands. They indeed are all under the Virgin umbrella, but they are generally not subsidiaries. I'm over them to see if one company can't help another, but otherwise they are independent. Some people like the idea of growing fiefdoms – companies that brag about sales of over $5 billion a year – but there is no logical reason to think that there is anything good about huge companies. History in fact shows the opposite. Those huge corporations with tentacles and divisions and departments become unwieldy, slow growing, stagnant. Some chairmen want them like that so that one

division's loss can make up for another's profit, but we'd rather have a lot of exciting companies that are all making profits – as are all of ours.[16]

The Virgin group has been likened both to a brand franchising operation and to Japanese *keiretsu* where member companies have financial and management links and share a common sense of identity. The reality, according to *Management Today*,[17] is somewhere between the two. Will Whitehorn, Branson's long-time strategist and business developer, describes Virgin as "a branded venture capital organization."

Although the formal linkages between the companies are limited to Branson's share-holdings, his presence or influence on the companies' board of directors, and the common use of the Virgin brand, there is also an informal corporate organization. Branson's London residence in Holland Park acted as an improvised corporate office where a small core of Branson advisors and senior executives spent time. These include:

- Will Whitehorn, originally Branson's press spokesman and head of PR, but widely regarded as Branson's second-in-command and sounding-board for issues of strategy and new business development.
- Rowan Gormley joined the Virgin group as Corporate Development Director after working as an accountant with Arthur Andersen & Co. He led Virgin's move into financial services in 1995 as chief executive of Virgin Direct. In January 2000, he become Chief Executive of Virgin Wine.
- Brad Rosser was Branson's head of new business development. An accounting and finance major from Australia with an MBA from Cornell, he was previously employed by Australian entrepreneur Alan Bond and by McKinsey & Company. He subjected new business proposals to rigorous criteria as to whether they fit the Virgin business model: "The products must be innovative, challenge authority, offer value for money, be of good quality, and the market must be growing."
- Michael Herriot, at 55, was one of the eldest of Branson's top management team. He was hired from Grand Metropolitan in 1989 to head up Virgin Hotels (a position he held throughout 2001).
- Rory McCarthy was business partner, friend, and soul mate of Branson. Having set the world hang-gliding altitude record as well as starting up a string of companies, he had similar drives as Branson. His McCarthy Corporation held 33 percent of V2 and 50 percent of Virgin Helicopters.
- Tom Alexander was recruited by Branson from BT Cellnet to head up Virgin Mobile.
- Gordon McCallum joined Virgin in 1997 as Group Strategy Director. He was formerly a McKinsey & Company consultant. In 2001 he was appointed to the board of Virgin Mobile USA.
- Frances Farrow joined Virgin Atlantic as Commercial Services Director from City law firm, Binder Hamlyn. She became chief executive of Virgin USA Inc. and a member of the board of Virgin Mobile USA.

A key feature of the Virgin group was the roles which senior executives played and the way in which they interacted. Although their formal positions were as executives of the individual operating companies, a number were long-time Branson associates who participated more widely in the management of the group. For instance, while heading up corporate services at Virgin Atlantic, Frances Farrow's legal background meant that she provided much wider legal advice within the Virgin group. Similarly, although Rowan Gormley's formal positions were with Virgin Direct and Virgin Wine, he was a source of new business leadership and strategy expertise for the group as a whole. Thus, although the Virgin group had no corporate structure, Branson and his senior executives and advisors did, in effect, form a team which exerted overall financial control, guided strategy, assessed new business ideas, and determined new appointments.

A key aspect of this informal integration and control was the Virgin culture. This was defined almost entirely by Branson's own values and management style. It reflected his eccentricity, sense of fun, disrespect for hierarchy and formal authority, commitment to employees and consumers, and belief in hard work and individual responsibility. The group provided an environment in which talented, ambitious people were motivated to do their best and strive for a higher level of performance. While the working environment was informal, anti-corporate, and defined by the pop culture of its era, expectations were high. Branson expected a high level of commitment, the acceptance of personal responsibility, and long hours of work when needed. Financial rewards for most employees were typically modest, but non-pecuniary benefits included social activities, company-sponsored weekend getaways, and impromptu parties.

The apparent chaos of the Virgin group, with its casual style and absence of formal structure and control systems, belied a sharp business acumen and forceful determination of the Virgin group. It was easy for more traditional business enterprises to underestimate Virgin – a key error of British Airways. Virgin possessed considerable financial and managerial talent, and what Virgin lacked in formal structure was made up for by a strong culture and close personal ties. The Virgin organizational structure involved very little hierarchy, offering short lines of communication and flexible response capability. Employees were given a great deal of responsibility and freedom in order to stimulate idea generation, initiative, commitment, and fun. The lack of a corporate headquarters and the small size of most of the Virgin operating companies were intended to foster teamwork and a strong entrepreneurial spirit.

■ BRANSON'S CHARACTER AND BUSINESS PHILOSOPHY ■

As the creator of Virgin and its unique corporate culture, and the primary promoter of its image and entrepreneurial spirit, Richard Branson was synonymous with Virgin. Robert Dick referred to Virgin as a "counter-cultural enterprise" and to Branson as a "hippie entrepreneur." To many of his generation he embodied the spirit of "New Britain." In a country where business leaders were members of "The Establishment" and upholders of the existing social structure, Branson was seen as a revolutionary. Despite a privileged family background (his father was a lawyer and Richard attended a private boarding school), Branson had the ability to transcend the social classes which traditionally divided British society and segmented consumer markets. As such, he was part of a movement in British culture and society that has sought to escape the Old Britain of fading empire, class antagonism, Victorian values, and stiff-upper-lip hypocrisy. In the remaking of British society in its post-imperial era, Richard Branson can be viewed – along with musicians such as the Beatles, politicians like Margaret Thatcher and Tony Blair, and other new-age entrepreneurs such as Anita Roddick of Body Shop – as an important change agent.

His informality and disrespect for convention were central to his way of business. Branson's woolly sweaters, beard, windswept hair, and toothy grin were practically a trademark of the Virgin companies. His dislike of office buildings and the usual symbols of corporate success was reflected in the absence of a corporate head office and his willingness to do business from his family homes – the Manor in Oxfordshire, a Maida Vale houseboat, and later his Holland Park house.

His lack of a clear distinction between work and his social and family life is reflected in the fact that his cousins, aunts, childhood friends, and dinner-party acquaintances were all drawn into business relationships with him. His approach to his business relationships was that work should be fun and his employees should gain both pleasure and sense of fulfillment from their role in creating enterprises. Branson has experienced few problems in paying quite modest salaries to the great majority of Virgin employees. According to Robert Dick:

> Much of the operating style was established not so much by design but the exigencies of the time when Virgin was getting started. It has proved to be a successful model that Branson can replicate. His philosophy is to immerse himself in a new venture until he understands the ins and outs of the business, and then hand it over to a good managing director and financial controller, who are given a stake in it, and are then expected to make the company take off. He knows that expansion through the creation of additional discrete legal entities not only protects the Virgin group, but also gives people a sense of involvement and loyalty, particularly if he trusts them with full authority and offers minority share holdings to the managers of subsidiaries. He is proud of the fact that Virgin has produced a considerable number of millionaires. He has said that he does not want his best people to leave the company to start a venture outside. He prefers to make millionaires within.[18]

His use of joint ventures was an extension of this model reinforced by his dealings with the Japanese. Branson was impressed by the Japanese approach to business, admiring their commitment to the long term and the way they took time to build a business through organic growth rather than acquisition. His only major acquisition was the parts of British Rail that formed Virgin Rail. Prior to that Branson had made only two significant acquisitions: Rushes Video for £6 million and the forerunner to Virgin Express. He saw similarities in the Japanese *keiretsu* system (multiple companies interlocking through managerial and equity linkages in a collaborative network) and the structure he created at Virgin, with around 200 mostly small companies, which combined "small is beautiful" with "strength through unity." He explained this and other business maxims that he believed to be necessary for success in a speech to the Institute of Directors in 1993. "Staff first, then customers and shareholders" should be the chairman's priority if the goal is better performance. "Shape the business around the people," "Build don't buy," "Be best, not biggest," "Pioneer, don't follow the leader," "Capture every fleeting idea," and "Drive for change" were other guiding principles in the Branson philosophy.

Branson's values of innocence, innovation, and irreverence for authority were apparent in his choice of new ventures. He drew heavily on the ideas of others within his organization and was prepared to invest in new start-ups even in markets that were dominated by long-established incumbents. His business ventures, just like his sporting exploits, reflected a "just live life" attitude and a "bigger the challenge, greater the fun" belief. In identifying opportunity he was particularly keen to identify markets where the conservatism and lack of imagination of incumbent firms meant that they were failing to create value for customers. Branson entered markets with a "new" and "anti-establishment attitude" that sought to offer customers a better alternative. An example of this was Virgin's entry into financial services. Into a business that was long regarded as conservative and stuffy, Branson hoped to bring "a breath of fresh air."

What did these principles mean for the types of markets that Virgin entered and the kind of strategy that Virgin adopted? Will Whitehorn identified a number of common themes:

- "Challenging markets"
- Taking competition to the next level"
- "Sticking it to the Big Boys"
- "Quality"
- "Value for money"
- "Challenge"[19]

At the same time, the affection of the British public towards Branson reflected the fact that Branson was a traditionalist as well as a radical. Branson's values and his sense of fair-play were consistent with many traditional values that defined the British character. His competitive battles against huge corporations like British Airways and Coca-Cola link well with the English heroes who have battled against tyranny and evil: King Arthur, Robin Hood, and St George. His fights against British Airways' dirty-tricks campaign, and his resisting unethical practices in competing for the franchise to run the National Lottery, resonate well with the British sense of fair play. Even his willingness to appear in outlandish attire reflected a British propensity for ludicrous dressing-up whether at fancy-dress parties, morris dancing, or the House of Lords.

■ MARKETING ■

The Virgin brand was the group's greatest single asset. What the brand name communicated and how it enhanced the products to which it was applied was complex. It had connotations of value for money, but also linked with concepts of style and broader social values, too. Most importantly, the brand was not associated with any specific products or markets – it allowed Virgin to cross product and market boundaries more easily than almost any other brand name. While Marks & Spencer was successful in extending its St Michael brand from clothing to food, Ralph Lauren extended his brand from clothing to cosmetics, toiletries, and accessories, and Harley-Davidson applied its brand to clothing, toiletries, cigarettes, and cafés. No company had extended its brand to so diverse a range of products and services as airlines, railroads, cosmetics, financial services, music, and soft drinks.

Much of the brand value could be attributed to Richard Branson and his persona and style. The values and characteristics that the Virgin brand communicated are inseparable from Richard Branson the entrepreneur, joker, fair-playing Brit, and challenger of giants. The differentiation that the Virgin brand offered was linked to the innovation and offbeat marketing approach that characterized the different Virgin start-ups. A key aspect of Branson's business enterprises was the difference in competitive approach between Virgin and the established market leaders in the sectors where it competed. Thus the difference between Virgin Atlantic and BA, between Virgin Cola and Coke, and between Virgin Direct and the leading banks was not just the characteristics of the product offered, it was also about the companies and how they related to their customers. As Virgin moved increasingly into international markets, the ability of the Virgin brand to attract consumers was less obvious. If the appeal of Virgin was the humor, style, fun, and irreverence that Richard Branson epitomized, Virgin had to consider how well this image could cross the boundaries of national culture. Although Branson was well known in Europe and North America, in many respects he was a quintessentially British character who was a product of time and place.

With the rapid diversification of the 1990s, and the significant number of start-ups that had achieved neither profitability nor significant market penetration, the group was considering the extent to which the Virgin brand had become overextended. The head of brand identity at consultant Landor Associates commented: "He's still way too unfocused. He should get out of businesses that don't fit the Virgin/Branson personality, such as beverages, cosmetics, certainly financial services, or come up with another brand name for them."[20] Other marketing experts suggested that Virgin's brand-stretching had damaged the goodwill associated with the Virgin name and compromised the core values it was founded on. Applying the Virgin name to rail services has been especially damaging – Virgin's vision of offering the traveling public new standards of speed and customer attentiveness had been swamped by the problems of Britain's privatized but poorly integrated rail network. The wisdom of applying a brand that had been identified with dynamic start-up business to the renaming of a former public sector monopoly was a source of much reflection within Virgin.

Despite his renown, Branson, too, might be waning in market appeal. Was there a risk that, having seen Branson as flight attendant, Branson in a wedding dress, Branson with successive prime ministers, and Branson attempting to fly around the world in a hot-air balloon, the public was beginning to tire of his exploits?

This emergence of these concerns during 1996–7 had encouraged a move to refocusing within Virgin. The executive team identified a number of "core businesses" where it wanted to see growth: Virgin Atlantic, Virgin Express, Virgin Rail, and the international expansion of its retail and cinema businesses. "We are going to consolidate around these core areas," says Whitehorn, "because we have a lot to do with them."[21]

The telecom and internet revolution of the late 1990s changed all that. During 1997–2001, Virgin had embarked upon a number of new businesses mostly built upon the opportunities provided by wireless telecommunications and the internet. By 2002, most commentators believed that a new phase of refocusing was inevitable.

■ LOOKING AHEAD ■

In May 2002, the Virgin group of companies was faced with two main issues. In the short term was the cash crunch that resulted from the presence of several perennial loss-making businesses within the Virgin portfolio and the effects of the 2001–2 economic downturn that had adversely affected Virgin's travel businesses. Virgin had already sold equity in several of its businesses to external partners; the most obvious route for additional large-scale cash injections would be to take some of Virgin's companies public. However, the current investment climate was not favorable for initial public offerings, and Branson was reluctant to run the risk of a disappointing stock market reception for any Virgin company.

Longer term, there were fundamental strategic questions about the future shape and rationale for the Virgin group. What kind of enterprise was Virgin? Was it a brand management and franchising company, an incubator of start-up businesses, a vehicle for Richard Branson's personal ambitions, or a novel form of conglomerate? Was Virgin a unified, if diversified, business or a loose confederation of many independent businesses?

Whatever the identity and rationale of the Virgin group, it was not apparent that the existing structure or organization fitted with any of these categories:

- If Virgin was a brand-franchising organization, then the critical role for the Virgin group was to develop and protect the brand and maximize the licensing revenues from its use by other companies. Clearly Branson would need to play a role in promoting the brand, but it was not necessary that he should have any strategic, operating, or ownership role in the companies using the brand.
- If Virgin is to be an incubator of new start-ups, then there needed to be a more systematic approach to evaluating new business opportunities and monitoring their progress and development.
- If Virgin was a conglomerate, then did this imply a stronger corporate role? What kind of strategic planning and financial controls were needed to ensure that value was not being dissipated? And could Virgin really perform across so wide a range of businesses?

Whichever path Virgin followed, it appeared that organizational changes would be needed in order to manage inter-company linkages. Although Branson liked to maintain that the different companies were independent and "stood on their own two feet," the reality was somewhat different. Some companies had been strong cash generators, others were heavy loss makers. At present, financial relationships between the companies were ad hoc, and Branson was proud of the fact that no consolidated financial statements were prepared, even for internal management purposes. Moreover, changes to Britain's capital-gains tax laws threatened to eliminate the advantages of multiple, offshore holding companies. Indeed, to obtain the tax benefits from Virgin's loss-making businesses, there were clear advantages in consolidation. Key questions also surrounded the management of the Virgin brand. To the extent that the brand was a common resource, how could it be best protected? The experiences of Virgin Rail had shown that adverse publicity from one company could negatively impact the overall status of the Virgin brand.

As always, the future of the Virgin group could not be considered without taking account of Branson himself. What kind of role did he anticipate now that he approached his 52nd birthday? If Branson was to become less active as chief entrepreneur, public relations director, and strategic architect for the Virgin companies, who or what would take his place?

NOTES

1. "Behind Branson," *The Economist*, February 21, 1998, pp. 63–6.
2. "The future for Virgin," *Financial Times*, August 13, 1998, pp. 24–5.
3. Michael Harrison, "Is Branson's honeymoon finally over?" *The Independent*, London, February 21, 1998, p. 3.
4. "Behind Branson," *The Economist*, February 21, 1998, pp. 63–6.
5. Tracey Boles, "Another big idea from the apostle of small," *The Business*, May 5/6, 2002, p. 9.
6. "Branson moots Virgin floats," Agence France-Presse, May 26, 2002.
7. Richard Branson, letter to *The Economist*, March 7, 1998, p. 6.
8. It is well known that Branson is one of Britain's richest individuals, with a net worth exceeding $1 billion. Branson also spent a night in Dover police cells when arrested for excise duty offenses after he sold through his Virgin store a batch of Virgin records intended for export to Belgium. The case was settled out of court.
9. Robert Dick, "The house that Branson built: Virgin's entry into the new millennium," INSEAD, Fontainebleau, France, 2000.
10. *Forbes*, February 24, 1997.
11. *Journal of Commerce*, January 26, 1998.
12. James Doran, "Branson plans 135m buyback of Virgin stores," *Scotland on Sunday*, March 22, 1998, p. 1.
13. Peter Robison, "Briton hopes beverage will conquer Coke's monopoly," *Bloomberg News*, December 14, 1997.
14. "The future for Virgin", *Financial Times*, August 13, 1998, pp. 24–5.
15. The only formal executive role that Branson holds is as CEO of Virgin Atlantic.
16. Robert Dick, "Branson's Virgin: the coming of age of a counter-cultural enterprise," Insead, Fontainebleau, 1995.
17. Chris Blackhurst, "At the court of King Richard," *Management Today*, May 1998, pp. 40–5.
18. Robert Dick, "The house that Branson built: Virgin's entry into the new millennium," INSEAD, Fontainebleau, France, 2000.
19. Will Whitehorn, Talk to Georgetown MBA students, London, March 16, 2000.
20. Melanie Wells, "Red Baron," *Fortune*, July 3, 2000.
21. Alan Mitchell, "Virgin in financing U-turn," *Marketing News*, April 17, 1997.

General Electric: Life After Jack

Robert M. Grant

When Jeff Immelt took over as Chairman and CEO of General Electric on September 1, 2001, he had no doubts that his predecessor, Jack Welch – "living legend," "best manager of the past half-century," would be a tough act to follow. But little did he realize just how tough it would be.

When Immelt addressed GE shareholders at the 2002 share owners' annual conference on April 24, 2002, GE's share price was below $33, compared with a peak of $60 in August 2000. GE was suffering from external events such as the global economic slowdown of 2001 and the fallout from the September 11 terrorist attacks in the US, but the primary problem was a rise of a tide of skepticism over GE's spectacular performance. In February 2002, GE announced record earnings for the previous year – net income was up 11 percent over the previous year – and return on equity was a robust 26 percent.

However, the post-Enron wave of cynicism over corporate financial reporting had drawn GE into its wake. After being lauded by analysts for its smooth earning growth, rumors of earnings manipulation by GE circulated among the investment community. More specific criticisms were directed at the way in which GE was able to disguise the true risks of its businesses by consolidating the financial statements of its industrial businesses within its financial services business, GE Capital. In March 2002, Bill Gross, of the IPCO fund management group, showed that GE was more a financial services company rather than an industrial enterprise. However, by supporting GE Capital with its industrial business, GE Capital had been able to operate on a narrow capital base and maintain a triple-A credit rating. In addition, GE's famously reliable earnings estimates were also subject to doubt. Given the slowing demand affecting several of GE's industrial business, there was concern that the 2002 earnings forecast would be achieved only through manipulating the earnings data.

While investors held little hope that Immelt could ever match the incredible 50-fold increase in GE's market value that Welch had achieved, the management community was more interested in the changes in corporate strategy, organizational structure, and management systems that Immelt would initiate. Welch had been a revolutionary and an autocrat. He had swept away most of GE's carefully constructed structure and its greatly admired corporate planning system. He had relentlessly challenged GE managers for improved operational and financial performance; he had created a GE management style based almost entirely upon his own personality, values, and beliefs. His management innovations at GE had exerted a huge impact upon management thinking and management practices throughout the whole corporate sector. Whole courses at business schools had been devoted to GE's approach to strategic planning, human resource management, knowledge management, international management, acquisition management, financial management, and quality management.

In the short term Immelt knew that his number one priority was to restore the confidence of the investment community in General Electric, particularly in relation to its financial structure and financial reporting. But looking further ahead, Immelt realized that his primary challenge was coming to terms with Welch's legacy at GE. Each of GE's CEOs had been associated with successfully adapting GE's strategy and management systems to the challenges of the particular era. Between 1950 and 1963, Ralph Cordiner had responded to the opportunities of post-war growth to diversify GE into a range of new markets and new technologies. His successor, Fred Borsch (1963–72), had reorganized GE around nine major growth sectors within which each business formed a strategic business unit. During 1972 to 1981, Reginald Jones established GE's highly regarded and widely imitated system of strategic and financial planning which reconciled strong central control with high levels of operational autonomy for divisions and business units. Jack Welch's contribution had been to adapt GE to a world of uncertainty, intense competition, and rapid competition. In building an organization and a management culture which reconciled the benefits of massive corporate size with flexibility and responsiveness, Welch undid much of Jones's management systems in favor of a system based upon personal accountability and high levels of performance expectations.

■ GENERAL ELECTRIC COMPANY ■

The General Electric (GE) that Jeffrey Immelt inherited in 2001 was widely regarded as one of the world's most successful companies of all time. It is the only company to have remained a member of the Dow Jones industrial index since the index was first created. Throughout its history, it has been associated with near-continuous growth and above average profitability. Table 15.1 shows profitability under successive CEOs.

GE was founded in 1892 from the merger of Thomas Edison's Electric Light Company with the Thomas Houston Company. Its business was based upon exploiting Edison's patents relating to electricity generation and distribution, light bulbs, and electric motors. During the twentieth century it became not only the biggest and most diversified industrial corporation in America, but "a model of management – a laboratory studied by business schools and raided by other companies seeking skilled executives."[1] Two decades under Jack Welch's leadership had only enhanced GE's reputation for effective management. In 2001, *Fortune* magazine named GE as America's "most admired company" for the fifth year in succession, and the *Financial Times* identified GE as the "world's most respected company" for the fourth consecutive year.

Table 15.1 GE's profitability under different chief executives

CEO	Av. annual pre-tax ROE
Charles A. Coffin, 1913–22	14.52%
Gerald Swope/Owen Young, 1922–39	12.63%
Charles E. Wilson, 1940–50	46.72%
Ralph J. Cordiner, 1950–63	40.49%
Fred J. Borch, 1964–72	27.52%
Reginald H. Jones, 1973–81	29.70%
John F. Welch, 1981–2001	25.81%
Jeffrey R. Immelt 2001–2	(16.8%)[1]

[1] September 2001 to June 2002.

The dates given for each CEO are for the financial years that correspond most closely to each CEO's tenure.

Source: www.ge.com.

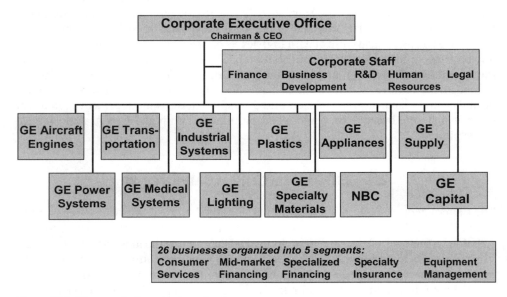

Figure 15.1 GE's organization structure, 2oo2
Source: Based on information in General Electric Annual Report, 2oo1.

GE was not only one of the world's biggest companies, it was also one of the world's most diverse. While most of the conglomerates of the 1980s – Hanson, ITT, Seagram, Philips, General Mills, and United Technologies – had either undergone massive refocusing or broken themselves up entirely, GE had remained a broadly diversified company spanning a wide range of businesses from jet engines to mortgage banking. Figure 15.1 shows GE's major businesses.

GE's ability to thrive as a broadly diversified corporation was one of the wonders of the business world. Since the early 1990s, diversified firms had been handicapped by the "conglomerate discount" – the capital markets had capitalized their earnings at lower multiples than for single-business companies. The only solution was to refocus or break up. For GE this issue has never arisen; GE's remarkable financial performance was such that it had never been under pressure to spin off individual businesses or dismember itself completely. This superior performance is evident in GE's capacity to achieve both growth and profitability throughout the economic cycle (see table 15.2), and in its financial stability – GE had maintained its triple-A credit rating for 44 consecutive years.

As Immelt emphasized to shareholders, it was the combination of these different businesses with their different cyclical characteristics that allowed GE to sustain its earning growth:

> We have four strong, powerful long cycle businesses: Power, Medical, Engines, and Transportation. These businesses are strong, number one, with multiple levers to grow earnings through technology and services. Our Power business had led the way through the past few years of gas turbine growth and as that turbine market subsides, our Power business will thrive by servicing an installed base that has grown five-fold. Our Medical franchise has unlimited opportunities driven by world-class technology, favorable demographics, and global distribution. Our Aircraft Engines business gets even stronger every year as we continue to invest in new engine platforms and technology. The importance of these long cycle businesses is that they give you steady earnings growth over time, with stable product cycles and rapid service growth.
>
> We also have a leadership franchise in our short cycle businesses, like NBC, Plastics, Materials, Consumer, and Industrial businesses. These have been hardest hit by the downturn but so far in 2002 we are seeing encouraging signs of recovery . . .
>
> We have the world's most diversified financial service business with consumer finance, mid-market financing, insurance, equipment management, and specialty segments. We're growing assets at GE Capital by 15 percent . . . The importance of GE Capital is that it can use GE's financial and industrial strength to generate superior returns over time . . .
>
> The GE portfolio was put together for a purpose – to deliver earnings growth through every economic cycle. We're constantly managing these cycles in a business where the sum exceeds the parts.[2]

However, for all the emphasis on the complementary performance characteristics of GE's different businesses, it was also apparent that there were clear differences in terms of both growth and profitability between them (table 15.3).

■ THE WELCH HERITAGE ■

This ability of GE, not just to drive performance in the individual businesses, but also to create a corporation where the sum exceeds the parts, was the hallmark of Jack Welch's tenure as GE's chairman and CEO. Welch's contributions to the restructuring of GE's business portfolio, its organizational design, and its management systems will be described in subsequent sections, but underlying all these contributions was Welch's revolutionary impact on GE's culture and its management style.

Table 15.2 GE's performance 1991–2001

	2001	2000	1999	1997	1996	1995	1994	1993	1992	1991
Revenues ($bn)	125.9	129.9	111.6	90.8	79.2	70.0	60.1	55.7	53.0	51.3
Net earnings ($bn)	13.7	12.7	10.7	8.2	7.3	6.6	4.7	4.3	4.7	2.6
Return on av. shareholders' equity	26.0%	27.3%	26.4%	25.0%	24.0%	23.5%	18.1%	17.5%	20.9%	12.2%
Total assets ($bn)	495.0	437.0	387.4	304.0	272.4	228.0	194.5	251.5	192.9	166.5
Long-term borrowings ($bn)	79.8	82.1	73.5	46.6	49.2	51.0	37.0	28.2	25.3	22.6
Employees at year end ('000)										
United States	158	168	167	165	155	150	156	157	168	173
Other countries	152	145	143	111	84	72	60	59	58	62
	n.a.	n.a.	n.a.	n.a.	n.a.	n.a.	5	6	42	49
Discontinued operations										
Total employees	310	313	310	276	239	222	221	222	268	284

	1990	1989	1988	1987	1986	1985	1984	1983	1982	1981
Revenues ($bn)	49.7	54.6	50.1	48.2	42.0	28.3	27.3	26.8	26.5	27.2
Net earnings ($bn)	4.3	3.9	3.4	2.9	2.5	2.3	2.3	2.0	1.8	1.7
Return on av. shareholders' equity	20.2%	20.0%	19.4%	18.5%	17.3%	17.6%	19.1%	18.9%	18.8%	19.1%
Total assets ($bn)	152.0	128.3	110.9	95.4	84.8	26.4	24.7	23.3	21.6	20.9
Long-term borrowings ($bn)	20.9	16.1	15.1	12.5	10.0	0.8	0.8	0.9	1.0	1.1
Employees at year end ('000)										
United States	183	243	255	277	302	236	248	246	n.a.	n.a.
Other countries	62	49	43	45	71	68	82	94	n.a.	n.a.
	53	n.a.	n.a.	n.a.	n.a.	n.a.	n.a.	n.a.	n.a.	n.a.
Discontinued operations										
Total employees	298	292	298	322	373	304	330	340	367	404

n.a. = not available.

Source: General Electric Annual Reports.

Table 15.3 GE's divisional performance, 1997–2001

	Revenue 2001 ($ billions)	Profit 2001 ($ billions)	Av. return on assets 1999–2001 (%)	Revenue growth 1997–2001 (%)	Profit growth 1997–2001 (%)
Aircraft Engines	11.4	2.6	24.2	46	91
Appliances	5.8	0.6	23.8	0	−17
Industrial Products & Systems	11.6	1.8	26.2	7	11
Materials	7.1	1.6	18.0	3	−2
NBC	5.8	1.6	31.6	12	31
Power Systems	20.2	5.2	28.3	153	305
Technical Products & Services	9.0	2.0	28.5	84	99
GE Capital	58.4	5.6	20.6	46	71

Source: GE Annual Report 2001.

During his 20-year tenure, Welch had remade GE in his own image. The culture and management style that he had fostered were reflections of his own personality and values. Welch attributes his management style to two formative influences: his mother and ice hockey. Welch credits his mother with nurturing self-confidence, determination, and strong values. He credits ice hockey with developing competitive spirit, confrontation, and camaraderie.

From the outset, Welch set lofty goals for GE: in 1981, as the newly-appointed chairman and chief executive, he outlined his vision:

> A decade from now I would like General Electric to be perceived as a unique, high-spirited, entrepreneurial enterprise . . . a company known around the world for its unmatched level of excellence. I want General Electric to be the most profitable, highly diversified company on earth, with world-quality leadership in every one of its product lines.

For 20 years, Welch continually pushed his subordinates for more. In the early days he continually reiterated his goal of creating a company that was "better than the best." This meant not just imposing " stretch goals" upon business-level managers, but encouraging GE's employees – at all levels – to embrace ambitious targets for themselves:

> Shun the incremental and go for the leap. Most bureaucracies – and ours is no exception – unfortunately think in incremental terms rather than in terms of fundamental change. They think incrementally primarily because they think internally. Changing the culture – opening it up to the quantum change – means constantly asking not how fast am I going, how well am I doing versus how well I did a year or two before, but rather, how fast and how well am I doing versus the world outside. Are we moving faster, are we doing better against that external standard?

Stretch means using dreams to set business targets – with no real idea of how to get there . . . We certainly didn't have a clue how we were going to get to 10 inventory turns [a year] when we set that target. But we're getting there, and as soon as we become sure we can do it – it's time for another stretch.[3]

Welch's early years at GE were a war on bureaucracy. Formality, elaborate PowerPoint presentations, complex strategic plans, were ways in which managers avoided reality and avoided coming to grips with painful decisions. Welch favored confronting reality, acknowledging disagreement, and reconciling conflict through open argument. "Constructive conflict" was his key tool. Welch would force his managers to defend their views, even if that meant getting into shouting-match arguments. "Jack will chase you around the room, throwing arguments and objections at you," said one executive. "Then you fight back until he lets you do what you want, and it's clear you'll do everything you can to make it work."

He spelled out his management philosophy in an interview with *Harvard Business Review*:

Good business leaders create a vision, articulate the vision, passionately own the vision, and relentlessly drive it to completion. Above all else, though, good leaders are open. They go up, down, and around their organization to reach people. They don't stick to the established channels. They're informal. They're straight with people. They make a religion out of being accessible. They never get bored telling their story.

Real communication takes countless hours of eyeball to eyeball, back and forth. It means more listening than talking. It's not pronouncements on a videotape; it's not announcements in a newspaper. It is human beings coming to see and accept things through a constant interactive process aimed at consensus. And it must be absolutely relentless. That's a real challenge for us. There's still not enough candor in this company.

I mean facing reality, seeing the world as it is rather than as you wish it were. We've seen over and over again that businesses facing market downturns, tougher competition, and more demanding customers inevitably make forecasts that are much too optimistic. This means they don't take advantage of the opportunities change usually offers. Change in the marketplace isn't something to fear; it's an enormous opportunity to shuffle the deck, to replay the game. Candid managers – leaders – don't get paralyzed about the "fragility" of the organization. They tell people the truth. That doesn't scare them because they realize their people know the truth anyway.

We've had managers at GE who couldn't change, who kept telling us to leave them alone. They wanted to sit back, to keep things the way they were. And that's just what they did – until they and most of their staffs had to go. That's the lousy part of this job . . . The point is, what determines our destiny is not the hand you're dealt; it's how you play the hand. And the best way to play your hand is to face reality – see the world the way it is – and act accordingly.

For a large organization to be effective, it must be simple. For a large organization to be simple, its people must have self-confidence and intellectual self-assurance. Insecure managers create complexity. Frightened, nervous managers use thick, convoluted planning books and busy slides filled with everything they've known since childhood. Real leaders don't need clutter. People must have the self-confidence to be clear, precise, to be sure that every person in their organization – highest to lowest – understands what the business is trying to achieve. But it's not easy. You can't believe how hard it is for people to be simple, how much they fear being simple. They worry that if they're simple, people will think they're simpleminded. In reality, of course, it's just the reverse. Clear, tough-minded people are the most simple.

Simple doesn't mean easy, especially as you try to move this approach down through the organization. When you take out layers, you change the exposure of the managers who remain. They sit right in the sun. Some of them blotch immediately; they can't stand the exposure of leadership.[4]

By the end of the 1980s, Welch's ideas about management were summarized in the slogan "Speed, Simplicity, Self-Confidence":

We found in the 1980s that becoming faster is tied to becoming simpler. Our businesses, with tens of thousands of employees, will not respond to visions that have sub-paragraphs and footnotes. If we're not simple, we can't be fast . . . and if we're not fast, we can't win. Simplicity, to an engineer, means clean, functional, winning designs, no bells or whistles. In marketing, it might manifest itself as clear, unencumbered proposals. For manufacturing people, it would produce a logical process that makes sense to every individual on the line. And on an individual, interpersonal level, it would take the form of plain-speaking directness, honesty.

But just as surely as speed flows from simplicity, simplicity is grounded in self-confidence. Self-confidence does not grow in someone who is just another appendage on the bureaucracy; whose authority rests on little more than a title. People who are freed from the confines of their box on the organization chart, whose status rests on real-world achievement – those are the people who develop the self-confidence to be simple, to share every bit of information available to them, to listen to those above, below and around them and then move boldly.

But a company can't distribute self-confidence. What it can do – what we must do – is to give each of our people an opportunity to win, to contribute, and hence earn self-confidence themselves. They don't get that opportunity, they can't taste winning if they spend their days wandering in the muck of a self-absorbed bureaucracy.

Speed . . . simplicity . . . self-confidence. We have it in increasing measure. We know where it comes from . . . and we have plans to increase it in the 1990s.[5]

■ RECONFIGURING THE BUSINESS PORTFOLIO ■

Although Welch was resolutely determined to retain GE's identify as a broadly diversified corporation, he was clear that GE's business portfolio should, first, be focused around a limited number of sectors and, second, these sectors should be attractive in terms of their potential for profitability and growth. During the early part of his chairmanship, Welch announced his intention only to retain businesses that held number one or number two positions within their global markets. His intention was to focus GE's resources on its best opportunities: "My biggest challenge will be to put enough money on the right gambles and no money on the wrong ones. But I don't want to sprinkle money over everything." This involved increasing GE's emphasis upon technology-based businesses and service businesses. Welch sold off its consumer electronics business, mining interests (notably Utah International), small household appliances division, semiconductors, and radio stations.

GE's acquisitions included a few major ones such as RCA, NBC, Kidder Peabody, and CGR, and a host of smaller companies. During 1997–2001, GE made over a hundred acquisitions in each year. By far the largest sector for acquisition was financial services. During the 1990s, GE Capital's phenomenal growth was built upon continuous acquisition of businesses in leasing, consumer and commercial credit, insurance, and other areas of finance. The result was the emergence of GE Capital as one of the world's biggest financial services companies.

For all GE's expertise in identifying acquisition targets and then integrating them into GE's structure and systems, not all were successful. Kidder Peabody was a disaster for GE, and the acquisition of Montgomery Ward was viewed by some outsiders as a mistake. Most recently, GE's biggest takeover, Honeywell, was unconsummated because of opposition from the European Commission on antitrust grounds.

■ CHANGING THE STRUCTURE ■

The changes in the portfolio transformed the product-market face of GE and increased its growth potential. However, to realize this potential required revitalizing the management systems and management style in order to generate drive and ambition. Achieving this required changes to GE's structure. Under Welch, GE eliminated several layers of management and large numbers of administrative positions. In particular, Welch disbanded GE's sectors, requiring the leaders of GE's 13 businesses to report directly to the CEO. The office of the CEO was expanded, and a Corporate Executive Council (CEC) was created to provide a forum for GE's business-level chiefs and senior corporate officers. Further organizational layers were eliminated both at headquarters and within the businesses. Decision making was pushed down to the operating units.

> We are now down in some businesses to four layers from the top to the bottom. That's the ultimate objective. We used to have things like department managers, section managers, subsection managers, units managers, supervisors. We are driving those titles out . . . We used to go from the CEO to sectors to groups to businesses. We now go from the CEO . . . to businesses. Nothing else. There is nothing else there. Zero.
>
> When you take out layers, you change the exposure of the managers who remain. They sit right in the sun. Some of them blotch immediately – they can't stand the exposure of leadership. I firmly believe that an overburdened, overstretched executive is the best executive, because he or she doesn't have time to meddle, to deal in trivia, or to bother people. Remember the theory that a manager should have no more than six or seven direct reports? I say the right number is closer to 10 or 15. This way you have no choice but to let people flex their muscles, to let them grow and mature.[6]
>
> Empowering line managers meant reducing the power – and number – of staff. Welch's goal was to "turn their role 180° from checker, inquisitor and authority figure to facilitator, helper and supporter of the businesses . . . Ideas, initiatives and decisions could now move quickly. Often at the speed of sound – voices – where once they were muffled and garbled by the gauntlet of approvals and staff reviews."[7]

The result was massive reductions in numbers of employees. Between 1980 and 1990, GE's headcount fell from 402,000 to 298,000. The biggest cuts were at the upper levels of the organization: at corporate headquarters and within sectoral administration. In some areas employee numbers increased – particularly in overseas operations. Welch's ruthless attack on bureaucracy and administrative costs earned him the nickname "Neutron Jack" – the building remained, but the people had gone.

■ CHANGING MANAGEMENT SYSTEMS AND PROCESSES ■

Strategic Planning

The changes in GE's structure were aimed at creating a more flexible and responsive corporation. This goal also necessitated changes in GE's highly developed management systems. In particular, Welch led a major overhaul of GE's much celebrated and widely emulated strategic planning system. The framework of an annual planning cycle was retained, but the staff-led, document-driven process was replaced by a less formal, more personal process. Instead of the big planning reports, Welch asked each business head to prepare a slim "playbook" that summarized the key strategic issues that the business faced, and how it intended to address them. This document provided the basis for a half-day, shirtsleeves review in mid-summer when Welch and key corporate officers would engage in discussion and debate with the top management team of each businesses. On the 1986 meetings, Welch commented:

> We asked the 14 business leaders to present reports on the competitive dynamics in their businesses. How did we do it? We had them each prepare one-page answers to five questions: What are your market dynamics globally today, and where are they going over the next several years? What actions have your competitors taken in the last three years to upset those global dynamics? What have you done in the last three years to affect these dynamics? What are the most dangerous things your competitor could do in the next three days to upset those dynamics? What are the most effective things you could do to bring your desired impact on those dynamics?
>
> Five simple charts. After those initial reviews, which we update regularly, we could assume that everyone at the top knew the plays and had the same playbook. It doesn't take a genius. Fourteen businesses each with a playbook of five charts. So when Larry Bossidy is with a potential partner in Europe, or I'm with a company in the Far East, we're always there with a competitive understanding based upon our playbooks. We know exactly what makes sense, we don't need a big staff to do endless analysis. That means we should be able to act with speed.[8]

Financial Planning and Control

Supporting GE's strategic planning system was a sophisticated financial budgeting system which centered on the annual budget. Budget preparation began in July and involved extensive negotiation between the operating units, the intervening groups and sectors, and the corporate headquarters. Once the budget was set, managers were locked in to meet it "at all costs" regardless of changes in the marketplace. It was generally agreed that the system had undesirable consequences, such as gaming to set low targets, and cutting long-term development to meet short-term targets. Because managers were locked in to figures established 18 months before, the budgeting system often inhibited adjustment to external changes and gave little information of management performance.

Welch's commitment to a performance-driven organization meant that financial targets were of critical importance. However, the key was to create shareholder value rather than accounting profits per se. In addition, it was essential that the system should permit the performance of divisional and business unit managers to be assessed. Two changes were made. First, the controller's office prepared a set of financial objectives for each operating unit in order to reflect more realistically each unit's prospects and to reduce gamesmanship in target-setting. Second, the budgets (now called operating plans) were subject to revision as economic or competitive conditions changed. Thus, line managers could propose changes to the plans once the original assumptions on which they had been based could be shown to have changed. Performance evaluation was then made against the revised targets.

Central to the changes in financial control was the idea that performance was not about "making the budget." It was about raising performance expectations to be "as good as possible": The primary task of the businesses, emphasized Welch, was to produce earnings. As a guideline, Welch proposed that GE's earnings should grow at between one-and-a-half and two times the growth of GDP.

Human Resource Management

The key to GE's long-term development and performance was the development of its management talent. GE had a well-developed system of management appraisal and development which Welch retained. He believed that giving managers greater profit-and-loss responsibility earlier in their careers would be conducive to an even greater flourishing of managerial talent. But to encourage risk taking and higher levels of performance aspiration required more powerful incentives. Welch believed in giving more recognition to individual contributors and higher rewards to those who produced superior results:

> A flat reward system is a big anchor to incrementalism. We want to give big rewards to those who do things but without going for the scalps of those who reach for the big win but fail. Punishing failure assures that no one dares.[9]

Welch redesigned the bonus system to reach deep into middle management. The bonuses became much more discriminating. The typical 10 to 15 percent bonuses for senior managers were replaced by 30 to 40 percent bonuses for far fewer managers. In addition, stock options were extended from the top echelon of management to a much wider range of managerial and technical employees. By 1996, Welch was able to report that the number of employees receiving stock options had increased from 400 in the early 1980s to 22,000 by the end of 1995: "Today, stock option compensation, based on total GE performance, is far more significant than the salary or bonus growth associated with the performance of any individual unit or business. This aligns the interests of the individual, the Company, and the share owner behind powerful, on-company results."[10]

Welch believed that a performance-driven organization would not only encourage GE's managers to perform up to the limits of their capabilities, it would also nurture those capabilities. Welch firmly believed that GE's ability to outperform its peers ultimately depended upon having outstanding employees. GE could offer opportunities for career development and the acquisition of skills and expertise that no other company could match:

Our true "core competency" today is not manufacturing or services, but the global recruiting and nurturing of the world's best people and the cultivation in them of an insatiable desire to learn, to stretch and to do things better every day. By finding, challenging and rewarding these people, by freeing them from bureaucracy, by giving them all the resources they need – and by simply getting out of their way – we have seen them make us better and better every year.

We have a Company more agile than others a fraction of our size, a high-spirited company where people are free to dream and encouraged to act and to take risks. In a culture where people act this way, every day, "big" will never mean slow.

This is all about people – "soft stuff." But values and behaviors are what produce those performance numbers, and they are the bedrock upon which we will build our future.[11]

Maintaining a vigorous, performance-driven culture required putting managers under continual pressure, including ongoing weeding-out of weaker performers. GE's system of evaluation was renowned for its thoroughness and its ruthlessness:

In every evaluation and reward system, we break our population down into three categories: the top 20%, the high-performance middle 70% and the bottom 10%. The top 20% must be loved, nurtured and rewarded in the soul and wallet because they are the ones who make magic happen. Losing one of these people must be held up as a leadership sin – a real failing. The top 20% and middle 70% are not permanent labels. People move between them all the time. However, the bottom 10%, in our experience, tend to remain there. A Company that bets its future on its people must remove that lower 10%, and keep removing it every year – always raising the bar of performance and increasing the quality of its leadership. Not removing that bottom 10% early in their careers is not only a management failure, but false kindness as well – a form of cruelty – because inevitably a new leader will come into a business and take out that bottom 10% right away, leaving them – sometimes midway through a career – stranded and having to start over somewhere else. Removing marginal performers early in their careers is doing the right thing for them; leaving them in place to settle into a career that will inevitably be terminated is not. GE leaders must not only understand the necessity to encourage, inspire and reward that top 20%, and be sure that the high-performance 70% is always energized to improve and move upward; they must develop the determination to change out, always humanely, that bottom 10%, and do it every year. That is how real meritocracies are created and thrive.[12]

■ CORPORATE INITIATIVES ■

One of the distinctive characteristics of Welch's system of management was his use of periodic new corporate initiatives as mechanisms to drive particular aspects of company-wide performance Thus, while strategic planning, financial control, and human resource management provided the basic systems for managing GE, about every two years, Welch would announce a major new initiative designed to energize the company and drive its performance in a particular direction. Over time these initiatives would become absorbed into the ongoing management systems of GE.

Work-Out

The idea for GE's "Work-Out" process began with the no-holds-barred discussion sessions that Welch held with different groups of managers at GE's Management Development Institute at Crotonville, New York. Impressed with the energy and impetus for change that these sessions generated, Welch initiated a company-wide process called "Work-Out."

The idea was to create a forum where a cross-section of employees could speak their minds about the management of their business without the fear of retribution by their superiors. Typically, the sessions assembled a cross-section of 50 to 100 of the business's employees for meetings that ran for two or three days. In an environment that Welch likened to an old New England town meeting, the group would be asked to openly and honestly review the management process and practices in their part of the operation. Initially they focused on unproductive or bureaucratic behaviors which had limited their personal effectiveness. At the end of each Work-Out, the group's manager returned to hear the findings and recommendations, and could either accept or reject them on the spot, or appoint a team to report back with more data by a given date. Welch believed that Work-Out could achieve fundamental changes in management:

> Work-Out has a practical and an intellectual goal. The practical objective is to get rid of thousands of bad habits accumulated since the creation of General Electric . . . The second thing we want to achieve, the intellectual part, begins by putting the leaders of each business in front of 100 or so of their people, eight to ten times a year, to let them hear what their people think. Work-Out will expose the leaders to the vibrations of their business – opinions, feelings, emotions, resentments, not abstract theories of organization and management. Ultimately, we're talking about redefining the relationship between boss and subordinate.
>
> These Work-Out sessions create all kinds of personal dynamics. Some people go and hide. Some emerge as forceful advocates. As people meet over and over, though, more of them will develop the courage to speak out. The norm will become the person who says, "Damn it, we're not doing it. Let's get on with doing it. This process will create more fulfilling and rewarding jobs. The quality of work life will improve dramatically."[13]

Initially, Work-Out focused on eliminating bureaucratic practices ("low-hanging fruit"). Over time, Work-Out sessions evolved to the evaluation and redesign of complex cross-functional processes – often involving suppliers and customers as well as GE employees.

The Boundary-less Organization

Welch reacted strongly to descriptions of GE as a conglomerate. But for GE to be greater than the sum of it parts required utilizing its product and geographical diversity to improve performance within each business. The key to transforming diversity into strength, believed Welch, was the frictionless transfer of best practices and other forms of learning within GE. But to achieve this required eliminating – or at least making permeable – GE's internal boundaries, as well as increasing openness to external learning. By 1990, Welch was developing the vision of a new GE organization that would be a truly "boundary-less" company. His boundary-less company was one in which both external barriers and internal barriers became blurred:

> In a boundary-less company, suppliers aren't outsiders. They are drawn closer and become trusted partners in the total business process. Customers' vision of their needs and the company's view become identical and every effort of every man and woman in the company is focused on satisfying those needs. The boundary-less company blurs the divisions between internal functions; it recognizes no distinctions between "domestic" and "foreign" operations; and it ignores or erases group labels such as "management," "salaried," and "hourly" which get in the way of people working together.[14]

Unbounding GE required changes in structures, attitudes, and behaviors that would permit the "integrated diversity" that Welch envisaged. Examples of boundary-less behavior were widely publicized and praised:

> Two years ago, one of our people spotted a truly innovative method of compressing product cycle times in an appliance company in New Zealand. After testing it successfully in our Canadian affiliate, we transferred the methodology to our largest appliance complex in Louisville, KY. It has revolutionized processes, reduced cycle times, increased our customer responsiveness, and reduced our inventory levels by hundreds of millions of dollars. Teams from all of our manufacturing businesses are now living in Louisville so we can spread the New Zealand-to-Montreal-to-Louisville learning to every business in GE.[15]

Globalization

All of GE's businesses were given global responsibility, which meant exploiting international growth opportunities and exploiting the advantages of global reach in terms of exploiting global-level economies of scale and increased learning opportunities. Global diversity played an important role in allowing GE to cope with economic problems that affected particular countries or regions, and take advantage of the opportunities that such downturns offered. For example, as "financial contagion" affected much of Asia during 1997–8, GE was seeking acquisition opportunities:

We've been down this road before. In the early 1980s, we experienced a United States mired in recession, hand-wringing from the pundits and dirges being sung over American manufacturing. We didn't buy this dismal scenario; instead, we invested in both a widespread restructuring and in new businesses . . . Europe looked a lot like the United States in the 1980s, and in need of the same remedies: restructuring, spin-offs, and the like. So, while many were "writing-off" Europe, we invested heavily, buying new companies and expanding our existing presence . . . "GE Europe" is now a $20.6 billion operation. Our revenues have more than doubled from 1994 to 1997; net income has tripled to more than $1.5 billion; and growth is accelerating as the European recovery progresses . . . Mexico in the mid-1990s was a similar story . . . GE moved, acquiring 10 companies and investing more than $1 billion in new and existing operations. The result was revenue growth of 60% and a doubling of earnings in the two years following the crisis. Today we are determined, and poised, to do the same thing in Asia we have done in the United States, Europe and Mexico: invest in the future.[16]

Six Sigma

From 1998 to 2000, Welch's Six Sigma program was its dominant corporate initiative and primary driver of organizational change and performance improvement. Welch described it as his next "soul-transforming cultural initiative." The methodology of defining, measuring, analyzing, improving, and then controlling every process that touches a company's customers until it reduces defects to 3.4 per million was borrowed from Motorola. However, at GE it was with unprecedented fervor across an unprecedentedly broad front. In four years some 100,000 people were trained in its science and methodology, and by 2001, GE was able to report: "Now Six Sigma is the way we work. We all speak a common language of CTQs (critical-to-quality), DPMOs (defects per million opportunities), FMEAs (failure mode effect analysis), and Needs Assessment Maps (to name just a few)." Across every one of GE's businesses major gains in performance ranking from reduced waste and lower operating costs to faster customer service and improved financial management were reported.

Digitization

Welch was a late convert to the electronic business. However, once converted, he became a raving evangelist, urging his line managers and launching his "destroy-your-business.com" initiative in 1999. Each organizational unit was encouraged to visualize how it might be crushed by the dotcom juggernaut. The result was widespread discovery of opportunities to use the internet to improve internal processes and better serve customers. By spring 2001, Welch reported:

As we said in our 1999 letter, digitization is transforming everything we do, energizing every corner of the Company and making us faster, leaner and smarter even as we become bigger. In 2000, these words began to turn into numbers, as we sold over $7 billion of goods and services over the net and conducted over $6 billion in online auctions. Digitization efforts across the Company will generate over $1.5 billion in operating margin improvements in 2001.[17]

GE's Operating System

By 2002, these different initiatives had been institutionalized to the point where GE referred to them as its "operating system." Thus, referring collectively to Work-Out, Boundarylessness, Globalization, Six Sigma and Digitization, GE described an integrated system for performance improvement:

> The GE Operating System is GE's learning culture in action. It is a year-round series of intense learning sessions where Business CEOs, role models and initiative champions from GE as well as outside companies, meet and share intellectual capital.
>
> The central focus is always on sharing, and putting into action, the best ideas and practices from across the Company and around the world.
>
> Meetings take place year-round, in an endless process of enrichment. Learning builds from previous meetings, expanding the scope and increasing the momentum of our Company-wide initiatives.
>
> Driven by the Company's values – trust, informality, simplicity, boundary-less behavior and the love of change – the Operating System allows GE businesses to reach speeds and performance levels unachievable were they on their own.
>
> The GE Operating System translates ideas into action across three dozen businesses so rapidly that all the initiatives have become operational across the Company within one month of launch, and have always produced positive financial results within their first cycle.[18]

■ JEFF IMMELT ■

Jeffrey R. Immelt was appointed CEO of GE at the age of 44, and heading up GE's plastics business and medical systems. He has an economics and applied math degree from Dartmouth and an MBA from Harvard. He claims that his own experience of GE extends beyond his two decades with the firm – his father spent his entire career at GE. At GE Appliances, GE Plastics, and GE Medical Systems, Immelt acquired a reputation for turning around troubled units, driving customer service, and exploiting new technologies. He also demonstrated the ability to motivate others – an aptitude that he had revealed as an offensive tackler for Dartmouth's football team in the 70s.[19]

As Welch's successor at GE, Immelt was broadly happy with most of the managerial and organizational innovations that his predecessor had introduced. At the same time he was acutely aware that the management system that Welch had created was closely linked with Welch's own personality. Immelt's personality and style were different from Welch's. *Business Week* observed: "Where Welch ruled through intimidation and thrived as something of a cult figure, Immelt opts for the friendlier, regular-guy approach. He prefers to tease where Welch would taunt. Immelt likes to cheer people on rather then chew them out. That style has given the 46-year-old chief a very different aura within GE. He may not be a demigod, but it's his man-of-the-people nature that draws praise from the top ranks to the factory floor."[20] Immelt knew that his different style of leadership would have important implications for his role as CEO and the ways in which he would influence GE's strategy, structure, and systems. However, Immelt believed that the major changes that he would initiate at GE would be a result of the changing environment that GE faced and the shifting priorities that it faced.

Between September 2001 and May 2002, Immelt had devoted himself primarily to shoring up confidence among customers and investors and within the company in the aftermath of the various shocks to the US and to business opinion. At the same time he was developing his strategic thinking about the future of GE. During the first four months of 2002, his speeches and interviews emphasized four main areas of development:

- *The Business Portfolio.* Like Welch, Immelt believed that GE needed to reposition itself to maximize growth opportunities and to achieve growth targets through sound acquisitions. Among the low-growth parts of GE's portfolio, many analysts believed that appliances and lighting would be early candidates for divestment. However, while acknowledging that their growth was low, Immelt confirmed that, "We'll stay in those businesses. They both return their cost of capital."[21] At the same time, further industrial acquisitions would be needed in order to keep GE balanced – if the rapidly growing GE Capital was to account for more than half of GE's earnings, then GE's risk status and earnings multiple might be adversely affected. Immelt committed to GE to continue to acquire high-margin, high-growth companies that expand GE's base: "We don't acquire companies just because we can. We don't go for unrelated fields. We acquire companies that give us new growth platforms where GE capability can improve financial performance and build shareholder value."[22]
- *Technology.* Immelt has remarked on the fact that he represents a different generation from Jack Welch, and that his generation has a much closer affinity for technology. He has identified technology as a major driver of GE's future growth and has emphasized the need to speed the diffusion of new technologies within GE and turn the corporate R&D center into an intellectual hothouse.
- *Internationalization.* Like Welch, Immelt believes that GE's major opportunities for organic growth will be in its overseas operations – particularly in China, India, and Europe. However, to better exploit these opportunities Immelt believes that GE's upper management will need to become more international and more diverse.
- *Marketing and customer service.* A key feature of Immelt's career at GE was the extent of his customer orientation and the amount of time he spent with customers building relationships with them and working on their problems. Looking ahead, Immelt saw GE using IT and redesigned processes to become increasingly customer focused: "We're dramatically changing our resource base from providing support to creating value. Every business has functions that add high value by driving growth. These are the functions that deal with the customer, create new products, sell, manufacture, manage the money and drive controllership. Call that the front room. Every business has back room support functions that sometimes are so large and bureaucratic they create a drain on the system and keep us from meeting our customer needs and keep us from growing. So we're going to take more of the back room resources and

put them in the front room – more sales people, more engineers, more product designers. We're changing the shape of this company and we're doing it during a recession."[23]

No one, either inside or outside GE, had any doubt that Immelt would not be a supremely effective leader for GE. The main questions concerned Immelt's ability to take GE to the next level – whatever that next level might entail. When Welch took over GE in 1981, it was certainly successful, but there was also tremendous scope for improvement within GE's sprawling, bureaucratic empire. For Immelt it was not so easy to identify opportunities either for improving existing opportunities, or to create new opportunities with the potential to lift GE to heights that Welch had never imagined.

NOTES

1. "Can Jack Welch reinvent GE?" *Business Week*, June 29, 1986, pp. 40–5.
2. Jeff Immelt's 2002 Annual Report to Share Owners, Waukesha, Wisconsin, April 24, 2002, pp. 4–5.
3. GE Annual Report, 1993, p. 5.
4. Noel Tichy and Ram Charan, "Speed, simplicity, and self confidence: an interview with Jack Welch," *Harvard Business Review*, September/October 1989.
5. Ibid.
6. "GE 1984," HBS Case No. 385–315.
7. Tichy and Charan, Welch interview, *Harvard Business Review*, 1989.
8. Ibid.
9. Ibid.
10. Jack Welch, address to 1989 shareholders' meeting.
11. Chairman's letter, General Electric Annual Report, 2000.
12. Ibid.
13. Tichy and Charan, Welch interview, *Harvard Business Review*, 1989.
14. GE Annual Report, 1990.
15. Ibid.
16. Chairman's letter, General Electric Annual Report, 1997.
17. Chairman's letter, General Electric Annual report, 2000.
18. The GE Operating System (www.ge.com).
19. "Running the house that Jack built," *Business Week*, October 2, 2000.
20. "The days of Welch and roses," *Business Week*, April 29, 2002.
21. "This is just about the best gig you can have," *Business Week*, September 5, 2001.
22. Jeff Immelt's 2002 Annual Report to Share Owners, Waukesha, Wisconsin, April 24, 2002, p. 8.
23. Ibid.

case sixteen

AES Corporation: Rewriting the Rules of Management

Robert M. Grant

God made us all a certain way. We're all creative, capable of making decisions, trustworthy, able to learn, and perhaps most important, fallible. We all want to be part of a community and to use our skills to make a difference in the world.

Dennis Bakke, CEO, AES

We broke all the rules. No overtime. No bosses. No time records. No shift schedules. No assigned responsibilities. No administration. And guess what? It worked!

Oscar Prieto, AES manager and director of Light Servicios de Electricidade, Brazil, October 1998

Spring 2002 presented AES Corporation, the world's largest independent power generator, with the most difficult business circumstances in its 21-year history. After almost uninterrupted growth and a steeply rising market valuation that had taken AES into the S&P 500 in 1998, AES's world had been shaken to its foundations by three major shocks. The first was the Californian power crisis of 2001. Although AES was only a minor player in electricity trading, as an independent power producer with plants in California it was caught up in the recriminations, lawsuits, and regulatory investigations that had followed California's electricity debacle. More generally, the California power crisis threatened continuing deregulation of the US electricity sector – it was this deregulation that had provided the rationale for AES's founding and the business opportunities for its continued growth. Second, AES had been caught up in the wake of Enron's collapse at the end of December 2001. Although AES's direct losses resulting from Enron's bankruptcy amounted to a mere $15 million, the sudden demise of this giant of the energy sector had a profound impact on investors' risk perception and upon the legitimacy of a range of previously accepted business practices, including off-balance-sheet financing. The third crisis impacting AES was Argentina. Argentina represented one of AES's largest overseas interests with over $1 billion invested. The meltdown of the Argentine economy had rendered these investments all but worthless and had had knock-on effects on AES's power interests in Brazil. The gloom affecting AES's Latin American operations was further increased by the mounting crisis in Venezuela. Finally, the aftermath of the September 11, 2001 terrorist attacks on the US had created further uncertainties for AES's global interests. With investments in several Muslim countries – in particular Pakistan and Kazakhstan – AES was again subject to greatly increased financial, political, and physical risk.

These factors had combined to ensure AES's entry into the infamous "90 percent club" – those companies (mainly technology, media, and telecommunication companies) that had lost more than 90 percent of their stock market value. After touching $70 a share in September 2000, AES's share price had fallen below $4 in February 2002, driven lower by sales by CEO and founder Dennis Bakke who was forced to liquidate a quarter of his 5.8 percent equity stake in order to meet margin calls. The sharp decline in AES's market value had placed considerable strain on AES's finances, making it increasingly difficult for AES to access the capital markets. In February, ratings on AES's unsecured debt were cut to below investment grade.

These combined pressures had forced an abrupt reversal of strategy at AES. After two decades of continuous and rapid expansion, the company was forced to retrench. In a series of measures announced in February 2002, AES began the desperate task of shoring up its finances and protecting itself against an increasingly hostile external environment. Capital expenditure was cut from $1,280 million to $790 million, over $1 billion in asset sales was announced, and AES was to begin withdrawing from some of its most risky areas of business – including Latin America and spot market sales.

For founder and CEO Dennis Bakke the most troubling aspect of the sudden strategic shift was not the abandonment of AES's ambitious growth targets. He believed that AES possessed the financial and management strengths needed to survive the current financial pressures. His concerns related much more to his personal mission to build AES as a different kind of company. Under the leadership of its two co-founders, Roger Sant and Dennis Bakke, AES had rejected profit and shareholder wealth as its raison d'être and committed itself to the pursuit of integrity, fairness, fun, and social responsibility. These principles were embedded in a management system which the *Wall Street Journal* referred to as "empowerment gone mad."[1] Its unique organization was referred to by board member Robert Waterman (of *In Search of Excellence* fame) as an "adhocracy." There were no staff functions or corporate departments; almost all traditional management functions were devolved to workers at the plant level.

So long as AES was a darling of Wall Street, investors and analysts were happy to accept AES's lofty values and its founders' disdain for profit. But the events of 2001 and early 2002 had changed all that. AES's values and unique management system which had been so effective in encouraging employees' loyalty and commitment, generating initiative and entrepreneurial drive, and promoting unmatched levels of operational efficiency was now having to come to terms with a very different environment.

But circumstances in 2002 were much changed. The independent power sector which had boomed with privatization and deregulation was no longer flush with opportunity and optimism. The California power crisis, the collapse of Enron, and the problems of power producers in several emerging market countries had cast a pall over the entire sector. Meanwhile, competition had greatly intensified within the sector. While AES had been a pioneer of independent power production, it was now a crowded sector. Competitors for electricity supply contracts included independent power producers (IPPs) such as AEP, Calpine, and Reliant Resources; traditional utilities such as Duke Power, Dominion Resources, Consolidated Edison, Electricité de France, and British Energy; gas companies such as Vectren, Centrica, and Gaz de France; and oil majors such as BP Amoco, ExxonMobil, and Shell.

Moreover, AES was no longer a small, entrepreneurial start-up. By the end of 2001, AES had 179 plants in operation or under construction in 31 countries of the world, with a total employment of about 38,000. Growth had increased the complexity and diversity of the company: from a single plant in Texas, its operations now extended from the Ukraine to South Africa; it had gone from coal-fired plants to gas-fired and hydroelectric plants; from supplying power on long-term contracts to utilities, AES had expanded into power distribution and producing electricity for competitive markets on spot and short-term contracts. Growing scale and scope was placing increasing strains on AES's informal, ad hoc style of management, while AES's principles, with their basis in traditional American values of equality of opportunity, openness, and individualism, had to adapt to the diverse cultures where AES did business – traditional Islamic societies such as Pakistan, socialist systems such as China, and the oligarchic societies of Latin America.

■ AES'S ORIGINS AND DEVELOPMENT ■

In January 1982, Roger Sant and Dennis Bakke founded Applied Energy Systems based in Arlington, Virginia. Their purpose was to take advantage of a 1978 Public Utility Regulatory Policy Act (PURPA) that required utilities to purchase power from independent energy producers. Sant and Bakke believed they could build a business in a niche segment of the enormous power-generation industry.

At first glance, Sant and Bakke seemed a rather unlikely pair to start what has become a large international energy company. Although both held Harvard MBAs, their experience was primarily public sector. Sant headed the Ford Administration's energy conservation efforts and Bakke served as a chief aide. Following government service, they moved on to the Mellon Institute's Energy Productivity Center, where they spent several years researching various techniques for energy conservation. It was during this time that the pair came up with the idea of starting their own company.

Sant and Bakke had a very difficult time raising money at first, because nobody took them very seriously. According to Bakke, "[we] had the worst possible background for raising money . . . first government and then academic experience. It looked to investors like a combination of inefficiency and ivory tower."[2] However, Sant and Bakke had one key advantage: as a result of their involvement in drafting PURPA, they were among the first to recognize the opportunity for independent generators to produce power at much lower costs than the established utilities.

Sant and Bakke raised $1.3 million from private investors and began looking for deep-pocketed partners. From 1981 to 1985 Sant and Bakke sought alliances with Arco, IBM, and Bechtel to name but a few. In 1985, the founders decided to go it alone and built their first power plant adjacent to an oil refinery in Houston, Texas, using petroleum coke (essentially a waste product) for fuel. Because AES agreed to link the price of the electricity generated to the price of natural gas (which subsequently fell sharply), the plant was not profitable. However, the second and third plants that AES built "weren't disastrous, and four, five and six turned out to be superb. By 1989 it was clear that we had reached viability."[3]

In 1991, AES went public. With a stronger equity base it was ready to look at opportunities overseas. Because of the rapid growth in electricity demand in many emerging markets, inadequate generating capacity, and the trend towards privatization, Sant estimated that over 70 percent of AES's opportunities lay outside the US. The fast-growing Asian markets for electricity, especially the huge potential markets of India and China, were especially attractive. In the early 1990s AES inaugurated its international strategy by acquiring two plants in Northern Ireland and one in Argentina. International expansion involved participating in the auctioning of state-owned electricity companies by governments, and bidding for long-term power supply contracts from governments which were opening the generating end of their electricity industries to competition. During the mid-1990s, AES's biggest new investments in power generation were in Kazakhstan and China. The 1996 acquisition of Light Servicios de Electricidade, Brazil, was a major strategic departure for AES: this was its first entry into the distribution end of the power business. Overseas expansion was primarily through the acquisition of existing power-generating facilities rather than building new plants. A similar transition was occurring in the US. Changes in utility regulations at the state level resulted in some utilities selling off their generating facilities – AES was among the most prominent bidders for these facilities.

Between 1998 and 2001, AES continued to expanded rapidly both at home and overseas.

- In 1998, AES acquired or built 34 plants, including major facilities in Bangladesh, India, Mexico, California, and New York, and bought electricity distribution companies in Buenos Aires, Georgia, and Sao Paulo.
- In 1999, AES acquired its first US utility, Cilcorp, hydroelectric generating facilities in Brazil, and DRAX, one of the world's largest coal-fired power plants located in England.
- In 2000, AES acquired a major Venezuelan utility and well as plants in Chile and Colombia.
- In 2001, AES continued its expansion into large utilities with the acquisition of PALCO. In addition, AES expanded into the Ukraine and Cameroon.

Tables 16.1 and 16.2 show AES's plants and distribution facilities at the end of 2001.

Table 16.1   AES's generating plants, December 2001

	Fuel	Year of acquisition or start-up	Location	Gross MW	AES equity interest (%)
Contract generation facilities					
North America					
Kingston	Gas	1997	Canada	110	50
Beaver Valley	Coal	1987	USA	125	100
Thames	Coal	1990	USA	181	100
Shady Point	Coal	1991	USA	320	100
Hawaii	Coal	1992	USA	180	100
Southland-Alamitos	Gas	1998	USA	2,083	100
Southland-Huntington Beach	Gas	1998	USA	563	100
Southland-Redondo Beach	Gas	1998	USA	1,310	100
Warrior Run	Coal	2000	USA	180	100
Ironwood	Gas	2001	USA	705	100
Red Oak	Gas	2002	USA	832	100
South America					
Tiete (10 plants)	Hydro	1999	Brazil	2,650	53
Gener-Termoandes	Gas	2000	Argentina	633	99
Uruguaiana	Gas	2000	Brazil	450	100
Uruguaiana	Gas	2000	Brazil	150	100
GENER-Norgener	Oil	2000	Chile	277	99
GENER-Centrogener (9 plants)	Hydro	2000	Chile	756	99
GENER-Electrica de Santiago	Gas	2000	Chile	379	89
GENER-Guacolda	Coal	2000	Chile	304	49
Europe/Africa					
Kilroot	Coal	1992	UK	520	92
Medway	Gas	1996	UK	688	25
Tisza II	Gas	1996	Hungary	860	100
Elsta	Gas	1998	Netherlands	405	50
Ebute	Gas	2001	Nigeria	290	95
Kelvin	Coal	2001	South Africa	600	100
Asia					
Khrami I	Hydro	2000	Georgia	113	0
Khrami II	Hydro	2000	Georgia	110	0
Mktvari	Gas	2000	Georgia	600	100
Wuhu	Coal	1996	China	250	25
Hefei	Oil	1997	China	115	70
Jiaozuo	Coal	1997	China	250	70
Yangcheng (3 plants)	Coal	2001	China	1,050	25
OPGC	Coal	1998	India	420	49
Lal Pir	Oil	1997	Pakistan	351	90
PakGen	Oil	1998	Pakistan	344	90
Meghnaghat	Gas	2002	Bangladesh	450	100
Barka	Gas	2003	Oman	427	85

Table 16.1 *continued*

	Fuel	Year of acquisition or start-up	Location	Gross MW	AES equity interest (%)
Ras Laffan	Gas	2004	Qatar	750	55
Kelanitissa	Gas	2002	Sri Lanka	165	100
Mt. Stuart	Oil	1999	Australia	288	100
Ecogen-Jeeralang	Gas	1999	Australia	449	100
Ecogen-Yarra	Gas	1999	Australia	510	100
Haripur	Gas	2001	Bangladesh	360	100
Caribbean					
Mirada III	Gas	2000	Mexico	484	55
Puerto Rico	Coal	2002	USA	454	100
Itabo	Gas	2000	Dominican Republic	587	24
Los Mina	Oil	1996	Dominican Republic	210	100
Andres	Gas	2003	Dominican Republic	310	100

Competitive supply facilities

North America

	Fuel	Year of acquisition or start-up	Location	Gross MW	AES equity interest (%)
Deepwater	Coal	1986	USA	143	100
Placerita	Gas	1989	USA	120	100
NY-Cayuga	Coal	1999	USA	306	100
NY-Greenidge	Coal	1999	USA	161	100
NY-Somerset	Coal	1999	USA	675	100
NY-Westover	Coal	1999	USA	126	100
Mountainview Existing	Gas	2001	USA	126	100
Huntington Beach 3&4	Gas	2002	USA	450	100
Granite Ridge	Gas	2002	USA	720	100
Greystone	Gas	2002	USA	500	100
Wolf Hollow	Gas	2002	USA	720	100
Lake Worth	Gas	2003	USA	210	100
Mountainview Development	Gas	2003	USA		

South America

	Fuel	Year of acquisition or start-up	Location	Gross MW	AES equity interest (%)
San Nicolás-CTSN	Coal	1993	Argentina	650	88
Rio Juramento-Cabra Corall	Hydro	1995	Argentina	102	98
Alicura	Hydro	2000	Argentina	1,000	100
Parana	Gas	2001	Argentina	845	100
Caracoles	Hydro	2004	Argentina	123	100

Europe/Africa

	Fuel	Year of acquisition or start-up	Location	Gross MW	AES equity interest (%)
Borsod	Coal	1996	Hungary	171	100
Tiszapalkonya	Coal	1996	Hungary	250	100
Ottana	Oil	2001	Italy	140	100
Belfast West	Coal	1992	UK	120	98
Indian Queens	Gas	1996	UK	140	100

Table 16.1 *continued*

	Fuel	Year of acquisition or start-up	Location	Gross MW	AES equity interest (%)
Barry	Gas	1998	UK	230	100
Drax	Coal	1999	UK	4,065	100
Fifoots	Coal	2000	UK	360	100
Songo Songo	Gas	2003	Tanzania	112	49
SONEL	Hydro	2001	Cameroon	800	51
Asia					
Ekibastuz Gres	Coal	1996	Kazakhstan	4,000	100
Altai-Leninogorsk CHP	Coal	1997	Kazakhstan	418	100
Altai-Semipalatinsk CHP	Coal	1997	Kazakhstan	840	100
Altai-Shulbinsk Hydro	Hydro	1997	Kazakhstan	702	100
Altai-Sogrinsk CHP	Coal	1997	Kazakhstan	349	100
Altai-Ust Kamenogorsk Heat Nets	Coal	1997	Kazakhstan	310	0
Altai-Ust-Kamenogorsk CHP	Coal	1997	Kazakhstan	1,464	100
Altai-Ust-Kamenogorsk Hydro	Hydro	1997	Kazakhstan	331	100
Caribbean					
Bayano	Hydro	1999	Panama	150	49
Bayano	Hydro	2003	Panama	110	49
Esti	Hydro	2003	Panama	120	49
Chivor	Hydro	2000	Colombia	1,000	96
Colombia I	Gas	2000	Colombia	90	62
Large utilities					
North America					
CILCORP-Duck Creek	Coal	1999	USA	366	100
CILCORP-Edwards	Coal	1999	USA	772	100
CILCORP-Indian Trails	Gas	1999	USA	19	100
IPALCO-Georgetown	Oil	2001	USA	79	100
IPALCO-Eagle Valley	Coal	2001	USA	341	100
IPALCO-Petersburg	Coal	2001	USA	1,672	100
IPALCO-Stout	Coal	2001	USA	944	100
South America					
Light-Fontes Nova*	Hydro	1996	Brazil	144	24
Light-Ilha dos Pombos*	Hydro	1996	Brazil	169	24
Light-Nilo Pecanha*	Hydro	1996	Brazil	380	24
Light-Pereira Passos*	Hydro	1996	Brazil	100	24
CEMIG (35 plants)	Hydro	1997	Brazil	5,068	21
CEMIG-Miranda	Hydro	1997	Brazil	390	21
CEMIG-Igarapava	Hydro	1998	Brazil	210	21
Caribbean					
EDC-generation (4 plants)	Gas	2000	Venezuela	2,265	87

Source: AES, 10K report, 2001.

Table 16.2   AES's electricity distribution businesses, December 2001

Distribution facilities	Year acquired	Location	Number of customers served	Gigawatt hours	AES equity interest (%)
Asia					
Eastern Kazakhstan REC	1999	Kazakhstan	291,000	1,455	0
Semipalatensk REC	1999	Kazakhstan	178,513	1,117	0
Telasi	1998	Georgia	370,000	2,200	75
Kievoblenergo	2001	Ukraine	763,000	3,840	75
Rivnooblenergo	2001	Ukraine	383,000	1,700	75
Cesco	1999	India	600,000	2,102	48
North America					
IPALCO	2000	USA	433,010	16,256	100
Cilicorp-Electricity	1999	USA	193,000	6,743	100
South America					
Light*	1996	Brazil	2,800,000	19,981	24
CEMIG	1997	Brazil	4,680,000	32,179	21
Eletropaulo*	1998	Brazil	4,657,306	34,789	50
Sul	1997	Brazil	935,125	7,390	96
Eden	1997	Argentina	278,854	1,886	90
Edes	1997	Argentina	141,281	834	90
Edelap	1998	Argentina	279,568	2,102	90
Caribbean					
EDC-distribution	2000	Venezuela	1,131,552	9,724	87
CLESA	1998	El Salvador	226,000	669	64
EDE Este	1999	Dominican Republic	350,000	2,990	51
CAESS	2000	El Salvador	443,430	1,697	70
DEUSEM	2000	El Salvador	43,362	75	69
EEO	2000	El Salvador	162,496	339	83
Europe/Africa					
SONEL	2001	Cameroon	452,000	3,020	51

Source: AES, 10K report, 2001.

The result of this expansion was not only a substantial expansion in the size of AES between 1998 and 2001, but also increasing complexity of the business as AES diversified its activities within the power sector. During 2001, AES recognized four lines of business activity:

- *Contract generation*. AES's traditional business was producing electricity supplied on long-term contracts (5 to 30 years) to distribution companies. By

Table 16.3 Revenues and gross profit by line of business, 2000 and 2001

	Revenue ($ billion)		Gross profit ($ billion)	
	2001	2000	2001	2000
Contract generation	2.5	1.7	0.83	0.77
Competitive supply	2.7	2.4	0.44	0.56
Large utilities	2.4	2.1	0.74	0.54
Growth distribution	1.7	1.3	0.30	0.13

Source: AES, 10K report, 2001.

matching the electricity supply contracts with long-term fuel purchase contracts, AES fixes its gross margin.

- *Competitive supply.* As electricity markets have become increasingly deregulated, so AES has expanded its involvement in such markets. AES's competitive supply line of business comprises generating facilities and retail supply businesses that sell electricity directly to wholesale and retail customers in competitive markets. These generating facilities sell a major part of their output into power pools, into daily spot markets, or on short-term contracts. The prices paid for these competitive supplies can be unpredictable and volatile.
- *Large utilities.* During the late 1990s, AES began acquiring large electrical utilities – regulated monopolies supplying electricity within specific geographical areas. At the end of 2001, AES owned five integrated utilities: two in the US, two in Brazil, and one in Venezuela. These utilities combine generation, transmission and distribution capabilities.
- *Growth distribution.* AES separates into a separate line of business distribution facilities that offer significant potential for growth because they are located in developing countries or regions where the demand for electricity is expected to grow at a higher rate than in more developed areas. As well as offering considerable opportunity, these businesses also present special challenges with regard to political risk, outdated equipment, non-technical losses (e.g., theft), safety, and non-payment. "Growth distribution" businesses include those in Argentina, Brazil, Cameroon, Dominican Republic, El Salvador, Georgia, Kazakhstan and Ukraine.

Table 16.3 shows revenues and gross profit earned by AES's four lines of business.

■ PERFORMANCE ■

AES's financial and operating performance during the 1990s placed the company among the top-performing firms of the decade, not only in its sector, but across the stock market as a whole. As a result, AES has been prominent among *Fortune* and

Washington Post lists of companies with fastest growing and best returns to shareholders. In the three years to April 1998, returns to shareholders averaged 80 percent a year.

This performance amazed many observers, since, not only is electricity generation far from being a glamor industry, but profitability and shareholder returns are not the primary yardsticks through which AES monitors and assesses its own performance. AES's assessment of its progress over time focuses upon four measures:

- Shared values – How did we do in having an organization that is fun, that is fair, that acts with integrity, and that is socially responsible?
- Plant operations – How safe, clean, reliable, and cost-effective were our facilities?
- Assets – What changes occurred in our assets, including AES people, during the year? This intends to measure the company's project development and construction progress as an indicator of future earnings potential.
- Sales backlog – What happened to our backlog of contract revenues during the year?

In terms of setting performance targets for the future, these tend to be a mixture of efficiency, employee satisfaction, community development, project development, and growth objectives. For example, AES's goals for 1998 were stated in "Our Wish List" published in the 1997 Annual Report. These included:

- Continuing progress in adapting to and living the AES principles and values
- Creating the most fun workplace since the beginning of the industrial revolution, and eliminating hourly payment systems
- Adding 10 to 15 new businesses to the AES portfolio
- Engineering a breakthrough in slow development businesses such as Ib Valley (India), Puerto Rico, and Nile Power (Uganda)
- Maintaining 100 new business ideas in the development pipeline
- Making our 1998 budgeted net income and cash flow

Operationally, AES plants have performed among the best in their industry. AES's US plants typically operate at around 95 percent capacity, compared to an industry average of 83 percent. Nor is operational excellence restricted to new plants. AES's West Belfast power station has achieved 95 percent availability in some years, remarkable for a 43-year-old facility.

Despite a history of growth, profitability, and operational excellence, AES is no stranger to crisis and its efforts have been successful. As already noted, its first power station was unprofitable from the start. In 1992, AES flirted with disaster when its Shady Point generating facility in Oklahoma was discovered to have been discharging polluted water and to have falsified the samples it provided to the Environmental Protection Agency. In the same year, AES was forced to abandon its rebuilding of a power plant at Cedar Bay, Florida following a dispute with state officials and the local community. These events caused AES's share price to fall by half.[4] Several of AES's acquisitions have proven disappointing: the 1997 acquisition of Destec's international

Table 16.4 AES's performance, 1991–2001

	2001	2000	1999	1998	1997	1996	1995	1994	1993	1992	1991
Revenue ($ million)	9,327	7,534	4,117	3,257	2,227	835	679	533	519	401	334
Sales backlog ($ billion)	n.a.	217	138	116	98	51	41	43	27	29	n.a.
Net income ($ million)	273	795	357	441	299	125	107	98	71	56	43
Earnings per share ($)	0.52	1.66	0.84	1.11	0.79	0.40	0.35	0.33	0.25	0.20	0.16
Total assets ($ billion)	36.7	33.0	23.2	12.9	11.1	3.6	2.3	1.9	1.7	1.6	1.4
Long-term debt:											
Non-recourse ($ billion)	14.7	12.7	9.5	4.5	4.5	1.6	1.1	1.0	1.1	1.1	n.a.
Recourse ($ billion)	4.9	3.5	2.2	1.6	1.1	0.5	0.1	0.1	0.1	0.1	n.a.
Stockholders' equity ($ billion)	5.5	5.5	3.3	2.4	2.0	0.7	0.6	0.4	0.3	0.2	n.a.
Equity generating capacity (thousands of MW)	50.8	n.a.	n.a.	n.a.	4.6	3.4	2.1	1.5	1.5	1.2	0.7
Return on average equity (%)	4.9	17.9	12.6	20.2	17.1	19.7	22.6	28.3	29.2	35.1	48.6

Sources: Annual Reports, UBS Securities Equity Research.

generation resulted in poor returns, while AES acknowledged that its venture in Ukraine had been an expensive error.

However, these problems had a limited impact on AES's financial performance; the problems that AES encountered during 2001 had a bigger impact. During 2001, revenues grew by a healthy 24 percent, mostly from acquiring new businesses and adding new plants. Revenue from existing operations grew by a more modest 5 percent. Net income fell sharply from $795 million in 2000 to $273 million in 2001 as a result of lower market prices in the UK, decline in the Brazilian Real resulting in currency transaction losses of $210 million, losses from closed telecom activities of $194 million, and higher sales, general and administrative expenses.

Table 16.4 summarizes some key indicators of AES's performance during 1991–2001.

■ STRATEGY ■

AES described itself as: "a global power company committed to serving the world's needs for electricity in a socially responsible way."[5] It describes its strategy as:

- Supplying energy to customers at the lowest cost possible, taking into account factors such as reliability and environmental performance;
- Constructing, acquiring, and operating projects of a relatively large size in geographically dispersed markets;
- To the extent available, maximizing the amount of non-recourse financing;
- When available, entering into longer-term power sales contracts or other arrangements with electric utilities or other customers with significant credit strength;
- Where possible, participating in distribution markets that grant concessions with long-term pricing arrangements; and
- When available, entering into hedging, indexing, or other arrangements to protect against fluctuations in currency, fuel costs and electricity prices.

The Company also strives for operating excellence as a key element of its strategy, which it believes it accomplishes by minimizing organizational layers and maximizing company-wide participation in decision making. AES has attempted to create an operating environment that results in safe, clean and reliable electricity generation, distribution and supply. Because of this emphasis, the Company prefers to operate all facilities and businesses which it develops or acquires; however, there can be no assurance that the Company will have operating control of all of its facilities.

The Company attempts to finance each domestic and foreign project primarily under loan agreements and related documents which, except as noted below, require the loans to be repaid solely from the project's revenues and provide that the repayment of the loans (and interest thereon) is secured solely by the capital stock, physical assets, contracts and cash flow of that project subsidiary or affiliate. This type of financing is usually referred to as non-recourse debt or project financing . . .[6]

■ VALUES AND PRINCIPLES ■

AES's unique organization and management systems are the direct result of the values upon which the company was established and continue to define every aspect of its management. These values reflect the personal beliefs of the two founders, Sant and Bakke. Both men were brought up in strongly religious families: Bakke as a Baptist, Sant a Mormon. Bakke was raised on a farm in Washington State. From the age of five he had worked in the fields and by the time he was 18 he had built up a herd of 29 beef cattle. Bakke's attitude to enterprise and material possessions was strongly influenced by ideas of Christian stewardship, which emphasized responsibility, building for the future, and sharing good fortune with others. Sant attended Brigham Young University and spent two years as a missionary with Native Americans in Wisconsin. Over time, Sant became less committed to the church and increasingly active in the environmental movement.

From the outset, both men viewed AES as an opportunity for them to pursue their values and effect a fundamental change in business practices. In a section of its 10K report entitled "Principles, Values and Practices," AES states:

> A core part of AES's corporate culture is a commitment to "shared principles or values." These principles describe how AES people endeavor to commit themselves to the Company's mission of serving the world by providing safe, clean, reliable and low-cost electricity. The principles are:
>
> • Integrity – AES strives to act with integrity, or "wholeness." AES people seek to keep the same moral code at work as at home.
> • Fairness – AES wants to treat fairly its people, its customers, its suppliers, its stockholders, governments and the communities in which it operates.
> • Fun – AES desires that people employed by the Company and those people with whom the Company interacts have fun in their work. The Company believes that making decisions and being accountable is fun and has structured its organization to maximize the opportunity for fun for as many people as possible.
> • Social Responsibility – Primarily, the Company believes that doing a good job at fulfilling its mission is socially responsible. But the Company also believes that it has a responsibility to be involved in projects that provide other social benefits, and consequently has instituted programs such as corporate matching of individual charitable gifts in addition to various local programs conducted by AES businesses.
>
> AES recognizes that most companies have standards and ethics by which they operate and that business decisions are based, at least in part, on such principles. The Company believes that an explicit commitment to a particular set of standards is a useful way to encourage ownership of those values among its people. While the people at AES acknowledge that they won't always live up to these standards, they believe that being held accountable to these shared values will help them behave more consistently with such principles.
>
> AES makes an effort to support these principles in ways that acknowledge a strong corporate commitment and encourage people to act accordingly. For example, AES conducts annual surveys, both company-wide and at each business location, designed to measure how well its people are doing in supporting these principles through interactions within the Company and with people outside the Company. These surveys are perhaps most useful in revealing failures, and helping to deal with those failures. AES's principles are relevant because they help explain how AES people approach the Company's business. The Company seeks to adhere to these principles, not as a means to achieve economic success but because adherence is a worthwhile goal in and of itself.[7]

Sant and Bakke recognize that these values cannot easily be reconciled with the concept of a shareholder-focused, profit-maximizing corporation, and both leaders have made it very clear where their priorities lie:

> Where do profits fit? Profits . . . are not any corporation's main goal. Profits are to a corporation much like breathing is to life. Breathing is not the goal, but without breath, life ends. Similarly, without turning a profit, a corporation too, will cease to exist . . . At AES we strive not to make profits the ultimate driver of the corporation. My desire is that the principles to which we strive would take preeminence.[8]

AES's commitment to its values, at the expense of shareholder gain where necessary, is indicated by the proviso which AES inserts in all of its prospectuses for new security offers which identifies AES's values as a source of investor risk:

> The Company seeks to adhere to these principles, not as a means to achieve economic success, but because adherence is a worthwhile goal in and of itself. However, if the Company perceives a conflict between these principles and profits, the Company will try to adhere to its principles – even though doing so might result in dominated or forgone opportunities or financial benefits.[9]

The AES principles and the way they are implemented reflect a set of assumptions about human nature. Sant and Bakke believe in the ultimate goodness of people – "Man is made in the image of God," declared Bakke.[10] Hence, within organizations, people can and should be trusted to exercise responsibility, and at the same time should be held accountable. Critical to the ability to motivate people is the innate desire of people to make a contribution to society. This implies that, for an organization to be effective and to harness human effort and ingenuity, the organization must be committed to a wider social purpose. These views are at variance with many of the assumptions upon which many traditional management systems and techniques are based and imply a different approach: "[t]he people in AES are not principally economic resources. We are not tools of the corporation. Rather we hope the corporation is structured to help individuals make a difference in the world that they could not otherwise make."[11] AES's annual employee surveys are an indicator of the importance which is accorded to the company's principles and values. Dennis Bakke has commented that he devotes more attention to studying the annual employee surveys than the annual financial statements.

■ ORGANIZATIONAL STRUCTURE AND MANAGEMENT SYSTEMS ■

AES's organizational structure and management systems manifest the company's values and principles. AES describes the key features of its organization in its statement of values:

> In order to create a fun working environment for its people and implement its strategy of operational excellence, AES has adopted decentralized organizational principles and practices. For example, AES works to minimize the number of supervisory layers in its organization. Most of the Company's plants operate without shift supervisors.
>
> The project subsidiaries are responsible for all major facility-specific business functions, including financing and capital expenditures. Criteria for hiring new AES people include a person's willingness to accept responsibility and AES's principles as well as a person's experience and expertise. Every AES person has been encouraged to participate in strategic planning and new plant design for the Company. The Company has generally organized itself into multi-skilled teams to develop projects, rather than forming "staff" groups (such as a human resources department or an engineering staff) to carry out specialized functions.

Many people have asked us about our team structure and how it works. To begin with, there is no one person in charge of teams and there is no Human Resources department. Teams are the basis of our structure, and they encompass the four values of our company. They are fluid; many people are members of more than one team at one time. A team is somewhat autonomous; all decisions about a project are made within that team, with final say granted to that team. Decisions are made not from the top-down, but from the bottom-up. Furthermore, responsibility is pushed to the lowest level possible, encouraging everyone to be part of a decision. As a result, each team member views the project in terms of a whole. Colleagues and team members must trust each other to follow through to the best of their ability.

Because people are what make up AES, we have decided not to resort to an organizational model. Instead, we give you the following comments from AES people regarding teamwork. In general, AES teams work extremely well in both achieving a common goal and having fun while doing so. The following ideas provide insight on what makes teams work well and what can stimulate true and productive teamwork.

"Teams imply friendship; not only the ability but the desire to work together. Starting with the wonderful example set by the original AES team, Roger and Dennis, working together in small groups has been a natural way to get big things done while preserving the dignity of each person." Tom Tribone

"There are two reasons why teams are successful at AES: the type of people we have here and the environment in which they work. People at AES tend to be independent and thrive in a loose environment where roles and responsibilities are not always clearly defined. The environment at AES is one where responsibility is pushed down to the lowest level possible, encouraging everyone to take ownership for not only their piece of the project, but for the project in its entirety." Michael Cranna[12]

This is not to say that AES lacks formal structure altogether. The most striking feature of its organization is the few layers of hierarchy: until recently there were only three organizational layers between the front-line employees and the CEO. AES is divided into regional organizations or "groups." These groups comprise the different plants, each of which is headed by a plant manager. Within each plant there are typically seven areas or "families," each of which is headed by a superintendent.

Figure 16.1 shows AES's formal structure at the beginning of 2002.

No Functional Departments

The company does not have a legal, human resources, or any other department. Decisions in such matters are made by teams at the plant level, which oftentimes have little or no experience in those decision areas. A few years ago, CFO Barry Sharp estimated that the company had raised $3.5 billion to finance ten new power plants. But, he added, he was personally responsible for raising only $300 million of that sum. The rest was secured by decentralized, empowered teams. When AES raised 200 million pounds sterling (about $350 million) to finance a joint venture in Northern Ireland, two control room operators led the team that raised the funds.[13] The same goes for other areas of financial management. Treasury operations are decentralized to the individual plant level, where they are performed by teams of non-specialists:

BOARD OF DIRECTORS
Chairman
(RogerSant)

EXECUTIVE COMMITTEE			
	CEO		
	(Dennis Bakke)		
COO	COO	COO	COO
Growth & Distribution Business	Contract Generation	Competitive Supply	Large Utilities
(Paul Hanrahan)	(John Ruggirello)	(Stuart Ryan)	(Barry Sharp)

CORPORATE OFFICERS		
General Counsel SVP & CFO	SVP, Investor Relations and Business Development	SVP, Financial Forecasting and Corporate Issues
(William Lurashi) (Barry Sharp)	(Kenneth Woodcock)	(Roger Naill)

OPERATING DIVISIONS	
AES Americas (Brazil, Venezuela) (Paul Hanrahan)	AES Horizons (Ireland, Low Countries, Scandinavia, Baltic States) (Ann Murthow)
AES Andes (Argentina, Chile) (Joe Brandt)	AES Oasis (Middle East, South Asia) (Shahzad Qasim)
AES Aurora (Mexico, Central America, Caribbean) (Sarah Susser)	AES Orient (China) (Bill Rucius)
AES Coral (Panama, El Salvador) (Ned Hall)	AES Pacific (Southern California) (Mark Woodruff)
AES Electric (England, Wales, France, Italy) (Michael Armstrong)	AES Sao Paulo (Brazil) (Luiz Travesso)
AES Endeavor (N.E. USA, E. Canada) (Dan Rothaupt)	AES Sirocco (Balkans, Turkey, North Africa) (Mike Scholey)
AES Enterprise (Mid-Atlantic USA) (Dan Rothaupt)	AES Silk Road (former Soviet Union) (Garry Levesley)
AES Great Plains (USA Midwest) (Lenny Lee)	AES Transpower (Australia, N. Zealand, S.E. Asia) (Haresh Jaisinghani)
	Think AES (retail and telecom) (Tom Tribone)

Figure 16.1 AES's company structure
Source: AES, 1oK report, 2oo1.

His hands still blackened from coal he has just unloaded from a barge, Jeff Hatch picks up the phone and calls his favorite broker. "What kind of rate can you give me for $10 million at 30 days?" he asks the agent, who handles Treasury bills. "Only 6.09? But I just got a 6.13 quote from Chase."

In another room, Joe Oddo is working on J.P. Morgan & Co. "6.15 at 30 days?" confirms Oddo, a maintenance technician at AES Corp.'s power plant here. "I'll get right back to you."

Members of an ad hoc team that manage a $33 million plant investment fund, Messrs. Oddo and Hatch quickly confer with their associates, then close the deal. "It's like playing Monopoly," Mr. Oddo says as he heads off to fix a leaky valve in the boiler room, "Only the money's real."[14]

Similarly, there is no human resources department. At the corporate level there are no staff specialists dealing with salary ranges, or annual review procedures, or personnel policies, or contract negotiations with unions. There is a person whose responsibility is to track 401k retirement plan benefits and send out the necessary reports, but that's about it at the corporate level. Everything else is devolved to the individual divisions, and within these it is the teams within each plant that handle almost all the human resource functions.

The company operates without any written policies or procedures. Issues such as hiring practices, leave periods, and promotion criteria, which in more conventional companies would be spelled out in a "Policies and Procedures" handbook, are left at the employees' discretion. When trying to find out how much time she could take off after the birth of her daughter, a Project Director for AES Puerto Rico discovered that the company did not have a policy about maternity leave. After investigating what other "AES people" had done, she decided to do what made sense for both herself and the business requirements of the project. In the end she decided to take three months, but she made herself available at critical points in the project's execution.[15]

Virtually all human resource decisions are made at plant level, and within the plant, decisional-making authority is among the different teams. For example:

- *Recruiting.* The recruiting process is done at the plant level, without any support or guidelines from corporate headquarters. AES people at all levels are committed to the hiring process, and everyone can participate in it. The process generally involves an initial résumé review, and a phone interview followed by a group interview. Interviews usually do not include technical questions. Instead, they focus on characteristics that help determine how the candidate will fit with the company's culture and values. There is little importance given to the candidates' educational background or experience, as greater emphasis is placed on the candidates' desire to learn, contribute, and grow, as well as their personal values and self-motivation.
- *Training and development.* In line with corporate values, AES employees are empowered to make decisions about their own development. Training is mostly done on-the-job, through open communication channels and embedded advice-seeking practices. However, AES people are free to take outside classes and they are reimbursed for them, as long as the courses are work-related.
- *Career paths.* Regarding development, there are no established career paths. Rather, the company encourages flexibility, which is a necessary requirement in such a dynamic industry. Because one of the company's shared values is to "have fun," employees are encouraged to move within the company if they feel their current assignment is "boring." Job vacancies are always posted and promotion decisions are made at an area superintendent's meeting.
- *Compensation and benefits.* AES does not have a set salary schedule for any given job, and salaries are determined based on what others are being paid inside and outside the company. Raises are given every year and superintendents usually determine them in an annual meeting. Most AES people put their retirement savings in company stock, and the company matches up to 5 percent of the person's salary in the retirement plan.

This emphasis on multi-functionalism is central to AES's concept of making work fun. The key is to make people's work fulfilling by continually providing challenge and learning experiences. Moreover, argues Bakke, specialization does not promote efficiency or better decision making: "As soon as you have a specialist who's very good, then everyone else quits thinking," Bakke says. "The better that person is, the worse it is for the organization. The information goes through the specialist, so all the education is to the person who knows the most."[16]

Moreover, AES relies heavily on outside expertise. A key aspect of the system of empowerment is that individuals and teams are encouraged to seek out the best advice available, whether it is within the company or outside. In relation to finance, while AES's financial management and project management teams lack great depth in financial expertise, they draw upon the knowledge of bankers and financiers. In any event, Bakke's view is that most management expertise, whether functionally specialized or general management skill, is not inherently difficult. Motivation, attitude, and a willingness to learn are more important determinants of ultimate performance.

The "Honeycomb"

AES refers to its organizational structure as a "honeycomb." The idea is that each plant comprises a number of small, flexible, self-managed teams who are able to operate cooperatively and efficiently without any centralized direction. At the basis of this structure is the belief that organizations do not need to be managed. Thinking, motivated people can manage themselves and undertake the communication and mutual adjustment needed to coordinate complex tasks. According to Dennis Bakke, the key to effective decentralization is keeping the basic units of organization small:

> I think of AES as a conglomeration of small communities. And I don't think there's any company in the world that's so big that you can't organize this way. Even a plant with 400 people can be broken down into smaller groups. It's a small enough community that there is the ability to have an accountability structure within it, you know, a social structure as opposed to a military structure. We will break down the Kazakhstan plant into four units. How can we stay small and be big? By breaking the organization into groups with chief operating officers.[17]

The principle of self-organization imposes a very different role on managers from the conventional management model. Indeed, the term "manager" is seldom heard within AES; it is at odds with the principle of letting people decide for themselves. The example comes from the top. "The most difficult thing for me as CEO," confided Bakke, "is not to make decisions." If individuals are to develop, they must be given responsibility and allowed to learn:

> [T]he modern manager is supposed to ask his people for advice and then make a decision. But at AES, each decision is made by a person and a team. Their job is to get advice from me and from anybody else they think it's necessary to get advice from. And then they make the decision. We do that even with the budget. We make very few decisions here [indicating the headquarters office]. We affirm decisions.[18]

Sant has made similar observations:

> If Dennis and I had to lead everything, we couldn't have grown as much as we have. People would bring deals for us to approve, and we would have a huge bottleneck. We've shifted to giving advice rather than giving approval. And we've moved ahead much faster than we would have otherwise."[19]

One consequence of this approach is the small size of AES's corporate headquarters. At any point in time there may be between 40 and 70 AES employees at the Arlington office, but in terms of actual corporate staff, these number only about 35.

In terms of performance, one of the most important advantages of the AES system is that it permits speed in decision making, preparing bids, and completing projects. AES abounds with a folk history of teams and individuals given huge responsibilities or thrust into unique and unexpected situations. Consider the following:

- Oscar Prieto, a chemical engineer with two years' experience with AES, was visiting AES headquarters in May 1996 when he was asked by Thomas Tribone to join a meeting: "I've got 14 people from France and some guys from Houston coming to talk about buying a business in Rio de Janeiro. We've only got two AES people. Could one of you show up?" The meeting with Electricité de France and Houston Light & Power concerned a possible joint bid for one of Brazil's largest utilities, which was being privatized. Within a month, Tribone was on his way to Paris to negotiate an agreement with Electricité de France. The deal was concluded, and by 1997 Tribone had moved to Rio to become one of the utility's four directors and a key player in a succession of deals in which AES acquired a string of power plants and distribution facilities in Brazil and Argentina.
- The development of the $404 million Warrior Run power plant in Cumberland, Maryland was undertaken by an AES team of ten people who handled all the work necessary leading up to the plant's groundbreaking in October 1995. They secured 36 different permit approvals involving about 24 regulatory agencies and arranged financing that involved tax-exempt bonds and ten lenders. Within the industry, such a project would typically involve well over a hundred employees.
- Scott Gardner joined AES in 1992 right after graduating from Dartmouth College. Gardner joined a team developing a $200 million cogeneration plant in San Francisco. "It involved a lot of work and few people to do it," he says. "I took on tasks that ranged from designing a water system to negotiating with the community to buying and selling pollution credits." Gardner also helped lead a bid for a $225 million cogeneration plant in Vancouver, British Columbia. When a comparable deal emerged in Australia, Gardner volunteered for that assignment. Two weeks later, he was on his way to Brisbane. "My task was to understand an unfamiliar regional power system, develop a design for the plant, and prepare a financial and technical bid document – all in six weeks," he says. When Gardner's proposal made the final round of competition, his division manager had him negotiate the terms of the $75 million deal.

"The stress was incredible, but I was having fun," he says. His bid won. "I held a press conference and was interviewed by local TV stations," says Gardner, who has since left AES to attend business school. "I had to pinch myself to be sure this was happening."[20]

- Paul Burdick, a mechanical engineer, had only been at AES briefly when he was asked to purchase $1 billion in coal. "I'd never negotiated anything before, save for a used car," he said. Burdick spent three weeks asking questions of people both within and outside of the company on how to accomplish the task. At AES, he says, "You're given a lot of leeway and a lot of rope. You can use it to climb or you can hang yourself."[21]

- Ann Murtlow, a chemical engineer with no experience in pollution abatement, was given the job of buying air-pollution credits. She had already purchased the option to buy $1 million in credits when she discovered that the option she had bought was for the wrong kind of credit and useless to AES.

The Relationship with Employees

The AES principles and its concept of the honeycomb organization imply a different type of relationship between those employed and the corporation than that which characterizes most companies. To begin with, the absence of functional specialists and the ideas about self-organization require a tremendous amount of information-sharing. According to the company, employees are given full access to the company's operating and financial information. Because of the extent of employee access to information that would normally be confidential at other companies, AES lists all its employees as "insiders" in its submissions to the SEC.

One of AES's current crusades is to eliminate the distinction between salaried and hourly paid employees and to put all employees on a salaried basis. The 1997 Annual Report stated the goal of eliminating hourly payment systems. By the end of 1998 considerable progress had been made with more than half of AES's US employees salaried – despite the restrictions imposed by Federal health and safety legislation which perpetuates staff/worker distinctions. The primacy that AES accords its "people," as the company refers to its employees, is emphasized by its practice of listing of every employee's name in the back of the AES Annual Report. However, once AES's total employment passed the 6,000 mark, this was no longer feasible.

AES and the Environment

AES's deep commitment to the environment extends well beyond Chairman Sant's personal involvement in environmentalist issues and his active roles in the World Wildlife Fund and as a member of the Environmental Defense Fund. Because building and operating power plants is not one of the world's most environmentally friendly endeavors, AES tries to compensate for the emissions it generates. When the company constructed a coal-fired plant in Montville, Connecticut, it calculated that it would generate 15 million tons of carbon dioxide over its estimated life of 40 years. The company then captured national attention when it announced that it would plant 52 million trees in Guatemala to offset the Connecticut's plant carbon dioxide emissions. According to AES Executive Vice-President Robert F. Hemphill: "Making electric power historically has had a relatively high level of environmental assault. We are not planting trees as part of our strategy to make us a more valuable company, we're doing it because we think it's a responsible thing to do." AES's average company-wide emission levels are 40–60 percent of permitted rates. These actions are of course in line with one of the company's four core values: social responsibility.[22]

Emphasis on responsibility to the environment and to local communities is viewed as integral to the efficient running of power plants. Professor Jeff Pfeffer of Stanford Business School describes a visit to the Thames, Connecticut power plant:

> A visitor to the plant is immediately struck by its cleanliness, and the people who work in the plant are proud of its appearance. The walls of the plant exterior are very light colored (off-white), so that any dirt would be immediately visible. The color of the walls was intentionally chosen to encourage respect for the physical environment and cleanliness. The place where the coal is unloaded from the barges that bring it up the Connecticut River is also immaculate. The coal handling system is covered to avoid excess dust or debris getting into the surroundings and the loading dock and surrounding area is swept by a mechanical sweeper after the once a week delivery. There is no smell of sulfur in the air, and in fact, no odor at all. The attitude to cleanliness extends inside the plant as well. For example, there are two lunch rooms, both have stoves, microwave oven, cooktops, refrigerator, and dishwasher which makes them more than a typical plant eating area. Quite elaborate meals are cooked there. Both lunch rooms are clean with no dirty dishes sitting around. The cabinetry is of excellent quality and appearance as are the appliances. The turbine rooms are also immaculate.[23]

The Challenge of Multiculturalism

As more and more of AES's business becomes located outside the US, and non-US citizens far outnumber US citizens among AES's employees, an increasingly important challenge is to retain AES's culture as the company grows. The company acknowledges that even the stated value of having fun is difficult to accomplish with so many people with many different backgrounds. By the end of the 1990s, fewer than 8 percent of AES people were native English speakers. The principles of equality, teamwork, empowerment, and individual initiative are also likely to be more difficult to implement in traditional Islamic societies such as Pakistan, and countries with a socialist heritage such as China, Kazakhstan, Ukraine, and Georgia.

Nevertheless, AES remains committed to its principles not just for its US, but for its worldwide operations. Bakke firmly believes that the AES principles are universal and are not culturally specific either to the US or to the West in general. AES's experience so far is that its own corporate culture can be transplanted in many different national cultures. The challenges presented in running one of the world's biggest (and once one of the most dilapidated) coal-fired power stations in Kazakhstan, and turning around heavily bureaucratized, former state-owned utilities in South America have provided remarkable test-cases in AES's ability to export its company culture. The results have often been amazing. Even though AES has been unable to eliminate the distinction between salaried and hourly paid employees within the US, in England, Argentina, and Pakistan it has moved to an all-salary workforce.

Instilling the AES culture into the 100-year-old Light Servicios de Electricidade involved, first, a generous severance package to cut the workforce by half, second, the careful selection of young, motivated engineers and supervisors to take key positions as facility supervisors, and finally, the devolving of decision-making power to them. At Light's Santa Branca facility, Oscar Prieto chose Carlos Baldi, a 34-year-old engineer, to lead the plant. "I knew he was the right person," says Prieto, "He was young, eager to do more." After agreeing to shared goals and expectations – zero accidents, thrifty construction budgets – Prieto turned Santa Branca and a $35 million upgrading project over to Baldi. After a short while, Baldi was managing in the same way with his project and team leaders.[24]

■ 2002: RETRENCHMENT AND RESTRUCTURING ■

During the first quarter of 2002, CEO Dennis Bakke was forced to shift his attention from the issues that consumed his attention – AES's ability to maintain its values and live its principles – in order to address the fallout from Enron, Argentina, Venezuela, September 11, and the California power crisis that was increasingly dragging down AES. In a press statement released on February 20, AES announced a major shift of strategy. In the expectation that AES would be unable to access the capital markets in 2002 for additional parent capital, it would be forced to rely on its internally generated cash flows to fund operations and capital expenditures. The major retrenchment measures included:

- Reducing capital spending by $490 million in 2002 through eliminating or curtailing a number of construction projects.
- Selling existing businesses, including Cilcorp, its Illinois-based utility in Illinois, a share of Ipalco, a utility in Indiana, and several overseas plants. Its biggest retrenchments were to be its withdrawal from its merchant generation businesses under which AES sold electricity on to the spot markets in UK, New York and California, and a major pullback from Latin America.

However, several analysts were doubtful as to AES's ability to command a fair value for the assets it was putting up for sale. In a note to clients, Ronald Barone of UBS Warburg wrote: "The markets in which AES operates are depressed and there are a number of other companies that are already looking to dispose of similar assets."

Bakke recognized the extent of the company's strategic reorientation: he opened his conference call to analysts with the simple statement: "Our world has changed." In the accompanying press release he stated: "We are taking aggressive action to restructure and de-leverage AES. Given today's market climate we are going to rely on the cash flows of our solid operating businesses. We have taken additional steps to provide a more substantial liquidity cushion. We believe the actions we have announced will provide for a more conservative business model." His comments were echoed by

Chairman Sant: "The Board of Directors has unanimously approved this plan to de-leverage AES and position us for the future. The cutbacks in construction capital expenditures, the accelerated sale of businesses and selective project financings leave us stronger from a cash perspective with expected results in the short term. All of these steps are being taken in parallel with the cost-cutting efforts of AES businesses around the world. We believe these steps will leave us with a better-capitalized and stronger company with less earnings volatility. AES in the future will be less concentrated in Latin America and have greater emphasis on contract generation."[25]

To permit restructuring and cost reduction, organizational changes were also made. In addition to AES's regional organization through 17 groups that operated in different parts of the world, an executive office was created comprising Bakke as CEO together with four newly created chief operating officers – each with responsibility for one of AES's four lines of business. The reorganization was intended to: "enhance operating performance, including further reductions of operating costs and revenue enhancements . . . Each COO is directly responsible for managing a portion of the Company's geographically dispersed businesses as well as coordinating Company wide efforts associated with one of the Company's business segments. In addition, two special offices, the Cost Cutting Office and the Turnaround Office, have been created to bring improved focus and coordination to the management of expenses across the Company and to improve or dispose of businesses that AES believes to be under-performing businesses from a return on capital perspective, respectively. Each of these offices reports to the Executive Office."[26]

The Outlook

March 2002 was a hectic month for AES's senior managers. At home the Enron affair continued to drag in ever more companies from the US energy sector, while abroad troubles in Argentina, Venezuela, India, and Pakistan called for ongoing crisis management. As managers struggled to restore AES's financial strength and bolster confidence in the company's viability, some pondered the longer-term implications of recent events for AES's longer-term vision and identity.

Faced with threats to its very existence, AES's commitment to "integrity, fairness, fun, and social responsibility" had taken a back seat to the pressing needs for liquidity and investor confidence. Was this a temporary shift forced by temporary crisis, or was it part of the inevitable maturity of a young, idealistic company?

For those who, like Bakke and Sant, shared the vision of an alternative type of enterprise, the lessons of history were not encouraging. Many companies, from Kellogg & Company to Apple Computer, had been formed with a vision of redefining relationships between business and society, investors and employees, and workers and managers, yet almost all had evolved towards the dominant model of the shareholder-oriented capitalist corporation. Was it inevitable that growing organizational size and an increasingly competitive environment forced all organizations to renounce individuality and innovation in management ideas in favor of standard management principles?

Certainly, the business environment of 2002 was very different from that which had faced AES during the 1980s and 1990s. AES's ability to grow at so remarkable a rate was the result of specific circumstances: worldwide electricity generation was undergoing deregulation, privatization, and internationalization. By 2002, this process was largely completed. Indeed, in some countries (including the US) the momentum towards regulatory reform had halted – possibly even reversed. Meanwhile, competition was increasing on all sides and the business was becoming more complex. The simple model of producing electricity and selling it on long-term contracts to utilities and distributors was being superseded by more open competition involving competitive energy markets and more complex transactions (including spot and futures contracts, swaps, and an array of their energy derivative products). Among AES's competitors in these energy markets were major companies such as Shell, ExxonMobil, Bechtel, and ENI who possessed not only massive financial resources, but an array of other resources and capabilities too, from political influence and hydrocarbon reserves to expertise in complex risk management techniques.

AES's unique organizational structure, management systems, and corporate culture had served it well. Although unorthodox, not only in the power industry, but in the corporate sector generally, the AES approach had shown itself to be highly effective both in the efficient operation of power stations and in supporting the entrepreneurial capabilities required for winning power supply contracts all over the world. Moreover, as an early mover in the international power business (it began operating plants overseas in 1992), AES has acquired a greater depth of experience in bidding for power contracts and operating power plants in more countries of the world than any other company. Moreover, because of its very low rate of employee turnover and open internal communication, it has been very effective in retaining this expertise and sharing it internally.

The long-term question facing Bakke and his senior management team was whether the combination of internal growth and external turbulence meant that the AES management philosophy had reached the limits of its effectiveness and henceforth AES would need to temper its enthusiasm for fun and social responsibility with more conventional management controls and greater responsiveness to Wall Street.

NOTES

1. "A power producer is intent on giving power to its people," *Wall Street Journal*, July 3, 1995, p. A1.
2. "Arlington's AES Corp. leads a battery of US energy companies overseas," *Washington Post*, May 22, 1995.
3. "The principles behind its power," *Washington Post*, November 2, 1998, p. F12.
4. An account of this period is found in "AES Honeycomb A" (HBS Case 9-395-132) and "AES Honeycomb B" (HBS Case 9-395-122).
5. AES Corporation, 10K submission to the Securities and Exchange Commission for 2001.
6. Ibid.
7. Ibid., p. 12.

8. Dennis W. Bakke, "Erecting a grid for ethical power," *The Marketplace*, May/June 1996, p. 5.
9. AES Corporation, 10K submission to the Securities and Exchange Commission for 2001.
10. Personal meeting, April 2000.
11. Dennis Bakke and Roger Sant, Annual Letter to Shareholders, *1997 AES Corporation Annual Report*.
12. AES Corporation, 10K submission to the Securities and Exchange Commission for 2001.
13. Alex Markels, "Power to people," *Fast Company*, 13 (March 1998), p. 155.
14. "A power producer is intent on giving power to its people," *Wall Street Journal*, July 3, 1995, p. A1.
15. Jeffrey Pfeffer, "Human resources at the AES Corporation: the case of the missing department," Graduate School of Business, Stanford University, 1997, p. 14.
16. *Wall Street Journal. Op. cit.*
17. Pfeffer, op. cit.
18. "The power of a team: Arlington's AES Corporation," *The Washington Post*, February 12, 1996, p. F12.
19. Markels, op. cit, p. 160.
20. "The power of a team: Arlington's AES Corporation," *The Washington Post*, February 12, 1996, p. F12.
21. "A power producer is intent on giving power to its people," *Wall Street Journal*, July 3, 1995, p. A1.
22. "Power plant builder tries to reenergize environmental image," *The Washington Post*, July 6, 1992, p. F1.
23. Pfeffer, op. cit, pp. 6–7.
24. Markels, op. cit, p. 164.
25. AES Corporation, Press Release February 19, 2002.
26. AES Corporation, 10K submission to the Securities and Exchange Commission for 2001, p. 3.

Index